# TRANSNATIONAL WRITING EDUCATION

Arguing that writing teachers need to enable students to recognize, negotiate with, deconstruct, and transcend national, racial, ethnic, and linguistic boundaries, this volume proposes a "transnational" framework as an alternative approach to literacy education and as a vital component to cultivating students as global citizens. In a field of evolving literacy practices, this volume builds off the three pillars of transnational writing education—translingualism, transculturalism, and cosmopolitanism—and offers both conceptual and practice-based support for scholars, students, and educators in order to address current issues of inclusion, multilingual learning, and diversity.

**Xiaoye You** is Professor of English and Asian Studies at The Pennsylvania State University, USA, and Yunshan Chair Professor at Guangdong University of Foreign Studies, China.

# ESL & Applied Linguistics Professional Series
Eli Hinkel, Series Editor

**Reflective Practice in English Language Teaching**
Research-Based Principles and Practices
*Steve Mann, Steve Walsh*

**Teacher Training and Professional Development of Chinese English Language Teachers**
Changing From Fish to Dragon
*Faridah Pawan, Wenfang Fan, Pei Miao*

**Research on Reflective Practice in TESOL**
*Thomas S.C. Farrell*

**Teaching English to Second Language Learners in Academic Contexts**
Reading, Writing, Listening, Speaking
*Jonathan M. Newton, Dana R. Ferris, Christine C.M. Goh, William Grabe, Fredricka L. Stoller, Larry Vandergrift*

**The Politics of English Second Language Writing Assessment in Global Contexts**
*Edited by Todd Ruecker, Deborah Crusan*

**Transnational Writing Education**
Theory, History, and Practice
*Edited by Xiaoye You*

For more information about this series, please visit: www.routledge.com/ESL—Applied-Linguistics-Professional-Series/book-series/LEAESLALP?page=2&page=1

# TRANSNATIONAL WRITING EDUCATION

Theory, History, and Practice

Edited by Xiaoye You

NEW YORK AND LONDON

First published 2018
by Routledge
711 Third Avenue, New York, NY 10017

and by Routledge
2 Park Square, Milton Park, Abingdon, Oxon, OX14 4RN

*Routledge is an imprint of the Taylor & Francis Group, an informa business*

© 2018 Taylor & Francis

The right of Xiaoye You to be identified as the author of the editorial material, and of the authors for their individual chapters, has been asserted in accordance with sections 77 and 78 of the Copyright, Designs and Patents Act 1988.

All rights reserved. No part of this book may be reprinted or reproduced or utilised in any form or by any electronic, mechanical, or other means, now known or hereafter invented, including photocopying and recording, or in any information storage or retrieval system, without permission in writing from the publishers.

*Trademark notice*: Product or corporate names may be trademarks or registered trademarks, and are used only for identification and explanation without intent to infringe.

*Library of Congress Cataloging-in-Publication Data*
Names: You, Xiaoye, 1974– editor.
Title: Transnational writing education : theory, history, and practice / edited by Xiaoye You.
Description: New York : Routledge, 2018. | Series: ESL & applied linguistics professional series | Includes bibliographical references and index.
Identifiers: LCCN 2018004107 | ISBN 9780815383499 (hbk) | ISBN 9780815383505 (pbk) | ISBN 9781351205955 (ebk)
Subjects: LCSH: Academic writing—Study and teaching. | English language—Study and teaching—Foreign speakers. | Multilingualism.
Classification: LCC P301.5.A27 T73 2018 | DDC 808/.042—dc23
LC record available at https://lccn.loc.gov/2018004107

ISBN: 978-0-8153-8349-9 (hbk)
ISBN: 978-0-8153-8350-5 (pbk)
ISBN: 978-1-351-20595-5 (ebk)

Typeset in Bembo
by Apex CoVantage, LLC

In memory of Professor Chao Zheng (郑超), a pioneer in transnational writing education

# CONTENTS

*Preface*          *x*
*Acknowledgements*          *xv*

1  Introduction: Making a Transnational Turn in Writing
   Education          1
   *Xiaoye You*

## PART I
## Theory          **19**

2  Rhetorical and Linguistic Flexibility: Valuing Heterogeneity
   in Academic Writing Education          21
   *Christiane Donahue*

3  Transnationalism and Translingualism: How They
   Are Connected          41
   *Suresh Canagarajah*

4  Writing Is the Question, Not the Answer: A Critical
   Cosmopolitan Approach to Writing in Neoliberal Times          61
   *Anne Surma*

**viii** Contents

## PART II
# History 77

5 Translanguaging in Hiding: English–Only Instruction
and Literacy Education in Nepal 79
*Shyam Sharma*

6 "Today the Need Arises" اليوم قد مسّت الحاجة : Arabic
Student Writing at the Turn of the 20th Century 95
*Lisa R. Arnold*

## PART III
# Practice 113

7 Potential Phases of Multilingual Writers' Identity Work 115
*Shizhou Yang*

8 Effects of Study-Abroad Experiences on L2 Writing:
Insights From Published Research 138
*Miyuki Sasaki*

9 From Activity to Mobility Systems: Tracing Multilingual
Literacies on the Move 156
*Steven Fraiberg*

10 Technology-Mediated Transnational Writing Education:
An Overview of Research and Practice 170
*Zhiwei Wu*

11 English Teacher Identity Development Through a
Cross-Border Writing Activity 187
*Yufeng Zhang*

12 The Affordances of Facebook for Teaching ESL Writing 203
*June Yichun Liu*

13 Teaching English Academic Writing to Non-English Major
Graduate Students in Chinese Universities: A Review and
a Transnational Vision 222
*Yongyan Li, Xiaohao Ma*

Contents **ix**

14 Epilogue: A Perspective on Transnational Writing
   Education From a New York City Subway Train          244
   *Brooke Ricker Schreiber*


*About the Editor*                                      *253*
*About the Contributors*                                *254*
*Index*                                                 *256*

# PREFACE

Embracing translingualism, transculturalism, and cosmopolitanism as the theoretical pillars, this volume advances transnational writing education in theory building, historical inquiry, study abroad research, information technology-mediated pedagogy, and cross-national scholarly exchange. With obvious overlaps, the chapters are organized under theory, history, and practice. The volume has crossed geographic, disciplinary, and linguistic boundaries: it brings together scholarly voices from Asia-Pacific nations, from writing studies and second language writing; it accommodates diverse "arts of the dwelling place" (You, 2016), a space where scholars co-construct knowledge for a better future through critique, collaboration, multilingualism, code-meshing, translation, and non-verbal representations.

The volume opens with an introduction by Xiaoye You, who defines transnational writing education as efforts made to enable students to recognize, negotiate with, deconstruct, and transcend national, ethnic, and racial boundaries in the teaching of writing, ultimately cultivating flexible and responsible global citizens. After reviewing the formation of nationalism and its relationship to writing instruction, You sketches out three key constructs—translingualism, transculturalism, and cosmopolitanism—in the hope of establishing a transnational framework for writing education. Next, published studies are reviewed to identify pedagogical projects and strategies that have clearly advanced the transnational agenda. Finally, new areas of research and teaching are proposed and the contributions of this volume in moving writing education towards a transnational turn are highlighted.

The next three chapters work towards deeper theory building. In Chapter 2, Christiane Donahue focuses on "trans" understandings of writing and English, using examples from European and US writing work in higher education, to consider what linguistic, rhetorical, and cultural values we should teach our students in transnational contexts. These are considered in the context of new evolutions in world dynamics that have highlighted growing interconnectedness and globalization. The chapter raises questions about the relationship between what we see in writing research and what we teach about writing in multilingual contexts, as well as between academic expectations versus professional ones for language use and writing. Five models for language and writing in this transnational context are presented and compared: translingualism, metrolingualism, *plurilinguisme*, cosmopolitanism, and heteroglossia. Finally, implications for research and for teaching grounded in these models are considered.

In Chapter 3, Suresh Canagarajah suggests that in the context of globalization, all writers occupy a space that is liminal—i.e., between communities, languages, and nations. Such positioning motivates in them a search for identities and literacies that go beyond bounded, static, and territorialized constructs and norms. This liminal space is referred to as transnational. This chapter demonstrates how inhabiting a transnational space is connected to adopting translingual communicative practices. Many complex explanations account for what motivates some to occupy this transnational social space and attain translingual dispositions, while others desire bounded spaces, territorialized identities, and language ownership. The chapter illustrates the connection between translingualism and transnationalism through a literacy autobiography of a Tibetan student in a Midwestern American university. The chapter will also demonstrate the functions of literacy narratives in facilitating a translingual awareness and transnational positioning.

In Chapter 4, Anne Surma reminds us that writing studies as a field has benefited tremendously from a neoliberal economy which values writing as a commercially useful skill and service. However, this politico-economic relationship puts the field in a conundrum: As the language of ethics and the relational, communal world are conflated with or subsumed by the language of economics, the role and practice of writing as a human, social, and politically democratic endeavor may be severely constrained by the very technologies that are claimed to support and extend its communicative and social reach. Drawing on the ideas of critical cosmopolitanism, Surma considers how it might be possible that we as teachers, students, researchers, and citizens write and relate to others in the public domain without resorting to the techniques of the self-serving entrepreneur.

Two chapters present historical inquires. In Chapter 5, Shyam Sharma assesses the effects of English-only instruction on writing education in Nepal, a site little known to scholars of applied linguistics and writing studies. His case study reveals that educational policies as well as market forces favor writing in English, even though it has limited social value and only benefits a minority of people in Nepal. Working from the premise that multilingual education should be promoted as a means for social good, Sharma argues that when English is viewed as the only ticket into the globalized economy, the promotion of English writing skills could only worsen gaps in curriculum and pedagogy and result in more overall harm than good to Nepalese society.

Building on her published work on writing education at Syrian Protestant College, in Chapter 6, Lisa Arnold analyzes a selection of student-authored articles appearing in nine Arabic-language publications between 1900 and 1906 at this English-medium college. These publications provide evidence that students interacted with each other regularly through writing outside of the classroom. These interactions articulate students' values and beliefs about writing, including what they believed writing could (or should) do. They wrote about writing to make sense of its power, to facilitate dialogue and critique, to educate and advise their peers, and to negotiate educational, cultural, and linguistic borders.

Sharing with Canagarajah a concern for students' translingual subjectivity, in Chapter 7, Shizhou Yang develops an interdisciplinary framework for tracing and facilitating multilingual writers' identity work. He first critiques the present scholarship for paying inadequate attention to the continuities of multilingual writers' identities. Then, drawing from poststructuralism, dialogism, and narrative theory, he identifies concepts such as investment, performing, reflecting, re-visioning, co-authoring, and outside witness, for tracing identity development. For illustration, Yang introduces an extracurricular writing group that he organized at an ethnic university in China. Tracing a Bai student's autobiographic writing across multiple samples, Yang is able to reveal the phases in which, with the brokerage of the writing group, the writer developed a translingual subject position. While previous studies, including Canagarajah's chapter, have focused on individuals who have physically crossed national borders, Yang's study reveals how a writer develops a translingual subject position within the borders.

Two chapters focus on issues of study abroad. In Chapter 8, Miyuki Sasaki helps us understand how study-abroad experiences may affect students' L2 literacy development. She starts her chapter by recounting the study abroad experiences of five Japanese women in the second half of the 19th century to establish some bases of language development in relation to study abroad. Then she surveys studies published over the last decade on the impact of study abroad on students' writing in the target language. Studies she reviewed suggest that discernable effects have been found on students' writing in terms of overall essay quality, rhetorical patterns, and composing strategies.

Also examining study-abroad contexts, in Chapter 9, Steve Fraiberg articulates a framework for tracing students' literacy practices across semiotic, social, and geographic borders. This framework attends to the politics of mobility: who moves, when they move, how they move, and to what effect. The mobile literacies approach articulates challenges and offers an alternative to structuralist and container models that have often undergirded academic and disciplinary literacies scholarship. To ground the analysis, Fraiberg focuses on a case study of a Chinese international student and the ways she mobilizes an array of human and non-human actors into her academic literacy practices. Together these actors form part of a complex literacy sponsorscape mediating the formation of her academic and disciplinary identities and literate activities.

Three chapters explore the affordances of technology in breaking down boundaries in the teaching of writing. In Chapter 10, Zhiwei Wu reviews the research and practice in technology-mediated transnational writing education published over the last two decades. After outlining the research outcomes and surveying practice cases in Europe, Asia, Australia, and North America, he identifies three issues prevalent in the existing research and practice: the (un) witting endorsement of Standard English as the privileged language of communication, the unexamined relations between "mere literacy" and multiliteracies, and the institutional confinement of transnational participants. He urges future researchers and practitioners to make three perspectival changes: from a nationalist approach to a cosmopolitan approach; from a monolingual focus to multilingual, multimodal, and multicultural foci; and from institutionally sanctioned access to participatory engagement.

While Canagarajah's chapter introduces literacy autobiography as a means of leading preservice teachers to develop a transnational positioning, in Chapter 11, Yufeng Zhang introduces how she used a tele-collaborative activity for developing such a positioning among preservice English teachers at an American university. She involved her teachers in reading and discussing essays written by undergraduate students from a Chinese university, communicating with the essay writers, and reflecting on their teaching philosophy. By examining the teacher-student correspondence, classroom discussions, and the teachers' reflections, she was able to trace the evolution of teacher identity, which moved from a bounded to a less bounded frame of language and culture.

In Chapter 12, June Yichun Liu examines the affordances of Facebook for academic literacy development in a first-year English course at a Taiwanese university. In the course, Liu created a Facebook space for fifty students to share their writing as well as life experiences. After sorting students' posts into academic writing and non-academic writing, Liu found that these two types of Facebook discourse shaped the students' academic writing in significantly different ways. Further, she found that the writing strategies used by students on Facebook demonstrate a developed awareness of genre and register, and that some students consciously moved between or fused genres or registers for creativity. Such language practice demonstrates their emergent translingual subject positions.

Responding to Donahue's (2009) call for writing studies to become aware of research published in local languages, in Chapter 13, Yongyan Li and Xiaohao Ma survey Chinese-medium scholarship on how English academic writing has been taught to non-English major graduate students in Chinese universities. After scrutinizing twenty-six articles published between 2005 and 2016, they find that academic English writing courses are widely offered in universities specialized in science, engineering, agriculture, and medicine. Since genre pedagogy was introduced into the country in the 1990s, a good number of efforts have been made to localize Western pedagogical ideas. However, most of the articles have focused on the teaching of abstract writing instead of teaching other parts of a research article, an observation that indicates a gap in teacher knowledge or experience with this genre and the urgent need of teacher development. Li and Ma conclude their survey by contemplating on how the notion of translingualism could inform the growing field of English for Research and Publication Purposes.

In the Epilogue, Brooke Ricker Schreiber outlines the specific insights she sees in this collection which can support teachers in facilitating their students' crossing of multiple boundaries within and beyond the classroom. In particular, she focuses on mining the knowledge generated by the volume for concrete pedagogical suggestions: specific ways of engaging students in negotiating language standards, reflecting on their own translingual and transcultural experiences, and working for institutional change.

## References

Donahue, C. (2009). "Internationalization" and composition studies: Reorienting the discourse. *College Composition and Communication, 61*(2), 212–243.

You, X. (2016). *Cosmopolitan English and transliteracy.* Carbondale, IL: Southern Illinois University Press.

# ACKNOWLEDGEMENTS

Language teachers in the U.S. and around the world are experiencing a paradigm shift as they recognize the global connectivity of English education and multiplicity of language practices. This volume represents one response, among many, from teachers and scholars who are concerned about teaching English writing amidst the paradigm shift.

As the worldwide mobility of people, capital, products, and language resources increases, the fields of applied linguistics and writing studies have responded proactively. One of the responses is the launch of the Writing Education Across Borders (WEAB) Conference, which brought together scholars from applied linguistics, education, rhetoric, and writing studies. The first conference was held in State College, Pennsylvania in September 2011, and the second one in Guangzhou, China in May 2016. This volume has resulted from the conversations that converged around these meetings. My sincere gratitude goes to the then-Penn State Confucius Institute and the Penn State Center for Democratic Deliberation for sponsoring the first conference, and the Guangdong University of Foreign Studies Faculty of English Language and Culture for sponsoring and organizing the second one. Colleagues who also contributed to the success of these meetings include Haiyang Ai, Xian Zhang, Alissa Hartig, Yumi Matsumoto, Chao Zheng, Ruiying Niu, Lin Jiang, Huhua Ouyang, and Yinyin Du.

I would like to thank the contributors of this volume for engaging each other during and after the conferences. I also want to thank Jay Jordan, Dwight Atkinson, Sheng-Hsun Lee, and an anonymous reviewer for commenting on parts of the volume. I would also like to thank Routledge editor Karen Adler and the ESL & Applied Linguistics Professional Series editor Eli Hinkel for their encouragement and guidance, and my research assistant Alex Bilger for his copy-edits.

Substantial revisions of portions of the following books appear in this book: Chapter 7: Shizhou Yang (2013), *Autobiographical Writing and Identity in EFL Education* (New York: Routledge); and Chapter 9: Steven Fraiberg, Xiqiao Wang, and Xiaoye You (2017), *Inventing the World Grant University: Chinese International Students' Mobilities, Literacies, and Identities* (Logan, UT: Utah State University Press).

I would like to dedicate this volume to Professor Chao Zheng (郑超). Trained as an applied linguist, he launched the first English Writing Teaching and Research Conference in Guangzhou in 2001, which later became the national organization and annual conference in China. He headed the Intermediate English Writing Teaching Division at Guangdong University of Foreign Studies for more than a decade. Under his leadership, the division's intermediate writing course was awarded the titles of "国家精品课程" (National Excellent Course) and "国家级精品资源共享课" (National Excellent Resources-Sharing Course) by the Chinese Ministry of Education. Professor Zheng and I established a telecollaborative writing program in 2009, enabling Chinese, U.S., and New Zealand university students to converse with one another on issues of English, writing, and culture. By the end of 2017, the program had administered thirty exchanges, shaping the worldviews and literacy experiences of nearly a thousand students. Professor Zheng and his work will be missed.

## References

Yang, S. (2013). *Autobiographical writing and identity in EFL education.* New York: Routledge.

Fraiberg, S., Wang, X., & You, X. (2017). *Inventing the world grant university: Chinese international students' mobilities, literacies, and identities.* Logan, UT: Utah State University Press.

# 1

# INTRODUCTION

## Making a Transnational Turn in Writing Education

*Xiaoye You*

As language educators, we are increasingly confronted by tensions between cultural identities and shifting language practice. These tensions, heightened by war, economic disparity, migration, and the resurgence of nationalism intertwined with racism and xenophobia in Europe and the United States, have stirred up widespread anxieties about our shared future. Social media have only perpetuated the anxieties. As a foreigner teaching in the U.S., I myself was disturbed by, and then shared, Facebook reports about white girls in an Arizona high school wearing letters to form the racial slur "NIXXER" after taking yearbook pictures (Benson, 2016), about a twelve-year-old Menominee student in Wisconsin being suspended from school for speaking in the Menominee language while in class (Campbell, 2016), and about a Black church in Mississippi being set on fire and spray painted with the words "Vote Trump" before the general election (Green, 2016). When I taught a summer course in Shanghai a few years ago, I ran into ethnocentrism as well. A disgruntled man shouted at me in a university cafeteria: "都是中国人，你干嘛说英语?" (We're Chinese. Why do you speak English?).

Individuals who have been directly affected by these events, like myself, probably have pondered questions like: What has language done to me and others? Who am I? And who do I want to become? Conceivably, these questions would prompt their reflections on the boundaries of nation, ethnicity, race, and political affiliation, on whether it is possible to live between or cross these boundaries. As language educators, these events raise similar questions to us and beg other challenging ones: What can *we* do to alleviate these tensions? Are we willing to negotiate with or even depart from these boundaries, boundaries that have long framed our pedagogy, assessment, and administration? In other words, how do we cross borders, and facilitate border crossing for our students? Some of these boundaries fall broadly under or are related to nationalism. Historically, as part of colonial and nation-building projects, notions of race and ethnicity along with

## 2 Xiaoye You

strict linguistic boundaries were developed to differentiate "us" from "them." These artificial categories, enforced in and through language, have structured social experiences and permeated educational systems. Educators in applied linguistics and writing studies need to imagine and actuate a social future beyond what these limiting frames can offer us. This volume will explore conceptual frames, literacy practices, and classroom instructions that challenge, negotiate with, and transcend nationalism and its derivatives.

In this introduction, I will cluster some of these alternative frames and practices broadly under "transnationalism," a notion that both highlights and works to build connections, crossings, and spaces between the existing national, ethnic, racial, and linguistic boundaries. Ethnicity and race are indexed by the term "transnational" because, due to colonial legacies, they are often territorialized in relation to the state. For instance, the U.S. is held by some as belonging to white people, as the racialized incidents reported above insinuate. I define transnational writing education as efforts made to enable students to recognize, negotiate with, deconstruct, and transcend these boundaries in the teaching of writing, ultimately cultivating flexible and responsible global citizens. While "transnational" has been widely used in higher education these days to refer to study programs spanning across two or more countries (Wilkins, 2016), it is used in this volume to accentuate the need for cross-border practice, space, identity, and disposition in writing education. With an orientation geared towards social equality and justice on a global scale, transnational writing education is ethical and ideological work.

To embrace a transnational frame, we need to understand how our dominant frame, broadly called nationalism, came into being and has shaped our work. We also need to identify constructs that can bolster the transnational frame, which can provide support for writing pedagogy, assessment, and administration. In addition, we need to identify workable strategies from previous fights against nationalism, racism, and sexism to build our writing education tool box. In this introduction, I will take stock of the advances that applied linguistics and writing studies have made in these areas, and suggest future directions for research and pedagogy. I will first review the formation of nationalism and its relationship to writing instruction. Then I will sketch out three key constructs—translingualism, transculturalism, and cosmopolitanism—in the hope of establishing a framework for transnational writing education. Next, I will review published studies to identify pedagogical projects and strategies that have clearly advanced the transnational agenda. Finally, I will propose new areas of research and teaching and highlight the contributions of this volume in moving writing education towards a transnational turn.

## Nationalism and Writing Education

The formation of nations always involves constructing boundaries—geographic, cultural, ethnic, and racial. This was the case with ancient nations, such as Qin

China (221BCE–206BCE). The Great Walls were built to demarcate the geographic and cultural borders between the Han and the northern pastoral nomadic tribes. The Qin government issued standards for almost every aspect of life, including measurements and language, such as the size and shape of script and the length of chariot axles. The ultimate purpose is to identify those who conform to the standards as "us," and those who don't, "them." Deeply intertwined with European colonialism, the formation of modern nations has very much followed the same path for building "fences." Native peoples were often described as "them," as barbarians, savages, or degraded races that need to be salvaged by the civilized colonizers. Modern nations always came into being in response to whom their subjects identified with, the privileged colonizer or the wretched colonized. Along with this national subject formation always came both real and imagined boundaries.

As part of an "imagined community" (Anderson, 1991), national subjects are indoctrinated by a bounded perspective of language and nation, or monolingualism. Within the monolingual frame, it is assumed that one communicates with members of an "imagined community," sharing a national language and a national culture; other languages are considered ethnic or foreign and best kept at home or in the classroom (Dicker, 2003). An example of monolingual nationalism is still common in the teaching and research of writing these days: Whatever languages or dialects have mediated a writing activity, when we focus on a multilingual writer's first language, we often assume it is the national code. In case someone chose to study me drafting this introduction, for instance, that person would likely focus on the mediation of Putonghua (China's official code) or of the Putonghua-based writing system. However, my first language is not Putonghua but Hakka. I draw on elements of Hakka, Southwest Mandarin, Putonghua, classical Chinese, and English in my composing process. Such translingual practice, i.e., drawing resources from one's linguistic repertoire, has also been noted by Suresh Canagarajah and Shizhou Yang in their contributions to this volume about a Tibetan and a Bai student from southwestern China writing in English. In multilingual societies, students' languages and dialects do not always coincide with the officially sanctioned codes.

The monolingual perspective, sponsored by the state, has long shaped the literacy classroom. In the U.S., historical accounts abound (e.g., Dayton, 2005; Horner & Trimbur, 2002; NeCamp, 2014; Spack, 2002; Wan, 2014; Webster, 2010). For instance, studying public discourse and beliefs about literacy during the Progressive Era (1890–1920), Dayton (2005) unveiled the conflicts between the monolingual, nationalist pedagogy sponsored by the Americanization programs and the community-based pedagogy sponsored by the labor union programs. In Americanization program classes, immigrants were destabilized and unsure of their class allegiances, and then they learned about the values and mannerisms of the American middle class. The cultural assimilationist expected passivity from students and taught them literacy in its most narrow, utilitarian form. Writing was presented to students as a skill with narrowly defined rules, best learned by repetition. In contrast, the union educators encouraged the students to use their multilingual literacy to meet their diverse, community-based needs and goals. They emphasized small-group learning and student discussion instead of drills, memorization, or lectures. Their pedagogy focused on student leadership, preparation for real-world work, activism, and cultural plurality. Dayton's description calls our attention to the distinction between the two types of programs, one inspired by nationalism and the other by class consciousness, in improving immigrant workers' literacy levels.

When English is taught outside traditionally English-dominant countries, the nationalist ideology often persists. English is viewed as a foreign language, a language of the other, and the acquisition of it as a source of power/prestige. It is presented to students for functional purposes, such as trade or diplomacy; the national language, on the other hand, is viewed as embodying the national essence and good for imaginative and creative work. Such was the case with English in China over the last one and a half centuries. When English composition was first introduced in Chinese colleges in the late 19th century, for instance, controlled composition and current-traditional rhetoric prevailed (You, 2010). In both approaches, Standard English was emphasized. While embracing these approaches, Lawrence W. Faucett (1927) and Chuangui Ge (1941), two composition specialists influential in Republican China (1912–1949), assigned English writing to a narrower domain than Chinese writing in their composition textbooks. Like the Americanization program educators, Faucett and Ge aligned the two approaches with the training of practical, business, and professional genres. For example, Faucett stated that "Many students have been taught literary English in the Far East when their own aim was to secure English for business or professional purposes" (p. 34). Similarly, Ge suggested that students acquire skills in practical genres that they would encounter in their disciplines and future professions.

Along with monolingualism comes the notion of "native speaker" and its derivatives, such as non-native speaker, language learner, and second-language writer. Native speaker identity is also territorialized to index a particular race and national identity regardless of language status (Holliday, 2006; Phillipson, 1992). In many language teaching contexts, native speaker norms are emphasized. In the teaching of English writing to non-native speakers, for instance, native speakers are seen as the target audience and the arbiter of language use. The best known example is probably the research and teaching centered in contrastive rhetoric. When Kaplan (1966) studied the essays of several hundred international students at the University of Southern California, he was interested in identifying their "thought patterns" based on their lingua-cultural background. Unfortunately, the patterns that he generalized came to be reified; English essay patterns were promoted as the native speakers' (read as the white American middle-class) favorite and the target of learning for non-native speakers. This influence lingers until today. When dealing with academic English writing, teachers tend to invoke a Western or Anglo-American audience, treating it as homogenous with rhetorical expectations different from the non-native writer's (see classroom studies such as Petrić, 2005; Walker, 2006; Xing, Wang, & Spencer, 2008).

## Translingualism, Transculturalism, and Cosmopolitanism

Recent conversations in applied linguistics, cultural studies, and philosophy have pointed out ways to move beyond nationalism in imagining a more socially just future. Important to literacy education are such constructs as translingualism, transculturalism, and cosmopolitanism. Arising from both historical human experiences and observations on the flows of people, artifacts, products, and literacy practices in globalization, these constructs provide ways for literacy educators to understand, cross, and sometimes transcend the boundaries that have circumvented students' reading and writing, and to help forge just social relations.

*Translingualism* emphasizes the fluid and artificial boundaries among languages and across modes of representation in human communication (Blackledge & Creese, 2010; Canagarajah, 2013a; García, 2009; Jordan, 2015). Our sense of language and dialect has been deeply influenced by nationalism, which has taught us rigid rules and forms within lingua-cultural boundaries. In practice, languages are neither discrete nor stable but rather dynamic and negotiated, and writing necessarily involves the negotiation of language differences. In translation studies, Liu (1995) used the term "translingual practice" to study how new words, meanings, discourses, and modes of representation arose, circulated, and acquired legitimacy in early modern China as it contacted/collided with European and Japanese languages and literatures. Using the same term in studies of spoken and written interactions, Canagarajah (2013a, 2013c) intends to break down the boundaries of linguistic codes in a speaker's communicative repertoire. He emphasizes two key points in human communication: first, communication transcends individual languages because languages are always in contact and mutually influencing each other; and second, communication transcends words and involves diverse semiotic resources and ecological affordances. In his contribution to this volume, Canagarajah takes a step further by arguing that translingual practice is deeply connected to a transnational positioning.

*Transculturalism* is the next critical lens in transnational writing education (Guerra, 1997, 2015; Pratt, 1991; Zamel, 1997). First defined by the South American scholar Fernando Ortiz, transculturalism refers to the process of *métissage* (mixing of peoples) as a distinctive character of a culture in the Americas, which developed from both native and immigrant populations. Ortiz views transculturalism in its earliest stage as a synthesis of two phases taking place at the same time: a deculturalization of the past and a métissage with the present. As a biological and cultural métis, one is always part of the dialectic with the Other.

Cuccioletta (2001) suggests that the process of recognizing oneself in the Other will lead to a cosmopolitan citizenship: "This citizenship, independent of political structures and institutions, develops each individual in the understanding that one's culture is multiple, métis, and that each human experience and existence is due to the contact with *other*, who in reality is like, oneself" (p. 9, emphasis in the original). Building on translingualism and transculturalism, I proposed the construct of transliteracy, emphasizing that in globalization everyone is a cultural and linguistic métis, but with salient socio-historical differences. When being respected and taken seriously, one has to, and can, come to recognize oneself in the Other through reading and writing across languages, engaging diverse cultural discourses, and shuttling between communities (You, 2016).

While translingualism and transculturalism describe language and cultural practices people already engage in, *cosmopolitanism* refers to a cross-border disposition to be inculcated in teachers and students. Although the term "cosmopolitanism" has been attributed to Diogenes the Cynic, an ancient Greek, the same ideal can be found in many cultures, such as in the writings of Confucius in China (Chan, 2002), of Immanuel Kant in Germany, and of W. E. B. Dubois, Martin Luther King Jr., and Barack Obama in the U.S. (Mullen, 2004; Selzer, 2010). Of its various formulations, cosmopolitanism carries a fundamental meaning: though sometimes defined by kindred relations, ethnicity, nation, race, or class, all people are first and foremost members of the human race, and as such are morally obligated to those outside their categories; further, they have the agency to develop and sustain new allegiances across cultures, communities, and languages. Taking an antiessentialist stand, the cosmopolitan perspective reminds us of the historicity, artificiality, and rhetoricity of these cultural categories, and more importantly, the historical effects of these categories. In writing studies, this perspective enables us to perceive human connectedness as being deeply underpinned in the various accents, styles, and uses of language in everyday life and literary culture. Linguistic, cultural, and ethnic differences are not things to be contained, but matters to be respected and appreciated. They need to be explored in pedagogy and research, to recover and protect the multifaceted, intricate human connections severed by artificial borders.

Together, translingualism, transculturalism, and cosmopolitanism constitute the theoretical pillars of transnational writing education. Translingualism calls our attention to how we use language and other systems of representation in communication, effectively tearing down the façade of language boundaries, and by extension, that of national, ethnic, and racial boundaries. Transculturalism reminds us that we are always culturally hybrid by nature, however we define "culture." We are always in a state of diaspora if there was ever a "home" in the first place. The way we encounter, blend in, and reconstitute various cultures challenges the idealized original "us." Cosmopolitanism offers an ethical imperative for literacy education. In addition to educating our students as national subjects, we must educate them at the same time as responsible global citizens. Further, as articulated by Surma (2013) and others, in writing studies cosmopolitanism can serve as a form of resistance to, or a critique of, the destructive aspects of globalization, particularly of the neo-liberal market economy, in current societal developments (see Surma's chapter in this volume for an elaboration). Therefore, what transnational writing education does is reexamine human history to distill lessons of crossing boundaries ethically and effectively in communication and cultural lives, and import such lessons into our education endeavors. In the remainder of this introduction, I will survey writing education in the past and the present to distill such lessons, and to suggest directions for future teaching and research.

## Transnational Writing Education in the Past

Transnational writing education has a long history. Since ancient times, the teaching of writing could often end up being transnational because teachers and students travelled across geographic and cultural borders and constructed social relations transcending these borders (Alberca, 1994; Berlin, 1984; Miller, 1997; Seeley, 1991). The spread of classical Chinese in Japan, for instance, took place largely through migration and travel. Chinese and Korean immigrants brought classical Chinese into Japan in the 5th century, which became its first major writing system. While for a long time it was only available to the elite class as a foreign language, over time its users appropriated it, along with imported Chinese texts, for their practical and imaginative purposes. When the oldest extant chronicle in Japan, 古事記 (Kojiki), was composed in the 8th century, Confucian and local historiographic methods were fused and the practice of writing with Japanese syntax while using kanji (Chinese characters), partially as phonograms, was firmly established (Seeley, 1991). The engagement with Chinese texts enabled the Japanese literati to transcend their geographic and cultural borders. Similarly, Miller (1997) traced the teaching of college writing in the U.S. to the establishment of college English studies in British cultural provinces in the mid-18th century. English literature, composition, and rhetoric were introduced into colleges throughout these provinces, which saw English studies as a means to upward social mobility through cultural assimilation. In the educational centers of England, however, the introduction of English represented a literacy crisis brought on by provincial institutions that had failed to maintain classical texts and learned languages. A similar literacy crisis occurred in the late-19th-century U.S.: colleges found incoming students unprepared for the writing ability required in academic work, which gave rise to the first-year writing requirement. In those early years, pedagogical approaches were introduced from Britain, and students often transcended national borders by engaging European authors on topics of moral philosophy and art in their writing assignments (Berlin, 1984; Jolliffe, 1989).

While writing education has almost always been transnational, historically the state reinforces monolingual nationalism through its apparatuses. In schools, this ideology gets perpetuated through pedagogy, assessment, and administration. Research dealing with the transnational aspect of writing education has also been shaped by this ideology. For instance, the rise of teaching ESL writing in the U.S. was connected to the influx of immigrant and international students after WWII. However, research dealing with ESL writers for a long time focused on enabling those students to adapt to their new national home by acquiring native speaker norms (Silva & Matsuda, 2001). When teaching and research are united under monolingual nationalism, teachers and students tend to develop bounded, static perspectives to identity, culture, and language, sometimes leading to indifference, biases, and bigotry towards the other. Over the last two decades, scholars in applied linguistics and writing studies have recognized the detrimental effects of this language ideology in the teaching of writing (Lu, 1994; Horner & Trimbur, 2002; Matsuda, 2006), and sought ways to engage students in identifying, negotiating with, and transcending linguistic and cultural differences (Horner, Lu, Royster, & Trimbur, 2011).

In recent years, scholars who identified with the three theoretical pillars of transnational writing education have undertaken a series of studies to examine the recent history of writing instruction outside the U.S., such as China (You, 2010), Indonesia (Engelson, 2011), Syria (Arnold, 2014), and Jamaica (Milson-Whyte, 2015). Invariably, these scholars discovered that teachers and students struggled in their negotiation with monolingual norms and forged translocal subjectivities through writing across languages and discourses. In her study of language attitudes, policies, and pedagogies at Syrian Protestant College (present-day American University of Beirut) in the 19th century, for instance, Arnold (2014) notes the change around 1880 of the college's medium of instruction from Arabic to English. The faculty initially wrote and translated texts for, and taught their courses in, Arabic. Then they switched to English because they believed that teaching in Arabic had not proven to be "the best means of Christianizing and civilizing the East" (p. 283, cited in Arnold, 2014). Additionally, as the student population and faculty hires diversified, Arabic was not always a language known to them. It is important to note that before and after the change of language of instruction, students and faculty were forced to negotiate and switch between English, Arabic, French, and other languages across the college curriculum as writers, readers, and speakers. Their translingual literacy practice enabled them to construct identities beyond territorialized lingua-cultural norms.

## Transnational Writing Education in the Present

The number of studies addressing issues of writing education from a transnational perspective is increasing. These issues include the development of viable pedagogical projects and writing programs (Marko, 2012; Martins, 2015; Starke-Meyerring, 2005; You, 2016), racial justice in writing assessment (Inoue & Poe, 2012), research collaboration across national borders (Donahue, 2009), and the

Introduction **9**

establishment of translingual norms in scholarly writing (Hartse & Kubota, 2014; Horner, NeCamp, & Donahue, 2011). These issues have been approached from both the applied linguistics and writing studies fields. However, published studies in English tend to be U.S.-centered thus far, either because the scholars or publishing venues are located in the country or because such education programs were initiated there. In this section, I briefly survey published pedagogical projects that have adopted a translingual-transcultural perspective.

Over the last two decades, applied linguistics scholars have increasingly recognized the fluid and contested boundaries between cultures (Atkinson, 2004; Belcher, 2014; Canagarajah, 2006, 2013b; Connor, 2011; Kubota, 1999; Matsuda, 1997). As contrastive rhetoric gradually moved to intercultural rhetoric, for instance, Connor (2011) identified three concepts as good practice in teaching L2 writing at the university level. They include cross-cultural contrasts in contexts, interactional accommodation, and dynamic cultures and genres. Interactional accommodation aligns with a translingual perspective to communication, emphasizing that languages are dynamic and negotiated. Key to Connor's conceptualization of culture is her adoption of Holliday's (1999) notion of "small culture," which aligns with transculturalism. While large culture denotes ethnic, national, and international group features, small culture portrays "any cohesive social grouping" (p. 237). Small culture is a dynamic, ongoing group process, in which members develop a discernible set of behaviors and understandings related to group cohesion. In forming a small culture, members bring with them residues of other small cultures.

Pedagogical studies carrying the spirit of intercultural rhetoric have been few. One exception is Abasi (2012), who examined the attitudes of American learners of Persian towards the rhetorical differences between two political commentaries, one written in Persian and the other translated into Persian from English without changing the original organizational structure. To help his students avoid stereotyping and essentializing the Persian writing style, Abasi invited a former Iranian journalist to come to his class to give a first-person account of the circumstances that gave rise to the Persian text, which was negatively judged by Abasi's students. Liebman's (1988) study also carried the spirit of intercultural rhetoric. In her classes involving both American and international writers, students worked as both researchers and participants to test Kaplan's (1966) hypothesis that speakers of different lingua-cultural backgrounds may organize texts differently. Despite their general agreement with Kaplan in the end, the students voiced objections, challenging the essentialized view of rhetorics promoted by Kaplan's hypothesis. Liebman found that, through this classroom experience, students gained increased awareness of the rhetorical choices available in any language. Furthermore, students involved in writing about writing developed their metacognitive skills, particularly the skill of culturally decentering themselves.

In writing studies, the transnational perspective has garnered the most synergy in the area of professional communication. Starke-Meyerring (2005), for instance, proposed a framework for developing global literacies in professional communication programs. With attention to pluralized identities and blurred boundaries, increased interactions between local and global discourses, and ideological contestations surrounding neoliberalism and the ideal of a global civil society, her framework aligns with translingualism, transculturalism, and cosmopolitanism. To teach global literacies, she proposes reconsidering the distinction between national and international professional communication, emphasizing pedagogies of boundary work and transcontextual, critical literacies, and developing partnership networks for borderless learning environments. Indeed, global partnership programs have been widely adopted in the teaching of business and technical writing (Anderson, Bergman, Bradley, Gustafsson, & Matzke, 2010; Connor, Davis, Rycker, Phillips, & Verckens, 1997; Herrington, 2010; Sapp, 2004; Starke-Meyerring, 2005; Starke-Meyerring & Andrews, 2006; Starke-Meyerring & Wilson, 2008) but much less in other areas of writing studies (see Verzella & Tommaso, 2014, for first-year composition and Craig, 2014, for writing across the curriculum). While these programs involve students and teachers from two or more nations, who have to negotiate linguistic and cultural differences, the programs do not always succeed in cultivating students' intercultural sensitivity. After examining seven partnership programs in professional communication, Bégin-Caouette (2013) notes that power imbalances, in terms of language, technology, and resources, can undermine the success of such programs as alternatives to the current globalization master-discourse.

Some pedagogical projects informed by the three theoretical pillars have emerged in other areas of writing studies in the last few years (Canagarajah, 2011, 2015; Fraiberg, Wang, & You, 2017; Marko, 2012; Marko, Osorio, Sepenoski, & Catalani, 2014; You, 2016). Drawing on Appadurai's (1996) conceptualization of "scapes" in globalization, for instance, Marko (2012) argues for and practiced a pedagogscape. She wants to intervene in "the cultural flows of (imperialist, neoliberal) dominant cultural producers of a dominant global image about people, events and countries occupying less dominant positions of cultural flow" (p. 1). In her first-year writing class at Emerson College in the U.S., she involved faculty members and young emerging artists, architects, writers, historians, journalists, urban planners, filmmakers, television producers, and marketers at both Emerson and the Universidad Nacional de Colombia of Medellín in Colombia in multiple art and writing projects. Through collaboratively writing grants and other documents in English and Spanish, her Emerson students helped bring Colombian students and teachers to showcase those projects in the U.S. As another example of pedagogscape, Marko et al. (2014) designed an English course for Latin American immigrant maintenance workers who clean toilets at Emerson. As a class project, the students/workers wrote down their stories and perspectives about immigration and education. Their writings were pasted on a fifty-van caravan, which travelled across the U.S. to educate people about immigration and inclusive education at colleges and conferences. Marko's pedagogscape effectively engaged students in negotiating linguistic and cultural differences, leading them towards curiosity, respect, affinity, and responsibility for strangers.

In *Cosmopolitan English and Transliteracy* (2016), I advocate a transliteracy approach to the teaching of writing. This approach encourages students to negotiate across linguistic and cultural differences in making meaning, and at the same time to develop affinity with the other. I used this approach across several types of writing courses in China and the U.S. In a first-year writing course, for example, by engaging my students in conversing with multiple audiences, they experienced the challenges and possibilities of crossing cultural boundaries and assuming multiple identities in academic discourse. In an advanced English course for American students, I implemented a pedagogy aimed at fostering their translingual and transcultural sensibilities. I also introduced a model for training writing teachers in the context of globalization, grounded in a study of a cross-national partnership with colleagues in China. When confronted with language and cultural differences in their literacy activities, my students were led to develop respect and understanding for the other, demonstrating the viability of a cosmopolitan ideal in writing education.

## Transnational Writing Education in the Future

To move transnational writing education forward, interdisciplinary work is needed. Much work has thus far been taken up by educators in applied linguistics, education, and writing studies. As this volume will illustrate, other fields, such as computer-mediated communication, feminist studies, literary studies, mobility studies, and transnational higher education, have much to offer. In research and pedagogy, efforts are required across multiple areas: theory building, historical inquiry, study abroad research, technology-assisted cross-cultural pedagogies, and scholarly exchange across national, disciplinary, and linguistic borders.

While cognizant of the three theoretical pillars for transnational writing education, we need to continue exploring each construct and the connections between them. For example, in terms of translingualism and transculturalism, should they stay largely descriptive of what's on the ground, or could they be methodologies for research and pedagogy? The three concepts that Connor (2011) identified as important in intercultural rhetoric pedagogy (cross-cultural contrasts in contexts, interactional accommodation, and dynamic cultures and genres) suggest that translingualism and transculturalism can serve as methodologies for pedagogy. Classroom reports by Canagarajah (2011, 2015), Marko (2012), and You (2016) have also confirmed these concepts' pedagogical value. Cosmopolitanism suggests an ethical imperative in globalization and performs a critique of the neoliberal discourse in education. While the ultimate goal of celebrating cosmopolitanism in literacy education is to cultivate flexible and responsible global citizens, educators don't seem to have a good grip on what a

**12** Xiaoye You

good global citizen looks like. In this volume, Suresh Canagarajah's and Shizhou Yang's conceptual work on transnational positioning takes an important step towards constructing such a portrait. Continual exploration of the theoretical pillars and other related constructs will provide critical frames for future research and teaching.

History provides important lessons for us about conducting writing education ethically and effectively. While historical studies have thus far informed us about the transnational nature of writing instruction, we have to remember that every site has a unique sociocultural formation, which makes the challenges of teaching writing different in every context. Future studies can continue examining geographic sites little known to the international community of writing educators, including their sociocultural contexts; the ways in which monolingual nationalism has shaped assumptions of writing, writing pedagogies, and writing practices; and the ways that teachers, students, administrators, and policy makers struggled against this ideology (see Shyam Sharma's chapter in this volume on teaching writing in Nepal as an example). And we can study locations of writing education beyond the classroom (see Lisa Arnold's chapter on Arabic-language magazines as an alternative space for writing education).

Cross-national mobility of students and teachers is a defining feature of the higher education scene these days. Study abroad has long been celebrated, especially in Western universities, as an important form of international education (Clarke III, Flaherty, Wright, & McMillen, 2009; Williams, 2005). It is often claimed that through study abroad, students will increase their global awareness and intercultural competence critical for functioning in this interconnected world. Study abroad can enhance academic learning. Students can improve their learning of foreign languages as they interact with native speakers, and they can take courses that may not be offered in their home institutions. However, while much studied in applied linguistics, study abroad has received negligible attention in writing studies, often focused on ESL/immigrant students. As more students participate in study abroad, we need to understand how this experience may shape their reading and writing across languages and cultures (See Miyuki Sasaki's review chapter on the impact of study abroad on students' L2 written products and composing strategies, and Steve Fraiberg's chapter on how to trace students' mobilities, identities, and literacy practices in study-abroad contexts).

The ability of information technology to connect distant writers and classrooms is a critical condition for transnational writing education. Previous studies have revealed its affordances in helping students acquire target languages and rhetorical conventions. Much less known, however, is in what ways it may enable or hinder students in negotiating with linguistic and cultural boundaries and in constructing transnational identities. Published studies have focused on transnational identity formation outside the classroom (DePew, 2011; Depew & Miller-Cochran, 2010; Schreiber, 2015; You, 2011). Future studies can focus on the classroom by, for example, bringing the three concepts of intercultural rhetoric pedagogy (Connor, 2011) into technology-mediated instructional spaces (see

Zhiwei Wu's review chapter on cross-cultural telecollaborative activities and the challenges in fostering transnational positioning therein; Yufeng Zhang's chapter on how a cross-national online writing activity led pre-service English teachers to develop professional identities in a transnational frame; and June Yichun Liu's chapter on how Facebook enabled her students to develop genre and register awareness and form translingual subjectivity).

To move out of the national frame, as Donahue (2009) has suggested, we need to learn about scholarship and pedagogy outside of our national and linguistic bounds. Translation of scholarship and primary sources from non-English-dominant contexts into English is needed. Ezzaher (2015), Kirkpatrick (2005), and Wu and Swearingen (2016) translated classical rhetorical treaties from non-Western contexts into English. Yongyan Li and Xiaohao Ma's chapter is another exemplary effort; they introduced a body of scholarship published in Chinese on teaching academic English writing in China.

## References

Abasi, A. R. (2012). The pedagogical value of intercultural rhetoric: A report from a Persian-as-a-foreign-language classroom. *Journal of Second Language Writing, 21*(3), 195–220.

Alberca, W. L. (1994). English language teaching in the Philippines during the early American period: Lessons from the Thomasites. *Philippine Journal of Linguistics, 25*(1/2), 53–74.

Anderson, B. (1991). *Imagined communities: Reflections on the origin and spread of nationalism* (Revised ed.). New York: Verso.

Anderson, P., Bergman, B., Bradley, L., Gustafsson, M., & Matzke, A. (2010). Peer reviewing across the Atlantic: Patterns and trends in L1 and L2 comments made in an asynchronous online collaborative learning exchange between technical communication students in Sweden and in the United States. *Journal of Business and Technical Communication, 24*(3), 296–322.

Appadurai, A. (1996). *Modernity at large: Cultural dimensions of globalization*. Minneapolis: University of Minneapolis Press.

Arnold, L. R. (2014). "The worst part of the dead past": Language attitudes, policies, and pedagogies at Syrian Protestant College, 1866–1902. *College Composition and Communication, 66*(2), 276–300.

Atkinson, D. (2004). Contrasting rhetorics/contrasting cultures: Why contrastive rhetoric needs a better conceptualization of culture. *Journal of English for Academic Purposes, 3*, 277–289.

Bégin-Caouette, O. (2013). Globally networked learning environments as eduscapes for mutual understanding. *Critical Intersections in Education, 1*(2), 54–70.

Belcher, D. (2014). What we need and don't need intercultural rhetoric for: A retrospective and prospective look at an evolving research area. *Journal of Second Language Writing, 25*, 59–67.

Benson, P. (2016, January 22). Students disciplined after offensive photo surfaces with racial slur. *Hawaii News Now*. Retrieved from www.hawaiinewsnow.com/story/31034456/students-disciplined-after-offensive-photo-surfaces-with-racial-slur?sf19472172=1

Berlin, J. (1984). *Writing instruction in nineteenth-century American colleges*. Carbondale: Southern Illinois University Press.

**14** Xiaoye You

Blackledge, A., & Creese, A. (2010). *Multilingualism: A critical perspective*. New York: Continuum.

Campbell, J. (2016, September 5). Wisconsin Menominee student suspended for speaking in her native language. *Counter Current News*. Retrieved from http://countercurrentnews.com/2016/09/wisconsin-menominee-student-suspended-speaking-native-language/

Canagarajah, S. (2006). Toward a writing pedagogy of shuttling between languages: Learning from multilingual writers. *College English, 68*, 589–604.

Canagarajah, S. (2011). Codemeshing in academic writing: Identifying teachable strategies of translanguaging. *Modern Language Journal, 95*(3), 401–417.

Canagarajah, S. (2013a). *Translingual practices: Global Englishes and cosmopolitan relations*. New York: Routledge.

Canagarajah, S. (2013b). From intercultural rhetoric to cosmopolitan practice. In D. Belcher, & G. Nelson (Eds.), *Critical and corpus-based approaches to intercultural rhetoric* (pp. 203–226). Ann Arbor: University of Michigan Press.

Canagarajah, S. (Ed.). (2013c). *Literacy as translingual practice: Between communities and classrooms*. New York: Routledge.

Canagarajah, S. (2015). "Blessed in my own way": Pedagogical affordances for dialogical voice construction in multilingual student writing. *Journal of Second Language Writing, 27*, 122–139.

Chan, K. (2002). Both sides, now: Culture contact, hybridization, and cosmopolitanism. In S. Vertovec, & R. Cohen (Eds.), *Conceiving cosmopolitanism: Theory, context, and practice* (pp. 191–208). New York: Oxford University Press.

Clarke III, I., Flaherty, T. B., Wright, N. D., & McMillen, R. M. (2009). Student intercultural proficiency from study abroad programs. *Journal of Marketing Education, 31*, 173–181.

Connor, U. (2011). *Intercultural rhetoric in the writing classroom*. Ann Arbor: University of Michigan Press.

Connor, U., Davis, K., Rycker, T., Phillips, E., & Verckens, J. (1997). An international course in international business writing: Belgium, Finland, and the United States. *Business Communication Quarterly, 60*(4), 63–74.

Craig, J. L. (2014). Teaching writing in a globally networked learning environment (GNLE): Diverse students at a distance. In T. M. Zawacki, & M. Cox (Eds.), *WAC and second-language writers: Research towards linguistically and culturally inclusive programs and practices* (pp. 369–386). Anderson, SC: Parlor Press.

Cuccioletta, D. (2001). Multiculturalism or transculturalism: Towards a cosmopolitan citizenship. *London Journal of Canadian Studies, 17*, 1–11.

Dayton, A. E. (2005). *Representations of literacy: The teaching of English and the immigrant experience in early twentieth-century America*. Ph.D. Dissertation, University of Arizona.

DePew, K. E. (2011). Social media at academia's periphery: Studying multilingual developmental writers' Facebook composing strategies. *The Reading Matrix, 11*(1), 54–75.

Depew, K. E., & Miller-Cochran, S. (2010). Social networking in a second language: Engaging multiple literate practices through identity composition. In M. Cox, J. Jordan, C. Ortmeier-Hooper, & G. G. Schwartz (Eds.), *Reinventing identities in second language writing* (pp. 273–295). Urbana, IL: NCTE.

Dicker, S. J. (2003). *Languages in America: A pluralist view* (2nd ed.). London: Multilingual Matters.

Donahue, C. (2009). "Internationalization" and composition studies: Reorienting the discourse. *College Composition and Communication, 61*(2), 212–243.

Engelson, A. (2011). *Writing the local-global: An ethnography of friction and negotiation in an English-using Indonesian Ph.D. program*. Open Access Dissertations, Paper 463, University of Massachusetts, Amherst. Retrieved from http://scholarworks.umass.edu/open_access_dissertations/463.

Ezzaher, L. E. (trans.). (2015). *Three Arabic treatises on Aristotle's rhetoric: The commentaries of al-Farabi, Avicenna, and Averroes*. Carbondale, IL: Southern Illinois University Press.

Faucett, L. W. (1927). *The teaching of English in the Far East*. New York: World Book.

Fraiberg, S., Wang, X., & You, X. (2017). *Inventing the world grant university: Chinese international students' mobilities, literacies, and identities*. Logan, UT: Utah State University Press.

García, O. (2009). *Bilingual education in the 21st century: A global perspective*. Oxford: Wiley-Blackwell.

Ge, C. (1941). *Yingyu zuowen jiaoben [A textbook of English composition]*. Shanghai: Jingwen shuju.

Green, E. (2016, November 2). A black church burned in the name of Trump. *The Atlantic*. Retrieved from http://countercurrentnews.com/2016/09/wisconsin-menominee-student-suspended-speaking-native-language/

Guerra, J. C. (1997). The place of intercultural literacy in the writing classroom. In C. Severino, J. C. Guerra, & J. E. Butler (Eds.), *Writing in multicultural settings* (pp. 248–260). New York: MLA.

Guerra, J. C. (2015). *Language, culture, identity and citizenship in college classrooms and communities*. New York: Routledge.

Hartse, J. H., & Kubota, R. (2014). Pluralizing English? Variation in high-stakes academic texts and challenges of copyediting. *Journal of Second Language Writing, 24*, 71–82.

Herrington, T. (2010). Crossing global boundaries: Beyond intercultural communication. *Journal of Business and Technical Communication, 24*(4), 516–539.

Holliday, A. (1999). Small cultures. *Applied Linguistics, 20*, 237–264.

Holliday, A. (2006). Native-speakerism. *ELT Journal, 60*(4), 385–387.

Horner, B., Lu, M.-Z., Royster, J., & Trimbur, J. (2011). Language difference in writing: Toward a translingual approach. *College English, 73*(3), 303–321.

Horner, B., NeCamp, S., & Donahue, C. (2011). Toward a multilingual writing scholarship: From English only to a translingual norm. *College Composition and Communication, 63*(2), 269–300.

Horner, B., & Trimbur, J. (2002). English only and U.S. college composition. *College Composition and Communication, 53*(4), 594–630.

Inoue, A. B., & Poe, M. (Eds.). (2012). *Race and writing assessment*. New York: Peter Lang.

Jolliffe, D. (1989). The moral subject in college composition: A conceptual framework and the case of Harvard, 1865–1900. *College English, 51*(2), 163–173.

Jordan, J. (2015). Material translingual ecologies. *College English, 77*(4), 364–382.

Kaplan, R. B. (1966). Cultural thought patterns in inter-cultural education. *Language Learning, 16*(1–2), 1–20.

Kirkpatrick, A. (2005). China's first systematic account of rhetoric: An introduction to Chen Kui's *Wen Ze*. *Rhetorica, 23*(2), 103–152.

Kubota, R. (1999). Japanese culture constructed by discourses: Implications for applied linguistics research and English language teaching. *TESOL Quarterly, 33*, 9–35.

Liebman, J. (1988). Contrastive rhetoric: Students as ethnographers. *Journal of Basic Writing, 7*(2), 6–27.

Liu, L. (1995). *Translingual practice: Literature, national culture, and translated modernity— China, 1900–1937*. Stanford, CA: Stanford University Press.

Lu, M.-Z. (1994). Professing multiculturalism: The politics of style in the contact zone. *College Composition and Communication, 45*(4), 442–458.

Marko, T. (2012). *Proyecto Boston Medellín as pedagogscape.* Retrieved from http://mobility17.com/wp-content/uploads/2013/09/MarkoPBMasPedagogscape.pdf.

Marko, T., Osorio, M. E., Sepenoski, E., & Catalani, R. (2014). Proyecto Carrito: When the student receives an "A" and the worker gets fired: Disrupting the unequal political economy of translingual rhetorical mobility. *Literacy in Composition Studies, 2*(2), 21–43.

Martins, D. S. (Ed.). (2015). *Transnational writing program administration.* Logan, UT: Utah State University Press.

Matsuda, P. K. (1997). Contrastive rhetoric in context: A dynamic model of L2 writing. *Journal of Second Language Writing, 6*(1), 45–60.

Matsuda, P. K. (2006). The myth of linguistic homogeneity in U.S. college composition. *College English, 68*(6), 637–651.

Miller, T. (1997). *The formation of College English: Rhetoric and belles lettres in the British cultural provinces.* Pittsburgh: University of Pittsburgh Press.

Milson-Whyte, V. (2015). *Academic writing instruction for creole-influenced students.* Jamaica: University of the West Indies Press.

Mullen, B. V. (2004). *Afro-orientalism.* Minneapolis, MI: University of Minnesota Press.

NeCamp, S. (2014). *Adult literacy and American identity: The moonlight schools and Americanization programs.* Carbondale, IL: Southern Illinois University Press.

Petrić, B. (2005). Contrastive rhetoric in the writing classroom: A case study. *English for Specific Purposes, 24,* 213–228.

Phillipson, R. (1992). *Linguistic imperialism.* Oxford: Oxford University Press.

Pratt, M. L. (1991). Arts of the contact zone. *Profession, 91,* 33–40.

Sapp, D. (2004). Global partnerships in business communication. *Business Communication Quarterly, 67*(3), 267–280.

Schreiber, B. R. (2015). "I am what I am": Multilingual identity and digital translanguaging. *Language Learning and Technology, 19*(3), 69–87.

Seeley, C. (1991). *A history of writing in Japan.* Leiden, The Netherlands: E. J. Brill.

Selzer, L. (2010). Barack Obama, the 2008 presidential election, and the new Cosmopolitanism: Figuring the black body. *MELUS, 35*(4), 15–37.

Silva, T., & Matsuda, P. K. (Eds.). (2001). *Landmark essays on ESL writing.* Mahwah, NJ: Lawrence Erlbaum.

Spack, R. (2002). *America's second tongue: American Indian education and the ownership of English, 1860–1900.* Lincoln, NE: University of Nebraska Press.

Starke-Meyerring, D. (2005). Meeting the challenges of globalization: A framework for global literacies in professional communication programs. *Journal of Business and Technical Communication, 19*(4), 468–499.

Starke-Meyerring, D., & Andrews, D. (2006). Building a shared virtual learning culture: An international classroom partnership. *Business Communication Quarterly, 69*(1), 25–49.

Starke-Meyerring, D., & Wilson, M (Eds.). (2008). *Designing globally networked learning environments: Visionary partnerships, policies, and pedagogies.* Rotterdam, The Netherlands: Sense.

Surma, A. (2013). *Imagining the cosmopolitan in public and professional writing.* New York: Palgrave Macmillan.

Verzella, M., & Tommaso, L. (2014). Learning to write for an international audience through cross-cultural collaboration and text-negotiation. *Changing English, 21*(4), 310–321.

Walker, D. (2006). Improving Korean university student EFL academic writing with contrastive rhetoric: Teacher conferencing and peer-response can help. *Journal of Asia TEFL, 3*(4), 71–111.

Wan, A. J. (2014). *Producing good citizens: Literacy training in anxious times.* Pittsburgh: University of Pittsburgh Press.

Webster, A. K. (2010). "Still, she didn't see what I was trying to say": Toward a history of framing Navajo English in Navajo written poetry. *World Englishes, 29*(1), 75–96.

Wilkins, S. (2016). Transnational higher education in the 21st century. *Journal of Studies in International Education, 20*(1), 3–7.

Williams, T. R. (2005). Exploring the impact of study abroad on students' intercultural communication skills: Adaptability and sensitivity. *Journal of Studies in International Education, 9*(4), 356–371.

Wu, H., & Swearingen, J. (2016). *Guiguzi, China's first treatise on rhetoric: A critical translation and commentary.* Carbondale, IL: Southern Illinois University Press.

Xing, M., Wang, J., & Spencer, K. (2008). Raising students' awareness of cross-cultural contrastive rhetoric in English writing via an e-learning course. *Language Learning & Technology, 12*(2), 71–93.

You, X. (2010). *Writing in the devil's tongue: A history of English composition in China.* Carbondale, IL: Southern Illinois University Press.

You, X. (2011). Chinese white-collar workers and multilingual creativity in the diaspora. *World Englishes, 30*(3), 409–427.

You, X. (2016). *Cosmopolitan English and transliteracy.* Carbondale, IL: Southern Illinois University Press.

Zamel, V. (1997). Toward a model of transculturation. *TESOL Quarterly, 31*, 341–352.

# PART I
# Theory

# 2

# RHETORICAL AND LINGUISTIC FLEXIBILITY

## Valuing Heterogeneity in Academic Writing Education

*Christiane Donahue*

This chapter will focus on "trans" understandings of writing and English, using examples from European and US writing work in higher education, to reply to the collection's call to consider "how we might think about the global nature of writing education" in both teaching and research. It will do so in the context of new evolutions in world dynamics that have highlighted growing interconnectedness and globalization, and that have been much-discussed in the past couple of decades. These evolutions are in contrast to a strong tendency in the past several decades to build our understanding via the study of comparisons and contrasts that have tended to reify geographic and linguistic frontiers and to inform our teaching accordingly. I hope we might move differently in our exchanges if we shift the emphasis in the ways I believe are enabled by transnationally-situated models, moving towards embracing complexity and resisting seamless narratives of bordered difference. There is much to be done.

As I consider the changes leading to new global norms, I want to emphasize that the references I will make are to US and European trends and scholars, but my sense is that the issues I'll raise are in play beyond those two regional contexts. I note as well, as I do this, that there is always tension between research—**studying and analyzing**—the questions we take on here about heterogeneous language use and academic writing, as compared to **teaching** academic writing in these multilingual or translingual contexts. The tensions can be between institutional language norms and on-the-ground language practices, between practice and theory, or between description and action. My work in this area is grounded in my dedication to academic writing—to studying and teaching writing—in an increasingly complex world, and to the needs of the students in front of me each year. But it is also grounded in a somewhat activist stance towards changing world expectations via research that shows language practices on the ground.

A key gap in our research is any deeply data-driven evidence that institutional or educational norms are changing now. While extensive research has begun to show—and to celebrate—heterogeneous linguistic, discursive, and rhetorical practices that are clearly successful in some contexts, how we understand "successful" and what the realities on the ground are in terms of the *reception* of heterogeneous, translingual, heteroglossic, and cosmopolitan productions in non-literary and non-everyday or business settings, in particular in education, are far less empirically researched (see Rampton, 2008; Hill, 1999; Pennycook, 2010). I suspect these will need to develop side-by-side. That line of thinking leads to questioning the relationship between institutional norms within the academy and practices outside of the academy. It is possible that the evolving globalized, digital, and linguistic context of professional activities today is not well aligned with much of what we support within the higher education domain of writing instruction.

## And What About English?

Academic writing has been, of course, developing in English world-wide for decades now, and Englishes are a longstanding but rapidly expanding linguistic medium, though what is often not underlined is the degree to which the humanities, and to a lesser degree the social sciences, still value publication in multiple languages. But I hope to suggest, in line with scholars such as Horner, NeCamp, and Donahue (2011), Fraiberg (2010), Lillis and Curry (2010), Seidlhofer (2009), or Lillis, Hewings, Vladimirou, and Curry (2010), that this development does not mean we are looking at a future of transparent communication via single-language use—the picture is far more complicated. That is, the relative ubiquity of English in no way leads to transparency, simple communication, or the absence of multilinguality and multilingual influences.

Academic writing in the 21st century is likely to continue to develop in every language. Indeed, in countries such as China, the current on-the-ground sentiment is, "why would we switch entirely to English?" (Maubrey, personal correspondence). Imagining a future of only one academic language, as has been more and more frequently suggested in US and European scholarship as early as the 1990s (Coleman, 2006; Flowerdew, 1999; Tardy, 2004), flies in the face of the many national and international movements to save languages, maintain languages, grow languages, and grow speakers' and writers' pluralities (see, for example, the European policies about plurilingual development in elementary and secondary schooling as represented in the Common European Frame of Reference), as well as to develop and support university academic, research, or scientific writing in those languages. As we think about how academic writing works across languages, and how English might work in that context, all scholars who study writing need to focus on how language itself, in our rapidly-changing academic contexts, might be seen differently, and thus might transform academic writing.

## A "Trans" Understanding?

In the past few decades, much of the work studying language and writing in different cultural contexts has been grounded in contrastive rhetoric, later revised as intercultural rhetoric (Connor, 2004). That work, which focused initially in the 1960s on identifying key linguistic and discursive features of different cultures, sparked initially by scholars such as Kaplan (1966), had evolved over time to focus on the various variables that might play into such depictions, including discipline, genre, audience, mode, and so on, in carefully contextualized analyses of micro-moments in and across many languages and dialects. The work had begun predicated on discrete independent languages linked to national cultures, but over time we have seen that these linguistic and discursive borders—much like the national borders described earlier—are simultaneously grounded in a reality, at some level, while also being far more nuanced, flexible, porous, and layered than was initially imagined (see for example Dahl, 2004; Flottum, Dahl, and Kim, 2006; Lim Falk and Holmberg, forthcoming).

The types of approach just described were working to understand how writing might function in different cultural contexts (Kaplan, 1987; Severino, 1993). Each exposes some aspect of that work, but all prepare the ground for a more complex "trans" understanding of writing and language, one that moves beyond traditional comparative/contrastive work. Such an understanding is rooted in at least two frames: transnationalism, and a cluster of models for language practice including translingualism, cosmopolitanism, metropolitanism, plurilingualism, and heteroglossia. Each has been widely developed in the scholarly literature, some for decades, others for some fifteen or twenty years now or only quite recently. Here I will first describe transnationalism, then briefly summarize the main contours and cite some of the key lines of scholarship about the cluster of models for language practice. With those in mind, I will then suggest that in order to further our teaching and research agendas, we need to work within a transnational frame to integrate one or several of these models, or at least their shared threads.

### *Transnational Perspectives*

Transnationalism has evolved in recent years as the frame for thinking beyond nation-state borders in education, but of course also in many other domains— economics, anthropology, sociology, business, comparative literature (which can claim early roots), and digital humanities, among others. Transnationalism has been variously defined, but the main focus remains fairly traditional: trans- as

**24** Christiane Donahue

"across" or "through," and national as frontiered lands and governings; it is often linked to translingualism as the linguistic model most appropriate for a globalized transnational frame. The prefix "trans-" bears some scrutiny. It has been critiqued by Blommaert (2012), for example, who suggests that the "trans-" prefix is no better than the "multi-" or "pluri-" ones, being grounded in comparison and its emphasis on languages as separate discrete entities, a perspective specifically contested by translingual model proponents. But at least some roots of the "trans-" prefix allow for movement and for flexibility in unique ways that underscore fluidity, transformation, blurring, and blending. Even in its most frequent form, the prefix is not restricted to "across" distinct entities, but also includes "through," "beyond," "passing across," and even "changing thoroughly" as in *trans*formation or "able to come through" as in *trans*lucent (OED, "trans-"). In less-frequent but equally valid forms, trans- as an adjective means "surpassing or transcending" (as in "transhuman") (OED, "trans-"). In its scientific uses, "trans-" actually represents a relationship, in chemistry, and a new chromosomic form when two lifeforms are cross-bred, in genetics (OED, "trans-"). These various nuances of the prefix add value to translingualism and transnationalism as dynamic models that do not emphasize languages or nations as discrete entities.

A transnational frame shapes 21st-century research and teaching by exploring and analyzing the porosity of frontiers or their erasure, the re-lining of frontiers in unexpected ways, the stratifying of types of boundary, the role of trans-movement or boundary-crossing and the effects of that crossing on the boundaries themselves, literal or figurative, and the remediation of traditional national lines and issues. Nations are, of course, still a reality in some ways. Countries, governments, common customs, common origins, histories, federations, and sovereignties exist as legal, political, military, and cultural entities. And in fact, in recent political developments, seen especially in Europe and the US, nations and nationalism are returning with force, suggesting that our sense of linear movement forward is not the way society works, as a "new nationalism" evolves (Sabanadze, 2010; Elliott, 2016).

But at the same time, nations are not a reality. Every country is more or less bound up with all others; economies are globalized, with effects traveling across real and virtual frontiers (including quite unpredictable effects from informal, "spontaneous order" (Makoni, 2014) economies or virtual currencies); educational systems are both globally ranked and ever-more interrelated. The current European and US turn towards nationalism might well affect policies and trends, but cannot easily remove the build-up in interconnectedness we have seen in recent decades. For example, in terms of nations' boundaries, on the one hand, Italy or Colombia has relatively stable borders, unique governments, rules for entering, tax and labor laws; but on the other hand, the shops in the downtowns feature ubiquitous brands, remote rural farms might use international products and technologies to buy and sell around the world, the multinational corporations behind production are willfully borderless, often to great gain, and the average Internet user works and plays in almost any country without any significant obstacles.

These factors are further complicated by the way populations are diversifying within countries and communities. The UK has provided some of the most striking examples of this "superdiversity," as detailed for example in Blommaert (2012), Blommaert and Rampton (2011), Vertovec (2006), or Creese and Blackledge (2010), but the phenomenon is widespread even if not yet identified specifically as such by scholars in every global context. Superdiversity as a social phenomenon—the intense and rapidly-growing movement of peoples across large-scale and local frontiers (themselves becoming less and less stable), further enabled by technology, and the resulting social and economic diversity within countries, cities, towns, institutions, social classes, and groups themselves—is necessarily intertwined with questions of language diversity (Donahue, 2016 or Jørgensen, Karrebæk, Madsen, & Møller, 2011).

## And Language? Complexifying Perspectives

Language, of course, cannot be ignored in each of these transnational features—and has not been ignored over the decades. Indeed, we can explore language "boundaries" in the same way that we explore national "boundaries": as something that in one way exists, a way that has been socially constructed but is grounded in actual features, even if only stabilized-for-now (such-and-such a linguistic "rule" for example), and in another way, does not exist because everything is so mixed and fluid and dynamic in 21st-century communication (see also on this topic Blackledge & Creese, 2014; You, 2016; Fraiberg, Wang, & You, 2017; Mahboob & Barratt, 2014). Claire Kramsch suggests that "within a globalized economy, the changing landscapes of human migrations and the expanded time/space afforded by internet technology, speakers' and writers' workspace has become located **in language itself**, either as textual identity or as 'intercultural stance'" (2009, p. 248). That is, language has become the **site** of globalization and not simply a tool in it.

In what ways might English, specifically, be such a site of globalization? It is broadly used around the world but is in fact well established as a diverse set of Englishes, with both shared and distinct features and ways of working (consider Trudgill & Hannah, 2008; McKay, 2003; or Cheshire, Kerswill, Fox, & Torgersen, 2011). Recent attention to Englishes in the popular press confirms what scholars have been suggesting for some time—not only are what have traditionally been considered "dominant" Englishes no longer dominant in international circles (see for example "You Need to Go Back to School to Relearn English," Morrison, 2016), but for some time now English speakers who used another language before English outnumber those who began with English (Crystal, 2003; Tapia, 2010). Morrison notes that "it is now up to Anglophones to learn how to speak their [sic] language within the global community" (p. 1), and Tapia (2010)

**26** Christiane Donahue

among others suggests that "standard" English and the claim to "native" ability are no longer settled phenomena. The rebalancing can only have a powerful impact on global norms and values, and indeed those in this global context with deep and broad linguistic and discursive repertoires are at an advantage; those who are (apparently) monolingual can find it very challenging to reimagine the flexibility they may need to develop.

We know that mobility of people, and social and economic superdiversity, do demand this kind of mobility of *language resources*. The new fluid and dynamic environment demands that we cultivate new forms of competence (Kang, 2013). Ashraf (2018) notes that "Current research in multilingual countries supports local languages and recognizes plurilingual practices as proficiency" (p. 1), though she also suggests that other multilingual countries, for example Pakistan, focus entirely on mandating education in English. Deep language and literacy learning across cultural contexts demands mobility, flexibility, and the *adaptability of knowledge* across contexts. These are linguistic, discursive, and in more diffuse ways, cultural values that the more fluid and dynamic global context calls out. Several language and communication models engage these demands, five of which I will present here as particularly generative.[1]

Each of the models presented here is different, but what all of these various threads have in common is that they deal with complexity (Blommaert, 2014). Translingualism focuses on recent developments in resistance to monolingual ideologies and ties itself specifically to thinking about university writing and teaching practices; *plurilinguisme* flirts with connections to multilingualism and policy, and situates itself in language education far more than in the study of writing; metrolingualism resists traditional language boundaries as ideological constructions, and focuses on on-the-ground linguistic realities that play out in speech and writing; cosmopolitanism has predated by centuries these other trends, emphasizes crucially the moral aspect of our language questions, and is shared across many disciplines; and heteroglossia has its roots in linguistic and discursive phenomena, and emphasizes the nature of word and the inherent tensions both within and across languages. But they all ask us to reconsider the way(s) language(s) work, the "essence"—if we can even accept that it has an essence—of language(s) in our world today.

## *Translingualism*

Trans-language, like trans-nation, works across frontiers, both imagined and real. Translanguaging[2] and translingualism have taken on different meanings for different research communities, though in particular the communities of linguistics, writing studies, second language writing, and modern languages instruction. Here I am focused primarily on the meaning for US writing studies, though I believe we deeply need a larger conversation across all of these fields.

> For writing studies the translingual model foregrounds prioritizing 'what the writers are doing with language and why' over whether language use

is standard (Horner et al. 305); considers all languages in the presence of other languages (Pennycook) and internally heterogeneous; and calls on 'communicative competence' as the transformative ability to merge language resources (Molina, 1245), a mixed, meshed, negotiating re-use accompanied by a mindset of flexibility and de-centering (Canagarajah).

*(Donahue, 2016, n.p.)*

Canagarajah (2011) summarizes the model as:

com[ing] to stand for assumptions such as the following: that, for multi-linguals, languages are part of a repertoire that is accessed for their communicative purposes; languages are not discrete and separated but form an integrated system for them; multilingual competences emerges out of local practices where multiples languages are negotiated for communication; competence does not consist of separate competencies for each language but a multicompetence that functions symbiotically [. . .]; and proficiency for multilinguals focuses on repertoire-building.

*(p. 1)*

In this model, the "unmarked" case is language difference and internal heterogeneity: "The variety, fluidity, intermingling, and changeability of languages [is] the statistically demonstrable *norm* [emphasis mine] around the globe" (Horner, Lu, Royster, & Trimbur, 2011), and linguistic diversity is the "normal state of affairs" (Blackledge and Creese, 2014; see also Hall, Cheng, & Carlson, 2006, Kramsch, 2009 and others). It is interesting to note that Cook's work in second-language acquisition posited "multicompetence" as the way in which an individual's multiple languages are part of one overall language ecology, a system of connections; the individual is not simply adding languages on and seeking single-language competences, but rather working them all in the best way for whatever context. This closeness to some definitions of translingualism suggests to me that there are many overlapping origins and manifestations of the terms and concepts developing in different strands.

## Plurilinguisme

Other terms and models than translingualism broaden our understanding of these new norms, including (though this is in no way an exhaustive list) *plurilinguisme* in its most recent European form, metrolingualism, cosmopolitanism, or heteroglossia. In European circles, the term *plurilinguisme* has been evolving to address similar issues. This term, however, clearly has roots in the "multi" frame of reference; in policy statements and in modern language teaching journals, the term is most often used to refer to developing language ability in several languages, but not to the kind of ability explored in "trans" or "metro" perspectives. However, some European work has begun to claim *plurilinguisme* as the term

**28** Christiane Donahue

of choice in resisting traditional multilingual models, for example in the work of Molina (2011), Kramsch (2009), or Zarate, Kramsch, and Levy (2008).

*Plurilinguisme*, as Claire Kramsch suggests, puts "value on the multilingual ability to operate *between* languages" [emphasis mine] (Kramsch, 2009, p. 249), or on what Zarate et al describe as "more than the mere coexistence of languages [. . .] the transcultural circulation of values across borders, the negotiation of identities, the inversion, even inventions, of meanings, often concealed by a common illusion of effective communication" (2008, p. 249). It thus moves away from what Molina calls "additionist" views of language (2011), towards language as perhaps a multidimensional continuum. But it does still depict languages as individual entities, even as it fosters a fluid ability to work among and across languages as more valuable than entrenched ability in a languages/languages.

## Metrolingualism

Metrolingualism, as introduced by Otsuji and Pennycook (2010), seeks (as do most of the terms that have evolved in the past couple of decades) to move us beyond "multi-"lingual or "pluralization" perspectives, seen as mired in a model of languages that maintains them as discrete separate entities, each inextricably linked to nation, culture, and ethnicity (pp. 241–243) and imagined as "codes" that can be identified, for example in "codeswitching," as autonomous systems in mixed interaction (p. 241). These models are being replaced by a view that traditional language boundaries are ideological constructions, and that on-the-ground linguistic realities play out in speakers' and writers' uses of the linguistic-discursive resources they have (p. 241). Metrolingualism

> describes the way in which people of different and mixed backgrounds use, play with, and negotiate identities through language; it does not assume connections between language, culture, ethnicity, nationality, or geography but rather seeks [at a meta-level, then] to explore how such relations are produced, resisted, defied, or rearranged; its focus is not on language systems but on languages as emergent from contexts of interaction.
>
> *(p. 246)*

However, a metrolingual model posits a landscape in which stability (or Connell & Gibson's, 2003 "fixity") and dynamism (or fluidity) are in constant interaction in "creative linguistic conditions across space and borders of culture, history, and politics" (p. 243), suggesting that the celebration of hybridity most often associated with a translingual model must not erase the understanding that "fixed categories are also mobilized as an aspect of hybridity" (p. 244) or, as You (2016) notes, boundaries are "artificial yet still quite real" (p. 7). This aspect of the model, then, is particularly important in contrast to translingual current models that emphasize hybridity and fluidity alone, or at least in dominance.

Metrolingualism also insists on the reality of language fluidity in every context—rural or local as well as metropolitan or global.

## Cosmopolitanism

We can also turn to recently-developing proposals to use "cosmopolitanism" and "cosmopolitan English" as our frames for understanding the work of English, specifically, in the globalized context (You, 2016). As You suggests, cosmopolitanism is a centuries-old concept that has persisted from East Asian and Greek roots through to 20th-century frameworks, and that can help to unseat both monolingual ideology and the nationalism it is bound up in.

Cosmopolitan English, for You, is "English as it is actually used by individuals across the globe, each with differences inflected by his or her pronunciation, vocabulary, syntax, and/or discourse structure" (p. 10), and deeply connected to the same aspects of other languages, which opens it to trans-linguistic and trans-discursive alliances (p. 10). As we engage with cosmopolitan English, we understand the multiplicity (p. 11)—or perhaps Blommaert's complexity—of English, and we cannot avoid thus engaging in the meta-work of language function. This kind of function is exactly what French functional linguists have studied and foregrounded since the 1960s (cf. in different ways Martinet, Bally, Jakobson, François, Salazar-Orvig) though not specific to English.

As with metrolingual perspectives, cosmopolitanism can provide "alternative frames and approaches that both acknowledge the usefulness of boundaries" while "interrogat[ing] and break[ing] them down" (You, p. 5). Cosmopolitanism "challenges us to acknowledge but also to go beyond the interests of people who *traditionally claim entitlement* to a language" (p. 6, emphasis mine). For You, a key principle is the "willingness and ability to communicate across difference" (p. 9), the ability to engage in a kind of "reflective encounter" that in fact students today, often rich in financial resources, may not have experienced, as they are often underprivileged in terms of their linguistic and cultural resources.

There is an essential moral and humanistic ground to cosmopolitanism, one which I sense as different from the social justice ground of some other perspectives. You argues that people are "first and foremost members of the human race and as such are morally obligated to those outside their categories" (the constructed categories of race, class, nation, etc.) (p. 6). You also cites the ethics of globalization, the "imperative to develop both a mentality and an ability to engage strangers through creative meaning-making" (p. 9)—certainly not the stuff of institutionally normed educational language policies and curricula. Creative meaning-making, however, demands divergent language styles, including in and through English, no matter how ubiquitous it becomes, or perhaps even precisely because it is becoming so. What this looks like in everyday interactions is not parallel to what is accepted in those institutionally normed educational

## 30 Christiane Donahue

contexts, thus creating conflict between what scholars observe and what teachers tend to teach. But in part because, as You notes, linguistic difference is inextricable from class, race, and gender, the moral imperative cannot be ignored.

### Heteroglossia

Finally, UK scholars Blackledge and Creese (2014) have suggested a return to a Bakhtinian linguistic-discursive model of heteroglossia as a way to "better understand the diversity of linguistic practice in late modern societies" (p. 3), although the history of its evolution is clearly grounded in the specific context of Soviet Union era politics and ideologies. Heteroglossia is a frame for thinking about the nature of writing in multilingual contexts, with its dialogic characteristics of heteroglossia—multidiscursivity, multivoicedness, intralingual diversity, and intralanguage variation (Blackledge, Creese, & Takhi, 2013, p. 194). It is, they note, centered on developing a "culture of heteroglossia" that acknowledges multiple languages in play; sees them as resources, never problems; and is committed to multidiscursivity and multivoicedness.

For Bakhtin, heteroglossia included diversity in three domains: "speechness," "languageness," and "voicedness" (p. 4), each relevant to aspects of fluid language function. For Blackledge and Creese, heteroglossia allows us to address what Blommaert and Rampton (2011) propose: "*analytically* to focus on the variable ways in which linguistic features with identifiable social and cultural associations get clustered together whenever people communicate" (1), and to focus, as Blommaert (2012) urges, on "*complexity*, rather than [. . .] multiplicity or plurality" (p. 3; see also Blommaert, 2014). This focus creates a new way forward, beyond "pluri" or "trans." It also frees us from the idea that "code" is the best metaphor for language(s), emphasizing instead the shared fluid and dynamic nature of *language* when we consider *languages*.

Blackledge and Creese's explanation of Bakhtin's heteroglossic model highlights three key features that allow us to understand language's dynamic ways of working: indexicality, tension-filled interaction, and multivoicedness (p. 4); of these three, the third has been extensively developed in US writing studies and European linguistics, though not specifically as relevant to questions of diversity in language practices. Indexicality allows us to understand language as indexing "a certain point of view, ideology, social class, [or] profession" (p. 4) as it is used. "Tension-filled interaction," according to Blackledge and Creese, offers a way to understand the social tension inherent in all language interaction, in particular in terms of the constant tension—quite relevant to language policy, teaching, and practices today—between homogeneity and norms on the one hand, and diversity, decentralization, and heteroglossia on the other. Finally, multivoicedness evokes "linguistic diversity as the normal state of a language" (p. 10). I raise the opportunities heteroglossia might afford in the work on the new norms of linguistic flexibility because I see this avenue as a potential way forward that is both grounded in decades of linguistic work, and less attached to perspectives that have already drawn lines in the sand in terms of different understandings of language fluidity and diversity. It remains to be seen whether the heteroglossic model will be widely adopted.[3]

I find heteroglossic perspectives particularly relevant for their emphasis on politics and ideology as drivers of much of what they and translingualism press against; they "engage with the ways in which different linguistic forms, either within or between what we typically call 'languages,' are connected with particular ideological positions and world views" (Blackledge & Creese, 2014). Another sub-area of particular interest to me is the choices, in heteroglossic work, entailed in referencing or citation. In some ways every writer is highly challenged by "working polyphony," working with voices and discourses. But heteroglossic working of such things is triply complex, magnified by questions of translation and authority.

Another reason to consider the heteroglossic model as the most useful one for work on academic writing comes from the decades-long tradition of French functional linguistics (not Systemic Functional Linguistics), focused on language-in-use "as the source of language models rather than looking first to structures and then to their manifestations" (Donahue, 2008, p. 321). This linguistic frame focuses on utterances and uttering (*énonciation*), and on language acts, written or spoken, as acts of meaning-making. We might accept that there are generally two purposes ascribed to writing: communication and meaning-making. They are of course inextricably linked. But a focus on "communication" alone in writing or language use can suggest that meaning exists and needs only to be communicated effectively, rather than that the act of real communication is one of co-constructing meaning by all involved (whether in speech or in writing). This can have sweeping effects on language models in transnational contexts, if we are seeing discourse as the co-construction of meaning, and not just surface translative "communication."

This malleable language model drew me to a developing field—as we've noted, translingual in the US, more often plurilingual or heteroglossic in Europe, though with some subtle differences—focused on how we might best understand and study student writers (and others) in an increasingly mobile and superdiverse world and how we might best work with their writing in our varied contexts and heterogeneous settings. It meshes very well with heteroglossia and multi-competence, and posits language itself differently in ways that can only influence academic writing. Thus a "trans," or pluri- or metro- or cosmopole- or (perhaps best) a heteroglossic understanding of writing, while each of these perspectives is definitely different, models in some way writing in and across all languages, writing as related to languaging, and writing as embodying translingual, plurilingual, heteroglossic, or cosmopolitan concepts.

## Fostering Linguistic, Cultural, and Rhetorical Values in a "Trans" World

If we are teaching writing in English in the transnational, translingual world described above, what responsibilities might we have, and what linguistic, cultural, and rhetorical values might we hope to support and foster? I will argue next that the global field of "writing studies" as it evolves and interconnects across many diverse local disciplines and practices, if we are able to see writing studies as a way to name all work on university writing around the globe and across disciplines, has a particular responsibility—a responsibility that itself will take on quite diverse local shapes—to think differently about nation and language, to empirically research the real demands the world makes on writers and speakers of English(es), to study language itself as flexible meaning-making activity, and to teach differently as a result. I am certainly not alone in making these arguments! I build on many voices, from those cited throughout this text that seem familiar to those which are perhaps less well-known. But I am hopeful that the particular framing I have offered synthesizes some of that existing thinking in a way that is useful for pursuing new paths in research and teaching.

### *Research*

The first and most important research value is a resistance to our urge to (only) compare across languages and contexts. We have seen that traditions in contrastive rhetoric from the 1960s onwards emphasized at first the distillation of cultural differences in writing into limited sets of predictable features, not unlike the early developments in teaching genre via teaching sets of features. We also see today that such contrastive studies, while still a primary mode of research in fields such as applied linguistics, are considerably more nuanced and open-ended (see, e.g., Taboada, Suarez, & Alvarez, 2014). A second research value is to resist the strand of study, particularly lively in recent years, about codeswitching, codemeshing, or codemixing as ways to understand what multilingual individuals are doing linguistically and discursively. This strand could bear much further research than has been done to date, in particular in terms of better understanding sociolinguistic models of meshing, switching, or mixing in relation to those explored or promoted in applied linguistics or, again differently, in US writing studies. The slippage in both how these terms are used in a given field and how they are taken up across fields has led to real difficulty. While I do not have space to take up this question here, I believe it is central to ongoing work in this domain.

Other scholars have questioned, for some time now, the validity of seeing languages as "codes" at all (the very basis for codeswitching, meshing, or mixing), and have argued for a move towards studying and teaching meaning and meaning construction regardless of the language(s) in play (cf. Berthoff, 1999;

François, 2017; Blackledge et al., 2013; or Donahue, forthcoming, among others). Otsuji and Pennycook, in the *International Journal of Multilingualism*, suggest that

> a recent movement in bi- and multilingual studies has been to shift away from a focus on how distinct codes are switched or mixed, in favor of an interest in how boundaries and distinctions are the results of particular language ideologies and how language users manipulate the multilingual resources they have available to them.
>
> *(2010, p. 241)*

The structural approach of identifying languages as codes is indeed an approach that reifies them as discrete entities, much as "nation" does for politico-ideological entities (see also the critique of "polylanguaging" for its underlying grounding in structuralist assumptions about language, Orman and Pablé (2016), as a way to understand "code" models as implicitly structuralist). That structural choice undergirds many branches of linguistics today, but not all of them.

Scholars in support of a multicompetence model as proposed first by Cook (2008) talk about knowing the "rules of interpretation"; a competent writer has "the adaptability to select those forms of accuracy and appropriateness" for a context. To this some might say, "yes, and the 'academic context' is just such a context, and we hope to teach them the rules." But then we enter the huge body of research knowledge we have about just how heterogeneous "academic discourse" is across disciplines, subjects, genres, etc. etc., and the situation gets much muddier! This raises for us the question of our responsibility: is it to reproduce current institutional, educational, or gatekeeping editorial norms? Or to question them in light of global change? Much of the scholarship to date that is not in the contrastive rhetoric tradition has made claims about the degree to which rich language practices are quite different from the standardized, normed descriptions of language that drive, for example, school curricula or editorial decision-making. But I have not seen much empirical research analyzing instances of "linguistic success" in the traditionally highly normed contexts of education, for example.

A mobile, "trans" model also engenders another kind of competence: flexibility in the sense of openness to uncertainty (Horner, 2016, p. 10). All language users "let ambiguities pass" as needed; translingual speakers and writers might do so more markedly, Horner notes, but it is a difference of degree, not of kind (p. 18). In the introduction to their collection *Latest Trends in ELF Research* (2011), Archibald, Cogo, and Jenkins highlight Ehrenreich's use of what she calls "accommodation analyses" that show how, in diverse "lingua cultural" contexts, communication is in fact almost always successful only because of the *negotiating strategies* in use. This kind of research is exactly what we need in empirical research focused on identifying the "success factors" in play in a wide variety of meaning-making contexts, from low-stakes to high-stakes, from the everyday to the highly normed, from international business to local education, and so on.

In terms of our research paths, a guiding principle should be to move beyond seeking to establish features of various languages and "codes" towards instead taking on the responsibility of understanding the ways in which language is "doing its work," as French functional linguists would say, but understanding built from systematic data-gathering and analysis. I mentioned early in this chapter that little empirical work has been done to establish what is changing, not in "uses on the ground" (for which a rich body of scholarship is evolving) but in terms of **what is constituting "success"** and **in what domains**. It seems to me that we must clarify, empirically, the difference between new linguistic norms in everyday practice, across multiple contexts, and the "norms" of normed expectations in particular high-stakes settings: academia, schooling, or public service, for example. An empirical understanding of the linguistic, discursive, and rhetorical features of "success" in each context—which in turn engender social values—might better ground efforts to change what we consider it to be.

- We might focus our research on "usage-based ideas of multicompetence" rather than, or, in addition to, how two discrete systems are interacting.
- We should, according to Hall et al., study new populations; study specific communities of language learners; and carry out ethnographies of communication and longitudinal studies chronicling the development of individuals' communicative repertoires and how they are or are not successful. We are perhaps ready at this stage for less a celebration of the creativity of hybridity, and more a hard look at the interactions in high-stakes settings and their results. As Canagarajah underscores, drawing on Rampton (2008), Hill (1999), and Blommaert (2005), we know little about the reception of translanguaged utterances, the interpretation or response or recognition of the utterance.
- We might study actual strategies used by multilinguals in various academic settings, furthering the work of, say, Lillis and Curry or Fraiberg. But in so doing, we must take on the complications of different standards set for different groups and individuals in different social strata or contexts. The recent study by Fraiberg, Wang, and You (2017) is an excellent example of the kind of work needed, with its focus on Chinese international students' underground academic learning network using ethnographies of communication, actual strategies used by multilinguals in various academic settings, and the process of composing beyond products of translingual practice.
- Finally, we might study the process of composing in much more depth; current research has tended to focus on the products of multi-, trans-, or heteroglossic practice (Canagarajah, 2011; 2013).

## Teaching

Current developments in linguistic, rhetorical, and educational research thus push us to question our assumptions and to move beyond comparisons. In that move we open ourselves up to supporting students' values, including their possible interest in linguistic and rhetorical flexibility, and the possibility that these are in fact becoming global norms, the foundation of a "*trans*" understanding. The norms include linguistic flexibility, mobility, and design; and rhetorical flexibility, mobility, and design, all of which lead to and are inherently tied to cultural fluidity, a much-needed openness.

One way to think about fostering these norms—fostering acceptance of them in institutional-academic contexts, and fostering their growth among our student writers—is to adopt a new understanding of what it might mean to be "competent," one that redirects our attention away from specific language features to strategies, tools, and meta-awarenesses. The "multicompetence" model for writers and speakers (Hall et al., 2006, based on Cook's earlier work) depicts *language* knowledge as "dynamic constellations of linguistic resources" that emerge through constant use, rather than "a priori components belonging to stable, a-contextual language systems" (p. 226). Hall et al. critique formal linguistics for not being able to account for multilingual uses, instead idealizing the pure monolingual speaker. Which language model we value matters to our teaching, of course.

I don't believe we can simply take theoretical frames and the results of research and turn them towards what to teach—as each study is specific to a text type(s), a discipline(s), a context. But I do believe we can take the body of evolving research into the many ways texts work across difference, and the ways current conditions support translingual and multicompetent models, as ground for re-envisioning both researching and teaching academic writing in superdiverse contexts. It seems to me that leadership in translingual academic writing research and teaching means moving beyond using traditional monolingual competence as the baseline, as has been extensively argued by Canagarajah, Horner, Matsuda, Kang, and many others, and is implemented at sites such as the Luxembourg University Language Centre. At the same time, it's important to not make the assumption that multilinguals are "naturally" and intuitively multicompetent (Canagarajah, 2011); teaching differently involves all students from all language backgrounds.

While every local context demands its own frames, sensitivities, and goals, we can still advocate for a broader set of principles. Other chapters in this collection offer carefully constructed examples of specific practices; my focus here is on broader principles. Teaching—teaching academic writing, teaching language—is incredibly hard under superdiverse and translingual circumstances. Molina notes that the challenge for teachers working in academic discourse in a particular

**36** Christiane Donahue

language is, while teaching one language, "to conceive of all languages combined as a tool kit to be used in pluriglossic environments" (Molina, 2011, p. 1248).

I noted at the start of this chapter: We must reimagine what our students will need as they learn academic writing in any number of languages, shifting our focus to courses and interactions that emphasize flexibility and multi-competence, pluri- or translanguaging, strategy, choice, and design. But we must even more critically re-imagine our own attitudes and dispositions towards language, writing, and teaching. So doing, we would be developing a space, a place in which all of the characteristics of translingualism, heteroglossia, and multi-competence feel natural.

We might consider opening up the results from our studies to our students and generating insights with them about the implications. We must also intentionally create contexts in which student writers more easily "transfer"—in the sense of adapting and transforming—their language and writing knowledge across the many heterogeneous, diverse contexts in which they will work. Our classes should be designed to call out students' vast knowledge, to invite re-use, and to foster student writers' meta-abilities. Students also need to develop an attitude towards that "knowledge transfer"—that it is possible, and expected.

Is it possible that meta-awareness, both ours and our students', of language function, language use, language fluidity, flexibility in strategic choice-making, knowledge within and across languages, openness to uncertainty and a prime on co-constructing meaning over imagining native-speaker monolingual perfection as the goal—is the future?

Claire Kramsch outlines a three-part framework for creating a "third space" for language learners, a space that sets aside dichotomies like native-nonnative or L1–L2. She suggests a "third culture" pedagogy needs to give room to popular culture, to play and mischief, to "making do" with what one has and using imposed systems reflectively or in resistance; needs to encourage critical interaction with dominant academic perspectives and materials; and needs to employ a flexible, adaptable methodology.

More specifically, in terms of language, Molina (2011) notes, drawing from the Common European Framework, that the competent language user:

> does not keep [. . .] languages and cultures in strictly separated mental compartments, but rather builds up a communicative competence to which all knowledge and experience of language contribute and in which languages interrelate and interact. In different situations, a person can *flexibly* [emphasis mine] call upon different parts of this competence to achieve effective communication with a particular interlocutor. For instance, partners may switch from one language or dialect to another, [. . .] call upon the knowledge of a number of languages to make sense of a text, written or spoken, in a previously "unknown" language.

*(p. 4)*

These are the abilities that we believe a 21st-century academic writer will need. They demand that our research focus on establishing the workings of these abilities in different contexts and their relationship to successful or failed meaning-making in each context. They demand that our teaching focus on emphasizing a high degree of linguistic and rhetorical awareness and flexibility. They demand that we value these, and develop that valuing with our students but also with other stakeholders. They demand that we expect to have complicated responsibilities and that we rise to the challenge. And they demand constant vigilance as the norms of the world we study and the world for which we prepare our students shifts, complexifies, and evolves, including in the unpredictable directions that shape our work, such as the current trend *away* from "globalism" towards nationalism, at least in the US and Europe.

## Notes

1. Note that of course many fields such as English for Academic Purposes, L1–L2, applied linguistics, second language acquisition have long and strong traditions of research and teaching in relation to these questions. I am focused here on a particular set of frames and approaches that offer a different way of working through the questions, but I believe we do not do nearly enough work understanding the relationships among all stakeholder approaches.
2. This is not the "translanguaging" developed by Ofelia García (2014) in language studies, but the version developed more recently in translingual scholarship.
3. I highly recommend the Blackledge and Creese edited collection (2014), *Heteroglossia as Practice and Pedagogy*.

## References

Archibald, A., Cogo, A., & Jenkins, J. (Eds.). (2011). *Latest trends in ELF research*. New Castle on Tyne, UK: Cambridge Scholars Publishing.

Ashraf, H. (2018). Translingual practices and monoglot policy aspirations: A case study of Pakistan's plurilingual classrooms. *Current Issues in Language Planning, 19*(1), 1–21.

Berthoff, A. (1999). *The mysterious barricades: Language and its limits*. Toronto: University of Toronto Press.

Blackledge, A., & Creese, A. (Eds.). (2014). *Heteroglossia as practice and pedagogy*. Dordrecht, Germany: Springer.

Blackledge, A., Creese, A., & Takhi, J. (2013). Beyond multilingualism: Heteroglossia in practice. In S. May (Ed.), *The multilingual turn: Implications for SLA, TESOL and bilingual education* (pp. 191–215). New York: Routledge.

Blommaert, J. (2005). *Discourse: A critical introduction*. Cambridge: Cambridge University Press.

Blommaert, J. (2012). *Citizenship, language, and superdiversity: Toward complexity*. Paper 95 in Working Papers in Urban Language and Literacies, Kings College London.

Blommaert, J. (2014) From mobility to complexity in sociolinguistic theory and method. (Tilburg Papers in Culture Studies, Paper 103.) www.tilburguniversity.edu/upload/5ff19e97-9abc-45d0-8773-d2d8b0a9b0f8_ TPCS_103_Blommaert.pdf

Blommaert, J., & Rampton, B. (2011). Language and superdiversity. *Diversities, 13*(2), 1–22.

## 38 Christiane Donahue

Canagarajah, S. (2011). Translanguaging in the classroom: Emerging issues for research and pedagogy. *Applied Linguistics Review*, *2*, 1–28.

Canagarajah, S. (2013). *Translingual practice: Global Englishes and cosmopolitan relations*. Abington, UK: Routledge.

Cheshire, J., Kerswill, P., Foxa, S., & Torgersen, E. (2011). Contact, the feature pool and the speech community: The emergence of multicultural London English. *Journal of Sociolinguistics*, *15*(2), 151–196.

Coleman, J. A. (2006). English-medium teaching in European higher education. *Language Teaching*, *39*(1), 1–14.

Connell, J., & Gibson, C. (2003). *Sound tracks: Popular music, identity, and place*. London: Routledge.

Connor, U. (2004). Intercultural rhetoric research: Beyond texts. *Journal of English for Academic Purposes*, *3*, 291–304.

Cook, V. (2008). *Second language learning and language teaching*. London: Arnold.

Creese, A., & Blackledge, A. (2010). Towards a sociolinguistics of superdiversity. *Zeitschrift für Erziehungswissenschaft*, *13*(4), 549–572.

Crystal, D. (2003). *English as a global language* (2nd ed.). Cambridge: Cambridge University Press.

Dahl, T. (2004). Textual metadiscourse in research articles: A marker of national culture or of academic discipline? *Journal of Pragmatics*, *36*(10), 1807–1825.

Donahue, C. (2004). Student writing as negotiation: Fundamental movements between the common and the specific in French essays. In F. Kostouli (Ed.), *Writing in context(s): Textual practices and learning processes in sociocultural settings*. Amsterdam, The Netherlands: Kluwer Academic Publishers.

Donahue, C. (2008). Cross-cultural analysis of student writing: Beyond discourses of difference, *Written Communication*, *25*(3), 319–352.

Donahue, C. (2016). The trans in transnational-translingual: Rhetorical and linguistic flexibility as new norms. *Composition Studies*, *44*(1), n.p.

Donahue, C. (forthcoming). Writing, English, and a translingual model for composition. In K. Yancey, E. Wardle, R. Malenczyk, S. Miller-Cochran, *Composition, Rhetoric, and Disciplinarity*. Logan, UT: Utah State University Press.

Elliott, L. (2016). Brexit is a rejection of globalization. *The Guardian*, n.p.

Flottum, K. (2009). *Language and discipline perspectives on academic discourse*. Cambridge: Cambridge Scholars Publishing.

Flottum, K., Dahl, T., & Kinn, T. (2006). *Academic voices: Across language and disciplines*. Amsterdam: Johns Benjamin.

Flowerdew, J. (1999). Problems in writing for scholarly publication in English: The case of Hong Kong. *Journal of Second Language Writing*, *8*(3), 243–264.

Fraiberg, S. (2010). Composition 2.0: Toward a multilingual and multimodal framework. *CCC*, *62*(1), 100–126.

Fraiberg, S., Wang, X., & You, X. (2017). *Inventing the World Grant University: Chinese international students' mobilities, literacies, and identities*. Logan, UT: Utah State University Press.

François, F. (2017). *Récits et commentaires, tours et détours*. Limoges, France: Lambert-Lucas.

García, O. (2014). Multilingualism and language education. In C. Leung, & B. V. Street (Eds.), *The Routledge companion to English studies*. New York: Routledge.

Hall, J. K., Cheng, A., & Carlson, M. (2006). Reconceptualizing multicompetence as a theory of language knowledge. *Applied Linguistics*, *27*(2), 220–240.

Hill, J. (1999). Styling locally, styling globally: What does it mean? *Journal of Sociolinguistics*, *3*, 542–556.

Horner, B. (2016). Reflecting the translingual norm: Action-reflection, ELF, translation, and transfer. In K. Yancey (ed.). *A Rhetoric of Reflection*. Logan, UT: Utah State UP. 105-124.

Horner, B., Lu, M. Z., Royster, J. J., & Trimbur, J. (2011). Language difference in writing: Toward a translingual approach. *College English, 73*, 303–321.

Horner, B., Necamp, S., & Donahue, C. (2011). Toward a multilingual composition scholarship: From English only to a translingual norm. *College Composition and Communication, 63*(2), 269–300.

Jørgensen, J. N., Karrebæk, M. S. Madsen, L. M., & Møller, J. S. (2011). Polylanguaging and superdiversity. *Diversities, 13*(2), 23–37.

Kang, E. Y. (2013). Multilingual competence. *Teachers College, Columbia University Working Papers in TESOL & Applied Linguistics, 13*(2), 55–56.

Kaplan, R. (1966). Cultural thought patterns in intercultural education. *Language Learning, 16*(1–2), 1–20.

Kaplan, R. (1987). Cultural thought patterns revisited. In U. Connor, & R. Kaplan (Eds.), *Writing across Languages: Analysis of L2 text* (pp. 9–21). Reading, MA: Addison-Wesley.

Kramsch, C. (2009). *The multilingual subject*. Oxford: Oxford University Press.

Lillis, T., & Curry, M. J. (2010). *Academic writing in a global context: The politics and practices of publishing in English*. London/New York: Routledge/Taylor and Francis Group.

Lillis, T., Hewings, A., Vladimirou, D., & Curry, M. J. (2010). The geolinguistics of English as an academic lingua franca: Citation practices across English-medium national and English-medium international journals. *International Journal of Applied Linguistics, 20*(1), 111–135.

Lim Falk, M., & Holmberg, P. (forthcoming). Writing in a globalized world. In S. Plane et al. (Eds.), *Research on writing: Multiple perspectives* (pp. 163–186). Anderson, SC: Parlor Press.

McKay, S. (2003). Toward an appropriate EIL pedagogy: Re-examining common ELT assumptions. *International Journal of Applied Linguistics, 13*(1). 1–22.

Mahboob, A., & Barratt, L. (2014). *Englishes in multilingual contexts*. Dordrecht, Germany: Springer Scientific.

Makoni, S. (2014). Multilingualism: spontaneous orders and System D: a concluding note. *International Journal of Bilingual Education and Bilingualism, 17*(6):714–717.

Molina, C. (2011). Curricular insights into translingualism as a communicative competence. *Journal of Language Teaching and Research, 2*(6), 1244–1251.

Morrison, L. (2016). You need to go back to school to relearn English. *BBC online*. Retrieved from www.bbc.com/capital/story/20161215-you-need-to-go-back-to-school-to-relearn-english

Orman, J. and Pablé, A. (2016). Polylanguaging, integrational linguistics and contemporary sociolinguistic theory: A commentary on Ritzau. *International Journal of Bilingual Education and Bilingualism, 19*(5), 592–602.

Otsuji, E., & Pennycook, A. (2010). Metrolingualism: Fixity, fluidity, and language in flux. *International Journal of Multilingualism, 7*(3), 240–254.

Oxford English Dictionary. Entry prefix "trans-."

Pennycook, A. (2010). *Language as a local practice*. London: Routledge. Rampton, B. (2008). *Language in late modernity: Interaction in an urban school*. Cambridge: Cambridge University Press.

Sabanadze, N. (2010). *Globalization and nationalism: The cases of Georgia and the Basque country*. Budapest: CEU Press.

Seidlhofer, B. (2009). Common ground and different realities: World Englishes and English as a lingua franca. *World Englishes, 28*(2), 236–245.

Severino, C. (1993). The "doodles" in context: Qualifying claims about contrastive rhetoric. *The Writing Center Journal, 14*(1), 44.

Taboada, M., & Gómez-González, M. Á. (2012). Discourse markers and coherence relations: Comparison across markers, languages and modalities. *Linguistics and the Human Sciences, 6*, 17–41.

Taboada, M., Suarez, S., & Alvarez, E. (Eds.). (2014). *Contrastive discourse analysis: Functional and corpus perspectives.* Sheffield: Equinox.

Tapia, A. (2010). Non-native English speakers setting new standard. *New America Media online.* Retrieved from http://newamericamedia.org/2010/07/non-native-english-speakers-setting-new-standard.php

Tardy, C. (2004). The role of English in scientific communication: Lingua franca or Tyrannosaurus rex? *Journal of English for Academic Purposes, 3*(3), 247–269.

Trudgill, P., & Hannah, J. (2008). *International English: A guide to varieties of Standard English.* London: Hodder Education.

Vertovec, S. (2006). *The emergence of super-diversity in Britain.* Working Paper 06–25, University of Oxford School of Anthropology. Download WP-2006-025-Vertovec_Super-Diversity_Britain (PDF). Retrieved from https://www.compas.ox.ac.uk/2006/wp-2006-025-vertovec_super-diversity_britain/

You, X. (2016). *Cosmopolitan English and transliteracy.* Carbondale, IL: Southern Illinois University Press.

Zarate, G., Kramsch, C., & Levy, D. (2008). Introduction. In C. Kramsch, D. Levy, & G. Zarate (Eds.), *Précis du plurilinguisme et du pluriculturalisme* (pp. 15–26). Paris: Contemporary Publishing International.

# 3

# TRANSNATIONALISM AND TRANSLINGUALISM

## How They Are Connected

*Suresh Canagarajah*

As translingualism becomes more widely discussed and pedagogically implemented, some scholars argue that this is an unnecessary imposition on communication and education. They feel that this is an academic bandwagon, spawning a neologism that will quickly fade (see Matsuda, 2014; Kubota, 2014). However, translingual scholars counter that language contact, code meshing, and shuttling between repertoires are not an option, but a necessity, for voice and identity for everyone in the context of transnational relations (see Canagarajah, 2013a; Horner, Lu, Royster, & Trimbur, 2010). I see linguistic creativity and cosmopolitan identities emerging among both native English speakers and multilingual students in my classrooms, often practiced relatively spontaneously. Such translingualism seems mostly to be connected with students who are locating themselves in a different space for identity construction, ideological reflection, and communicative practice. These writers seem to occupy a space that is liminal—i.e., between communities, languages, and nations. Such positioning motivates in them a search for identities and literacies that go beyond bounded, static, and territorialized constructs and norms. I call this space *transnational*. I demonstrate in this article how inhabiting a transnational space is connected to translingual communicative practice. After defining the key terms and reviewing theoretical discourses that explain the connection, I illustrate from the literacy narrative and identity development of one of my students.

## Definitions

*Transnational* is different from other related terms such as multinational or international. *Multinational* is a constellation of nation-states. *International* is the relationship between two or more nation-states. Both terms frame the relationship

**42** Suresh Canagarajah

or collective around geographically bounded nations. However, the term transnational looks at relationships that transcend the nation-state. That is, there are social ties and relationships that are not constrained by or contained within nation-state boundaries. Though people are located within nation-state borders, many of their relationships, experiences, and affiliations are not bound by them. These are ties of liminality. They occur between and beyond boundaries and borders. Consider, for example, the relationship with my siblings and cousins in Australia, UK, UAE, and Canada. Having fled the ethnic conflict in Sri Lanka, we now live in different countries. However, our relationship takes place on another space that has little relevance to national borders. As we interact with each other via digital media, such as Viber, Facebook, and Skype, we inhabit another space that transcends nation-states, with an identity and life of its own. Note also that our relationship is not defined solely by our Sri Lankan Tamil homeland. The homeland is not our frame of reference, as it has changed irrevocably because of the ethnic conflict and we don't envision returning there. In this sense, *transnational* is also distinct from the construct *diaspora*. The latter term assumes the homeland (a distinct geographical place) as the frame of reference, even though community members might be living in different nation-states. This doesn't mean that the homeland is never relevant in transnational relations. The point is that it doesn't bind or limit one's social relationships and identities. From this perspective, as I will discuss below, one's life within their homeland can also involve mobility and transnational identities and connections.

To theorize this liminal social field, some geographers have constructed new terms, such as *transnational social space* (Faist, Fauser, & Reisenauer, 2013). They also distinguish between place and space. While *place* is a geographical entity, identified by physical boundaries and governed by the nation-state, *space* is liminal. It is socially constructed and affectively experienced. From this perspective, note that one doesn't have to leave one's usual habitation (i.e., traditional homeland, city, or village) to adopt a transnational positioning. What is critical is the imagined and virtual communities people form beyond their place to connect with others and treat their relationships, investments, and experiences as occurring in a transnational social space with its one liminal identity. This distinction is important, as transnationality doesn't require that all of us become migrants. Even those who are relatively sedentary can inhabit a transnational social space. They can be connected to communities beyond their own locality or country through other migrants or through digital media, information flow, and economic/production relationships.

Similarly, the term *translingual* is different from constructs such as multilingual or interlingual. *Multilingual* refers to multiple languages forming a repertoire, with the languages maintaining their separate identities. Terms such as code switching and code mixing conceptualize the interlingual relationship between languages while preserving their own structures. *Translingual* considers the languages in contact, generating new forms and meanings in synergy. It treats communication as constituted by mobile verbal resources that are appropriated by people and used beyond their separate language labels as suits their purposes. The notion of pure, standardized, or autonomous languages is an ideological construct. This traditional understanding of language doesn't relate to how verbal resources work in communicative practice. Notions of ownership and territorialization (i.e., language x belongs to community x and rooted in nation x) inform what I consider monolingual ideologies. They treat languages as separate, owned, and pure. In practice, our communicative repertoire and genres involve verbal resources from diverse labeled languages. Within translingualism as a form of practice and cognitive process, scholars use the term *codemeshing* (Young, 2004; Canagarajah, 2006) to discuss how multilingual verbal resources populate texts (treated as a product). In other words, translingualism is the process and codemeshing is the product. What this means is that translingual processes characterize all communicative practice even when words identified as belonging to different languages may not appear in the finished product. For example, one might translate ideas between languages mentally, even though the essay is in academic English.

The prefix "trans" therefore indexes the verbal relationships that transcend separately labeled languages. It also indicates that communication transcends words to include diverse semiotic resources (i.e., such as multiple modalities beyond the visual, and symbols from color, images, objects, and sound). Moreover, the prefix can be understood as treating communication as transforming established norms and relationships associated with a language. In each act of communication, speakers are reconfiguring contexts in order to represent their own voices and interests. As Bakhtin (1986) has stated, speaking involves populating words with one's own intentions. This activity can involve appropriating available semiotic resources and developing new indexicalities for meanings and values that are empowering and inclusive. For example, nonnative speakers of English might appropriate verbal resources from English and use English creatively with their other repertoires for communicative success to challenge notions of deficiency and construct new identities beyond their unequal status. Therefore, translingual is not about using language to conform to dominant meanings, conventions, contexts, and social relationships. It is about reconfiguring contexts through critical and creative language use.

In my experience as a teacher and writer, I see a connection between inhabiting transnational social spaces and engaging in translingual practices. Those who occupy a transnational social space develop the dispositions to engage in translingual communication. That is, the shuttling between community or nation-state boundaries seems to develop more cosmopolitan dispositions, identities, and interests, which cannot be satisfied by monolingual language ideologies or practices. Such writers aspire to develop genres, grammars, and voices that go beyond territorialized and autonomous languages. They fashion new indexicalities and conventions for voice, deriving from multiple semiotic systems. As

**44** Suresh Canagarajah

they occupy liminal spaces of communication, they also consider their identity construction and competence as ongoing. Their translingual practice involves progressive learning, repertoire building, and creativity.

Before we move further, some clarifications are in order. One might argue that language mixing is not new. Traditional sociolinguistic notions such as code switching and other processes such as creolization accommodate language mixing. However, these constructs assume the prior existence of labeled/separate languages providing the resources for mixing. Separate languages is the norm; mixing is the exception, and comes after the fact. In the translingual orientation, on the other hand, verbal resources are mobile and fluid. It is labeled languages that are after the fact and exceptional (see Canagarajah, 2013a, for an analysis of how this orientation makes a difference in meaning making practices). Similarly, the mixing of words with other semiotic resources, such as gestures or visuals, has also been theorized under the label of multimodality (see Kress, 2009). However, the multimodality orientation assumes that each mode has its own structure with predefined meanings available for meshing. Translingual orientation, on the other hand, considers all semiotic resources as mediating each other and taking on meanings that arise from situated practice. However, one must acknowledge that monolingual ideologies are still dominant, enforcing monolingual practices and policies, despite transnational conditions. What translingualism theorizes is communication at the level of practice. Despite monolingual ideologies, everyday communicative practice involves a negotiation of diverse verbal and semiotic resources. In fact, multilingual students and communities do face pressure from monolingual ideologies to shape their practices in a conforming manner. Transnational conditions don't lead automatically to translingual practices. As I will articulate below, it takes certain critical life events and social conflicts to generate the awareness among multilinguals to rise above monolingual ideologies and adopt translingual orientations.

To begin with, people encounter diversity as they shuttle across geographical and linguistic borders. They then experience conflict, alienation, pain, and disorientation. They might resolve this conflict in different ways. If targeting a more dominant language or community, they might initially desire the identity that language or community promises. In some cases, they might react negatively and withdraw to the identity that their home/native language provides. For a majority of people, however, the tension between semiotic systems leads to new forms of belonging in transnational social spaces. Finding existing bounded communities, identities, and languages constricting, they might seek more expansive practices of communication and identity. This can turn out to be an ongoing quest, as stability in a bounded place or semiotic system might not satisfy their translingual disposition. This quest is what Clare Kramsch (2009) labels "subject-in-process"—a progressive and enriching journey of self-realization and identity construction. It is difficult to provide a neat cause/effect explanation for what motivates some to occupy this liminal transnational social space and attain translingual dispositions, while others desire bounded spaces, territorialized identities, and language ownership. Many personal and social factors are involved in this process. My attempt below is to illustrate the connection between translingualism and transnationalism through a literacy autobiography (LA, hereafter) of my student, to support the theorization relating to this connection. The article will also demonstrate the function of literacy narratives in facilitating this translingual awareness and transnational positioning.

## Theorizing the Translingual Subject

The emergence of the translingual subject—i.e., a person who positions himself/herself in the liminal spaces between nation-states, develops a critical awareness of diverse languages and cultures, and treats identity construction as an ongoing process of hybridization—has not been studied well. Research on motivation, identity, and language acquisition in applied linguistics theorizes how people develop competence in a second language and a suitable identity, adopting a trajectory of accommodation to a target speech community. For example, some scholarship on motivation posits that those who have an *integrative motivation* (i.e., the desire to join or engage with the community that speaks that language) are more successful in learning a second language than those who demonstrate an *instrumental motivation* (i.e., learning the language for pragmatic goals such as passing a test or getting a job)—see Gardner & Lambert (1972) and Brown (1991) for a review. These constructs treat language learning and identity construction as a case of moving from community or nation-state to another, in a somewhat linear direction.

In contrast to this largely psycholinguistic orientation, more recent social orientations to motivation accommodate socioeconomic considerations. Adopting the metaphor of *investment*, Peirce (1995) theorizes that those who are invested in learning a language for social and economic goals (such as asserting their identity in the new community for the economic survival of their family, gaining a job that suits their accomplishments, etc.) are more successful in appropriating the second language for their interests. Such subjects are more agentive and resistant as they go on to develop hybrid identities. However, these studies have largely explored the appropriation of another language according to one's own values and interests from a specific locus, such as a nation-state. Also, hybridity is sometimes treated as an end point rather than a strategy for ongoing identity construction. Divergent from such approaches, Bhabha (1999) defines hybridization as a strategy of emergence, a practice (rather than an essential state) that always resists dominant discourses for empowerment in an ongoing and situated manner. His theorization of this definition is similar to Kramsch's notion of subject-in-process.

Why is it that some people find meaning in liminal language identities, while others wish to resolve their trajectory in favor of native speakerhood (either in the second language or first language)? Kramsch articulates a theoretical orientation that offers a useful starting point for this exploration. She develops this orientation in relation to the LAs written by students in Berkeley on their multilingual learning and identity experiences in courses on heritage language and intercultural studies. Many of these texts are written by "1.5 generation" students in the US, who are in some ways inhabiting liminal spaces between countries and communities. Understandably, they adopt the trope of liminality and translingual practices in their LA. Though many of these LAs are short (as students were asked to write a one-page narrative in some courses), we see considerable rhetorical and linguistic creativity in the writing. Many of them contain codemeshing, though Kramsch doesn't theorize or label them as such. She labels language mixing as codeswitching or hybridity, and theorizes them as rhetorical creativity. Despite these differences in terminology, the model she provides to explain her "multilingual subjects" I find relevant to those whom I call "translingual subjects," as the writers demonstrate shared dispositions and trajectories.

Kramsch borrows from Lacan, Kristeva, and Foucault to explain the emergence of the multilingual subject. I first introduce Kramsch's adoption of these theorists for her purposes in this section. In the next section, I suggest how I diverge from Kramsch's model slightly to accommodate the experiences emerging from my teaching and research.

Lacan (1977) theorizes identity construction for a child as involving objectifying her identity and separating herself from her association with her mother. For example, the child would find it difficult to grasp that the image in the mirror is herself. There is a gap between the image, her self, and her connection with the mother's world that would generate tension and alienation. Lacan theorizes the role of language in this process. Developing a social identity involves adopting language. Since language is systematized, Lacan considers it as belonging to the father's world of detachment and objectivity, different from the mother's world of empathy. For the child to move from her mother's world of personal empathy and unity to the father's world of objectivity and sociality also generates profound tensions. Though the child desires the power of the father's world, she also feels that this world involves subjecting herself to a language system that is not fully satisfactory or empowering. This identity construction process involves separation from the mother's world of empathy and wholeness. In this sense, Lacan explains how there is always a tension one has to live with in identity construction, between the rich, empathetic world of the mother and the objectifying, organized world of the father.[1]

If Lacan's theorization explains the tensions in identity construction and emergence, Kristeva (1986) theorizes the creative possibilities behind them. She develops the linguistic implications of identity construction by treating the mother's world as richly semiotic in relation to the father's world of normative language. She labels the father's world as *symbolic*, as it is more systematized, with language as the chief medium. The mother's world is considered *semiotic* in that it includes diverse expressive resources, such as myths, rhythm, and multimodal resources, which defy systematization. As the mother's world is embedded in time and space contingencies, Kristeva calls the mother's world *Chora*. Identity construction through the systematized resources of the father she labels *Theta*. As the child moves to learn language, she experiences a tension and alienation from the rich mythic world of the mother. The father's symbol system, though necessary for social communication, proves to be limiting in relation to the mother's rich and expansive semiotic world. However, this tension generates creativity, as identity construction involves constantly shuttling between both worlds, drawing from the semiotic world of the mother to construct new symbol systems and texts and seek coherence. Thus subjects fashion new social identities by drawing from the mother's semiotic world. Kramsch adopts this theorization to explain the creativity of multilingual students in their LAs. They experience tensions and alienation writing in English, as they are constantly reminded of the oneness that their home, family, and first language provide. These influences from the mother's world are constantly layered in their writing in English, generating new expressive systems and hybrid identities for them.

Kramsch also introduces Foucault to bring out the ideological implications behind language learning and biopolitics (Foucault, 1991). Foucault theorizes the role of myths (or ideologies, by analogy) in shaping one's subject position. While the evil myths of the father's world shape identities to serve the ulterior purposes of social institutions, good myths have resistant potential. They can provide a critical perspective on the father's world of symbol systems. The emphasis on myths as the focus on the effects on subject formation draws attention to the ideologies that inform the expressive systems of the father's and mother's worlds. Though some are good myths (such as those that inform the mother's world to represent rich diversity, new possibilities, and larger connectivities), others are limiting. They are controlled by the state and powerful institutions for shaping desirable or compliant subjects. This is the biopolitics or governmentality that is a potent weapon in the hand of neoliberal agencies. The father's world of language and discourses can be shaped by powerful institutions and agencies for their purposes through ideologies favorable to their interests. Finding subjecthood in these ideologies involves losing one's voice and agency. However, the mother's semiotic world of free-floating signifiers and expansive myths provide subjects a way to resist the limiting ideologies of society. This perspective resonates well with theorization by postcolonial scholars who see possibilities in hybrid and in-between identities. As we discussed earlier, hybridization is a strategy for emergence, facilitating new spaces for identity representation against dominant ideologies.

Kramsch goes on to employ this theoretical orientation to explain how the tension between languages explains the liminal spaces occupied by multilingual students who shuttle between languages. This orientation also explains for

**48** Suresh Canagarajah

Kramsch their creativity in constructing hybrid texts to find new textual homes to resolve their representational tensions. Her application of this orientation to multilingualism and writing goes as follows. The migrant students who are writing currently in the dominant local language, English, are adopting *symbolic self 1* (or S1). However, in writing as S1, they are reminded of the rich semiotic world of the mother. This is the S2, which seems to stand variably for good myths, rich semiotic worlds of the home, or the heritage language of the students. As S2 informs the writing in more engaged ways, the text provides a new tentative home that resolves the tensions for the writer in S3. The S3 is a reflexive position situated in liminal spaces, marking a subject-in-process. Thus, these orientations help explain the struggle for multilingual students as lying between L1 and L2 (i.e., first language and second language), home and school, or native community and host/immigrant community, respectively, as they attempt to construct hybrid identities and expressive systems.

The theoretical orientation articulated above offers Kramsch a three-part trajectory in identity construction for multilingual subjects. The three stages are desire, alienation, and subject in-process. Desire is the need to identify with the powerful symbol systems in society, such as English as a second language. Multilingual learners of English often attempt to approximate the norms and identities of native speakers. However, this desire is illusory for many reasons. One cannot identify completely with another symbol system. That system may not satisfy one's communicative interests fully, and native speakers may not accept a newcomer as an insider in their community. Such negative experiences can result in alienation and disillusionment from the second language. However, this tension can compel some multilinguals to draw from their other repertoires, good myths, and empowering language ideologies to engage in an ongoing process of hybrid identity construction. Kramsch labels this stage *subject-in-process*.

As Kramsch goes on to demonstrate, LAs provide multilingual students a space for critical reflection on their identity conflicts. They also provide an opportunity for new realizations and possible reconciliations. In many cases, the texts offer the construction of tentative subject positions, drawing from the different representational systems they are shuttling between. Their finished products provide them temporary homes, or textual models for identity resolution. These functions explain the personal and engaged nature of these LAs. Many multilingual writers in my classes often testify that they found the writing to be more than pedagogical exercises. The LAs become performative. They *are* the new identity the students seek or find satisfying. Some students discover identity positions in their LAs that guide their future social and academic life. In this sense, the LA provides blueprints for action for some students.

What motivates most multilingual students to adopt a transnational locus of enunciation and transition to translingual dispositions is what Kramsch calls "horizons larger than oneself" (2009, p. 98). It emerges that these writers are motivated by ethical, spiritual, and social visions that drive them to resist conforming to any of the symbolic systems or semiotic systems that inhabit their worlds. These could be the good myths associated with the mother's world. The in-between position to become "subjects in-process" is motivated by this larger vision. This is treated as a position of strength and creativity, despite the pain and difficulties involved in detaching oneself from established symbolic systems. The writers often derive this larger vision from their childhood semiotic world. For many students, these myths provide ethical, spiritual, moral, and aesthetic visions that help them resist limiting language ideologies and move towards transnational spaces and translingual practices.

## Some Qualifications and Applications

I interpret the theoretical framework introduced by Kramsch slightly differently to resolve some questions related to translingualism emerging from my students' writing. In my courses on teacher education for second language writing instruction, I treat the writing of an LA as an important pedagogical activity (see Canagarajah, 2013b for more background information). In a semester-long writing project, students develop their narratives in relation to the course readings and discussions. The LA is peer-reviewed and teacher-commented multiple times before the final submission. The objective is that students will develop a critical awareness of their literacy trajectories and learning strategies that would help them toward effective teaching. Though codemeshing is not mandated, I find that reflections from shuttling between multiple codes and communities motivate many students to move to a transnational positioning and translingual writing. Native English-speaking students also adopt codemeshed writing in a context where readings and peers help them discover their own transnational positioning.

In the LAs of my students, I find that the mother's world is not always informed by good myths. My students explain how the expressive life at home was invaded by limiting ideologies (informed by systematicity, norms, and rigidity) very early in their life. They testify to the possibility that L1 can also be informed by limiting myths. Therefore, their L1 (or their heritage language) cannot be romanticized as always empathetic and empowering. The writers of my LAs narrate how L1 was presented with norms and genres that tended to be restrictive for them, though it is associated with the heritage and family, which often tended to provide a nurturing and expansive world for the child. Some encountered these restrictive norms in schools, while others encountered them in homes, as elders taught puristic and standardized ways of using the L1, presenting an alienating experience. What this finding suggests is that we have to inquire into the policies, pedagogies, and ideologies accompanying the languages used in order to interpret their identity and expressive implications.

To make the Foucauldian notion of myths more specifically relevant to multilingual writing, I like to treat them as *language ideologies* (Kroskrity, 2000).

Language ideologies are values and assumptions about what constitutes a language, how it is used, and how it gains value. Evil myths are monolingual ideologies which treat languages as normative, separated from each other, owned by native speakers, and superior to other symbolic systems. I treat translingual ideologies as good myths that are more inclusive, creative, and critical. If we treat language ideologies as the issue of concern, we can also say that languages by themselves are not good or evil. It is the language ideologies associated with the use of any language that can make it limiting or creative. From this perspective, all languages tend to be fluid signifiers with immense creative potential in practice. It is not the symbolic resources in themselves but the language ideologies of teachers, parents, and politicians that turn languages into repressive and colonizing systems. Furthermore, any language can be associated with repressive or empowering language ideologies, whether L1 or L2. Similarly, semiotic resources, such as visual media, can also be organized into dominating and restrictive systems by ideologies. Though features of all languages and expressive systems have creative potential, we have to examine the ideologies they are associated with to consider their use, effect, and realization.

The above theoretical elaboration helps me adopt a more complex orientation that explains the experiences of my students. Consider the following possibilities:

- A language that for some students might be an alienating second language might be part of the mother's world of empathy and wholeness for others. For example, English can be treated as a symbolic system of the father's world for some multilingual students. For Anglo-American students, however, it is part of the mother's world and sedimented with empathy and warmth. Thus we can be open to languages playing creative or limiting roles based on the language ideologies they are associated with. These roles are not determined by the sequence of acquisition and cannot be essentialized to the language.
- The focus on language ideologies helps us to treat the L1 or L2, home or school, native or host community as not homogeneous. They are not creative or limiting all the time, or in themselves. What makes verbal and semiotic resources so are ideology constructions that shape them to be used in particular ways. This explains the possibility for my students that sometimes repressive language ideologies enter the mother's world itself as they learn the L1. On the other hand, some students do find creative potential in the father's world of schools and society when they are introduced to critical ideologies there.
- Native English speaker students or monolinguals can also develop translingual creativity in their languages. (We must note that monolingualism or native speakerism is also an ideology, not a state of affairs.) Even if someone speaks only English, he/she can experience the identity tensions and possibilities theorized above for multilinguals. That is because the tension

between good myths and bad myths (or monolingual and translingual ideologies) can get played out in the same language. Therefore, someone who speaks or writes only in English can still inhabit a transnational social space and practice translingual writing, depending on the language ideologies they adopt.

- However, there is some truth that those from historically more multilingual communities often tend to adopt more critical and creative communicative practices and translingual dispositions than those from less diverse communities. These possibilities derive from the opportunities for defamiliarization facilitated by the diverse languages in their repertoire for multilinguals. As they shuttle between languages, multilinguals have possibilities for understanding the limitations of territorialized language ideologies and other oppressive myths. It is also possible for multilingual communities outside the West, which have accommodated diverse semiotic and symbolic resources for centuries, to be more friendly to empowering and inclusive translingual ideologies. Though there is diversity everywhere in practice, the West has tended to be influenced by monolingualist ideologies since Enlightenment, adopting policies that are not friendly to multilingualism.
- In a similar way, it is possible for language practices of early childhood, associated with the family and home, to be informed by more expansive ideologies. The mother's world doesn't experience the limiting ideologies of social and political institutions too directly. The home and family can turn out to be a relatively safe space from repressive institutions and their limiting myths. The expressive resources here are relatively less systematized, unlike those of other social institutions. The mother's world also features rich semiotic resources, where communication involves symbols beyond verbal resources, such as sound, images, rhythm, and body. To some extent, these semiotic resources are part of one's prelinguistic development in infancy, and they remain one of expansive communicative possibilities. Therefore, with some qualifications, we can understand how the mother's world (i.e., home, family, community) might present resources for creativity and help resist limiting language ideologies.
- This orientation also suggests that identity and textual construction always involve mobility, even if one doesn't physically migrate. That is, the shuttling between the mother's and father's worlds, or home and school, family and social institutions, already involves mobility. There is thus a conflict between the mother's world of semiotics and father's world of language as "monolingual" or "native speakers" of any language grow up. This tension has creative and resistant possibilities. The mythic resources of the mother reveal how repressive and controlling the father's language system and ideologies are. The relatively immobile might thus gain glimpses into the unruliness, materiality, and mobility of symbol systems that they might exploit for creative expression in their first language itself. Therefore, inhabiting transnational

**52** Suresh Canagarajah

social spaces and practicing translingual text construction are not limited to multilingual and international students alone. We realize that mobility and the need for creative expressive systems for voice are universal needs for everyone in identity construction and communication.

## An Illustration

While I have a large corpus of LAs from both international and native English speaker students that demonstrates the development of a transnational locus, emergence of subject-in-process, and representation of translingual writing, I focus below on a student from Tibet who was doing a Master's degree in TESOL at Penn State University. The LA written by Yujie Jie[2] titled "Rediscovering Heritage Identity through Literacy" narrates the trajectories and experiences involved in growing up in a home and family rich in Tibetan language and culture, but becoming alienated during education in Chinese and English, and then rediscovering her heritage in the faraway United States. Though she returns to her heritage, her positioning is liminal as she now inhabits a context of diverse languages and cultures, and develops a hybridizing discourse. She also demonstrates a more cosmopolitan disposition in the end.

Yujie's narrative adopts a chronological structure and starts from her childhood in her small Tibetan village on the border with China:

> Like every child raised in the idyllic Tibet, my childhood was filled with abundant legends, sagas, myths and ghost stories, both inherited and recreated, over the past generations. The raconteur would always be a family's grandma who has a huge stock of fairy tales and sophisticated narrative skills. I believe my grandma's favorite was the story of King Gesar, narrated with rhythmized words and poetic sentences. The story based in Khampa opened self-introspection and the awakening of national consciousness in me. It taught me how our ancestors bravely fought against evil, how splendid and rich our culture, and how our great nation bred generations of noble people.

There is a rich evocation of the semiotic world that is part of her mother's world. We see her world populated by legends, myths, fairy tales, and spirituality. Though they are narrated or represented in Tibetan language, they are rendered in diverse modalities and genres. There is both narrative and poetry. Some are written and others are oral. Even the written texts are rendered effectively for the ear and imagination by the grandmother's narration. We do see a strain of national and ethnic pride conveyed by these texts, which might result in a rootedness in one's heritage, a natural part of identity formation for a child. However, this ethnic pride doesn't seem to develop exclusive identities, hatred for others, or a reductive nationalism in Yujie. All in all, this stage fits the description of the broad symbolic world of identification and harmony provided by the expansive world of the mother and its empowering ideologies.

As Yujie grows up, she is sent for her education to a neighboring Chinese town, where the dominant Mandarin is the medium of instruction. As she continues her secondary education in this school, she is also introduced to English language. Though these languages pluralize her repertoire, they are presented to her in normative ways, introducing monolingual ideologies. Similarly, though there is a crossing of geographical and community boundaries involved in her schooling, this doesn't result in reaching a transnational space. Both English and Mandarin are presented to her as associated with specific nation-states, England and China for example, with associated native speaker claims and ownership ideologies. Furthermore, the product-oriented teaching treats the languages as separate systems for acquisition. Also, these languages are presented in normative ways for her literacy development. Yujie narrates: In China, writing templates was one of the main ways that I learned to construct both my L1 [i.e., Mandarin] and L2 [i.e., English] essays. Both in elementary (1995–2001) and middle schools (2001–2007), my teachers would introduce or analyze the structure of an article, draw the structure on the blackboard, and then ask us to follow the structure and write a similarly structured composition. Such pedagogies would have inducted her into normative discourses, not providing her spaces for transforming meanings and forms. The rule-governed ways of writing also don't provide spaces to explore more hybrid identities and voices, constraining her to communicate according to established norms. Furthermore, since Tibetan was not taught, Yujie also doesn't get the opportunity to develop translingual repertoires or dispositions. As Yujie mentions: "The door of developing both Chinese and English literacy was opened, but the door of Tibetan literacy and identity was almost closed." She is therefore introduced to limiting language ideologies and symbolic systems of the father's world, very different from her upbringing of rich and fluid semiotic resources at home. She concludes thus about this stage of her literacy development: "The product-oriented instruction I experienced during the process of developing L1 and L2 literacies hampered my cognitive development."

However, we must not consider Yujie's then-localized place (China) as not open to diversity. There are alternate spaces she finds for different pedagogies and literacies, which encourage different orientations to language and literacy norms. She writes: "Later I became an undergraduate student in 2007 and changed my major to English in 2008. It was at that time that I realized the powerful role critical thinking plays in reading and writing, and how writing in turn influences the development of my critical thinking." At this stage, she engages in process writing, interacting with peers and instructors on feedback and negotiating meanings in texts. She becomes comfortable with the plurality of meanings generated by texts and peer interactions, and negotiates diverse interpretations. She also gets introduced to more diverse genres of writing, such

**54** Suresh Canagarajah

as poetry and fiction. Thus, she is introduced to good myths relating to more diverse and empowering forms of communication. There begin to emerge some cracks in the father's world of monolingual ideologies.

After thus narrating what she labels "in-school" literacies, Yujie titles the next section of her trajectory "out of school contexts." Here she discusses how, paralleling her school education in China, she was introduced to even more diverse genres and identities outside. Her transition statement between the sections is suggestive: "The in-school context helps me to be a proficient reader and writer in the academic setting. However, the out of school contexts helps me to develop another kind of literacy and identity." What emerges is that though the school literacies occluded her development in her heritage language and semiotic worlds, Yujie developed parallel out of school literacies that provided space for diversity. She narrates: "When I went to middle school in 2001, I spent all my pocket money buying lots of books. Interestingly, these books had nothing to do with studies. They were mostly children's literature. Novels written by Zhang Yueran, Guo Jingming who had talent in youth literature were growing in popularity among middle school students at that time." While these were in Chinese, she also took efforts to maintain some contact with Tibetan epics and legends by reading on her own. She felt "homesick" for her heritage semiotic world. She narrates that she went to a lama in a monastery close by and asked him questions about Tibetan Buddhism and traditions when her family couldn't help her: If I had questions and my family did not know how to answer, I usually went to the Monastery nearby my home. I asked the Lama questions about King Gesar and the Gods living up in the heavens. He always had insightful points and satisfactory answers. I was very impressed by the Lama's erudition. He told me that his secret weapon was reading. Thus I motivated myself to read more. The monastery becomes an alternate space to preserve her heritage.

Such experiences suggest that there are alternate *spaces* within constraining *places* where Yujie found different language ideologies and literacies. In these spaces, there were discourses and genres that facilitated the development of a more creative translingual disposition. Yujie says that as she went to college, she got acquainted with the internet, multimodality, and netspeak, which introduced her to non-normative communication. She says: "Developing literacy through the Internet not only helped me broaden my horizons, but also allowed me to see that cultural differences existed in new technologies and that it in turn influenced my literacy development." Thus, digital media provided her a space to explore alternative discourses and semiotic resources that facilitated more creativity and voice. They allowed her to step out of the father's world of normative language ideologies and rigid symbolic systems.

Ironically, it was after coming to the United States that these intimations of her lost mother's world of semiotics demonstrate stronger development, leading to her inhabiting a transnational space and developing translingual dispositions. Here, she is able to detach herself from the ideologies of her homeland and

Transnationalism and Translingualism **55**

see the world from a different point of view. She is able to reconnect with her Tibetan heritage more fully and develop her suppressed translingual creativity in a foreign land. Yujie finds that the Penn State library had resources for her to dig deeper into Tibetan myths and literature. She begins to read outside her academic requirements and sustain her interest in her heritage:

> "It was in our school library, that I first came to know the Karmapa, who is called our spiritual leader of the 21st century. This happened when I was reading Gaby Naher's Wrestling With the Dragon (2004). Robert Burns' ballads (1786), Byron's sonnets (1818–1823), even Tshaṅs-dbyaṅs-rgya-mtsho's poems (1683–1706), all these great works knitted a marvelous picture about life, love, and belief for me. Especially Tshaṅs-dbyaṅs-rgya-mtsho, who is the sixth Dalai Lama, made me quite curious about his mysterious life and passionate creations of poetries. Hence, I looked for any piece of relevant research about him and could not wait to read them."

These readings help her to reconnect with her lost semiotic world of her childhood and home.

However, these texts are read in translation in English. When she wants more knowledge of Tibetan traditions and literature, she faces a crisis. She realizes that she has lost her Tibetan proficiency to be able to read the originals and fully satisfy her evolving curiosity and interest. Her reaching out to members of the Tibetan diaspora doesn't help, as they too have lost their Tibetan proficiency. We see the onset of her identity crisis poignantly narrated below:

> Finally, when I got the courage to have a conversation with one of my friends who studies in the University of Hong Kong about grandma's stories-King Gesar one day in the second semester of my MA study, I found neither the Chinese nor English edition could satisfy me and revive my memories. It was then that I realized how regretful it was that I could not speak or write Tibetan. The education that I had received completely in Chinese had led to my attrition of Tibetan. I had become a Tibetan illiterate. I was pained when I realized that we have the longest epics of the world but I could not read them; we have the most thoughtful Buddhist works but I could not understand them; we have the remarkable fruits of a powerful civilization but I could not taste them. I realized that every fact I had acquired about Tibetan culture and history during my schooling relied on texts written in or translated into Chinese or English. Therefore, I decided to learn Tibetan.

Yujie realizes how alienated she is from her heritage. She also realizes the rich semiotic world of her home that is lacking in the symbolic worlds of English and Mandarin presented to her in schools. She is disenchanted from her previous educational trajectory that was motivated by identification with more power-ful languages and literacies represented by Mandarin and English, thus losing her Tibetan. Ironically, her identity crisis and longing for connection with her semiotic heritage are experienced far away from home, in the United States. Though she doesn't explain this irony, we can imagine how the new geographi-cal and national setting in the US might have exacerbated her sense of alienation. It might have also helped her defamiliarize herself from place-based limiting language ideologies of China. It is significant that she concludes with a forward-looking attitude. "I decided to learn Tibetan" suggests that her journey home (or to her heritage) has just begun. We are left with a subject-in-process.

While she returns gradually to her mother's semiotic world, albeit in falter-ing and insufficient ways as she lacks complete access to them, she finds in her heritage a paradoxical motivation for cosmopolitanism. She movingly narrates her present condition of writing the LA in her room in the US:

> Now, I am sitting by the window and writing this essay. The sunshine is pouring down upon me. I am suddenly reminded of the strong sunlight in my hometown, a small county in the roof of the world. I believe that these are the same shafts of sunlight I once enjoyed in my hometown, because it gives me warmth and strength when I am alone in this foreign country. I also believe that, like the sunlight, my Tibetan literacy and identity that largely developed in out of school contexts give me warmth and strength to master my in-school literacy development. The philosophy developed from Tibetan Buddhism actually influences the way in which I think of issues in academic reading and writing. It encourages me to view things from differ-ent angles, mixed with both a healthy skepticism and compassion.

We see her here occupying a liminal transnational social space. In this space is the "layered simultaneity" (Blommaert, 2005) of influences from multiple places. Though she is physically in the US, she is simultaneously also in Tibet. Buddhism provides her the "horizons larger than oneself"—i.e., the good myth in Foucauldian terms—to reconstruct her identities and literacies in more expan-sive ways. Her semiotic world of childhood provides her spiritual and attitudinal strength for her present challenges. She also realizes that it has silently sustained her through her educational and literate strategy all her life. She compares Bud-dhism to the sunlight that has strengthened her throughout. It is the same sun that shines on her whether she is in the US or Tibet. It symbolizes her liminal transnational social space that transcends national borders.

However, Yujie cannot return to her childhood world without changes. Her literate trajectory and educational experiences have changed her. She sees new meanings in Tibetan Buddhism, inspired by her translingual disposition. There-fore, her reading of Tibetan heritage is not nationalistic, motivated by limiting or territorialized ideologies. As she goes on to clarify, what Tibetan Buddhism offers her is a compassionate cosmopolitanism: at the core of Tibetan Buddhism is altruism. Dalai Lama once called for a compassionate approach to view issues because we are all so closely interconnected. His insightful view influences the way in which I think about the conflicts of ideologies, politics, and religion, even in academia. Now, when I write an essay, I will never take an extreme position as I did before because I know the ultimate reason why we make a claim is because we want to resolve problems, not make new problems. And every one who is involved in today's controversial problems deserves compassion because we are all same in human nature.

Paradoxically, then, her heritage inspires her to connect her other languages and literacies into a new whole, rather than keeping them segregated. She develops a pluralist outlook without abandoning her rootedness in her culture and traditions. While Tibetan Buddhism serves to provide her "horizons larger than oneself" to move to this expansive translingual position and liminal space (between and beyond diverse languages and communities), and adopt a cosmopolitan disposition, it also helps her to be located in her heritage language and culture. For this reason, we might call this also a form of rooted cosmopolitanism. This is a rootedness not in a bounded and limiting place, but in a rich heritage culture and semiotic world.

What is more interesting is that her LA embodies this new identity that Yujie is developing. The LA has not only been a medium to reflect on her trajectory and conflicts, but also serves as a model for the translingual identity she likes to adopt. Note that the LA straddles the academic and the poetic. While we see citations to support the pedagogies in her learning experience, we also read rhythmic, imagistic, and evocative lines such as the following: "I was pained when I realized that we have the longest epics of the world but I could not read them; we have the most thoughtful Buddhist works but I could not understand them; we have the remarkable fruits of a powerful civilization but I could not taste them." Yujie constructs a text that brings together her diverse repertoires and puts them into a new whole. Though the essay is written in English, she finds spaces to mesh Chinese and Tibetan in a guarded and strategic way in well-chosen textual spaces. Consider her use of Chinese in: "we used 神马 instead of 什么 ('what'), v587 instead of 威武霸气 ('powerful') to prove we belonged to the same Internet culture." She thus illustrates the creativity that involved constructing new indexicalities through visuals, numbers, and words. She concludes the essay aptly with a Tibetan word: "For me, my own literacy development is a gift. Through it, I taste three different kinds of languages and culture. Most importantly, it leads me to my home, the place where I truly belong-ཚང་།." In this sense, the text is codemeshed. It becomes metonymic of her new translingual identity.

Admittedly, the mixing of verbal resources other than English is minimal. However, the translingual nature of Yujie's writing doesn't depend only on the amount of non-English words meshed. The merging of the academic and the poetic, accompanying different registers of English, is also part of her textual

**58** Suresh Canagarajah

diversity and voice. More importantly, it is not the amount of words mixed that defines translingualism, but the strategic use of whatever resources for rhetorical significance. Furthermore, one might ask about the transferability of this writing practice. Can mixings in a literacy narrative be generalized to other genres of academic writing? What is of value here, once again, is not the amount and type of mixing, but the rhetorical strategies and dispositions behind this practice. As I have elaborated elsewhere, the rhetorical strategies, writing practices, and language awareness accompanying such usage can be expected to transfer to other contexts, when students find spaces for voice as relevant to those genres and contexts (see Canagarajah, 2015, pp. 137–138).

## Conclusion

As Yujie's LA shows, as writers adopt a transnational social field that is liminal, between communities and languages, they see the possibility of making new textual homes that are codemeshed. We thus see how transnationalism and translingualism are interconnected. The liminal transnational spaces provide scope for detachment from limiting language ideologies, connect writers with larger horizons for meaning making, identity construction, and writing, and facilitate the creativity that attempts to go beyond existing language systems and monolingual ideologies to construct new textual homes. Finding a subjectivity to existing language systems limiting, writers resolve to appreciate the fluidity of semiotic resources, and renew their identities and vision through linguistic experimentation as subject-in-process. They cannot return to their first language, culture, or family discourses because their new repertoires and ideological conflicts pose new communicative and ideological challenges. They cannot be resolved by seeking refuge in limiting languages or ideologies. For this reason, they are also dissatisfied with nationalist ideologies, labeled languages, and normative communication.

What this exploration suggests is that developing transnational identities or translingual writing is an ideological project. Fundamentally, it involves deconstructing the limiting language ideologies, being reminded of "horizons larger than oneself," and becoming comfortable with constructing identities and repertoires that are more creative and critical. Teachers can consider how they can help students remain committed to larger communicative, social, and identity goals as they learn languages and literacies. In some ways, this is a question of reminding students of the rich semiotic resources they bring from their homes and communities, which represent a diverse and ethical vision of life, informed by resistant and inclusive myths. In this sense, the pedagogical goal is not about introducing new ideologies to students, but helping them tap into the funds of knowledge (i.e., a rich world of myths, legends, and epics) they bring from outside the classroom. Such a pedagogy could also mean reminding students of the experiences and resources they bring from transnational social fields. The shuttling they have

## Transnationalism and Translingualism  **59**

already been doing between languages in these spaces has endowed them with a habitus, dispositions, and discourses that can help them negotiate new symbolic/language systems. Teachers can also unveil the ideologies informing the desired symbolic systems so that students draw from them selectively for their transnational identities and voices. In many ways, this is the project of critical thinking and pedagogies. This amounts to awareness-raising among students to encourage reflexivity for new identity construction and expression. Such a pedagogy can also involve deconstructing dominant language ideologies and limiting myths to expose their interests and implications.

Note that this pedagogical orientation involves seeing students as resourceful and bringing with them the repertoires and competencies for their self-fashioning. Such a pedagogy does not involve teaching forms and conventions in a product-oriented manner, but letting students discover their styles and texts in relation to their chosen trajectories of identity development. It must be emphasized that teachers must be careful not to impose their ideologies on their students. This might constitute the type of controlled symbolic systems of the father's world that can stifle the development of writers and students. In fact, the school already possesses its own symbolic system in the form of authorized discourses, genres, and registers that generate the conflicts that students often experience. It is possible, however, to construct classrooms and schools as ecologically rich safe spaces where students can explore the potential of different representational systems for identity and communicative purposes. This can be done in a flexible and non-impositional manner so that students can shuttle between diverse representational systems for their ongoing identity development, and appropriate them as suitable to their own interests as I have demonstrated elsewhere (see Canagarajah, 2013b).

## Notes

1. I treat the notion of mother's world and father's world as metaphors for two forms of language relationships. I complicate them later to show how these states cannot be essentialized, as there is considerable tension and diversity in how people experience these states.
2. I am using the actual name of the student, with her permission, as her essay is to be published in a collection of LAs.

## References

Bakhtin, M. M. (1986). *Speech genres and other late essays* (Trans. V. W. McGee). Austin: University of Texas Press.

Bhabha, H. K. (1999). Interview. Staging the politics of difference: Homi Bhabha's critical literacy. In G. A. Olson, & L. Worsham (Eds.), *Race, rhetoric, and the postcolonial* (pp. 3–42). Albany: SUNY Press.

Blommaert, J. (2005). *Discourse: A critical introduction.* Cambridge, UK: Cambridge University press.

## 60  Suresh Canagarajah

Brown, H. D. (1991). TESOL at twenty-five: What are the issues? *TESOL Quarterly, 25*, 245–260.

Canagarajah, S. (2006). The place of World Englishes in composition: Pluralization continued. *College Composition and Communication, 57*, 586–619.

Canagarajah, S. (2013a). *Translingual practice: Global Englishes and cosmopolitan relations.* Abingdon: Routledge.

Canagarajah, S. (2013b). Negotiating translingual literacy: An enactment. *Research in the Teaching of English, 48*(1), 40–67.

Canagarajah, S. (2015). "Blessed in my own way": Pedagogical affordances for dialogical voice construction in multilingual student writing. *Journal of Second Language Writing, 27*, 122–139.

Faist, T., Fauser, M., & Reisenauer, E. (2013). *Transnational migration.* Cambridge, UK: Polity.

Foucault, M. (1991). Governmentality. In G. Burchell, C. Gordon, & P. Miller (Eds.), *The Foucault effect: Studies in governmentality* (pp. 87–104). Chicago, IL: Chicago University Press.

Gardner, R. C., & Lambert, W. E. (1972). *Attitudes and motivation in second language learning.* Rowley, MA: Newbury House.

Horner, B., Lu, M., Royster, J. J., & Trimbur, J. (2010). Language difference in writing: Toward a translingual approach. *College English, 73*(3), 303–321.

Kramsch, C. (2009). *The multilingual subject.* Oxford: Oxford University Press.

Kress, G. (2009). *Multimodality: A social semiotic approach to contemporary communication.* London: Routledge.

Kristeva, J. (1986). Revolution in poetic language. In T. Moy (Ed.), *The Kristeva reader* (pp. 89–136). New York: Columbia University Press.

Kroskrity, P. (Ed.). (2000). *Regimes of language: Ideologies, polities, and identities.* Oxford: James Currey.

Kubota, R. (2014). The multi/plural turn, postcolonial theory, and neoliberal multiculturalism. *Applied Linguistics, 33*, 1–22. August 2014 published online. doi:10.1093/applin/amu045

Lacan, J. (1977). *Ecrits: A selection* (Trans. A. Sheridan). New York: Norton.

Matsuda, P. K. (2014). The lure of translingual writing. *PMLA, 129*(3), 478–483.

Peirce, B. N. (1995). Social identity, investment, and language learning. *TESOL Quarterly, 29*(1), 9–32.

Young, V. (2004). Your average nigga. *College Composition and Communication, 55*, 693–715.

# 4

# WRITING IS THE QUESTION, NOT THE ANSWER

## A Critical Cosmopolitan Approach to Writing in Neoliberal Times

*Anne Surma*

## Introduction

What does it mean to write and to evaluate writing in the contemporary context of the university in a neoliberal environment?[1] This chapter reflects on a significant challenge facing writing practices generally, and in the higher education context in particular. Other scholars have written extensively and powerfully about the significance of writing as a social practice, rather than as a product conceived in reductively instrumental, calculable, or commercial terms (see, for example, Barton, Hamilton, & Ivanic, 2000; Berlin, 2003; Cooper, 1986). As well, the interests of many of the authors in this volume on transnationally and translingually oriented writing practices are informed by the complexities of the social places and spaces of writing today (see, for example, Canagarajah; Donahue; Wu; this volume). Based on those understandings, on my conception of public and professional writing as ethical, imaginative and rhetorical praxis (Surma, 2000, 2005), and drawing specifically on my concept of critical cosmopolitanism tailored to the field of writing (Surma, 2013), I consider how it might be possible (as a teacher, student, researcher and citizen) to write, and relate to others, near and far, in the public domain, *without* resorting to the techniques of the self-serving entrepreneur: the atomized subject privileged under neoliberalism. In such an environment, along with other social practices, writing is frequently valued and evaluated principally in terms of its instrumental properties and potential: as a quantitatively assessable function and "techno-rationalist" (Lankshear, 1997, p. 313) skill, and as a vehicle for achieving measurable "results." I thus examine the constraints on and the possibilities for writing as a self-consciously critical challenge to the normative prescriptions of the neoliberal agenda.

In a context of neoliberalism (as outlined below), to teach writing, to learn writing, to research writing and to do writing in our world—across the borders of private and public, local and global, national and international, selves and others, now and then—is insistently to *ask questions* of the texts we imagine, write, read, share, interpret and respond to. I suggest that a critical cosmopolitan perspective can help us to ask provocative and critical questions of writing, in order to reflect on the contradictions and complexities of such a challenge. I also illustrate, by means of a specific example, how this approach is more important than ever, when a techno-rationalist, "outsourcing" approach to writing practice (and particularly to shaping and correcting writing) in the academy has gained significant traction. Students and teachers have reported the benefits to their learning of grammar and editing software (see, for example, Moore, Rutherford, & Crawford, 2016; Saadi & Saadat, 2015), and these benefits are to be lauded. Nonetheless, I suggest that the concentration on the mechanical and measurable aspects of writing encouraged by the use and prevalence of such technologies demands that we also give redoubled attention to the qualitative—social, ethical, political and discursive—dimensions of writing for academic, professional and community purposes.

## The Neoliberal Project

The neoliberal project originates in the work of economist and philosopher Friedrich von Hayek and economist Ludwig Von Mises in the 1920s and 1930s (Davies, 2014, p. 3), spreading from Austria into London, Germany, the rest of Europe and the USA over the following decades. From the late 1970s onwards its impacts have been pervasive in cultures across the world.

Neoliberalism is a belief in the centrality of free markets and economic calculation as the basis of determining or judging the value of all human social and political activities (Brown, 2015; Davies, 2014, p. 4). For Hayek, the role of markets was

> to coordinate social activity without intervention by political authorities or "conscious" cooperation by actors themselves . . . The virtue of markets, for Hayek, was their capacity to replace egalitarian and idealist concepts of the common good that he believed could lead to tyranny. (Davies, 2014, p. 1)

In 1947, Hayek and like-minded colleagues founded the Mount Pèlerin Society, and they committed to challenge Keynesian economics and the planned economies of socialist countries. Over subsequent years, numerous networks and institutions were purposefully designed and established internationally to promote and embed neoliberal ideas among financial, business and academic elites. During both the 1970s, a period that saw challenges to the welfare state and to the role

Writing Is the Question, Not the Answer **63**

of government in guiding the economy to ensure protection of the state's most vulnerable citizens, as well the 1980s, witness to the rise of Thatcherism and Reaganism, neoliberal ideas began to direct and shape economic and social policies (Dean, 2009, pp. 52–53; George, 2000). Consequently and progressively, the role of government has increasingly become to serve, bolster and extend commercial and market interests, and to restructure all public services on the model of a quasi-market rationality. By extension, under this model, human beings are reconceived as primarily "market actors," every area of activity as a market and "every entity (whether public or private, whether person, business, or state) . . . governed as a firm" (Brown in Shenk, 2015). Thus, the political and ethical dimensions of individual and community lives, as well as the messiness and ambiguity of the human and social worlds, are inimical to the neoliberal project.

In this environment, in the latter decades of the twentieth century and into the twenty-first century, the university, which was traditionally understood as serving a public good, has been radically and progressively transformed into an enterprise by government policy, market and institutional reforms (Holborow, 2015, pp. 98–104). The university is now frequently represented and promoted as a matter of individual investment and (economically demonstrable) private return or reward. As Steven Ward explains, this transformation has deeply affected the role and status of knowledge, knowledge formation and the privileging of certain discipline areas over others in the university. He points out that "fields that directly contribute to marketability or neoliberal-style governability [. . .] thrive at the expense of more theoretical, critical or speculative areas which have a considerably lower 'exchange value' or direct convertibility" (2012, p. 122). In other words, knowledge and knowledge practices that may be readily commodified and their economic benefits calculated are more likely to be accommodated and supported as useful areas of university study.

By extension, Ward and other scholars (Brown, 2015; Collini, 2012; Giroux, 2014; Hil, 2015; Holborow, 2015; Holmwood, 2011) have (directly and indirectly) expounded at length on the deleterious impacts of a neoliberalized education system on democracy and the democratic flourishing of communities. The neoliberal credo that individuals are personally responsible for their own improvement, for example, masks the structural inequalities that continue to distinguish so-called successful from unsuccessful students as they go through their school education (Tronto, 2013, p. 131). At the tertiary level, an environment encouraging critical inquiry and reflection, pivotal to effecting positive social change, is jeopardized by practices that privilege the bottom line (Giroux, 2014, pp. 1–28). Ultimately, the abandonment of the aim of educating people for democratic citizenship by a neoliberal agenda that cannot account for the value of such education other than in economic terms, reduces the raison d'être of the university to a provider of job training and private wealth generation (Brown, 2015, pp. 175–200).

## The Impacts of Neoliberalism on Writing and Writing Studies in the University

In this context, what is the purpose and value of the practice and discipline of academic and professional writing in the university, except to respond to local and global market demands? It can be argued that the field of writing has benefited from the neoliberal environment, in which writing is now recognized and valued as a commercially useful skill and service. Moreover, the centrality of writing to students' development of their capacity to work and thrive in diverse professional environments also seems to have been acknowledged. However, as the languages of ethics and of the relational, communal world are conflated with or subsumed by the language of economics so that, for example, terms such as "value" or "skill" have been co-opted by neoliberal discourse (Urciuoli, 2008), the role and practice of writing in the academy and beyond, as a human, social and politically democratic (and not merely technical) endeavor, may be compromised by the very technologies that are claimed to support and extend its communicative and social reach.

Before introducing the critical cosmopolitan approach to writing and demonstrating how it might mitigate the impacts of an instrumentally driven approach to writing, it is important to highlight the influence of neoliberalism, its pervasiveness in our globalized world and thus in the academy, and its particular relevance to a discussion of writing. Political scientist Wendy Brown makes the connection directly when she reflects on how far the process of "neoliberalization" has advanced:

> Even its critics cannot see the ways in which we have lost a recognition of ourselves as held together by literatures, images, religions, histories, myths, ideas, forms of reason, grammars, figures, and languages. Instead, we are presumed to be held together by technologies and capital flows (2015, p. 188).

Similarly, and as George Monbiot wryly comments, so thoroughgoing has our immersion in neoliberalism become that we seem to accept the idea "that this utopian, millenarian faith describes a neutral force; a kind of biological law, like Darwin's theory of evolution" (Monbiot, 2016, para. 3).

In this context, we can see how in relation to writing as a discipline, the value of students developing specific communication skills—conceived as separable techniques that can be applied to achieve specific (typically commercial) writing goals—becomes an attractive possibility. Or, as Bonnie Urciuoli (2008) comments:

> In skills discourses, social acts are recast in a transactional or entrepreneurial frame and actors' segmented selves are recast as assemblages of productive elements, as bundles of skills. All these aspects of social action

and personhood are skills insofar as they are divorced from their users' everyday social context and recast, entextualized, inculcated, and assessed by experts for work applications.

*(p. 224)*

As skills become marketable in this way, it is unsurprising that business and commercial enterprises have sought to exploit the public and professional practices of writing and communicating across different domains, modes and platforms. For instance, William Davies remarks that while corporations such as Facebook cannot "own" verbal languages, they can seek "to privatize the means of communication" (Davies, 2015, para. 16). In other words, the "free," open-access social media platforms by means of which we write to one another, including Facebook (and WhatsApp, which Facebook acquired in 2014), are privately owned. Thus, corporations can be seen to shape or even determine the forms, structures, content and styles of texts (such as Twitter); regulate what counts as legitimate and apparently original writing (through plagiarism software such as Turnitin); and prescribe and evaluate standards of what is deemed good and correct writing (through grammar and editing software such as Grammarly). Nonetheless, while this regulatory function of social media platforms does not preclude writers from using their individual voices to interact with others productively and meaningfully in transnational contexts, as chapters in this volume persuasively demonstrate (see Wu; Liu; this volume), it is important to remain alert to the ways in which such platforms also regulate, standardize or otherwise constrain communicative practices from achieving their cosmopolitan potential.

Indeed, as Vojak, Kline, Cope, McCarthey, and Kalantzis's (2011) study of writing assessment software (such as Criterion and WriteToLearn) shows, most typically "new technology is being used to reinforce old practices" (p. 108). These authors argue that such assessment software is designed to treat writing as a product rather than as a process, and is programmed to assess writing's formal or surface accuracy rather than, for example, its socially situated meanings and effects. The brief overview of and example from grammar and editing software Grammarly (below) finds something similar. Therefore, as I propose in the following section, in a neoliberal context a critical cosmopolitan perspective provides an important counterbalancing approach to those technologies that might serve (albeit indirectly) to entrench and limit what passes for the good and the correct in relation to institutionally sanctioned writing practices in the university.

## A Critical Cosmopolitan Approach to Writing

What does a critical cosmopolitan approach to writing consist of and how can it help orient us to writing that considers carefully its qualitative—particularly its social and ethical—texture?[2] Critical cosmopolitanism, as I develop and apply the concept, building on the work of Gerard Delanty (2006), can be broadly defined as a challenge to the destructive aspects of globalization, constituting a communicative, dialectical response to them. While the processes of globalization have accelerated the movements and flows of people, finance, trade, services and communications across state and continental boundaries, its impacts are experienced unevenly, both within individual states and across the globe. While for some people the opening up of boundaries has resulted in increased mobility, wealth and power, for many others it has resulted in increased poverty, insecurity and restricted opportunities for free movement. It is notable that the influence of neoliberal policies on globalization flows (particularly the global movement of capital) has been substantial (Ward, 2012, p. 39).

Delanty uses the term critical cosmopolitanism to outline a form of resistance to, or "a normative critique" of, globalization. From this perspective, Delanty conceptualizes the social world "as an open horizon in which new cultural models take shape" (2006, p. 27). It involves individuals, groups and societies interacting with each other within and across borders, territories, networks and temporalities and, in the process of doing so, undergoing, as Delanty suggests, "transformation in light of the encounter with the Other" (2009, p. 252). It is important to note that the critical cosmopolitan subject imagined here is *not* the "strategic cosmopolitan" (Mitchell, 2003), the individual driven by the thrills of global competition, the chameleon who readily orients and re-orients herself to exploit shifting social, cultural and temporal contexts according to expediency and the pursuit of (financial) interests of the neoliberal agenda. Neither is the critical cosmopolitan subject the "rootless cosmopolitan" that Stuart Hall (2006) describes, one of the global elite, free from cultural and ethical attachments. Instead, the critical cosmopolitan subject is situated in a specific spatio-temporal context, with the ties, loyalties, commitments and obligations involved in that positioning, and at the same time alert to her real and dynamic connection and responsibilities to (often unknown) others and others' lives within and across local, national and international boundaries. For the critical cosmopolitan subject, then, the ethical, interdependent dimensions of living and communicating in the world with others near and far, familiar and unfamiliar, are pivotal.

The reflective, critical and dialogic disposition of critical cosmopolitanism is reflected in Delanty's comment that it involves "the creation and articulation of communicative models of world openness in which societies undergo transformation" (2006, p. 35; see also Delanty, 2009, pp. 251–252). Thus, as Xiaoye You, puts it, a cosmopolitan perspective "enables us to perceive human connectedness as being deeply underpinned in the various accents, styles, and uses of language in everyday life and literary culture" (You; this volume, p. 6). In a globalized world, writing, as a means of interacting with, representing or marginalizing the lives, worlds and concerns of others has a potential reach and impact unimaginable just a few decades ago. Writing may thus be conceived and practiced as a process through which the individual and social relationships that constitute the cosmopolitan world can be imagined, enacted, critiqued and transformed.

Writing necessarily involves interlocutors in obligations and responsibilities that they may not have actively sought and that they may wish or choose to ignore, but that are nonetheless real. The focus or concerns of writing may well be immediate, local, clear and specific, but its impacts may well also be long-term or retrospective, global, uncertain and wide-ranging. Critical cosmopolitanism underscores the idea that writers do writing in ethically ambivalent contexts, that they confront and work within the constraints (whether economic, political, professional, institutional, legal, cultural, ethnic or social) and conventions of their subjective or representative positions. It also highlights the way in which writing that merely rehearses and reiterates the same prejudices, or that entrenches the I/we while obscuring or objectifying the other/you, or that refuses to acknowledge the repercussions it may generate, is lifeless, worthless writing. Writing that doesn't engage (with) others, whose lives and wellbeing it affects, that doesn't expect and enable the responses of others, is likely to be merely promotional, abstract or both.

In order that it is grounded in the realm of human, lived experience, the critical cosmopolitan approach to writing that I delineate here thus incorporates some of the practices and values of a feminist ethics of care. While theorists of cosmopolitanism such as Delanty refer briefly to the importance of care to the cosmopolitan imagination (see, for example, 2009, p. 7), it is scholars such as Virginia Held and Fiona Robinson, extending a feminist ethics of care into the global arena, whose work represents what I read as a specifically imaginative expression of a contextualized cosmopolitanism. Broadly speaking, the key tenet of feminist care ethics is that strong relationships and flourishing local and global societies are reliant on the concrete ties of interdependence and care that bind human beings and communities together. As Robinson (2009) says, a feminist ethics of care treats human beings "not as autonomous subjects, but as being embedded in networks and relationships of care" (para. 14). This approach to ethics determinedly situates discussions about relations between self and other at the center of what we might imagine as valuable and important in both private and public life. Held (2006) puts it succinctly when she remarks that people are always and everywhere "relational and . . . interdependent" (p. 156). Held also argues that an ethics of care helps highlight the connections between people as emotionally rich and mutually sustaining relations of interdependence, not as exclusively rationally based or as centered on the lone individual. It is the emotions, she argues, such as empathy, sensitivity and responsiveness, that are better guides to what we should or shouldn't do, in moral terms (p. 157). As practice and as a value, an ethics of care "advocates attention to particulars, appreciation of context, narrative understanding, and communication and dialogue in moral deliberation" (pp. 157–158). Held's discussion of an ethics of care in a global

## 68 Anne Surma

context (p. 156) also reminds us how some of our responsibilities to care are not chosen, but are nonetheless real, and emerge from our social positioning and historical embeddedness. This means too that caring relations "are not limited to the personal contexts of family and friends. They can extend to fellow members of groups of various kinds, to fellow citizens, and beyond. We can, for instance, develop caring relations for persons who are suffering deprivation in distant parts of the globe" (p. 157).

So if writing is one means by which the social relationships that constitute a cosmopolitan resistance to the neoliberal agenda can be enacted, imagined, realized, critiqued and transformed, what does it entail in practical terms? A critical cosmopolitan orientation to writing demands that we ask some crucial questions of the texts we write and read. These include the following: How does the writing voice (its discursive and rhetorical predilections and emphases) position the text in relation to imagined readers? Which discourses are privileged, and how is rhetoric harnessed to impress a specific perspective on readers? To what extent do the writer and the writing situate or imagine individual, social and organizational relationships and activities across different cultural, social and temporal contexts? What are the relations of dependence and interdependence elided or made visible in the text? Is the writing self-referential, or does it gesture outwards, to others, to the wider world? Does the writing trace the ethical connection between self and other, self and world? How might this writing be variously read or re-read from the place and time of the other? I now seek to harness some of these questions in exploring an increasingly pervasive approach to writing practices in universities across the world.

## A Critical Cosmopolitan Challenge to Instrumental Approaches to Writing

The university, as outlined above, has been transformed in a number of ways by the policies, priorities and practices of neoliberalism. Alongside those changes, the technologizing of knowledge, learning and teaching practices has accelerated and radically altered the modes, sites, processes and even the content of their enactment. While such technologies have provided students, teachers and researchers with expanded and easy access to all manner of texts and archives, for collaborative research and so-called flexible learning across multiple sites, they have also served the neoliberal agenda, especially in their orientation to market demands, and when they are deemed as enhancing possibilities for efficiency, productivity, competition, growth and profit.

Lucas D. Introna (2016), in a discussion of the neoliberal reforms in education that have, among other things, reconstituted academic writing as "the production and ownership of commodities," observes that universities now "conceive of students as potential customers for their programs in a competitive market" (p. 32).[3] In this light, Introna considers the ways in which algorithmic-based technologies that govern practices of writing in the university, such as the plagiarism detection software Turnitin (the case study focus of his discussion), determine and validate those practices as "calculable" (2016).

Put differently, and as I outlined at the beginning of this chapter, writing in (and beyond) the academy is frequently conceived, from an institutional perspective, as a tool for performing expedient transactions. Consequently, as teachers of writing we face real practical and political challenges in encouraging and enabling students to consider their texts as *other than* artifacts whose value can be quantitatively measured, or whose accuracy can be calculated in an essentially instrumental fashion. This instrumentality diminishes the possibilities for helping students to approach and write their texts to others and for others with care. Just as software such as Turnitin, according to Introna (2016), "makes originality of ownership calculable" (p. 33), privileging the use of grammar and editing software over review processes that instead would focus on the qualitative, ethical and social dimensions of writing can reduce the very purpose, value and impacts of writing to a concern of (market and mathematical) calculability.

As mentioned above, digital capitalism's privatizing of the means of communication is now not only commonplace, but the realm of public communication has become almost unimaginable without such market-oriented legitimization and validation. The company Grammarly was established by Alex Shevchenko and Max Lytvyn in 2009.[4] With offices in Kiev and San Francisco, the company's CEO is a venture capitalist, Brad Hoover. To sustain and build on its claim to be "the world's leading automated proofreader" (Grammarly, 2017), Grammarly relies heavily on social marketing (particularly via Facebook and Twitter) to promote not only its prime product, the grammar checker, but associated products: a free browser extension (for Chrome and Safari); Grammarly Answers, an online "community" for writers' questions and answers on writing; Grammarly Handbook, an online guide of grammar and style; and the Grammarly Blog, which includes tips and commentary on writing. In this way, we thus see how Grammarly, and its current competitors (such as WhiteSmoke, CorrectEnglish, and WriteMonkey, to name a few) become the tools for rationalizing and governing the very substance and texture of written forms of communication, and how they may direct and transform understanding of why, what and how we write. Grammarly's use in the university sector is widespread, with (so the corporation claims) 600 universities and corporations around the world subscribing to its services (Grammarly, 2017). However, as Michelle Cavaleri and Saib Dianati (2016) point out, as yet, relatively little research has been carried on the applications and effects of the use of online grammar checkers (p. A–225).

According to Grammarly, once a user copies and pastes text into its online text editor,

> Grammarly's algorithms flag potential issues in the text and suggest context-specific corrections for grammar, spelling, and vocabulary. Grammarly explains

the reasoning behind each correction, so you can make an informed decision about whether, and how, to correct an issue.

*(Grammarly, 2017)*

As Introna (2016) points out, and as we see above, algorithmic action, "a significant form of action (actor) in contemporary society," thus seems to be "ordering social practices in both the private and the public sphere" (p. 37). In the excerpt from Grammarly's website here, the algorithms are attributed full agency as they "flag" language problems and "suggest" corrections. Moreover, the company's promotional blurb claims that "Grammarly's writing app finds and corrects hundreds of complex writing errors—so you don't have to" (Grammarly, 2017). This makes explicit not only the outsourcing of the writing process but also the transfer of the writer's responsibility for their writing to a paid service. As a result, the ethical relationship between self and other, which writing both enables and entails, risks being diluted or obscured.

Grammarly technology is programmed to identify spelling, grammar and punctuation errors; instances of "wordiness"; words overused in the lexicon; and any use of the passive voice. Nonetheless, Grammarly is often wrong in its assessments. An emerging writer or editor who is not conversant with the conventions of grammar, punctuation and spelling may well be misinformed by Grammarly, as the corrections it recommends are often either erroneous or misleading. For example, Grammarly highlights each instance of the use of the passive voice, suggesting that writers should not use the passive. This generalized rule for writing is both misleading and reductive. As well, any sentence that runs on for more than a couple of lines is identified as demonstrating wordiness, even if that sentence is suited to its readership and its purpose, and even if it is syntactically coherent and properly punctuated. Vocabulary is also frequently—and wrongly—corrected. All of this is unsurprising since the capacity of Grammarly as a context-sensitive technology is circumscribed. But more than that, the inscrutable, automatic, diffuse and naturalized algorithmic actions (Introna, 2016) of such software treat writing and editing as techno-rationalist skills, skills that may be learned once and then applied, template-fashion, to all writing situations. Writing and editing thus risk being treated by writers as exercises in providing standardized answers to instrumental problems.

As I hope has been made clear, Grammarly (and similar grammar and editing software) is neither designed, nor its technology programmed, to do more than fix largely mechanical and technical problems related to writing. Such corrective functions are not to be underestimated, according to empirical studies examining the benefits of such software for students' diverse writing needs (Liao, 2016; Moore et al., 2016; Saadi & Saadat, 2015; Yu, 2015).[5] However, precisely *because* these problems or errors are calculable and amenable to statistical evaluation, their perceived efficacy and their value in an environment that privileges measureable outcomes may well be overstated or, indeed, may inadvertently result in

Writing Is the Question, Not the Answer **71**

the obscuring of the substantive social and ethical dimensions of writing, revising and evaluating texts.

Grammarly and similar technologies support writers' efforts to improve their writing skills—where skills are calculable, measurable, and assessable in terms presented as statistically meaningful. However, what of the qualitative—social, ethical, and aesthetic—dimensions of texts, and of writing as process as well as product, dimensions not amenable to algorithmic calculation or assessment? In university environments where the use of such technologies comes not only to supplement, but increasingly to substitute for, textured, qualitative and dynamic approaches to and ways of learning (about and through) writing and writing research (Vojak et al., 2011), what questions might students, and might we all, risk forgetting to ask of our writing?

For example, will we ask about the voice(s) of the writer/the texts we write and read: who is speaking and how? Will we ask about interlocutors: who is being addressed? Will we ask about the relationship between the writing voice and her (real or imagined) interlocutors? Will we ask who or what kind of voice is being silenced in a given text? Will we ask about the ties of interdependence, obligation, power, privilege and responsibility that bind self and other? Moreover, apart from crudely defining and categorizing text types (academic, business, technical, medical, creative and casual), will we ask about the situation or the situatedness of the text: where and when it was written, why or in whose interests?

Such questions arguably become ever more urgent, in a "post-truth" world, as the text below—an excerpt from the transcript of a now infamous speech given by Donald Trump (2015), in which he announced that he would be running as a candidate for US President in 2016—illustrates (see Figure 4.1).

The excerpt has been run through Grammarly software. Identified as partly plagiarized text, the technology suggests the deletion of an apparently redundant phrase ("believe me"); highlights the repeated use of certain words ("economically," "problems," "bringing"); draws attention to the overuse of a word ("good," for which it suggests the substitution of the word "real"!); and recommends the insertion of commas in two places. The excerpt from the transcript is scored at 92%.

Let us remember, however, that the software is *not* designed to raise questions about the rhetorical situation, the voice of the rhetor, his appeal to, and the ethical relationship he sets up with, his immediate audience (as well as his secondary audience, including in particular the Mexican people about whom he speaks), or the discourses (of economics, of othering, of crime) that he privileges. But then that is because Grammarly treats a document as an abstract—amoral, ahistorical, acultural—product, evaluated by an "inscrutable" and "automatic" algorithmic code (Introna, 2016). As a result, Trump's text may indeed be described as largely "correct" when assessed according to statistically calculable measures.

What is therefore most telling are the problems that Grammarly of course cannot identify, the questions it cannot ask. This is not a complaint about

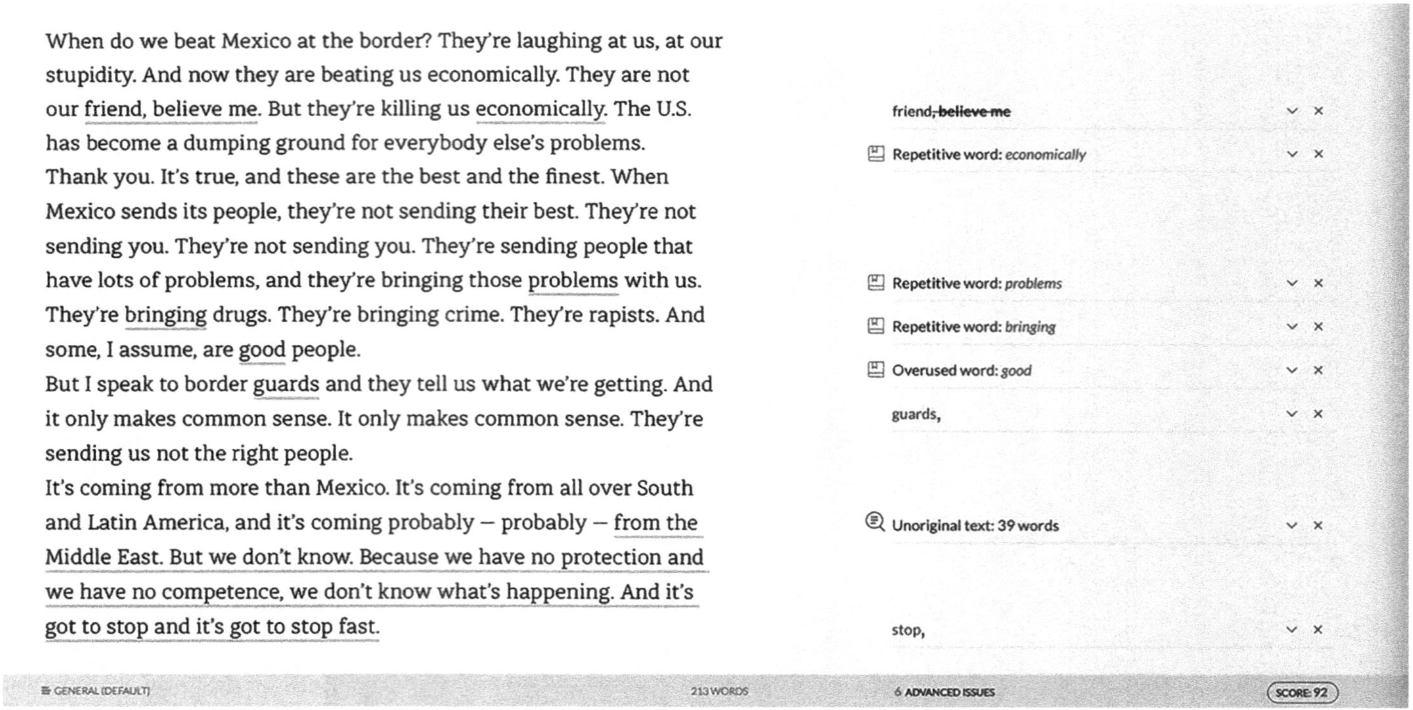

When do we beat Mexico at the border? They're laughing at us, at our stupidity. And now they are beating us economically. They are not our friend, believe me. But they're killing us economically. The U.S. has become a dumping ground for everybody else's problems. Thank you. It's true, and these are the best and the finest. When Mexico sends its people, they're not sending their best. They're not sending you. They're not sending you. They're sending people that have lots of problems, and they're bringing those problems with us. They're bringing drugs. They're bringing crime. They're rapists. And some, I assume, are good people.

But I speak to border guards and they tell us what we're getting. And it only makes common sense. It only makes common sense. They're sending us not the right people.

It's coming from more than Mexico. It's coming from all over South and Latin America, and it's coming probably — probably — from the Middle East. But we don't know. Because we have no protection and we have no competence, we don't know what's happening. And it's got to stop and it's got to stop fast.

friend, believe me ✕

🖵 Repetitive word: *economically* ✕

🖵 Repetitive word: *problems* ✕

🖵 Repetitive word: *bringing* ✕

🖵 Overused word: *good* ✕

guards, ✕

🔍 Unoriginal text: 39 words ✕

stop, ✕

**FIGURE 4.1**  Editing a Text Using Grammarly

Grammarly as a deficient technology. Rather, it is to point out that, as a critical, contingent, imaginative, ethical activity, writing cannot be meaningfully evaluated in terms *only* of its mechanical, instrumental properties, especially when those are divorced from their contexts of production and interpretation, their meaning and their impacts in the social world. In this light, therefore, Grammarly's (2017) claim to "improv[e] communication among the world's 2+ billion English writers" becomes a dubious assertion. Grammarly cannot live up to these claims to forge meaningful connections between writers across all manner of borders, unless, of course, communication is understood *only* as a transactional activity, where writing's purpose and aim is to achieve predetermined ends and to answer questions perfunctorily and unequivocally. Such technological approaches to "efficiently" and quickly fixing a complex social practice will do little to help students develop an understanding of or ask questions about the writing they produce for myriad purposes, and addressed to different readers in diverse contexts. Nonetheless, as Introna (2016) points out, such technological solutions have significant appeal, since as "calculative practices" they "are constitutive of domains of knowledge and expertise. They have a certain moral authority because they are taken to impose objectivity and neutrality in a complex domain that is already loaded with moral significance" (p. 39).

Our challenge as educators, then, is to teach our students to write in ways that are coherent and meaningful in relation to the demands of their communicative contexts, responsibilities and aims in the professional and public domains. It is, at the same time, however, to question the assumptions underlying the knowledge and representations of expertise (referred to above) in the apparently objective technological appraisal of texts and in the algorithmically driven resolution of writing problems. Students' (non-calculable) responsibilities as writers for their texts as forging connections with others across times and territories are realized through their consideration of questions posed in cosmopolitan contexts of ethical, discursive and rhetorical complexity.

## Conclusion

To be clear, as educators we have a responsibility to guide our students in learning to use the tools of writing—including grammar, syntax, vocabulary and punctuation—to produce a wide range of texts that can be acted on or responded to by their interlocutors. Grammar and editing software may be usefully harnessed by all writers to help us address some of our writing questions. However, if we treat these component tools of writing instrumentally, and as separable from writing in its, arguably fullest, critical cosmopolitan sense, if we limit our understanding of writing to its technical components in the interests of efficiency, of achieving results, then the notion of writing as an imaginative, potentially expansive, and other-oriented social activity will be impoverished. This is the challenge we face: to keep insisting on writing and communicating as

**74** Anne Surma

situated, critical and careful practices, which connect us to, and implicate us in, the words and worlds of others.

## Notes

1. This study treats the transformation of the university under neoliberalism as a global phenomenon. However, the discussion in this chapter is based largely on the university sector in Australia, and on research and studies from Australia, the US and the UK.
2. The discussion in this section draws directly on material in a longer reflection on writing from a critical cosmopolitan perspective in Surma (2013).
3. Introna's focus in his paper is on the use of algorithms: a set of mathematical instructions, which, when given to a computer, help calculate answers to specific problems by means of mechanical and recursive processes. Introna shows how algorithms, as "algorithmic actors," are incorporated into "practices . . . enacted as technologies of governance" (2016, p. 17). He investigates in particular the algorithmic action and effects on governing practices of the plagiarism detection software Turnitin, which he describes as "a mundane technology of government" (2016, p. 33).
4. Grammarly was listed as number fifty-five in Deloitte's 2014 Technology Fast 500, the fastest growing US companies (http://markets.financialcontent.com/stocks/news/cat egory?Category=2014+Deloitte+Technology+Fast+500)
5. It is notable that most studies relating to the benefits of grammar and editing software focus on students writing in English, and for whom English is an additional language.

## References

Barton, D., Hamilton, M., & Ivanic, R. (Eds.). (2000). *Situated literacies: Reading and writing in context.* London and New York: Routledge.

Berlin, J. A. (2003). *Rhetorics, poetics and cultures: Refiguring College English studies.* West Lafayette, IN: Parlor Press.

Brown, W. (2015). *Undoing the demos: Neoliberalism's stealth revolution.* New York: Zone Books.

Cavaleri, M., & Dianati, S. (2016). You want me to check your grammar again? The usefulness of an online grammar checker as perceived by students. *Journal of Academic Language & Learning, 10*(1), A223–A236.

Collini, S. (2012). *What are universities for?* London: Penguin.

Cooper, M. (1986). The ecology of writing. *College English, 48*(4), 364–375.

Davies, W. (2014). *The limits of neoliberalism: Authority, sovereignty and the logic of competition.* Los Angeles, London, New Delhi, Singapore and Washington, DC: SAGE.

Davies, W. (2015, September 11). Mark Zuckerberg and the end of language. *The Atlantic.* Retrieved from www.theatlantic.com/technology/archive/2015/09/silicon-valley-telepathy-wearables/404641/

Dean, J. (2009). *Democracy and other neoliberal fantasies: Communicative capitalism and left politics.* Durham and London: Duke University Press.

Delanty, G. (2006). The cosmopolitan imagination: Critical cosmopolitanism and social theory. *British Journal of Sociology, 57*(1), 25–47.

Delanty, G. (2009). *The cosmopolitan imagination: The renewal of critical social theory.* Cambridge: Cambridge University Press.

George, S. (2000). A short history of neoliberalism: Twenty years of elite economics and emerging opportunities for structural change. In W. Bello, N. Bullard, & K. Malhotra

(Eds.), *Global finance: New thinking on regulating speculative capital markets* (pp. 27–35). London: Zed Books.

Giroux, H. A. (2014). *Neoliberalism's war on higher education*. Chicago, IL: Haymarket Books.

Grammarly. (2017). *Grammarly*. Retrieved from www.grammarly.com

Hall, S. (2006). Cosmopolitanism. Interview with Pnina Werbner. *Film interviews with leading thinkers*. Cambridge: University of Cambridge. Retrieved from www.sms.cam.ac.uk/media/1119965?format=mpeg4&quality=360p

Held, V. (2006). *The ethics of care: Personal, political and global*. Oxford and New York: Oxford University Press.

Hil, R. (2015). *Selling students short*. Crow's Nest, NSW: Allen and Unwin.

Holborow, M. (2015). *Language and neoliberalism*. Abingdon, Oxon: Routledge.

Holmwood, J. (Ed.). (2011). *A manifesto for the public university*. London and New York: Bloomsbury Academic.

Introna, L. D. (2016). Algorithms, governance, and governmentality: On governing academic writing. *Science, Technology & Human Values, 41*(1), 17–49.

Lankshear, C. (1997). Language and the new capitalism. *International Journal of Inclusive Education, 1*(4), 309–321.

Liao, H. C. (2016). Using automated writing evaluation to reduce grammar errors in writing. *ELT Journal, 70*(3), 308–319.

Mitchell, K. (2003). Educating the national citizen in neoliberal times: From the multicultural self to the strategic cosmopolitan. *Transactions of the Institute of British Geographers, 28*(4), 387–403.

Monbiot, G. (2016, April 16). Neoliberalism: The ideology at the root of all our problems. *The Guardian*. Retrieved from www.theguardian.com/books/2016/apr/15/neoliberalism-ideology-problem-george-monbiot

Moore, K. A., Rutherford, C., & Crawford, K. A. (2016). Supporting postsecondary English language learners' writing proficiency using technological tools. *Journal of International Students, 6*(4), 857–872.

Robinson, F. (2009). EIA interview: Fiona Robinson on the ethics of care. *Carnegie Council*. Retrieved from www.carnegiecouncil.org/studio/multimedia/20090305-eia-interview-fiona-robinson-on-the-ethics-of-care

Saadi, Z. K., & Saadat, M. (2015). EFL learners' writing accuracy: Effects of direct and metalinguistic electronic feedback. *Theory and Practice in Language Studies, 5*(10), 2053–2063.

Shenk, T. (2015, April 2). Booked #3: What exactly is neoliberalism? Interview with Wendy Brown. *Dissent*. Retrieved from www.dissentmagazine.org/blog/booked-3-what-exactly-is-neoliberalism-wendy-brown-undoing-the-demos

Surma, A. (2000). Defining professional writing as an area of scholarly activity. *TEXT, 4*(2). Retrieved from www.textjournal.com.au/oct00/surma.htm

Surma, A. (2005). *Public and professional writing: Ethics, imagination and rhetoric*. Basingstoke, Hants: Palgrave Macmillan.

Surma, A. (2013). *Imagining the cosmopolitan in public and professional writing*. Basingstoke, Hants: Palgrave Macmillan.

Tronto, J. C. (2013). *Caring democracy: Markets, equality and justice*. New York and London: New York University Press.

Trump, D. (2015, June 16). Our country needs a truly great leader. Transcript. *Wall Street Journal*. Retrieved from http://blogs.wsj.com/washwire/2015/06/16/donald-trump-transcript-our-country-needs-a-truly-great-leader/

Urciuoli, B. (2008). Skills and selves in the new workplace. *American Ethnologist, 35*(2), 211–228.

Vojak, C., Kline, S., Cope, B., McCarthey, S., & Kalantzis, M. (2011). New spaces and old places: An analysis of writing assessment software. *Computers and Composition, 28*(2), 97–111.

Ward, S. C. (2012). *Neoliberalism and the global restructuring of knowledge and education.* New York and Abingdon, Oxon: Routledge.

Yu, B. (2015). Incorporation of automated writing evaluation software in language education: A case of evening university students' self-regulated learning in Taiwan. *International Journal of Information and Education Technology, 5*(11), 808–813.

**PART II**

# History

# 5

# TRANSLANGUAGING IN HIDING

## English-Only Instruction and Literacy Education in Nepal

*Shyam Sharma*

### Introduction

Alan Davies, the author of *The Native Speaker: Myth and Reality* and former Chair of the British Association of Applied Linguistics, was involved in teaching and research in Nepal since 1969 when he was appointed professor at Tribhuvan University. While he didn't work there for very long, he often returned for academic events until the 1990s, continuing to write about Nepal's English language policy (or lack thereof) and the undergirding political dynamics until he passed away in September 2015, drawing many insightful inferences for the field of applied linguistics at large. In an interesting story that helps to set the social and educational context for this chapter, Davies and two other British researchers, along with three local Nepalese counterparts, tried to present their professional recommendations based on their findings from a national survey of English language teaching in Nepal in 1984. The sponsors of the research, the Principal Private Secretary of the British Crown Prince and the Secretary of Nepal's Education Ministry (both former English teachers), wanted them to "adjust" the recommendations for adding (instead of reducing and delaying) English language in the grade school curriculum. Reflecting on that experience twenty-five years later, Davies (2009) wrote that English language played a far greater "sentimental" role than it did an "instrumental" one as a foreign language in Nepal. He noted that even though few people needed English in their daily lives and professions, a "symbolic" but powerful view of the language as a "magical" means of progress dominated Nepalese public imagination at the time. Strikingly, the local researchers also wanted "to have English on the curriculum [as] a mark of being modern, whether or not much learning took place" (p. 46). Like foreign agencies, the politicians and the public, they too found any

**80** Shyam Sharma

research-based "change in method, in textbook, in examination . . . [ultimately] irrelevant" (p. 46).

The romanticized view of English described by Davies is even more dominant in Nepalese society today. The number of private schools, which are synonymous with English-only instruction (EOI), has exploded[1] in the past few decades. Public schools, where more than three quarters of Nepal's largely poor families have to send their children (Sijapati, 2005), are switching to EOI in order to avoid an exodus of students to their private counterparts due to the widespread assumption that English-language instruction improves, as if magically, educational quality as well as economic opportunity (Baral, 2015). The country's official educational policy promotes, on paper, multilingualism involving local languages (Phyak, 2013), but it also assumes that using English as the language of content instruction will somehow promote multilingualism. Meanwhile, the strange social demand for EOI has been forcing schools, teachers, and students across the board to increasingly "hide" and suppress the use of local languages in the classroom. EOI was already a step ahead in colleges and universities, private or public, based on the assumption that "higher" education must be of "international standard." The recent shift from annual to semester-based education in tertiary education, whose official guidelines have promoted EOI, is pushing EOI toward universal use and the use of local languages in the classroom is becoming more stigmatized than ever before—while fluency in English among teachers and students has arguably not increased in recent times.

Using the case of Nepal, this chapter shows how particular power dynamics among languages involved in a certain multilingual context shape the ways that language users in that context can engage in unique translanguaging. I start by briefly describing the ironic twist in the history of Nepal where English evolved from a language used for excluding the general public against accessing formal education to one that excludes the national and local languages, even though they carry far more socioeconomic value for most people than English. Then I describe the current educational situation, which involves hiding and suppression of linguistic border-crossing in the classroom, showing how political and ideological dynamics are increasingly restricting teachers and students alike from drawing on the resources of local and other international languages in Nepal. Finally, offering a few specific strategies that may be adapted for avoiding pitfalls like those in Nepal in other contexts, I argue that educators must understand and improve what I call the "translingual condition" before promoting translanguaging as it is.

## Defining Terms in Context

Not all multilingual education promotes learners' languages and voice, and not all translanguaging offers them positive opportunities to use and enhance their language abilities. The particularities of a given translingual condition may harm as well as help learners. Let me begin by briefly defining the terms "multilingualism," "translanguaging," and "transnational" use of language in the Nepalese context.

With 123 languages spoken by 28.5 million people in Nepal, 41% of Nepalese are "multilingual" (Yadava, 2014) in that they use different local languages,[2] largely sticking to one at a time based on context, purpose, and audience. For example, multilingual speakers among the many ethnic minority communities use Nepali, the national lingua franca, when speaking to a Nepali-only speaker. In schools and colleges, teachers can—or, rather, could—use the national language, Nepali, or other local languages spoken by the majority of the class. With the exception of a few schools in the capital city that are attended by native English speakers[3] and a handful of other good schools in major cities, English is not a similarly adoptable choice. When it is enforced as the only means of instruction, that is, without ensuring that teachers and students are fluent in it,[4] adding this "international" language to the pool only takes away the freedom to choose what is best for a class, whether that is learning and writing in content courses or learning English language in required English language courses.

In the community, "translanguaging" involves Nepalese multilinguals switching, combining, and blending resources and strategies across different local languages that they share.[5] For example, a speaker of one of the many local/ethnic minority languages draws on the national language (Nepali) in a more or less fluid manner while speaking to another speaker of her home/local language. Such translanguaging involves "co-constructing meaning" (Canagarajah, 2013) by working different local languages into the process of conversation. When English is enforced as the only permitted means of communication, because few teachers and students are fluent in it, they borrow words and expressions out of sheer necessity, rather than by rhetorical choice. Worse, translanguaging in school and college classrooms is done against fear of punishment: teachers and students avoid it, or keep it short, preface it with apology or justification, frame it within humor, make it sound like a slip of the tongue, and so on. This phenomenon is a response to schools making rules that encourage children to go on a "witch hunt" of their peers followed by punishment from teachers and school administrators (Gaulee, 2012). In private conversations, teachers admit to using "a lot of translanguaging" for teaching, as a colleague said on the phone recently, and I remember doing it myself while teaching in Nepal for more than a decade. However, openly using or advocating local languages in the classroom can jeopardize a teacher's employment. Because local languages are suppressed in the educational context, students' ability to translate between languages, essential for professional success in most fields within the country, is generally declining. In fact, forcing a foreign language upon students for years doesn't promote proficiency in it, either. Based on the 1982–84 survey, Davies estimated that students' English vocabulary consisted of 500 words when they passed the tenth-grade national exam if they started learning it from the beginning of the eighth grade; starting it four years earlier added only 350 more words, with little change

## 82 Shyam Sharma

to overall fluency (p. 56). The situation for the average Nepali is not much better today, and for most high school and college students, English isn't a rich resource to draw on for translanguaging.

Finally, many Nepalese also engage in "transnational" communication by using Hindi,[6] Nepali, and many other world languages (as I will elaborate shortly), which they do far more frequently than by using English. And yet, policy makers, scholars, and the public alike assume English as the only language of international communication and a means of unlimited "opportunity" for anyone in a "modernized" national economy and a "globalized" world. These assumptions are used as justification for EOI. As such, the very attempt to define multilingualism, translingualism, and transnational communication in the Nepalese context exposes absurdities in the country's translingual condition. It is the implications of this contradiction that this chapter seeks to explore.

With regard to writing in and across languages, most people can—increasingly, *could*—write in Nepali, and many of them in other local languages. This ability is increasingly stymied because reading and writing in Nepali is relegated into one "compulsory" subject, and other local languages are only promoted in government policy documents (Phyak, 2013). Marginalization of national and local language throughout formal education has led to the demise of local scripts; in fact, with advancements in new technologies, Romanized keyboards, which have replaced native ones, only produce poorly approximate Nepali spelling.

Of course, "translanguaging" is desirable as an educational practice and objective if it looks like how it is generally described in its scholarship. For instance, in an essay contributed to a Nepalese English language teaching forum, García (2013) defines the term by using the case of emergent bilingual students who "select language features from a repertoire and 'soft assemble' their language practices in ways that fit their communicative situations" (n.p.). Building on the idea of "selecting" language features and "assembling" them as desirable, García's definition implies freedom and agency, voice and engagement, even social change:

> Translanguaging in education can be defined as a process by which students and teachers engage in complex discursive practices that include ALL the language practices of students in order to develop new language practices and sustain old ones, communicate and appropriate knowledge, and give voice to new sociopolitical realities by interrogating linguistic inequality.
>
> *(2013, n.p.)*

But as we can see from the definitions/descriptions of translingualism above, whether certain practices of it are educationally productive depends on the presence or absence of freedom and agency, positive or negative effects or influence of power and privilege, and so on.

As such, the case of Nepal, as I hope to illustrate in the rest of this chapter, provides an occasion to explore realities about "translingual" teaching/learning—as well as its "multilingual" background and promise for "transnational" communication—that undermine rather than help realize the ideals and potentials of translanguaging that language and writing educators desire to promote.

## Multilingual/Translingual English: A Troubling History in Nepal

English has a checkered and deeply political history in Nepal. Although English speakers had reached the country in the late 1700s, the newly unified nation's autocratic rulers started learning English as they developed a love-hate relationship with British colonizers in India in the mid-1800s. Similarly, while a permanent residence for a British envoy was established in Kathmandu in 1792, the language entered formal education when the first modern and also English-medium school, Durbar School, was established in 1853 (Stiller, 1993). The school was only meant for children of the ruling class in the capital: The Shah-Rana regime (1846–1951) wanted to keep the country politically isolated from the West. As Eagle (1999) states, "English and a Western-style education were not only a privilege of the elite, but a factor in reinforcing their despotic rule" (p. 284). English also facilitated geopolitical power struggles in the region. For example, Nepal's rulers supported the British during the 1857 Indian Mutiny in exchange for favors related to national sovereignty and to suppression of democratic forces at home.

In another striking case of politicization of English, an ultra-nationalist regime in the mid-20th century tried and failed to make English inaccessible to the public (Baral, 2015). When a Shah king took over in 1960, he imposed a national policy of Nepali-only, effectively banning English in education, while also seeking to destroy local languages in a rather callous manner.

> If the younger generation is taught to use Nepali as the basic language then other languages [of ethnic minorities] will gradually disappear, the greater the national strength and unity will result . . . Local dialects and tongues other than Nepali should be vanished [banished?] from the playground as early as possible in the life of the child.
> (Nepal National Education Planning Commission, 1956, p. 11)

But as Nepal established diplomatic relationships with the Western world, more and more aristocrats around the royals sent their children to English-speaking countries (or to high-end private schools in India), prompting increasing imitation from the upper middle class. While the democratic movement partially succeeded in 1990, before completely overthrowing monarchy in 2006, the myth that English is the ultimate means of expression and freedom, opportunity and progress, globalization and technological advancements had become rampant across the society.

**84** Shyam Sharma

The romantic view of English did become a self-fulfilling prophecy for a small minority, but as Nepalese language scholars have been writing during the past decade (e.g., Gaulee, 2012; Khati, 2015; Phyak, 2013, 2016; Sharma, 2016), it also helped to destroy a functional public education by perpetuating powerful myths which make English beneficial for a minority of families while being an obstacle against learning and economic opportunity for the majority. The promise of English as an economic "key" to global opportunities—because the ability to write/speak and communicate across national borders only happens in English—has practically turned it into what is locally called a "padlock" that most people cannot economically open, as well as a door for a minority. So, instead of assuming that all kinds of multilingualism or every context of transnational communication—or, for that matter, any act of translanguaging—is by default ideal and beneficial, educators must ask critical questions in particular contexts. Leki (2001) recommends that we ask questions such as "why" we require writing in a foreign language and to "challenge or resist where appropriate the hegemony of center ideas and techniques [meaning those from dominant countries], take students where they are in their writing expertise and move them forward, and help learners create texts that match their expanding intellectual abilities" (p. 206). In contexts like Nepal's, asking critical and ethical questions that Leki has suggested means asking what languages are used by most learners at home, in the community, and in their future professions in a particular society. Does one of the languages involved dominate and help destroy others? Does the dominant language, local or foreign, offer equitable access to all, promise realistically similar opportunities in the future, and/or allow learners to develop fluency in other languages—as well as translingual skills where they can use and improve all their languages?

With the above questions in mind, let me describe the state of writing education in Nepal's secondary and tertiary education.[7] First, the imposition of English-only instruction (EOI) severely affects the teaching of content (see Baker, 2011; Cummins, 2006): teachers are unable to explain lessons, articulate their own ideas, and engage students—who in turn have little to write about. Scholarship based on classroom observations has consistently reported teachers of content subjects saying that they can't teach well in English (esp. Baral, 2015; Phyak, 2016; Phyak, "pedagogical resource," forthcoming). A math teacher told Baral: "Neither I nor my students feel satisfied after explaining concepts of mathematics in English" (p. 44). As You (2016a) observed in a study based in China, instructors in Nepal could best help students "cross literacy regimes" if they could build on linguistic and epistemological resources from home languages/cultures. Unfortunately, as other languages are increasingly suppressed, teachers and students cannot harness the potentials of translingualism.

Second, students cannot understand what their teachers are able to describe or express in English. Below is how an instructor at a regional university described what happens when he has to limit himself to English in the classroom:

टवाँ परेर हेर्न थाले भने main point फ्याट्ट नेपालीमा translate गरिदिन्छु—अनि मजाले बुझ्छन । [If they seem *completely* confused, I *quickly* translate the main point (into our local language) and then they *easily* understand.]

*(Skype conversation, April 20, 2016)*

Noting that his students would benefit the most if he could use Nepali as a default medium, he added that if he at least had the freedom to use it as needed, he wouldn't need to wait until students seemed confused. The point he was making is illustrated in the sentence above that was spoken to me, as it was also illustrated in the following one: "माध्यमलाई strategically use गर्ने हो भने पढाई धेरै effective हुन सक्छ" [If we use the medium/language strategically, learning can be highly effective]. I could feel during the conversation how the freedom to use Nepali syntax made his sentences flow naturally, while inserting English words like "main point," "translate," "strategic use," and "effective" added semiotic substance and richness. Having to do the opposite in his classroom would be far less productive (e.g., see Phyak, 2016; Phyak, "pedagogical resource," forthcoming). Furthermore, the Nepali words that he did "not" translate were the most striking. What I translated above as "seem completely confused" was literally said as "look at you with mouths wide open"; my translation of "quickly" was said with an expression that evokes the visual effect of an object suddenly falling to the ground; and my word "easily" was said in a Nepali term that conveys the connotation of "pleasure." As You (2016a) has indicated, whenever translanguaging can be done at levels that are accessible to students, it can also be a political act of resistance, respect, inspiration, and justice for students. This was clear from both how my interviewee described the inhibited translanguaging in his classroom and the uninhibited translanguaging that he and I could do. As Nepali speakers, English teachers, and scholars interested in translanguaging, we were able to connect and engage ideas and each other on multiple levels. Thus, for teachers to be able to avoid unethically dragging learners into spaces where they cannot understand, engage in, or enjoy learning, translanguaging must be uninhibited. It is not translanguaging itself that is beneficial to communication; it is the conditions that allow it to harness the power of language and affect positive results in life and society.

Third, when students are unable to understand content and directions, and when they cannot say what they mean in a foreign language that they rarely use outside school, they cannot contribute to class discussion, solve problems, and generate ideas toward writing. When they resort to local language, to the extent permitted, they do so with fear and hesitation and don't exploit or develop their language abilities well. Especially because translanguaging in writing cannot be hidden as well as it can be in speech, students suffer serious consequences. For instance, of the nearly 300,000 public school students in the national high school board exams of 2015, only 28% passed, with 74% failing in English (*Himalayan News*, 2015). Not only are students unable to write what they know, evaluators have also been found to give lower scores to papers written in Nepali language (Mathema & Bista, 2006). The new semester-based education in tertiary education carries a participation grade, as well as shifting focus toward writing-intensive formative assessments. It used to be that high school and college students could choose to write in one language or another; in this "multilingual" system, their writing would be sent to examiners assigned to read whatever single language they marked at the top of the sheet. In subjects like math and science, they also had the option of "translanguaging" by combining and blending languages. Today, while most Nepalis are unable to afford private, English-medium schools (Sijapati, 2005, p. 29), public schools are switching to EOI, aggravating student failure and jeopardizing their own existence.

Thus, ground realities in Nepal make English-dominated multilingualism more ideological than educational, more illusory than practically useful, and more riddled with side effects than benefits. Using education to create an artificial "multilingualism"[8] has been counterproductive, and the "translanguaging" that happens in that situation adds little positive value. In fact, because a foreign language of highly unequal power is used for officially excluding other languages, the translanguaging becomes distorted—being done in hiding and shame, fear and guilt—and unproductive for teaching and learning.

## Transnational English in Nepal: More Ideology Than Education

The whole premise of English-only instruction (also called "English education") is that English is "the" international language. But facts fly in the face of this assumption, and adopting it as such hasn't changed the reality, beyond opportunities for a minority and self-perpetuating false promises for the rest. Let me discuss how the appeal of English has obscured the reality that there are many other languages that offer greater transnational communicative and economic opportunities to far more people.

To begin, thousands of Nepalese migrant workers who leave for cities in the Middle East and across Asia must learn Hindi, Arabic, Korean, Japanese, and Chinese—which they do outside formal schooling. The latest census data (2011) showed that 7.3% of Nepali citizens[9] work and live abroad, mostly in India among "absentee" populations,[10] followed by the Middle East (75% among "labor migration") and Malaysia (MLE, 2014). Labor migration to English-speaking countries is insignificant, while Nepalese studying abroad[11] are a fragment by comparison, with 39,000 workers leaving home in 2011 (UNESCO, 2017). Beyond far smaller numbers of opportunities in a few professional fields such as media, diplomacy, and business—which tend to favor the elite—English language proficiency plays a largely "bonus" role in international communication for the vast majority of Nepalese. Hindi is used by millions for communicating across the open border with India in the south; thousands more people in the global diaspora learn German, French, and other European languages than they do English. So, the closer we get to Nepal's language politics, the uglier the advocacy of EOI, implemented in the name of promoting multilingualism and "global opportunity," turns out to be.

But the case of Nepal is not entirely new. Prendergast (2008) described a similar, eventually failed experiment in post-communist Slovakia, where blindly embracing English didn't fulfill the dreams of most people simply because larger political problems still determined opportunities and progress for the individual and the society. Prendergast noted that "power structures will not stop creating hierarchies, unequal opportunities, and information asymmetry from which only a few benefit" (p. 148). In much the same ways, English creates less opportunity for the masses than other world languages in Nepal, at home or abroad. But the sheer geopolitical power behind English has created artificial conditions of use, giving the public the impression that it is globally the most beneficial language to learn. From an educational perspective (especially if we view education as a social cause), even if facts better supported the valorization of one language over all others, scholars and teachers ought to adopt an ethical outlook and practice respect for learners by asking "not whether English [is] a world language," as Prendergast urges. The question, she suggests, is "what kind of world, good or bad, yet to be envisioned, will be shaping [English]" (p. 148). Educators must be a part of a world that can shape English in a positive way. They must promote what Phillipson and Skutnabb-Kangas (1996) call "the ecology-of-language paradigm" that is built on local language diversity, while promoting English and other world languages as well. Without "granting linguistic human rights to speakers of all languages" (p. 429), societies cannot achieve any of the social goals of teaching a national or international language or languages.

Nepalese language scholar R.A. Giri (2011) made an important point about the Nepalese context: "Nepal, once a mecca for linguists because of its vast linguistic and cultural resources, is in socio-political trouble" (p. 198). Behind that trouble, he noted, are "invisible language politics" that favors the national language; English adds yet another layer to those politics, driven by a confluence of global and local political and socioeconomic forces. Giri shared a powerful illustration of this problem with the example of a poor couple who avoided speaking their home language in front of their children while going to extremes to send them to an English medium school: "I would rather skip meals to be able to send my children to an English medium school. . . . There is no use of our language. So, what's the point in learning it?" (p. 204). Most Nepalese parents, like the couple above, increasingly believe today that "English education" will get their children into the "transnational" world of communication and opportunities—which it probably would if it didn't undermine the quality of their education in the first place.

Nepal's case of "forced" multilingualism and "suppressed" translingualism (as opposed to their naturally occurring instances or educationally purposeful

## 88 Shyam Sharma

implementations) shows how languages can be used for preventing learners and society alike from realizing the potentials and ideals that multilingual and translanguaging learning are generally associated with. Beyond a handful of elite private schools, the translanguaging that happens in Nepal, essentially under duress, seems worth rejecting and replacing. Ironic as this may sound, a national language policy seems necessary for requiring Nepali and local languages as mediums of instruction, for if some languages are imposed at the cost of others, the resulting "multilingualism" can be detrimental, "translingualism" unproductive, and the "transnational" potentials of an important international language divorced from the reality of life for the majority of people in the society. In *Shaping Language Policy in the U.S: The Role of Composition Studies*, Wible (2013) urges teachers to think about "why" they want to promote multilingual/translingual skills as well as "how." It seems to me that cases like Nepal's prompt us to further ask "whether" we should accept and practice translanguaging as it is, or if we should instead focus on changing the translingual condition in the first place, if it is detrimental to education and society.

## Avoiding Pitfalls, Harnessing Potentials

In "The Fortunate Traveler: Shuttling Between Communities and Literacies by Economy Class," Canagarajah (2001) describes the advantage of learning a new language. The author tells us that he at first found it "exhilarating to join the exclusive club of bilinguals . . . as [he and his parents] teamed up to put others into disadvantage" (p. 24). But he remembers quickly realizing the need to be "politically sensitive enough to question the unfair power enjoyed by [a] language." As Canagarajah suggests, once we as educators become aware, we must "understand the need to teach English critically and share its resources widely in [our] communit[ies] to democratize possibilities" for as many people as we can (p. 24). Here I respond to Canagarajah's important call by describing a few ways to prevent dominant languages from undermining multilingualism, destroying translanguaging, and creating false hopes of transnational communication in educational contexts like that of Nepal, drawing some potentially relevant implications for other contexts.

First of all, scholars can play the most important role in helping to change the course and promoting translanguaging as a natural process in teaching and learning. In contexts like Nepal's, they can do so by aligning their work with ongoing social changes, building on the increasing respect for minority languages and cultures brought about by democratic revolution, and using emerging scientific evidence and social science research about the benefits of multilingualism and translingual skills. Language experts can create and find professional opportunities by tapping into the forces of global neoliberalism, urbanization and emigration, and global hegemony of English—instead of just responding to market demands for English—in order to help disrupt privilege and power and enhance

Teachers' roles are equally important. They can help revive or start bilingual testing, which will help students understand prompts; they can also allow students to write translingually, which helps enhance their "identity, confidence, and self-concept" (Sohamy, 2011, p. 419). Especially in private institutions, teachers can help shape informal curricula and academic support beyond the classroom, start new conversations, organize workshops and conferences, and integrate social-media based writing into teaching. As Pandey (2006) writes in a reflective account of his education in Nepal, "literacy learning is imbricated in the larger politics of a society" (p. 246); educators can make the greatest impact if they are aware of political and social forces in their attempt to affect change through promoting translingualism.

Governments can and must play a role as well. As a few governments such as Tanzania's (Lugongo, 2015) and Ghana's (Poteat, 2016) have done recently, they can reverse course on EOI by preventing or discouraging private schools from enforcing the practice. Some governments, such as Nepal's has recently done, have also tried requiring public servants to send their children to public schools; while this isn't itself a democratic strategy, the idea behind it could be used for developing better strategies to promote translingual skills through formal education. Governments can also provide resources and support to "budget private schools" (Caddel, 2007) for teaching different languages, helping them move away from "memorization at the expense of criticality, creativity and relevance to the problems being faced in the real life" (Baral, 2015, p. 5) and into translingual learning and teaching practices.

Non-government organizations and professional associations can also play important roles: while these agencies typically have more to gain by promoting the language of power, they can also pursue the opposite mission by aligning their business, cultural, and political objectives with the promotion of more than one language. After all, improving education by promoting linguistically and culturally inclusive approaches can help them better achieve their long-term goals. This was indeed the move made by the British Council in January 2018, which released a statement, withdrawing its support for "English medium instruction" (EMI) and instead recommending an "English as [separate] subject" (EaS) approach to teaching English. Acknowledging that "it takes pupils six to eight years to develop the cognitive and academic language proficiency (CALP) needed to support learning across the curriculum," the organization stated its decision to no longer support EMI in or just after the lower primary level, as it has been adopted in South Asia and Sub-Saharan Africa. Due to a "shallow

**90** Shyam Sharma

foundation" of English to sustain learning in other subjects, the Council agreed with research studies showing that EMI can "impair" learning especially "in the formative years" of education (Simpson, 2017, p. 3).

Translingual skill, it is worth noting here, is not a particular objective to be achieved by imposing "translanguaging" as pedagogy or practice in a top-down manner. In the context of Nepal, it is what teachers and students spontaneously do when they are not prohibited and punished for using the different languages at their disposal. Translingualism is also critiqued as simply a new terminology for old ideas such as code-switching and code-mixing, or that it has little to say about particular aspects of language education such as writing pedagogy. In the context of Nepal, translanguaging is the broadest, most flexible way to describe how teachers and students would exploit local languages alongside English, if allowed, in the service of teaching/learning content subjects, as well as language and writing. Nepal's particular multilingual context and its particularly damaging English-only educational practice makes translanguaging useful and necessary. Its justification may be different in different linguistic contexts.

More generally, as the case of Nepal shows, if historical, political, economic, and cultural forces behind a dominant language—whether national or international—are narrowing access to education at large, scholarship and pedagogy must be used for countering harmful ideologies and romanticization of a particular language. Only then can we realize the potentials of multiple languages and using them together and dynamically.

## Conclusion

Nepal is a small country half a world away from where most conversations about translingual and transnational writing education are taking place today, and the history and roles of English there are perhaps too unique to draw many broad inferences. However, I hope that the case of "translanguaging in hiding" created by an extraordinary role played by English, a foreign language in Nepal, will help generate perspectives that will help illustrate relatively abstract issues of language and education elsewhere as well.

The Nepalese case is not just a striking illustration of English—and therefore both translingual and transnational language and writing education—as a function of global linguistic hegemony. It is also a case of vicious cycles of unequal access and privilege created by local historical, political, and socioeconomic forces. As Phyak (2016) notes, many "developing countries worldwide are, like Nepal, embracing the ideology of English-as-a-global-language and English-as-a-social-capital and giving it a significant space in education with the imaginary hope to help students participate in a global competitive market education" (p. 213). If language policy professionals are not cautious, their justification of English medium education can reproduce "social inequalities in terms of class, caste/ethnicity, and race," promoting "differential access to both material and educational resources" (p. 213). As such, educators must take such dynamics into account in order to truly promote translingual and transnational writing skills in ways that will benefit more than the already privileged segments of society. Especially in countries where many people are poor and marginalized, only realistic understanding, an ethical mindset, and a willingness to debunk myths can help educators promote translingualism and increase access to English (or another dominant language) as a means of educational and economic opportunities and political or cultural capital.

Without a doubt, translingual practice can help improve teaching, learning, and assessment, but it does so when the underlying sociopolitical conditions are positive. Ricento (2015) reminds scholars of language and language policy that they need a level of "sophistication in political economy" to be able to "critically address the effects of neoliberalism on language policies and practices in many parts of the world today" (p. 31). As he rightly notes, "English is not the inherent hegemon, nor the de facto oppressor, nor the ticket to social or economic mobility, nor the crucial factor in promoting a global demos that it is claimed to be" (p. 49). Instead, it is for scholars to envision and develop an "overarching framework to account for English both as a means of social mobility and as an inhibitor of local development, especially in those low-income countries" (p. 49). The call for chapters for this book similarly asked contributors to explore issues in the same direction: "What research and pedagogical projects will help break down barriers and create opportunities to address standards, values, and practices in writing?" the editor asked. Even as he acknowledged the "global nature of writing education," he added, "How can we . . . promote a more inclusive view of writing that enables our students to draw upon their own linguistic and rhetorical resources . . .?" (You, 2016b). Research and scholarly conversations tend to travel from economically developed nations and uncritically shape the same in developing nations. While responding to the call by examining a context from the global periphery of Nepal, this chapter has hopefully contributed a different perspective to transnational scholarship about translanguaging at large from the other direction.

## Notes

1. Ministry of Education data compiled by Bhatta and Budathoki (2013) show that the number of private schools in the country rose from roughly 2,600 in 1990 to 12,600 in 2010, with the number of students increasing from approximately 225,000 to nearly 960,000.
2. 44% speak Nepali as a home language, with 32% speaking it as second language; 59% are, mostly Nepali-speaking, monolinguals (Yadava, 2014).
3. About 2,000 people in Nepal speak English as a home language (2011 Census data, cited in Yadava, 2014).

# 92 Shyam Sharma

4. In the case of grade schools, English is also required for student-to-student communication, often enforced through corporal punishment. In fact, English through English-only instruction can be very ineffective as well (see Kerr, 2011).
5. This includes English, usually broken, in the case of younger generations, especially in urban areas, that experienced EOI.
6. Hindi is India's national language and is spoken fluently by many Nepalese, including by most across Nepal's densely populated southern border.
7. Given the paucity of scholarship on writing education per se in Nepal, I build on current general conversation in Nepal on language education in both secondary (with focus on high school) and tertiary levels.
8. Advocates of "English education" also argue that English could be a unifying national lingua franca, alleviating political tensions among the language groups, while ignoring educational problems it has caused.
9. That is nearly 2 million out of a population of 27 million, a number that has doubled since the previous census in 2001.
10. There is no exact number in the census due to the open border.
11. International education typically involves English, but only a minority of total study abroad students are accepted in English-speaking countries; Japan, for instance, receives a third of the total.

## References

Baker, C. (2011). *Foundations of bilingual education and bilingualism* (5th ed.). Bristol: Multilingual Matters.

Baral, L. (2015). *Expansion and growth of English as a language of instruction in Nepal's school education: Towards pre-conflict reproduction or post-conflict transformation.* Master's thesis in Peace and Conflict Transformation, Arctic University of Norway.

Bhatta, P., & Budathoki, S. B. (2013). Understanding private educationscapes in Nepal. *Privatization in research initiative.* Open Society Foundations. Retrieved from www.periglobal.org/sites/periglobal.org/files/WP-No57-01-24-2014-FINAL.pdf

Caddell, M. (2007). Private schools and political conflict in Nepal. In P. Srivastava, & G. Walford (Eds.), *Private schooling in less economically developed countries: Asian and African perspectives* (pp. 187–207). Didcot, UK: Symposium.

Canagarajah, A. S. (2001). The fortunate traveler: Shuttling between communities and literacies by economy class. In D. Belcher, & U. Connor (Eds.), *Reflections on multiliterate lives* (pp. 23–37). Clevedon, UK: Multilingual Matters.

Canagarajah, A. S. (2013). *Translingual practice: Global Englishes and cosmopolitan relations.* London: Routledge.

Cummins, J. (2006). Identity texts: The imaginative construction of self through multiliteracies pedagogy. In O. García, T. Skutnabb-Kangas, & M. Torres- Guzman (Eds.), *Imagining multilingual schools: Languages in education and glocalization* (pp. 51–68). Clevedon: Multilingual Matters.

Davies, A. (2009). Professional advice vs. political imperatives. In J. C. Alderson (Ed.), *The politics of language education: Individuals and institutions* (pp. 45–63). Bristol: Multilingual Matters.

Eagle, S. (1999). The language situation in Nepal. *Journal of Multilingual and Multicultural Development, 20,* 272–327.

García, O. (2013, July 1). Translanguaging to teach English. *ELTChoutari.* Web blog. Retrieved from http://tinyurl.com/y99apcge.

Gaulee, U. (2012, January 1). Millennium development goals, education for all and the issue of dominant language. *ELT Choutari*. Web blog. Retrieved from http://tinyurl.com/y8kjh4ut.

Giri, R.A. (2011). Languages and language politics: How invisible language politics produces visible results in Nepal. *Language Problems and Language Planning, 35*(3), 197–221.

Himalayan News (2015, June 15). Institutional schools fared better: Pass percentage more than three times compared to community academies. Kerr, R. (2011). Filling a training gap. In L. Farrell, U. N. Singh, U. N., & R. A. Giri (Eds.), *English language education in South Asia: From policy to pedagogy* (pp. 136–146). New Delhi: Cambridge University Press. Khati, A. (2015, August 9). EMI in Nepal: A passport to a competitive world or a commodity to sell? A case study. *ELT Choutari*. Retrieved from http://tinyurl.com/ya293eg9

Leki, I. (2001). Material, educational, and ideological challenges of teaching EFL writing at the turn of the century. *International Journal of English Studies, 9*(2), 197–209.

Lugongo, B. (2015, February 18). Tanzania dumps English as language of instruction. *Observer*. Retrieved from http://tinyurl.com/yb8wxtpm.

Mathema, K. B., & Bista, M. B. (2006). *Study on student performance in SLC: Main report*. Ministry of Education and Sports Education Sector Advisory Team. Retrieved from www.moe.gov.np/assets/uploads/files/SLC_Report_Main_English.pdf

Ministry of Labor and Employment. (2014). *Labor migration for employment: A status report for Nepal* (2013/14 fiscal year). Retrieved from https://asiafoundation.org/resources/pdfs/MigrationReportbyGovernmentofNepal.pdf

Nepal National Education Planning Commission. (1956). *Education in Nepal: Report of the Nepal education planning commission. Kathmandu*. Nepal: Nepal Government.

Pandey, I. P. (2006). Literate lives across the digital divide. *Computers and Composition, 23*(2), 246–257.

Phillipson, R., & Skutnabb-Kangas, T. (1996). English only worldwide or language ecology? *TESOL Quarterly, 30*(3), 429–452.

Phyak, P. (2013). Language ideologies and local languages as the medium-of- instruction policy: A critical ethnography of a multilingual school in Nepal. *Current Issues in Language Planning, 14*(1), 127–143.

Phyak, P. (2016). Local-global tension in the ideological construction of English language education policy in Nepal. In R. Kirkpatrick (Ed.), *English language education policy in Asia* (pp. 199–217). New York: Springer.

Poteat, L. (2016, March 28). Ghana to remove English as teaching standard in schools. *Afro*. Retrieved from http://tinyurl.com/y9fwuohw

Prendergast, C. (2008). *Buying into English: Language and investment in the new capitalist world*. Pittsburgh: University of Pittsburgh Press.

Ricento, T. (2015). Political economy and English as a "global" Language. In R. Thomas (Ed.), *Language policy & political economy: English in a global context* (pp. 27–47). Oxford: Oxford University Press.

Sharma, S. (2016, November 16). Myths about English. *Republica*. Retrieved from www.myrepublica.com/news/9189

Sijapati, B. (2005). Perils of higher education reform in Nepal. *Journal of Development and Social Transformation, 2*, 25–33.

Simpson, J. (2017). English language and medium of instruction in basic education in low- and middle-income countries: A British Council perspective. *Position Paper*. Retrieved from https://tinyurl.com/yalad6n4

Sohamy, E. (2011). Assessing multilingual competencies: Adopting construct valid assessment policies. *Modern Language Journal, 95*(3), 418–429.

Stiller, L. (1993). *Nepal: Growth of a nation.* Kathmandu: Human Resource Development. Research Center.

UNESCO. (2017). Outbound mobility ratio by host region. *UIS Stat: UNESCO.* Retrieved from http://data.uis.unesco.org/#

Wible, S. (2013). *Shaping language policy in the US: The role of composition studies.* Carbondale, IL: Southern Illinois University Press.

Yadava, Y. P. (2014). Language use in Nepal. *Population monograph, 2* (pp. 51–72). Kathmandu: CBS and UNFPA.

You, X. (2016a). *Cosmopolitan English and transliteracy.* Carbondale, IL: Southern Illinois University Press.

You, X. (2016b). Call for proposal. *Transnational writing education: Theory, history and practice.*

# 6

## "TODAY THE NEED ARISES"
اليوم قد مسّت الحاجة

## Arabic Student Writing at the Turn of the 20th Century

*Lisa R. Arnold*

### Introduction

> Today and every day, the need arises for the presence of an honest magazine that
> scolds, lectures, and entertains rather than one that flatters others with fake words . . .
>
> اليوم و في كل آن نحن في حاجة الى جريدة صادقة تؤنّب و تؤدّب و تسلّي و لا تتحبب
>
> ("Today," 1906)

As Xiaoye You points out in the introduction to this volume, "writing education"—even in monolingual contexts—"has almost always been transnational" (p. 7). Historical accounts of transnational writing education *as such* are necessary because they add context and grounding to the practical realities and challenges that contemporary educators face. Then and now, educators working in transnational environments, or toward transnational ends, must understand and confront differences in political, linguistic, and ideological traditions and structures. In order to be effective, transnational writing teachers must also find ways to enable students to negotiate and appreciate these differences in and through writing—transnational histories of writing instruction highlight teachers' and institutions' previous successes and failures in doing just that. This chapter offers one historical case study that examines student writing in Arabic published between 1900 and 1906 at Syrian Protestant College (SPC). Through this study, contemporary scholars and educators can learn about the challenges and opportunities afforded by a transnational writing pedagogy.

Since 1899, students at SPC, which today is the American University of Beirut, have "published a magazine or newspaper for part of or almost every year," and "[i]n 1906 alone, the students published sixteen different papers, the largest output in any given year of the school's existence" (Anderson, 2011, p. 22). In analyzing a selection of SPC student writing published in this context at the turn of the 20th century, this chapter considers the following questions: What were students *doing*—how did they conceive of writing—in these early publications, and why? What roles did students negotiate in taking up positions as magazine writers and editors, and how did this contribute to their learning? How did student writers imagine their audience(s), and what did they hope their readers would take from their writing? What can teachers and researchers today learn about transnational writing education through an examination of this historical moment? In considering these questions, I hope this chapter provides an example of what historiography in writing education from a transnational perspective can look like.

A note on the Arabic-English translations throughout this essay: I have presented the original passage in Arabic directly under each quote in English. My rationale is three-fold: First, I believe including the original Arabic highlights the students' original voices, making the students' voices accessible to readers familiar with Arabic. Additionally, presenting both English and Arabic emphasizes the transnational nature of the students' writing education. And finally, making multiple languages visible throughout the text disrupts scholars' tendency to discuss multilingual students and subjects in a single language. At times, the English translation does not match the exact wording of the Arabic original, because the translation aims to capture the contextual meaning of the passage, rather than present a word-for-word or line-by-line translation. Occasionally, I have provided a fuller version of the passage in Arabic in a footnote in order to provide a more complete rendering of the original for Arabic-speaking readers. Because Arabic is read from right to left, all passages in Arabic are aligned to the right directly below the English. Titles of the publications are presented in the original Arabic (with the Arabic's transliteration in parentheses), next to the title's translation in English. I hope my presentation of the student texts and their translations serves to model the kind of multilingual academic convention that is necessary for transnational scholarship.

## SPC as a Transnational Institution

As an institution, SPC provides a compelling location for historical analysis because of its transnational—translingual, transcultural, and cosmopolitan—identity. Located in metropolitan Beirut (present-day Lebanon), SPC enrolled 535 male students, most from Greater Syria and Lebanon, but also Turkey, Greece, Cyprus, Persia (present-day Iran), Egypt, and elsewhere at the turn of the 20th century. The college, which was founded in 1866 by American Protestant missionaries, was the second American-style institution of higher education established outside of the United States; today, it is the longest-running such university. The majority of students were Christian, though a fair number were Muslim and Jewish.

The college curriculum—which emphasized the study of multiple languages—was based on the classical rhetorical model of education found at mid-19th-century

"Today the Need Arises" اليوم قد مسّت الحاجة **97**

Harvard, Amherst, and Yale; as I have explained elsewhere, SPC's focus on language and rhetoric differed from the trajectory of Harvard's more practical, liberal arts curriculum at around the same time (Arnold, 2014). Students studied the Bible and ethics, and they engaged in the study of English and Arabic, as well as French or Turkish. They were exposed to rhetoric and literary study, in addition to grammar and penmanship, in multiple languages (Bliss, 1900; Syrian Protestant College, 1900–01). In addition to their coursework, students wrote and spoke outside of their classrooms in extracurricular groups and student-authored publications, primarily in Arabic and English.

Throughout the college, students and staff negotiated across languages, both formally and informally. Arabic was the medium of instruction at SPC from its founding in 1866 until around 1880, when, as I have described elsewhere, the faculty shifted to teaching in English for political and practical reasons (Arnold, 2014). Even after English became the medium of instruction, though, Arabic and other languages remained a key part of the curriculum, and there was a distinct hierarchy on campus between Arab staff (native Arabic speakers) and non-Arab faculty (most of whom did not speak Arabic).[1] Students entered the college with varying levels of spoken and written fluency in English, Arabic, and French, among other languages. Because Arabic is a diglossic language, those students who had spoken fluency in a local dialect may not have been proficient in the formal written language.

## SPC in Regional and Historical Context

As one student writer explained in the introduction to the first issue of الحظ (al-Haz), or *Luck*, magazine, newspapers went "viral" on campus at the turn of the twentieth century (I. Attieh, 1901). The reason(s) for the emergence of these student-authored publications—or even the prevalence of their circulation, who authorized their publication, and who read them—is not immediately clear. However, it is likely that students chose to write because of the rise of print media in the local and regional community, as well as the legacy of the college itself. The newspaper industry was increasingly prevalent in Beirut, Damascus and—as the Ottoman Empire placed restrictions on the local press—Cairo, where journalists enjoyed more freedom thanks to Egypt's autonomy (Dajani, 1992, pp. 26–31). As print media proliferated, so too did the promotion of what is commonly referred to as Arab nationalism and identity (but what might be better termed today as Arab transnationalism)—what is commonly known as النهضة (al-nahda), which translates to "the awakening" and is often called the "Arab Renaissance."

Throughout the 19th century, as the Ottoman Empire struggled to maintain its colonial influence and power over much of the Arab world, ideologies of Arab nationalism—or "the idea that the Arabs are a people linked by special bonds of language and history (and, many would add, religion), and that their political organization should in some way reflect this reality" (Khalidi, 1991,

p. vii)—gained traction. Christian and Muslim writers from across the region helped articulate a nationalist self-view, largely in comparison with, or in contrast to, "the West." Elizabeth Kassab (2010) explains that the writing published during the *nahda* revolved around questions related to civilizations' "rise and fall," political justice, science, religion, and gender (pp. 20–22).

At around the turn of the 20th century, SPC students would have been well aware of *nahda* writers' calls to "reclaim [Arabic] history and language as pivotal elements defining who they were"—these calls were published in local and regional newspapers and magazines (Anderson, 2011, p. 12). Additionally, by the time student-authored publications began to flourish at the college, a number of the college's graduates had become writers in their own right.

## SPC's Student Writing

According to educational historian Betty Anderson (2011), and corroborated by my own reading of the archives, SPC students wrote in English, Arabic, French, and even Armenian for a variety of reasons—for student societies or class assignments, on their own or in groups (pp. 22–23). In their writing, students explored a wide range of topics, many of which align with *nahda* themes, centering on questions about religion and morality, social and cultural behaviors and practices, politics and national identity, gender and education, and progress and modernity. They wrote in a multitude of genres—editorials, short informational essays, biographies, personal anecdotes, fables and allegories, poetry, fiction, photo essays, and more. The archives suggest that student publications were overseen by members of the faculty, but it is not clear what role faculty played in monitoring or censoring the content of each issue; due to most faculty members' lack of fluency in Arabic, Arabic-language publications were likely only read or reviewed by Arabic-speaking staff and students.

Below, I analyze a selection of articles, published in nine Arabic-language publications between 1900 and 1906, which focus specifically on writing. As writers and editors of their own newspapers and magazines, in this selection, students adopt the role of instructing their peers—in the arts of writing and critique, moral and ethical behavior, and how writing and a writer's character could bring about progress and change in the college, community, and society *writ large*. These examples provide evidence that students interacted with each other regularly through writing outside of their classrooms. These interactions articulate students' values and beliefs about writing, including what students believed writing could (or should) *do*. Importantly, while there is some focus on writing in a number of English-language magazines and newspapers, the focus in the English publications is less explicit, seeming to take the value of writing for granted, rather than something to be negotiated and deployed for specific (contested) purposes.

"Today the Need Arises" اليوم قد مسّت الحاجة   **99**

While the articles I analyze in this chapter represent only a handful of the hundreds of articles preserved in the archives, together, they present a context for what students believed they were *doing* as they composed print publications for distribution and consumption within the college. Without a doubt, students' writing about writing, particularly in Arabic, reflects not only their learning in the classroom, but also their understanding of the importance of magazine and newspaper circulation in the surrounding communities. Students wrote about writing to make sense of its power, to facilitate dialogue and critique, to educate and advise their peers, and to negotiate educational, cultural, and linguistic borders.

## *Writing (and Speaking) as a Mode of Instruction*

Many articles in the student-authored publications reference extracurricular writing and speaking activities at the college. Based on these articles, as well as descriptions of the curriculum in faculty minutes and presidents' reports, it seems that students were required to become involved in one or more "literary" or "scientific" extracurricular organizations as a part of their work as students. Although rarely explicitly described as such, at least some of the publications appear to have been extensions of the work of these extracurricular organizations. For example, one student writer, reflecting on "The College in Past and Present Days" in الحديقة (*al-Hadeeqa*), or *The Garden* (1903), explains that the college's recent development of associations and scientific clubs has helped support "students . . . working for the purpose of scientific progress, with a lion's might and pride." Additionally, the writer stresses, the "section involve[d] [in] working with writing and composition of different newspapers containing various subjects and purposes" is "considered [one] of the best educational sections of the college" ("The College," 1903).

نهضت التلامذة للنهضة العلمية نهوض الأسد من عرينهِ ....
على ان هناك فرعٌ من اعظم فروع التعليم الا و هو انشآء الجرائد المختلفة المقاصد و المتباينة المواضيع

Indeed, according to this author at least, "writing enlightens the mind" and promotes students' development ("The College," 1903).

من المراسلات و المناظرات ما يشحذ الاذهان و يذهب الافكار

Similarly, الكنانة (*al-Kanaaneh*), or *The Arrowhead*, published an article toward the end of the academic year that provides a history and description of the regular activities of العربية الجمعية العلمية , or the "Scientific Arab Association," and the authors indicate that part of the magazine's purpose was to "give way for the association to state its opinions, relevant to the success of the association and the progress of its members" ("A Look," 1901).

و قد سمح لمجلتنا هذه ان تفتح باباً مختصاً بالجمعية لابداء الارآء فيما يؤول الى نجاح الجمعية و تقدم اعضائها

Within these organizations and throughout the college, both speaking and writing were regular activities for students. In the Scientific Arab Association mentioned above, for example, the newspapers recounted the association's speeches, including "The Factors of Change in the University," "Our Purpose as Knowledge-Seekers," "Formation of Earth," and its "discussions," where participants considered questions such as "Do the Benefits of Acting Outweigh Its Harms?," "Can Love Lift Man Beyond the Pillars of Civilization?," and "Did the World Progress towards True Suffering or Happiness?" ("A Look," 1901). In المنارة (al-Manara), or *The Lighthouse*, the author(s) describe the magazine's plan to "write from different perspectives about the 'bad boys' of college, 'shocking events,' and many more" ("Today," 1906). The magazine also planned to "dedicate an issue to poetry writing, divided into amateur poetry provided by those who claim they can write and real poetry such as classical poetry" ("Today," 1906). And the editors of *Light: A Monthly Review*, an English-language magazine, recounted minutes of the college's various Arabic societies, the preparatory school and college's declamation contests, and the debating club (1906). Describing the month of June at SPC as "the most interesting month in the . . . academic year," the editors explain that "Every week, twice a week, and in the latter part, every day and in some cases twice a day, we have some sort of meeting. We have literary meetings, farewell meetings, meetings of sports, declamation contests, class day exercises, sermons, memorial meetings and so forth" (1906).

Based on these descriptions and others, we can see that students and teachers at the college valued both writing and speaking, and saw it as central to the work of the college. Outside of the classroom, students used newspapers and magazines, as well as speeches and declamations—which have been lost to time—to explore issues relevant to their lives, to refine their voices as speakers and writers, and, perhaps most importantly, to inform, instruct, and persuade their peers. One way of making sense of the extant writing is to examine those articles in which students positioned themselves as *teachers*: In those articles where they focused on writing as a subject, students instructed their peers about what they saw as "best practices" for writing and critique, through which development of one's moral and ethical character, as well as larger progress and change could occur.

## Writing's "Best Practices"

A number of articles published in the student newspapers focus on "best practices" for writing, particularly the writing of criticism. Although we cannot know where the student writers learned these practices, we can assume that they were connected to what they learned at the college—from teachers and from each other—as well as their reading experiences, in particular in reading publications authored by their peers as well as the larger community outside of college walls. In presenting their ideas about "best practices" in these articles, students take on the role of teacher and advisor, instructing their peers on the role(s) they should occupy as writers, how writing can work, and on how particular approaches to writing might be received.

"Today the Need Arises" اليوم قد مسّت الحاجة **101**

One of the primary concerns expressed by students revolves around the "art of criticism" (Yousef, 1900). Students, seemingly spurred by peers' critiques of their writing, debated across publications about what constitutes appropriate and fair criticism. For example, in response to apparent criticisms of speeches made at the Arab Society the week before, the editors of *Luck* magazine "caution" its readers "towards criticizing others, especially other student speakers who may be better in terms of intellect and sciences" ("A Word," 1901).

'الحظ' بها اعضاء هذه الجمعية الزاهرة متوخياً بها طريقة الاصلاح ليس اللوم و ما من حقوقه الانتقاد على من هم اطول منه باعاً في كل فن و اغلى متاعاً في كل علم و لكنها بعض.

Such warnings against criticism in general are not common in the archives—students seem, on the whole, prepared to receive and accept criticism from their peers. In fact, the editors of some English-language newspapers explicitly requested such feedback—editors of *Light*, for example, left one page at the end of each issue blank, for readers to leave their "suggestions and remarks" (1906). But in their exchanges, particularly in the Arabic-language publications, students articulate a variety of perspectives about what should be valued about writing, as well as the way critique should be rendered.

In an article published in ثمرات الأذهان (*Thamaraat al-'Azhhan*), or *Fruit of the Mind*, Abi Yousef (1900) notes that "[i]t has become a convention for our Arab writers to reject and reform the flaws in others' writing expressions, article sentences, speeches and books in terms of language, syntax and the different branches of linguistics."

و في عرف كتّاب لغتنا اظهار ما في ألفاظ أو جمل مقالة أو خطاب أو كتاب من العيب من جهة اللغة و الاعراب و فروع علوم اللغة و رفضه و اصلاحه لا غير.

Yousef (1900) takes issue with the attention paid to surface features of writing, arguing that such a focus is problematic in that it "teaches society to favor appearance over essence. They will prefer body to soul."

على أني لا أرى ذلك غاية الصواب فأنك تفضل العرض على الجوهر و لا اللباس على اللابس

Yousef's warning about the inappropriateness of paying attention to surface features in writing is important, in that it suggests that students, like most writers, hoped to receive feedback on the content of their writing. What's more, this warning suggests that students wanted their publications to be read not so much as final, flawless pieces, but as texts that could spur debate and exchange.

Yousef's complaints about what he saw as an inappropriate attention to the surface features of writing were echoed by other writers. Take, for example, A.K. Tijari's (1904) article in الغادة (*al-Ghada*), or *Grace*, magazine, in which he sparred with editors of الدائرة (*al-Daa'ra*), or *Circle*, arguing that their focus on word choice and meaning was misguided. Both Yousef's (1900) and Tijari's (1904) "instructions" to other critics suggest that they should value content over mechanics in writing—this suggestion might resonate especially because the student writers are also language learners who are practicing writing in Arabic in and through the publications they are authoring. Tijari (1904) is also troubled by critics' lack of appreciation for the intention of the writer under critique, whom Tijari

**102** Lisa R. Arnold

characterizes as intentional and thoughtful in choosing language and structure to convey his argument.

In addition to the problem of critiquing surface-level features of writing, Yousef (1900) argues that "this century's writers" have a propensity to critique the "manners, customs and behavior of the writer."

قلت أن من أغراض الانتقاد و تجنبه و تبين الصواب و اتباعه و لكنني لا أرى هذا من أغراض كتّاب هذا العصر و ان كانوا يدعونه ... انتقاد الأخلاق و العوائد و الطباع

He argues that such methods of criticism—essentially an *ad hominem* attack—work against both the writer and the critic, because critique offers an "opportunity [to provide] sincere amendment and assistance" (Yousef, 1900).

و نقدٍ كهذا يفنى ما أراد أن يصلح

This opportunity, he suggests, constitutes the larger value of critical writing—to provide constructive feedback and help to the developing writer.

While it isn't always clear who or what student writers were responding to as they articulated their beliefs about "best practices" for writing, four articles published in succession in *Grace* and *Circle* magazines allow us to better understand how students' exchanges across publications helped shape their beliefs. Across these four articles, writers in the two magazines offer critiques and responses meant to "instruct" their readers about the problems in their peer publication. The first of the series was published by a writer calling himself "The Sergeant" (الرّقيب) on January 15, 1904 in *Circle*. In this article, titled نحن و الغادة, or "Grace [Magazine] and Us" (1904), "The Sergeant" attacks *Grace* for its use of "colorful decoration and dress," characterizing the magazine as a temptress that "seduced young men, leading them on with her shallow love, like the rest of youthful women that look for a man to deceive and a fellow to fondle."

أقبلت الغادة في برود التزخرف و التبهرج و اخذت تقف للشبان بالمرصاد طامعة بقضهم الى ارادتها غنيمة باردةً و نحن لا نعذ لها فذلك شأن غانيات العصر اللّوات هنّ في مقتبل العمر و نضارة الصّبا كغادتنا المذكورة التي هي في ابن شبابها تنشد حباً تلاعبه و رفيقا تداعبه

Continuing, the author focuses on what he claims is *Grace*'s improper use of structure and semantics, suggesting that the magazine's "writers should look into dictionaries before publishing their articles" ("Grace," 1904).

فلتراجع حضرة غادتنا الحسناء.... محيط المحيط لعلها بمفردات اللغة تحيط و لا تأخذ الاشياء بالقدح (و اللّبيط)[2]

In the second article, نحن وتوارد الأفكار , or "The Confluence of Ideas and Us," published in *Grace* on January 28, Tijari (1904) responds to "The Sergeant." Here, Tijari (1904) urges "The Sergeant" to reveal his "motives behind shooting poisonous darts at *Grace*." Tijari (1904) hypothesizes that *Circle*'s critique was in response to *Grace*'s own published criticism. He defends *Grace*'s

> right to publish articles that contain criticism because it has a free conscience and is not afraid to alarm its people about flaws and mistakes they are doing. Its goal is to ensure reform; it has a sound taste in writing. . . .

In fact, the critiques it has written are real, and reflect its taste of what is important.

*(Tijari, 1904)*

ألأنها انتقدت او ما لها الحق في الانتقاد و هي حرة الضمير لا تروم الّا الاصلاح و ما هي فضل الجرائد اذا لم تنبه الشعب الى هفواتِهِ فالغادة كما لا يخفى على حضرتك ايها الرقيب سليمة الذوق. فالانتقاد الذي انتقدته هو حقيقي لان ذوقها دلّها عليه حقيقيٌّ لانه طرق اذني من [نعزُّ] ليس بقليل و من عدة ثقات.

Continuing, Tijari (1904) advises "The Sergeant" that a better approach to the critique would have been

if you knocked on the door of criticism in a loving and welcoming way instead of a tense and aggressive one; the first of those is better and more peaceful than the second you used; the latter drove the hearts of readers away from you.

الامتحانِ ام كان الافضل لك ان تلج باب الانتقاد بطريقة الِلم و الحب و ليس بطريقة الشحن و الحرب فالاولى بلا مراء افضل و اسلم مغبّة من الثانية التي استعملتها فنفرت منك القلوب

Tijari's (1904) advice demonstrates an awareness of the delicate rhetorical situation when it comes to critique writing. At the same time, it is not clear to what extent *Grace*'s previously published criticisms measured up to these suggestions, particularly since they drew the negative attention of *Circle* magazine.

In a response published on February 8, an "associate of The Sergeant" reiterated the problems with *Grace* and urged readers of *Circle* to "remember all the mistakes in language, the wrong grammar, the misspelled words and punctuation, and the improper choice of words," which constituted for the writer "the many pitfalls and traps that *Grace* pulled on its readers to believe" ("Secret," 1904).

الله. الم يأتك حديث الغادة الحسناء. يوم خبطت خبط عشواء في استعمال احرف الجر و شوارد الأفعال. و سخافة التراكيب و معاظلة الأقوال ارأيت كيف ابدلت الواو في "محيتهم" الياْء. و خالفت العلماء و الأدباء؟ و نصبت المثنى بالألف و ذلك جليّ للعيان في جملة "المشقة و السهر الطويل اللذان" الخ. ارأيت كيف بعض النادم على البنان افقهت كيف مغبّة اسير الحسان. ارأيت كيف يصبح اضحوكة الأنس و الجان و كيف استمحت لها على زلّاتها عذرا. و اسبلت على معاييرها سترا. فادعيت انه آية الأوانس و نابغة الكوانس[3]

The greatest fault of *Grace*, according to this writer, is that "the writing removed all sense from the language and composed a rotten and false impression of what eloquence really is" ("Secret," 1904).

نحن لا نطارحك الكلاّم سجالاً. و لا ننشد مناقشة و لاْ جدالاً. فما بالك تخطّيات سنة المناظرة. و نزعت الى التقريع و المهاترة فرقمت نفثات صدرك بلغةٍ لا تعرف. و بلاغة لا توصف لانها محط رحال التعسف و الغلط

For the writers of *Circle*, then, eloquence in writing is comprised of correctness in grammar and word choice—but this differs from the opinion of their peers.

On April 24, the editors of *Grace* magazine offered a final response to *Circle*'s February critique, in an article titled نحن والإنتقاد, or "Criticism and Us" (1904). In

**104**  Lisa R. Arnold

this article, the writers suggest that "the Eastern mentality"—an obvious reference to a common *nahda* rhetorical move contrasting "East" with "West"—is what has interfered with the positive reception of their critiques. The writers argue that the surrounding culture "has not yet reached a noble degree of advancement that equates criticism to peace and pure intention" ("Criticism," 1904).

و ذلك لاعتقادنا ان العقل الشرقي لم يصل الى درجةٍ ساميةٍ من التقدم يلاقي فيها الانتقاد بالسلم و صفآء النيّة

They explain that they consulted with a teacher who confirmed their understanding, and they state that they decided to publish criticism in *Grace* because they "thought it could offer means to the Eastern mind to advance, succeed, and discipline itself" ("Criticism," 1904).

و قررنا بعد ذلك ان ننشئ الجريدة ممسوحةٌ من الانتقاد الا ان يمن الله على العقل الشرقي بالتقدم و النجاح او تهذيب القويم

The writers then explain that they believed that this stereotype could not extend to everyone in the East, particularly to those students in the college, who "are the citizens of freedom and equity" ("Criticism," 1904).

فنحن ابناء الكلية ابنآء الحرية و المساواة

Emphasizing that they have been called to the work of writing, the authors write that "We must speak the truth and show what the conscience hides and our minds recommend. . . . We must announce the liberty of writing, and speak of what is right, even if it makes others cry" ("Criticism," 1904).

لا ينبغي لنا الّا المجاهرة بالحقيقة و نظهر ما يكنّه الضمير و يوصيه العقل و لو كان ذلك يغضب كثيرين من سخيفي العقول الذين يتمسكون باهداب ترهات الكلام و الحديث المموه الملفف المنمق المحشو كذباً و بهتاناً و نعلن لرؤوس الاشهاد حرية القلم و الضمير و نتكلم الصواب و لو كان كلامنا يبكي كثيرين

Within *Grace*'s extended defense of its publishing practices, we see the students articulating a higher purpose or exigency that motivates their writing— they see writing as a means to speak truth and exercise what they see as a part of the practice of "freedom and equity." Their defense also "instructs" their peers at the college about what they see as the roles students should occupy, especially as critical readers, writers, and thinkers.

## *Morality, Ethics, and Narratives of Progress and Change*

Just as student writers instructed their peers about "best practices" in writing, so too did they use writing to measure their peers' moral and ethical character, and as a tool for progress and change. For these student writers, good writing begins with the strong morality and ethics of the writer; without good character, progress and change is impossible at the individual, institutional, cultural, or state level. Student writers consistently expressed a goal of progress and change through writing, and they saw writing—and print publication as a whole—as a way through which political, cultural, educational, and economic reform could occur. Some students even reflected explicitly upon the role that magazines and newspapers—both in the college and outside of it—play in bringing about progress and change.

According to student writers, "excellence" in writing requires high standards of reasoning and eloquence—standards tied to the hard work and morality of the writers themselves. Describing the history and recent activities of the Scientific Arab Association, writers in *The Arrowhead* celebrated the association's ability to claim "the biggest team of journalists" in the East as a part of its legacy ("A Look," 1901).

الفريق الاكبر من الصحافيين على اختلاف مشاربهم

These men, according to the publication, are "eloquent in [their] speech and logical in [their] reasoning," traits that emerged because they had been "active in participating in the association, and kept in [their] heart[s] to reach excellence" ("A Look," 1901).

حيث ترى في كل منها و لو رجلاً بين الرجال يستميلك برقة حديثه و طلاقة لسانه و قوة برهانه و ثبات جأشه و رشاقة الفاظه و هذا الرجل ايها الادباء ليس الاّ ذاك التلميذ الذي من امدٍ ليس ببعيد كان عضواً عاملاً في هذه الجمعية و قد لعب دوره فيها فخرج و في قلبه ما ينزع به الى المعالي و الطموح الى اوج العلاء.

While they celebrated the association's legacy of well-spoken and judicious graduates, writers of *The Arrowhead* also reference teachers' and the college's apparent turn to "freedom of speech" as a sign of overall progress for the association and the college. They specifically praise the Scientific Arab Association president's recent efforts to "repeal the habit of censorship, cynicism, and deplorable writing in research" ("A Look," 1901).

الا و هو اولًا إبطال عادة التقريع و التهكم و استعمال الكلام المستهجن في المباحثات

Similarly, in his introduction to one issue of *The Lighthouse*, the editor expresses his "gratitude for the new system and doctrine, allowing us to have freedom of speech" ("Introduction," 1906).

و انا كنت في غنىً عن هذه المقدمة اذ قد تعوّدت منكم في الماضي الرضى و الاستحسان و تعودتم منها الصدق و الامانة. لولا اني احب ان اذكر ما وصلنا اليه من حريّة القول و العمل بفضل الدستور و النظام الجديد و اتوصل منه الى اهداء الجريدة الى كل نفس حرة تسعى وراء هذه الغاية

Without freedom of speech, truth—a virtue that ostensibly defines good writing—would not be possible. For writers of *The Lighthouse*, "an honest magazine" is one that "scolds, lectures, and entertains rather than one that flatters others with fake words" ("Today," 1906).

اليوم و في كل آن نحن في حاجة الى جريدة صادقة تؤنّب و تؤدّب و تسلّي و لا تتحبب

Indeed, the magazine aimed to "eliminate miscommunication between the college's writers, and set the records straight to the right stances advocated by each" ("Today," 1906).

لمنع سوء التفاهم بين ادباء الكلية و تحديد كل منزلته لئلا يشرد عن محجة الصواب

By achieving "its purpose of providing truth and good work," the magazine, its writers explain, will "gain reputation and credibility in the eyes of its readers" ("Today," 1906).

. . . تنال خطوة في اعين قرائها لانها تصدق الخدمة

And like the writers of *The Lighthouse*, the writers of *Grace* magazine connect truth and sincerity—values shared within the local and regional culture—to good writing. In defending their work against the aforementioned attacks of *Circle* magazine, the authors assert that:

> A newspaper has no true purpose if it disregards the voice of conscience. . . . There were times when we were confused in writing about a person or an association, especially with the sound of conscience at the back of our heads, calling us to write about the absolute truth, devoid of any personal bias or tendencies.
>
> *("Criticism," 1904)*

و ما هي فائدة الجرائد الاجتماعية اذا كانت لا تشير الى مواقع الخلل و تنبه القوام الى غفلاتهم و سقطاتهم و ما المنفعة منها اذا كانت تملأ صفحاتها بمدح هذا و شكر ذاك و تترك ما به الخير العام في زاوية الاهمال و النسيان. و ما الجدوى منها اذا اهملت صوت الضمير و تركت القول الخارج من القلب و كتبت القول المنمَق. و قد كنا نقع احياناً في حيرةٍ اذ نرى من الواجب ان نتكلم عن شخصٍ و جمعيةٍ ما و صوت الضمير ينادي بكتابة الحقيقة مجردة عن كل ميل و انحياز و قصدٍ ذاتي و في ذلك غضبٌ المكتوب عنه

These writers complain that in return for speaking the truth, "ugly words, abuses and mistrust came out of many fellow students," but they claim that they maintained their moral high ground and "returned the abuse with forgiveness and gratitude" ("Criticism," 1904).

فنتج عن الاخير سوء ظن و بغض و كلام قبيح و اساءات متعددة ما لم نكن نظنه يصدر من ابناء الكلية ابناءالكلية ابناء الحريّة. و قد قابلنا الاساءة بالصفح و الشكران.

Within their critique, these student writers seem to be providing guidance to their peers, stressing the value of morality—in this case, the value of "forgiveness and gratitude"—in writing. Implicitly, these writers suggest that a moral approach is the only way forward for journalism.

Along these lines, some student writers emphasize the importance of words matching actions. In an article titled "Why? لماذا Pourquoi" (which translates to "Why? Why Why" and is an interesting example of explicit translingual creativity), Elias Attieh (1906) criticizes the hypocrisy of newspaper editors, poets, writers promoting the study of Arabic, and others, whose practices do not follow their words. Attieh argues that these writers and speakers, who "only give time to thinking, writing, and giving absolute opinions about ways to build the country and help it" do not bring about change because their "sentimental poetry and eloquent words" are only words, not tied to actions.

اريد ان ادخل معكم في حديث قصير ارجوكم الاصغآء الّيّ و ان كنت ممن لا يتعدُ بهم في ابدآء الآراء يا ايها الذين تصرِفون الوقت في الافتكار و الكتابة فقط فيها يؤول الى خير البلاد و تنشرونه على رؤوس الاشهاد ظناً منكم انه يكفي لاصلاحها و لكن لماذا لا نرى نتيجة لتلك الجمل البليغة و الاشعار النفسية بالله

According to Attieh, "newspaper editors who encourage [readers] to stay in Syria will be the first to sail away . . . the famous poet, who enchants [readers] with words about patriotism," is not actually patriotic himself, and "the dear writer, who invites us to study the Arabic language and speak it, all we hear from you is 'bonjour,' 'bonsoir,' and 'good morning,' among many other foreign borrowings."

يا ايها الكاتب التحرير الذي تدعونا الى البقاء في سوريا لماذا [نرا] [sic] عندما تصير قادراً على تحصيل المعش [sic] تركب متن البحار تاركاً لنا صدى كتاباتك يرنُّ في الآذان و انت ايها الشاعرُ المطبوع يا من اذا نثرت علينا درر اقوالك تهجينا في تلك الساعة الى حب الوطن لماذا عندما تخرج لما نرى عليك غباراً ما كنت تدعونا اليه و انت يا أديبنا العزيز الذي تدعونا الى درس اللغة العربية و التكلم بها لماذا لا نسمع منك الا بونجور بونسوار يا مونشار good morning و غيرها من المقتبسات الاجنبية كأن لغتك ضيقة بمثل هذه المصطلحات

For Attieh, in other words, a writer's hypocrisy—or immorality—impedes national and cultural progress.

Some students also view "serious" writing as the only kind that can serve the dual purposes of morality and progress. For example, a writer published in حسناء الكلية (*Hasnaa' al-Kulliyeh*), or *Beauty of the College*, scolds his peers for avoiding Arabic magazines because they lack "funny jokes and humorous sayings" ("Magazines," 1903).[4]

الاعظم من رفقائنا التلامذة لا يستحسنون اهم جرائد العربية لعدم وجود نكت مضحكة و اقوال هزلية

On this subject, the writer argues that:

> There is no real benefit from reading a humorous phrase; the reader may smile for a few minutes, but this smiling is temporary and will be forgotten. However, if you read a wise or literary phrase, it will be imprinted in your mind and imagination for as long as you live, leading you to better knowledge and understanding.
>
> *("Magazines," 1903)*

فما فائدة جملة هزلية تبتسم لها شفتيك و لا يدوم ذلك الابتسام الا لوقت قصير حتى تنساها لا بل تتناساها لما ترى بها من الركامة و قصر لعقل. انما ما قولك في جملة حكيمة او ادبية تُخلّ في ذهنك و تنطبع على مخيلتك ما عشت فتقودك الى سواء السبيل

The writer advises his peers to value so-called "serious" writing by characterizing his peers as "students of loyalty and righteousness" who "seek science, facts, and true opinions" ("Magazines," 1903).

لسنا تلامذة ضحك و تقريق بل تلامذة وافين للمدرسة ساعين في طلب العلم الصحيح و الرأي القويم.

In conveying confidence about his peers' sincerity and intelligence, the writer indirectly teaches his peers what they should aspire to and how they should behave.

In the same article, the writer ties morality to the general purpose of magazines, which, he argues, "revolves around the need to spread awareness about reform, civilization, and culture" ("Magazines," 1903).

و ثانياً لاجل اصلاح بعض شؤُون وثب روح التمدن و توزيع نطاق الحضارة في [القط] الموجودة به.

For student magazines in particular, the author explains, the articles published bring about "progress"—they "benefit the readers, offering new knowledge" ("Magazines," 1903).

اولاً: ترقي ابناء كليتنا و تقديم بعض فوائد و مقالات علمية و ادبية تؤول الى نفع القرّاء

**108** Lisa R. Arnold

In this article, the writer articulates both the purpose of magazines and his expectations for readers and writers. In tying these together, the writer instructs his audience about the roles that all three play in driving a larger purpose of progress and change.

## Conclusion

Throughout these student publications, we witness the practical and pedagogical consequences of a transnational writing education: Students negotiate what it means to be a writer, a moral and ethical being, and someone who strives to promote individual, institutional, and cultural development. At times, students negotiate language and identity, as they criticize their elders' use of foreign words and the tendency to leave the region rather than improve it, while they also negotiate what it means to express oneself eloquently or coherently in Arabic. Student writers negotiate the roles of student and teacher, as they use these publications to facilitate dialogue, challenge their peers, and advise readers on the roles they should play and writers on the habits they should employ if they want to be heard. And students negotiate what the "viral" medium of print publication means to them. We witness, in other words, a constant and oftentimes productive negotiation of educational, linguistic, and cultural borders.

Taking a historical and transnational view of writing education at the turn of the 20th century allows contemporary scholars and teachers to consider the many ways in which our students might also negotiate the boundaries constructed around them—boundaries that are often reinforced or constructed by us. While SPC students no doubt experienced boundaries—the college campus was, and is, literally surrounded by walls, and student behavior was highly regulated by the American Protestant administration, which required staying on campus, attending chapel regularly, and studying the Bible—we see in the student-authored publications an engaged and energetic student population, eager to speak in spite of these literal and figurative borders.

We would benefit, therefore, from considering what these student publications can teach us about effective writing education. These student writers advise us to consider the following questions: How we might provide similar writing opportunities to our students, opportunities through which students can engage with each other in writing? In what ways can we encourage students to experiment with writing by occupying the role of teacher or critic? How can we support students as they practice using a variety of multimodal genres to communicate exchange? In what ways can we ensure that students have the opportunity to "play" with existing modes of communication while giving and receiving feedback? And how might we encourage students to both acknowledge and negotiate linguistic, institutional, and cultural boundaries through writing?

Beyond these questions, as the student writers in *The Lighthouse* magazine write in "Today the Need Arises" (1906), they are inspired to publish their magazine because they simply see the need for: "a platform in which SPC students can freely write about their opinions and ideas."

كثيراً مما نحبّ ان نقوله الى تلامذة الكلية لا نحب ان يعرف في الخارج[5]

These student writers may offer one final key in effectively promoting the value of writing in our classrooms: asking students themselves to identify the exigency for their writing.

## Acknowledgments

This chapter would not have been possible without the translations from Arabic to English (and commentary on the translations) by Ghada Seifeddine and transcription of the originals by Yasmine Abou Taha, both graduates of the American University of Beirut. I am deeply indebted to them for their involvement in this project and for their continued assistance. Additionally, I am grateful for the assistance of the librarians in the Special Collections and Archives section of the American University of Beirut's Jafet Library in facilitating access to the original documents presented here. I thank Ashleigh Petts for her help with coding the articles, as well as her thoughtful feedback and revision suggestions on this essay. And finally, I am grateful to Xiaoye You and Shyam Sharma for their insightful comments.

## Notes

1. Arab teachers were not given professorial-rank status until 1909 and did not receive voting rights or professional equity until the school changed its name and dropped its religious affiliation in 1920, becoming present-day American University of Beirut (Anderson 48).
2. The English translation provided here is not an exact translation of the original in Arabic. The full excerpt, which provides an extended critique of the original article published in *Grace*, is as follows:

قالت لأفض فوهافي الصفحة السّابعة عشرة (١) تصدُم او تُصدَم - لا فرق في ذلك - بحجر دجليه - و الصواب رجلاه لأن الفعل المجهول على الوجه الاول يلزم له نائب فاعل و هذا لا يكون ألّا مرفوعا و ان كلبت الوجه الثاني يجب ان تقول - تُصدم بحجر رجلاه - قياماً بواجب الفاعل الذي رغبت في خفضه كما استحلت خفض مقام الكرام. (٢) صفحة ٠٢ قالتُ - محيتهم - و الصواب محوتهم لأن الفعل وأدي فلتراجع حضرة غادتنا الحسناء... محيط المحيط لعلها بمفردات اللغة تحيط و لا تأخذ الاشياء بالقدح (و اللَّبيط). ثم قالت المشقة و السهر الطويل اللذان حضرتها فحضرتها لا تميز بين المفعول به و الجار و المجرور.... و كان اولى بها ان تقول الكلمات عملاً بالأحوال النحوية. و قالت ايضاً دور الملك الذي لم يسمعه و يفهمه فخيل لها ان الملك نفس الكلمات التي كانت تتلى بديل قوتها و يسمعه لا بد ما يقهم و يسمع النطق لا الناطق. صفحة ١٢ قالت اعزّها الله... تطلب للرفعه: فجعلت تطلب بمعنى طلبه. و لم يقل لنا للشيء فيا ما احيلى حذلقة الجيبة. و مما ورد لها من المحاسن قولها بوصف الملك اللحية و الشارب منعتاه: و الأحسن منعاه لان المذكر يغلب على المؤنث. و لعلها ودت ان تؤنث كل شيء لأنها انثى او ربما انفت من اللحية كما هي عادة الغادات... صفحة ٢٤ قالت ما شاء الله. اجيج مياه كثيرة: و عنت بذلك صوت المياه. و هذا على خلاف المشهور لان ذلك يستعمل للنار فيقال اجت النار اذا تلهبت و اج الماء اجوجا صار اجاجا اي مالحا. و ربما قصدت بذلك عجيج المياه. و انا على الحالين نسأل الله ان يفتح عيونها حتى تبصر فتعلم ان العيون ليست مفضحة كعين اجيج فان كانت هذه معرفتها في اللغة التي تدعى العصمة فيها فكيف بفن التمثيل الذي لا المّا لها فيه و لم يساعدها الطالع السّعيد برؤيته ألّا في تلك المرّة. و ايضاً عندما لمعت حضرة الآنسة الى حالة الشرق.... الحضرة و التعاسة المحدقة بهم: و الصواب (المحدقة به) لانها

**110** Lisa R. Arnold

كانت تخاطب الشرق بصفة المفرد ضاربة صفحاً عن اهله. صفحة ٦٢ قالت متّجهة لنقطة خصوصيّة:
فكا ينبغي ان نقول (الى) نقطة خصوصية اذ ان فعل اتجه كما يقول القاموس يتعدى بحرف الجر: الى:
فتأملوا. و في تلك الصفحة عينها قالت (سامحها الله) يسفه النسيم و لم تفقه معنى سفة فكانها لرفعة
ادابها توهمت النسيم شاتماً لاعنا و لا بدع فمن هام بشيء خال الكون بأسره يردده هذه بعض معاييب
الغادة التي طوينا عن اكثرها كشمأ تأدباً لانا لا نريد التعدي لابنة.... فنحن رجال فلتشمخ بانفها و لترفل
بمطارق الاعجاب ما شأت عملًا بقول الفارض.

3. Again, the English translation is not an exact translation of the original in Arabic. The full excerpt is as follows:

فيا حضرة التاجر. انا نرى الخسائر الفادحة اخذت عليك فقد تاجرت بعيوب "الغادة" و ما عدت الّا
بالنزر اليسير. فهل وضعته ما اخفيته في "البنك" لتنال "فائضاً" يستحق الذكر؛ مهلاً فقل لي اقالك
الله. الم يأتك حديث الغادة الحسنآء. يوم خبطت خبط عشوآء في استعمال احرف الجر و شوارد الأفعال.
و سخافة التراكيب و معاظلة الأقوال ارأيت كيف ابدلت الواو في "محيتهم" اليآء. و خالفت العلمآء و
الأدبآء؟ و نصبت المثنى بالألف و ذلك جليّ للعيان في جملة "المشقة و السهر الطويل اللذان" الخ.
ارأيت كيف يصبح النادم على البنان افقهت كيف مغبّة اسير الحسان. ارأيت كيف يصبح اضحوكة الأنس
و الجان و كيف استمحت لها على زلّاتها عذراً و اسبلت على معاييها سترا؛ فادعيت انه آية الأوانس و
نابغة الكوانس. اهملت لفظة "اهل" حين المعت الى حالة الشرق. و هذا هو العجب العجاب لعمر الحق.
فما نحن ممن اوتي علم الخفيّات. و لسنا في عداد ارباب التكهنات حتى ندري كنه السّرائر. و نعلم ما
تجنه الضمائر. و ما دار في خلدنا ان الغادة تنصب للقرّاء اشراك الألغاز بل عهدي بها سلسلة العبارة
جيدة الأستاذة....

4. The writer of this article is likely presenting a contrast between Arabic- and English-language magazines and newspapers, as the English-language newspapers (at least those published by students in the college) frequently contain jokes, humorous sayings, and proverbs.

5. The whole passage from which this quote is excerpted provides fuller context:

كثيراً مما نحبّ ان نقوله الى تلامذة الكلية لا نحب ان يعرف في الخارج اذ ربما يكون هذا داعياً الى
احتقارنا اذا علم ما يوجد بيننا من الادعاء الفارغ و الفخفخة الصبيانية و الطرق الدنيئة التي يتخذها
البعض سلماً الى الارتقاء و كنا نحن عنها غافلين الفخفخة

# References

Anderson, B. S. (2011). *The American university of Beirut: Arab nationalism and liberal education*. Austin: University of Texas Press.

Arnold, L. R. (2014). "The worst part of the dead past": Language attitudes, policies, and pedagogies at Syrian Protestant College, 1866–1902. *College Composition and Communication, 66*(2), 276–300.

Attieh, E. (1906, February 8). لماذا Why Pourqoi. المنتهون [*The abstainers*]. (Trans. G. Seifeddine). (Box 8, Student Manuscripts Magazines). Archives and Special Collections. Beirut, Lebanon: American University of Beirut Jafet Library.

Attieh, I. (1901, November 14). Introduction. الحظ [*Luck*]. (Trans. G. Seifeddine). (Box 4, Student Manuscripts Magazines). Archives and Special Collections. Beirut, Lebanon: American University of Beirut Jafet Library.

Bliss, D. (1900, July 11 and December 14). [Annual reports]. *Annual reports by the presidents to the boards of managers and trustees, 1866–1902*. Archives and Special Collections. Beirut, Lebanon: American University of Beirut Jafet Library.

Dajani, N. H. (1992). *Disoriented media in a fragmented society: The Lebanese experience*. Beirut: American University of Beirut Press.

Kassab, E. (2010). *Contemporary Arab thought: Cultural critique in comparative perspectives*. New York: Columbia University Press.

Khalidi, R. (1991). The origins of Arab nationalism: Introduction. In R. Khalidi, L. Anderson, M. Muslih, & R. Simon (Eds.), *The origins of Arab nationalism* (vii–xix). New York: Columbia University Press.

*Light: A monthly review.* (1906, June). (Box 10, Student Manuscripts Magazines). Archives and Special Collections. Beirut, Lebanon: American University of Beirut Jafet Library.

Seifeddine, G. (1901, May 27). الكنانة [*The arrowhead*]. A look at the Scientific Arab Association this year. (Box 3, Student Manuscripts Magazines). Archives and Special Collections. Beirut, Lebanon: American University of Beirut Jafet Library.

Seifeddine, G. (1901, December 5). الحظ [*Luck*]. A word of praise. (Box 4, Student Manuscripts Magazines). Archives and Special Collections. Beirut, Lebanon: American University of Beirut Jafet Library.

Seifeddine, G. (1903, January 20). الحديقة [*The garden*]. The college in past and present days. (Box 4, Student Manuscripts Magazines). Archives and Special Collections. Beirut, Lebanon: American University of Beirut Jafet Library.

Seifeddine, G. (1903, February 2). حسناء الكلية [*Beauty of the college*]. Magazines. (Box 6, Student Manuscripts Magazines). Archives and Special Collections. Beirut, Lebanon: American University of Beirut Jafet Library.

Seifeddine, G. (1904, January 15). الدائرة [*Circle*]. Grace magazine and us. (Box 7, Student Manuscripts Magazines). Archives and Special Collections. Beirut, Lebanon: American University of Beirut Jafet Library.

Seifeddine, G. (1904, February 8). الدائرة [*Circle*]. Secret word to the leader of literary chaos. (Box 7, Student Manuscripts Magazines). Archives and Special Collections. Beirut, Lebanon: American University of Beirut Jafet Library.

Seifeddine, G. (1904, April 24). الغادة [*Grace*]. Criticism and us. (Box 6, Student Manuscripts Magazines). Archives and Special Collections. Beirut, Lebanon: American University of Beirut Jafet Library.

Seifeddine, G. (1906, 10th issue). المنارة [*The lighthouse*]. Today the need arises. (Box 4, Student Manuscripts Magazines). Archives and Special Collections. Beirut, Lebanon: American University of Beirut Jafet Library.

Syrian Protestant College. (1900–01). [Course catalogue]. Course Catalogues, Syrian Protestant College, 1900–1905. Archives and Special Collections. Beirut, Lebanon: American University of Beirut Jafet Library.

Tijari, A. K. (1904, January 28). We, and the confluence of ideas. الغادة [*Grace*]. (Trans. G. Seifeddine). (Box 6, Student Manuscripts Magazines). Archives and Special Collections. Beirut, Lebanon: American University of Beirut Jafet Library.

Yousef, A. (1900, May 17). Transference: Speech made in the Arab League. ثمرات الأذهان [*Fruit of the mind*]. (Seifeddine, G., Trans.). (Box 4, Student Manuscripts Magazines). Archives and Special Collections. Beirut, Lebanon: American University of Beirut Jafet Library.

# PART III
# Practice

# 7

# POTENTIAL PHASES OF MULTILINGUAL WRITERS' IDENTITY WORK[1]

*Shizhou Yang*

## Introduction

Multilingual writing in the current era presents unprecedented opportunities for border crossing. The Internet and other modern communication technologies greatly facilitated the mobility and merge of texts, images, and sounds from diverse languages and cultures. Texts, often embodying such diversity, frequently cross geographic borders unseen in previous times. The phenomenon is so rampant that there is a need to adopt a "trans-" perspective in understanding individuals' creative use of various semiotic resources on the Internet (see e.g., Hartley & Qu, 2015). At a glance, one may assume some magic power of the Internet to free multilingual writers from restricting monolingual ideologies. But as Canagarajah (in this volume) points out, the most essential is actually the provision of some "alternate space," be it online or in an actual classroom, which allows a multilingual writer to construct. Relating to "transnationalism," the theme of this book, space-making is essentially a matter of crossing artificially created boundaries through teaching and/or research. As a result, individuals may take up an identity position as a hybrid, rather than purely as one or the other.

This vision of transnational writing education calls for refined understandings of multilingual writers' identity work. Current discussions tend to emphasize the multiplicity and change of the identity of language learners at large (e.g., Norton, 2000) and that of multilingual writers in particular, especially where change is significant (e.g., Cox, Jordan, Ortmeier-Hooper, & Schwartz, 2010). In contrast, little attention has been paid to possible continuities of multilingual writers' identities (see Menard-Warwick, 2005 for a critique), the less dramatic changes and identities beyond the L1/L2 binary (Cook, 1999). Take published memoirs of bilingual writers as an example. Collectively, their stories seem to suggest that all bilingual writers begin as "souls in exile" and end as "global souls" (Li, 2007). However, such an identity narrative cannot really reflect the actual processes of self-making by the numerous multilingual writers who have not had a chance to live in an English-speaking country and who are still struggling to learn the language. To capture their identity work, on site and in their particular sociocultural context, more theorization and research is still needed.

In this chapter, I introduce an integrated framework, drawing insights from poststructuralism, dialogism, and narrative practices, to gain a more nuanced understanding of multilingual writers' identity work. I then explore a multilingual writer's autobiographical writing using data from my doctoral research. My goal is to delineate potential phases of multilingual writers' identity work and reveal the tensions involved in border crossing, as well as the rewards that follow. While this is not a pedagogical account, it may provide insights into designing alternate spaces to provide transnational literacy education.

## Multilingual Writing and Identity Work

In the past two decades, a great number of qualitative studies have documented multilingual writers' experiences with academic literacy in English (Belcher & Braine, 1995; Casanave, 2002; Hungerford-Kresser, 2010; Liu, 2008; Shen, 1989; Starfield, 2002; Yi, 2013). Focusing on international students, immigrants, and refugees in the Anglophone "Inner Circle" countries, these studies show that to acquire academic literacy in a second language is not just a matter of developing technical skills in that language. Rather, it is a complex socio-psychological process in which learners re-construct their sense of self in a new discourse community. This process of remaking one's identity is referred to in this chapter as *identity work* (Snow & Anderson, 1987, p. 1348). I borrowed the term from sociologists to emphasize that identity is a form of social practice; that it is dynamic and ongoing; and that learners play agentic roles in what they become.

Multilingual writers' identity work has also been revealed through their published memoires. For instance, in her study of bilingual writers' autobiographies, Li (2007) suggests two main phases of being bi-literate. In the initial stage, bilingual writers are "souls in exile," estranged from their native language and culture. Through much intense struggle, in a later stage, they may become "global souls," drawing on "both languages" to construct their "multiple identities" (p. 160). Similarly, Steinman (2005) highlights bilingual writers' hybrid identities or accents found in their English autobiographical writing. Quoting Aciman, a bilingual autobiographical writer, Stainman wrote, "An accent marks the lag between two cultures, two languages, the space where you let go of one identity, invent another, and end up being more than one person but never quite two" (p. 76). These studies show that, so far as published memoirists are concerned, multilingual writing has the potential to enable the writers to adopt a transnational sense of self.

Also important is the sense of self as a writer that multilingual writers develop when engaging in autobiographical writing as a course (e.g., Brisk, 1998; Edelsky, 2003; Wu, 1994), sometimes embedded in academic writing programs (e.g., Park, 2013). For example, Edelsky's (2003) study on Spanish immigrant children's engagement with autobiographical writing in a dual language classroom shows that the students have taken up an identity as memoirists in their language use. Others (e.g., Cummins et al., 2005) have also found students developing more agentic writer identities. Such pedagogical use of autobiographical writing thus provides an alternate space for multilingual writers to tap into their diverse linguistic and cultural resources to create new writer identities.

In addition to academic literacy and autobiographical writing, multiliteracies studies have also provided an important approach to understanding multilingual writers' identity work. Several case studies find that multimodal literacy such as writing online may generate new and positive "textual identities" (Krămsch & Lam, 1999) among multilingual writers (e.g., Lam, 2000; Maguire & Graves, 2001). For instance, Lam's case study depicts how Almon, a Chinese immigrant teenager who was failing in his ESL class, constructed a more self-enabling identity within a transnational teen community. Almon combined his English use with multiple narrative roles and discourses online, such as advertising language and teenager forms of language use. Also, in his study of white-collar workers' literacy practices in an online community, You (2011) finds that the writers drew on multiple linguistic, cultural, discoursal, and modal resources to construct their "domestic diaspora" writer identities. Not surprisingly, it is generally expected now that multilingual writing teachers integrate and bridge their students' media literacy with academic literacy in order to provide learners with more identity options (CCCC Statement on Second Language Writing and Writers, 2009).

The above studies, mainly situated in the Inner Circle countries, have provided several important insights for studying multilingual writers' identity work. First, they show that traditional dichotomous and static categories such as "native" and "non-native" are insufficient to capture the complexity, richness, and dynamics of multilingual writers' identity work and their agency in the process. Second, learning to write in a second language does not necessarily make the writers feel inferior; provided with proper conditions, it can result in an enriched sense of self, e.g., by forming a "global soul" informed by more than one language (Li, 2007). Third, one should be open to "textual identity of the third kind" (Krămsch & Lam, 1999), i.e., emergent identities constructed by writers through their multilingual, multimodal and multidiscoursal literacy practices in their particular contexts (Freiberg & You, 2012).

Despite these advances, our ways of describing multilingual writers' identity work are yet to be refined. In their studies, applied linguists sometimes use "self-translation" to refer to the "painful process" of multilingual writers (more specifically, published memoirists) losing some existing identities while developing new ones (see Pavlenko, 2004, pp. 54–55). Writing scholars have also used similar terms such as negotiation and (re)construction (e.g., Cox et al., 2010).

## 118 Shizhou Yang

These terms are useful in suggesting the overall tendency of multilingual writers' identity work. However, they fall short of capturing the still happening, possibly less dramatic, identity work of multilingual writers who stay within the borders of their home countries. There remain some critical questions regarding how multilingual writers engage in autobiographical writing outside class, how they use such writing to mediate their identity work, and how their investment in autobiographical writing affects their sense of self as a writer. By proposing an interdisciplinary framework and illustrating it with a case study from China, this chapter sheds some light on these issues.

## Investment, Dialogical Self, and Narrative

The concept *investment* sets a cornerstone for a poststructuralist theory of learner identity. Norton views language learning as a way for learners to invest in their imagined communities (Norton, 2000; Peirce, 1995), and hence some imagined identities. "In essence, an imagined community assumes an imagined identity, and a learner's investment in the target language must be understood within this context" (Norton, 2006, p. 505). Investment is future-oriented, with a possibility for greater mobility. Multilingual writers invest or *participate* in particular literacy practices, which promise them "possibilities for an enhanced range of identity options in the future" (Norton, 2006, p. 505). The opposite is also true. If multilingual writers do not see connections between given literacy practices with expanded identity options, they are likely to resist the practices (Norton, 2001). Adopting an investment view of multilingual writers' identity work thus provides a sociocultural understanding of the writers as agents. As studies have also shown, multilingual writers are involved in the making of their selves through their ways of relating to particular literacy practices (e.g., Haneda, 2005; Norton & Williams, 2012; McKay & Wong, 1996). Therefore, investment can be a useful concept to describe the identity trajectory of multilingual writers.

However, investment as used in the present literature still seems too vague. To make investment more concrete, I propose the following considerations: first, one should quantify investment. Quantity, such as the amount of time put in a writing activity, may provide a general picture of the degree to which multilingual writers engage in literacy, understood as both events and practices. Second, one should contextualize individuals' investment by highlighting their available resources—that is, rather than comparing simplistically the amount of time, energy and monetary resources that learners put in a language learning activity, one should also consider the values of individuals' investment on their own terms. After all, the same amount of resources, say $100, may be one learner's monthly living allowance and another's pocket money. Only by knowing how invested resources are weighed in individuals' own life or learning scales can we know the true nature and significance of their investment. Further, one should

Multilingual Writers' Identity Work  **119**

consider the quality of investment, whether learners invest willingly or only do so grudgingly. Last, one should also consider the type of investment. In this, we need to consider the writer's sense of ownership, emotional engagement, and ideological stances in and through his or her writing. With investment understood in terms of its quantity, value, quality and type, we may arrive at more holistic understandings of the impact of an imagined identity on a multilingual writer's ways of writing.

Multilingual writers' identity work also occurs at the ideological level. Broadly speaking, identity work features the positioning of the *self* in relation to some *other* (Holquist, 2002), be it broad conceptions such as languages and cultures, or others' words. Essentially, such identity work is a matter of appropriating others' words as a way of forming one's own ideological position in the world (Morris, 1994, p. 78). One kind of positioning is passive, taking others' words as the final authority, with no questions asked. Such words function as "authoritative discourse." Another kind of positioning is active, working out the meanings, implications and reasons behind others' words. Such words are "innerly persuasive discourse." In both cases, there is room for multilingual writers to make others' words serve their own communicative purposes. The key lies in whether they can re-contextualize the borrowed words to make them "double-" or even "multi-voiced."

Multilingual writers' identity work can be further understood from a narrative perspective. Their identity work can be viewed as movements to new identity categories, conclusions, or imagined futures. As Bruner (1986), the cognitive psychologist, points out, what we know as reality is usually not the lived reality, but a narratively constructed one. Such storied reality includes both *the landscape of action*, i.e., sequentially linked events, and *the landscape of consciousness*, i.e., understandings of the world, events, people and self. White (2005), a co-founder of narrative therapy, goes so far as to suggest that each story is composed of two landscapes: one of action, and the other of *identity conclusions*, i.e., understandings of self as informed by the contemporary culture. Therefore, narrative is vital in revealing one's identity work, at least in how one sees oneself in relation to his or her lived experiences. Translated to multilingual writing, one's sense of self as a writer may refer to particular conclusions one draws based on one's actual writing experiences.

A few terms can be adapted from narrative practices to help map out multilingual writers' identity work. First of all, *performing, reflecting* and *re-visioning* (e.g., White, 2007) are three related movements in identity work. Applied to multilingual writing, performing refers to a "literacy event" (Heath, Street, & Mills, 2008), during which multilingual writers try on or experiment with images of themselves through writing a particular autobiographical text in a second language. Reflecting refers to either of the two activities: (1) learners generating identity conclusions about themselves in relation to their past experiences; and (2) learners revisiting and evaluating the social identity conclusions they experienced elsewhere by writing about them in a second language.

Re-visioning refers to learners redesigning their imagined futures through writing and is an advanced phase of identity work, which builds upon performing and reflecting. Importantly, narrative practices encourage a sociocultural view of identity work. Other related terms include "co-authoring" and "outside witness." Co-authoring refers to the fact that one's identity work involves the participation and influence of powerful others such as a counselor in a therapeutic session (White, 2007). "Outside witness" refers to an audience recruited from outside the core individuals such as the counselor and the client to witness and retell the client's significant stories. Both terms help capture multilingual writers' identity work as influenced by diverse social others.

Joining together investment, dialogical self and narrative practices, such a sense of multilingual writers' identity work deserves thick description, as through a case study.

## Methodology

### Context

The study took place in an extracurricular writing group that I led at Lakeview University (pseudonym) in southwest China. Although the university has several Chinese minority groups represented, ethnic cultures and languages seemed persistently disvalued on campus. Take ethnic Bai students as an example. It was a popular belief that, due to their accent, ethnic Bai students were not suited for learning English. A university leader also claimed that inventing a Bai script is of no use to the Bai people. In my observation of English classes, ethnic languages were not encouraged, although students sometimes used a Han Chinese dialect called Southwest Mandarin to engage in small group discussions.

To understand how ethnic Bai students would participate in autobiographical writing in English outside class, I visited different English classes during the breaks between classes. I introduced myself as a doctoral student from Australia, as I was back then, doing a research project to find out how ethnic Bai students write in English. I then invited the Bai students to a special meeting, with a free meal provided, to learn more about my research and to also meet with my American wife. A Chinese and English invitation was given to each Bai student. The Bai students responded to my invitation with enthusiasm. In the end, nineteen English major students joined the group. They came from three grade levels: freshman, sophomore and junior, and represented three ethnic groups: Bai, Yi and Han. The majority of the group members were ethnic Bai (fourteen students) and females (seventeen altogether). The gender imbalance reflected a common phenomenon in foreign language departments in today's China.

Lasting nine months, from March to December 2008, the group activities included two stages. During the first stage, which lasted sixteen weeks, the members were encouraged to work on their individual autobiographical projects in English. During the second stage, which lasted another sixteen weeks, the members were encouraged to focus on argumentative writing in English. To increase the students' opportunities to practice oral English, I mainly used English—occasionally Mandarin and dialect Chinese—to lead the weekly discussions. English being the dominant language of the writing group was a strategic choice because I assumed that a focus on Chinese writing would have less appeal to the English major students. However, my attitude towards ethnic Bai language and local languages was appreciative and sympathetic because I myself am an ethnic Naxi, speak a Chinese dialect, and had experienced struggles over my languages. My orientation towards ethnic languages and cultures contrasts with that of the college.

I usually held the meetings by seating ourselves in a circle in a classroom, or sometimes at my home. Every eight weeks or so, I would invite the students to share their best piece of writing with each other, and at these events, food was often provided and (international) visitors invited to attend.

## Data Collection and Analysis

Ethnographic approaches (Heath et al., 2008) were used to collect data such as writing samples, feedback, interviews, drawings, field notes, and video recordings of group meetings. Usually at group meetings, and sometimes over emails, the student members would share with me their writing samples, to which I would give handwritten or typed feedback. My field notes included plans before and reflections after meetings, as well as photos of publicity materials from the research site. Most meetings were video-recorded and the ones with the participants' active involvement transcribed.

Interviews included three main types: those focusing on the members' life experiences as a whole, as guided by McAdams' (1995) life story interview outline; those focusing on the members' previous literacy experiences, which included questions such as "What's learning to write in Chinese been like for you?"; and those focusing on the writing of particular samples, as guided by questions such as "How did you come to this topic?" and "What impressions of yourself would you like to leave for your reader through this text?"

Seeing writing as a situated activity, I also encouraged the members to write a short description about the context in which a particular sample was produced, which might entail time, place and emotions associated with writing the sample.

For my doctoral dissertation research, four members who actively participated in autobiographical writing in English were selected as case study participants. However, in the present study, I will only focus on one participant whom I call Beth. As a Bai, Beth is a fluent speaker of her ethnic language. However, she was not interested in learning the Bai script, neither the obsolete one based on Chinese characters, nor the newly invented system based on Latin alphabets.[2]

**122** Shizhou Yang

Instead, she was more interested in Chinese writing, and had wanted to take College Entrance again so as to major in Chinese rather than in English.

To understand Beth's possible identity work through autobiographical writing, I took the following steps. First, I identified Beth's autobiographical samples for the writing group. In this, we attended to not only linguistic features such as "I," "my," "mine" and "me" (e.g., "My feeling about 自传"), but also particular samples' connections with her personal experiences, emotions and hopes. I then coded the autobiographical writing samples, labeling them in terms of identity work involved, using open and axial coding (Strauss & Corbin, 1990) and narrative terms as a guide. Finally, I triangulated my initial analysis with other data: interview and video transcripts, reflective drawings and explanations, and field notes. From the consistent codes concepts of identity work are formed, resulting in the following report.

Second, I contextualized Beth's investment in autobiographical writing. This was done by analyzing interviews on her previous literacy experiences as well as on her life history. The former provides an understanding of whether there is any qualitative shift in Beth's ways of relating to autobiographical writing in the writing group. The latter provides an understanding of possible connections between her investment in autobiographical writing and imagined identity.

Third, I analyzed Beth's identity work in narrative terms. This is a step similar to the previous step as both draw on sample-related interviews. However, in revealing Beth's identity work in narrative terms, more attention is given to identity categories and conclusions appearing in her particular written narratives.

Fourth, I considered Beth's shifting sense of self as a writer in relation to her investment in autobiographical writing. Beth's reflective drawings at the end of the program, in which she compared her self-perceived changes, guided the analysis. Her writing samples were then analyzed for triangulation.

## Investment in Autobiographical Writing

Prior to joining the writing group, Beth made restricted investment in autobiographical writing in English. She said that she had written diaries largely in Chinese and only occasionally in English: "*Before joining the writing group, I basically didn't write anything except my mentor's assignments and diary . . . Of diary writing, one out of ten is in English,*" (I 2).[3] But due to her fear of "*making grammar mistakes in* [her] *writing*" with no one to correct them for her, she soon stopped keeping her diary in English.

> I wrote one or two passages in English. Then I felt I couldn't continue anymore; there might be grammar mistakes in my writing. Since I wouldn't give it to anyone to read and have it corrected, I was afraid to get it wrong and get into a habit. So, I quit.
>
> *(I 4)*

These comments suggest that multilingual writers' investment in autobiographical writing may be restricted by a lack of support in an institutional context.

In contrast, joining the writing group greatly boosted Beth's investment in autobiographical writing. During the nine months as a group member, Beth produced sixteen handwritten autobiographical samples in English for the group, a total of about 4,000 words. It surpasses her previous investment in autobiographical writing in both quantity and frequency.

There also seem to be qualitative differences in Beth's later investment in autobiographical writing. First, there was a sense of belonging and pride. As Beth wrote, "In this group . . . I could recognize a lot of schoolmates. . . . My senior high school of my mates are very admire me when I told them that I took a particular group. I'm so proud and happy. . . . a dream for me and my classmates" (Week-1 Writing. The typed texts follow similar spelling, spacing and punctuation as in the handwritten samples.). In the group, Beth wrote *with* familiar others from a privileged position, rather than as a marginalized soloist.

Second, Beth's investment was shaped by her imagined identity as a writer. By participating in the group's literacy practice, Beth hoped to realize her "literature dream": "I think written autobiography could continue my literature dream" (Week-1 Writing). Before coming to university, Beth's "literature dream" appeared to be attached to Chinese, in which she was well versed and positioned. For instance, she had written compositions in Chinese in the primary school, for which she had been praised by both her teacher and classmates. She had also read many Chinese classics. Unfortunately, she could not major in Chinese as she had hoped: "When I end my Entrance examine to university. my come forward is Chinese. But I don't know why reason my major became English" (Week-1 Writing). In China, universities assign students majors based more on their College Entrance Exam scores than on the students' choices. So when Beth joined the writing group to write her own autobiography, she was investing in an imagined identity, which is connected to and an extension of her Chinese writer identity.

Beth's investment in autobiographical writing provides a unique space for her identity work. In interactions surrounding her previous writing in college, Beth was frequently reminded of her linguistic deficiency. *"I just felt that my grammar—especially every time I handed in my composition, my book would be corrected all in red. And yet I tried—I studied and studied [the grammar], but whenever I used it, I just couldn't remember; I got it all wrong"* (1 I). Writing in and for the group, Beth was more concerned with meanings, even the possibility of multiple meanings of the same experience. As will be shown next, the kind of identity work she engaged in as mediated by her autobiographical writing assumes movement across diverse boundaries.

## Identity Work Through Autobiographical Writing

### Performing

At least in three occasions, Beth used autobiographical writing to textually perform some known identities of hers. In one of her only two diary entries shared with me, she wrote about her experience of being cheated by a stranger, "a woman, about 30 years old with black skin and short body." The woman wanted to borrow Beth's phone. Being cautious, Beth "refused" the woman's request but gave "my all changes" to her to call at a phone booth. When Beth told the story to her roommate, she finally realized that she had still been cheated.

> I'm very happy to help a strange man. So I called my domitry mates. But she told me I was cheated because ten minters ago, a woman used same way to cheat her money. After I described the appearance of the woman, my mates exclaim: a sam person.

Through this diary entry, Beth performed her social identity as "a pure girl," a description of her by her parents. As she wrote in the first two paragraphs of her diary:

> Today, I'm very angry because of I was cheated.
> When I became a university student, my parents always tell me: the society is complex and dark, you should learn to protect yourself. In the eyes of my parents, I'm a pure girl without enough social experience. In order to reduce worried of parents, I cautiously to living. Even though I'm so carefully, I still was cheated on this Sunday.

In other words, Beth's experience of being cheated by the middle-aged woman, as recorded in her diary, is not merely a recounting of her past experience. While telling the story, Beth dressed herself as "a pure girl," adopting the identity conclusion previously drawn by her parents. As her parents could only speak Chinese (I 2), the original words must have been "单纯的女孩," the Chinese equivalent of "a pure girl." Through her translation, Beth functioned as a translingual subject.

Beth's second diary entry features her speech in an oral English class. Her Canadian teacher had asked the class to give a "free talk" at the "teaching-desk" on a topic decided by drawing lots. Beth ended up with the topic: my dream job. Beth wrote in her diary, "In the class, I told my teacher and classmates, my 'dream' job is teacher so that I have regular income and peaceful life." It was very possible that Beth talked about a teacher dream simply because such an idea was easy to express or socially acceptable in a Chinese classroom. As Beth said about her future plan in an interview, *"My parents want me to be a teacher; because just as Tina (Beth's classmate) said, it is very stable*" (I 1). She performed an imagined teacher identity, first in front of her class through her "free talk" and then through her written narrative to an extended audience.

In a similar vein, Beth recreated through her autobiographical samples, "*A Teacher of Forty Minutes*" and its revisions, a teacher identity that she had performed during a village trip. As Beth wrote,

> After a short rest, we arranged the class schedule, I was arranged English class for grade 1. It was my first time to stood teaching-desk as a teacher. For children too young, I was afraid they can't accepted my teaching contents. So I changed my schedule. This is a successful and happy experience. I hope I could have more chances to donated my knowledge to others.

In this short narrative with only two paragraphs, Beth recounted an English teacher identity she had enacted at a primary school: someone who planned the lesson (e.g., "I changed my schedule") and transmitted knowledge ("donated my knowledge to others"). Beth's subsequent revision (17W_W), containing a total of five paragraphs with added details about the teaching process, helped make this teacher identity more "experience-near-and-particular" (White, 2007) than her first draft. For instance, she added a description of her interactions with her students:

> The ringing bell, I begun class. "Have you anyone could lend me a book?" I asked. "Teacher, me, me, me!" They said. Suddenly one little boy rushed platform. "Teacher, used mine! He said. I was so frighted because their head teacher looking me out of the window. I soon received his book and said: thanks for your books, please return your seat now! The case ended with happy. Because I saw a delighted exprssion on his face. After that, we begun sang ABC songs. They are so passional and active. The forty minutes teaching quickly passed away.

Through these details, Beth performed a teacher identity in the classroom. Her audience included her students, who addressed her as "Teacher" and eagerly lent her their books ("'Teacher, me, me, me!' They said"). It also included the "head teacher," who was "looking [at her] out of the window."

However, autobiographical writing may not be a transparent window into multilingual writers' performed identities. Different versions of the same story may involve different audiences from previous performances. So, even though the story appeared to be the same as the lived experience itself, through writing and sharing it with others, the writer actually performs a preferred identity to extended audiences. Take Beth's sample "A Forty Minutes' Teacher" (Week-19 Writing) as an example. It is her third revision of her story about the same

**126** Shizhou Yang

teaching experience. When she read it to the writing group, there were nine student members, two international visitors, and I. By hearing her story, we all became "outsider witnesses" (White, 2007) to Beth's "successful teacher" identity.

These examples show that autobiographical writing provides a space for multilingual writers to foreground, convey and share with the audience the identities or identity conclusions that they had experienced or constructed elsewhere, in some other language. This is consistent with Ivanič's (1998) view that writers often construct some "discoursal identity" or impressions of themselves as certain types of people through writing. The main difference here is that Beth used written narratives in a third language, rather than traditional academic writing in one's first language, to foreground her particular identities. Also, some continuity of identity occurs despite the use of a different language.

## Reflecting

In her autobiographical writing, Beth was also found to engage in significant identity work through reflection. In one sample, Beth foregrounded her experience of falling in water and generated an identity conclusion of herself as a curious girl. One "sunny" afternoon, Beth took a walk with a classmate to a lake on her university campus. The lake had "a bridge . . . and some wooden area." Walking on the wooden area against her classmate's advice, Beth "fell into water." She became "very afraid" when she realized that her "feet can't touch the bottom of lake." So, she started screaming. Fortunately, her classmate grabbed her hand and pulled her out. Soaking wet, Beth felt "cold and embarrassed" in front of the "so many students walking around the lake" (Week-15 Writing). Beth's fall was partly due to an external condition ("one part of wooden area suddenly loose") and partly, as Beth explained, due to her "curiousty." "My classmate told me don't went to wooden area, but *I was very curiousty* it. Old says: *curiousty kill cat*. That day, *the curiousty nearly killed me*." The western proverb "curiosity kills the cat," albeit inaccurately quoted, provided Beth with a cultural way of explaining her act and its consequences. She was, through reflection, a curious girl. Meanwhile, autobiographical writing, functioning as an alternate space, allowed her to merge her experience with a selected aspect of western culture.

Beth's identity work through reflection becomes more apparent as we consider her multiple drafts. Before sharing her complete story (Week-15 Writing) with me on June 20, Beth had worked on it twice during the meeting on June 13. The writing group had just read *The First Time to Say "I Love You!"* (Coffman, 2003, pp. 164–165) and reviewed the group's way of understanding voice as uniqueness in content, expression and structure (Video 14). I then asked the members to write something on the topic "the first time to . . ." that would show their uniqueness. Beth titled her draft "*fall into man-made lake*" (Week-13 Writing). She wrote the first half in black (Week-13 Writing), and during the time for revision, after sharing each other's drafts, Beth added several sentences in green (Week-14 Writing, see Figure 7.1).

Multilingual Writers' Identity Work  **127**

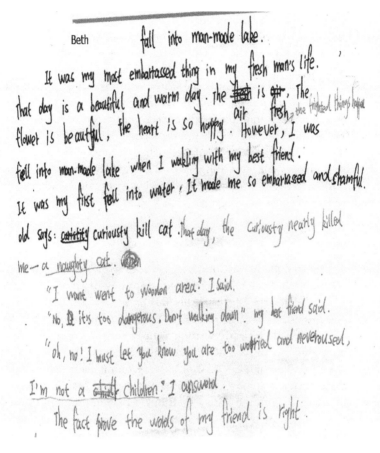

**FIGURE 7.1** "Fall into Man-Made Lake"

Beth's original writing was in two colors. Her first draft, written in black, starts with the title and ends with "curiousty kill cat." Her second draft, written in green, starts with "That day" and ends with "my friend is right." It was added by her when she was asked to revise her original writing. Together, Beth's writing shows her evolving understanding of herself in relation to her experience of falling in water. From the proverb she quoted inaccurately ("curiousty kill cat"), Beth seemed to suggest that she was curious. In her summary of that day's event, however, she called herself "a naughty cat" ("That day, the curiousty nearly kills me—a naughty cat"). Her reply to her classmate's caution shows still another possibility, that she was being adventurous ("Oh, no! I must let you know you are too worried and neveroused, I'm not a children"). This third possibility is viable for two reasons. For one thing, Beth's curiosity, which led her to fall into water, was linked to her embarrassment about falling in front of other students (Week-15 Writing). For another, Beth had written that she was "*afraid* of . . . gossipe" and needed others' approval to love herself (3W_W). Her tension between home and outside thus continued, but with a slight variation: playing it safe and being adventurous. In the end, Beth chose to foreground her curiosity ("I was very curiousty it . . . curiosity kill cat. That day, the curiousty nearly killed me"). And that is the identity she shared with the writing group through her final draft "*Fall into water*" (Week-15 Writing).

As shown by Beth's multiple drafts on her experience of falling in water, her autobiographical writing was a site of struggle between multiple identity options. These options became available to her through reflection, as mediated by her autobiographical writing. Accordingly, Beth engaged in significant identity work by actively working out which identity options to adopt and foreground, and which ones to submerge.

## Re-Visioning

In several instances, Beth was found to use autobiographical writing to re-vision her future self. Such re-visioning concerns how Beth wants to position herself in her readers' eyes regarding her future. First of all, Beth re-visioned herself as an English writer in terms of the imagined content she was to write about, as evident in Beth's early writing samples for the group. For instance, during the second meeting on March 21, I asked the members to give a preface to their "autobiographies" or simply write about their feelings towards writing their autobiographies. In response, Beth wrote "My Feeling of 自传 [Autobiography]," beginning with a draft in Chinese in the right upper-hand corner of the page, which expressed a sense of freedom about autobiographical writing:

> 在我的自传中，我会写些我想写我想要表达的一些东西，它可以是我的过去，也可以说是我未来的梦想，或者是一些我根本就不知道该不该和能不能写的东西，我对它有很大的期待。
>
> *(Week-1 Writing)*

> *In my autobiography, I may write what I want to write or express. It can be my past, or dreams for my future, and something I don't even know whether I should or can write about. I have a great expectation for it!*

This sense of freedom contrasts sharply with Beth's previous investment in English writing, which was extremely limited in both scope and content. As Beth revealed, she had written little in English except completing her mentor's assignments from "*previous TEM4* [a Chinese National English exam] *exams . . . including a big composition and a small one—a note*," (I 2). Moreover, such writing tasks were perceived by Beth as requiring her to state the positive only. "*The standard of test-oriented education is that you can only write about the positive aspects* [of issues]" (I 2). By this, Beth probably means that making critical comments about any official position would lead to lower test scores.

In Beth's case, re-visioning was found to closely link with reflection. Also in her diary entry 2 (Week-5 Writing), Beth first introduced a teacher identity she had performed before her class. She then asserted that her real "big dream" was to travel around the world. As Beth continued in her diary, "In fact, I want a high income job to travel aroud the world, I eager to experience different life and culture. It is my big dream." Two identities are mediated through autobiographical writing here: a teacher identity and a world traveler identity. In the space afforded by autobiographical writing, Beth re-visioned these identities. For instance, Beth's expression "In fact" introduced her reflection, basic as it was, on a teacher identity that she had performed through speaking. As a result of this reflection, Beth downplayed the position of her imagined teacher identity, which had taken a prominent place in her spoken English class. In addition, through her expression "In fact," Beth also ushered in her new imagined social identity as a traveler. She named this imagined traveler identity as "my big dream," which seemed to link with her travel dreams already mentioned in "My Feeling of 自传" (Week-3 Writing): i.e., "travelling around the world, especially to French. Japen."

## Impact of Autobiographical Writing on Beth's Writer Identity

Significant changes in Beth's sense of self as a writer can be observed in her self-portraits as well as her writing samples. During the thirty-second meeting, which was also the final meeting of the group, I asked the student member to represent their writing experiences before, during, and after their participation in the writing group. Multimodality was encouraged as the members should first use only images and then words. Beth drew a cup, a girl in a circle and a rainbow (see Figure 7.2), with captions and explanations for each.

Beth's cup image seems to suggest three dimensions of herself as a writer in English at the time she joined the writing group. First, she felt a sense of helplessness due to her lack of knowledge about writing in English. As she explained in an interview, "At the beginning, I'm like water, pure (pointing to and tapping near the cup), uh—*didn't know what to do and how to do*." Second, she seems to suggest that her writing was inadequate. As her first caption says, "My words and sentences are plain, the structure of my article is ~~losse~~ 松散. . . ." By *plain*, Beth appears to mean her English writing was dull or boring, unlike her Chinese writing, in which she could use "华丽的词藻" ("beautiful words") and express her insightful understandings (I 2). Third, she expressed a sense of unrealized personal agency ("but I want to write a good composition"),

130  Shizhou Yang

**FIGURE 7.2** Beth's Three Images and Captions

implying that she wanted to develop further as a writer but did not feel that she was yet doing so.

Beth's second image, a girl in a circle (with the circle originally in green), shows her confusion when interacting with multiple audiences. "I feel puzzled." she wrote in her caption. Further explanation reveals the source of her confusion: One of her writing samples had received contrasting comments from me, the writing group leader, and her Singaporean writing teacher. This incident suggests that unlike her earlier English diary entries, her later writing samples had an expanded audience, whose feedback shaped both her understandings of her writing and her sense of self as a writer. Importantly, Beth's confusion bridged her into her third image, a "rainbow." The transition resonates with a line from a Chinese pop song she had attempted to translate into English to describe her senior high school period, "Don't pass the wind and rain, how to see the ribon [rainbow]?" (不经历风雨，怎能见彩虹? Week-5 Writing)

The caption of Beth's rainbow image reveals her self-perceived changes as a writer. She first emphasized what I taught, "the Nicholas teach us how to write better . . . use exactly words . . . pay attention to structure. . . ." She then highlights what she could do by herself, "I can write the composition better than before." Especially worth noting is her mention of writing poems, both in Chinese and English, "even written poem. One Chinese poem and English poem." It suggests a sense of excitement associated with pursuing her "literature dream" in two languages. Last, Beth expressed a sense of increased confidence in communication through written English, "I can express my idea in my article generally, and use different ways to write about different things."

Similarly, Beth's last writing sample during the autobiographical writing stage also showed her growing confidence as a writer. During the fifteenth meeting on June 20, I asked the members to write for twenty minutes about their "auto-biographies." Beth wrote "A Wonderful Book" (Week-18 Writing) in response. Three features of *"A Wonderful Book"* stand out most strikingly for me, with reference to Beth's drawings and previous writing samples. First, Beth can now stand her ground/find her place to write her own "wonderful book." Her previous "literature dream" (Week-1 Writing) was becoming more substantial and personal, as evidenced by events and dreams that she already had written about in the writing group (e.g., "Fall into Man-Made Lake," "Provence Dream") and events yet to be written about (e.g., "travelling to Lijiang," being "cheated and betrayed by my friend," and "the earthquake in Wenchuan"). She is now a confident writer in English ("I'm a literary girl and always decorate colorful and peomful for my book and life"). It seems that her experience of writing auto-biographically for the group has partially allowed her to realize her "literature dream" and given her an increased sense of personal agency.

Second is Beth's description of the potential of her book. "If you read carefully, you will find it is a really wonderful book. Perhaps, you can more understand me." Beth thus saw her book leading to richer shared understandings about her than other limited and limiting views of her, e.g., someone who wanted to *"take remedial classes"* and whose writing in English was *"corrected all in red"* (1W_W). Therefore, autobiographical writing was, to Beth, a powerful medium to reposition her *self* as a complex person with many possibilities.

Third is an emerging sense of ownership in English writing. Previously, Beth had compared her English writing to a cup of water—"dull," uninteresting, for her lack of *"beautiful words."* Now, she was the owner of "a wonderful book written by myself," "decorate[d] colorful and peomful for my book and life." Her English writing now contains her beautiful dreams associated with both her writing (e.g., "literature dream") and life (e.g., "attic" dream, "provence dream," and "big dream" as a world traveler), as well as hopes and alternative possibilities. It can indeed be compared to a "rainbow," the third image she drew (see Figure 7.2) to represent how she had changed as a writer in the writing group. Her explanation during a video interview seems to suggest that her

**132** Shizhou Yang

English writing experiences in the writing group even had a life-enriching effect on her: "Now. . . . My life is like a rainbow—colorful and hopeful" (Video 32).

## Discussion and Conclusion

The study provides new insights regarding multilingual writers' identity work in a foreign language. Studies of published multilingual memoirists often suggest that writing in a second language constitutes a process of translating the self into another language and culture (e.g., Shen, 1989; Pavlenko, 2004), thus implying writing in L1 and L2 as distinct identity-making processes. An analysis of Beth's investment in autobiographical writing suggests otherwise. More specifically, Beth's views of self, first formed in her first and second languages (Bai and Chinese) were found to serve as basis for her to structure her stories (e.g., as a "pure girl"), to encourage her investment in autobiographical writing (e.g., "to continue my literature dream"), and to ultimately shape her sense of self as a confident writer in English (e.g., "If you read my book, you will saw a girl of both rose dreams and . . ."). Beth's case suggests that rather than running as parallel or successive tracks, L1 and L2 writing processes may be intertwined to enrich the writer's understandings of self. In this regard, pedagogical use of autobiographical writing, including that of literacy autobiographies (see Canagarajah in this volume), seems to open up an alternate space for multilingual writers to cross ethnic, linguistic, and cultural boundaries in their lives.

In at least three ways, Beth's study provides a more dynamic picture of multilingual writers' identity work than previously understood. First, even in her early stage of autobiographical writing, Beth integrated Chinese, her second language, both explicitly and implicitly. This suggests that becoming "global souls" (Li, 2007) does not have to be a final destination, nor should it be taken as an individual achievement. Instead, in a safe space for exploring a wide range of identity options, it is only natural to see the writer's diverse linguistic repertoire being manifested textually. This finding resonates with similar studies where the social context allows multilingual writers to draw on their multiple resources to construct some kind of "identity texts" that transcend a singular way of meaning-making (e.g., Cummins et al., 2005; You, 2011, 2016). In other words, "global souls" can be expanded to include a general state of being for all multilingual writers when they are practically "resourceful users" (Pennycook, 2012) of their languages, cultures and experiences.

Second, Beth's study also offers a new understanding about "souls in exile" (Li, 2007) among multilingual writers, especially in the foreign language context. For published memoirists, the term "souls in exile" captures an identity crisis accompanying their "critical experience" (Block, 2002) of geographical, linguistic and cultural relocation into some English-speaking countries. Their heightened sense of cultural and linguistic loss is triggered by crossing geographical boundaries. In contrast, multilingual writers in a foreign language context, as in Beth's case, usually stay within their national bounds. Much stayed the same for Beth. For instance, she could go about her daily life comfortably by speaking a Chinese dialect or Mandarin. She could even speak Bai with some of her classmates. Nonetheless, she was a "soul in exile" (Li, 2007) through what I call institutional dislocation. That is, in participating in her department's approach to English literacy, particularly by focusing on TEM-4 writing topics and on getting grammar right, Beth became disconnected from valuable parts of her cultural and language repertoire, such as her previous life and literacy experiences, dreams and evolving understandings of self, as well as the multiple languages she already knew. Such institutional relocation constrained Beth's identity options as a writer, making her only able to write from a position of linguistic deficit. Multilingual writers can be "souls in exile" when pedagogical practices cut them off from their past and future.

Third, Beth's use of Chinese and disuse of Bai in her autobiographical writing samples are also suggestive of her identity work as a tension-filled process. They highlight that a looking back, as afforded by autobiographical writing, may provide opportunities for multilingual writers to reconnect with their multilingual resources. However, to what extent multilingual writers use these resources is partially dependent on the writers' ideological orientations towards these resources. In Beth's case, Chinese, her second language, was her primary resource. She embedded Chinese in her autobiographical writing in multiple ways, ranging from individual words (e.g., "My strong 后盾 and source of happy") to long stretches of text, as in her introduction of "My Feeling of 自传." Sometimes, Beth utilized her Chinese expertise through translation. Besides describing herself as "a pure girl," following her parents' view of her, she also inserted "don't pass the wind and rain, how to see the ribon [rainbow]" (Week-3 Writing), her own translation of a Chinese pop song's lyrics, into her writing. A reason for Beth's frequent, and sometimes covert, use of Chinese might be because she already had an established writer identity in Chinese through formal education. Using Chinese allowed her to express what she could not in English.

In contrast, Beth never showed signs of using Bai, her ethnic minority language, in her autobiographical writing. One reason might be because Beth subscribed to a locally dominant language ideology which positions Bai literacy negatively. For instance, one of her departmental leaders once commented on the invention and promotion of a Bai script in a local community as creating unnecessary burden for the Bai people. According to this leader, the Bai people were culturally more "advanced" than other minority groups in the province, precisely because there was no Bai script to hinder the group's assimilation to the Han culture. Similarly, when Beth was asked about the new Bai script, she questioned the need: *"There was not a script for the Bai people before; why should there be one now?"* (I 2). After all, Bai was not her home language, as neither of her parents could speak it (I 2). She probably learned to speak Bai by interacting with other Bai in her hometown, including her grand parents. The lack of apparent evidence, however, does not mean that the Bai culture was not influencing Beth's autobiographical writing. As she wrote:

> When I writing my autobiography, the experience of my grown course is deeply effect me. This experience may myself, or I learnt from others. For example, my parents, my teachers, my friends. Of course, It will include some Bai culture.
>
> *(Week-20 Writing)*

Therefore, it can be said that, without leaving her home country, Beth still became a translingual subject as she engaged in autobiographical writing to negotiate her textual identity.

A dynamic model of multilingual writers' identity work can be observed in this study. A multilingual writer's imagined identity, a "literature dream" in Beth's case, invites her investment in autobiographical writing. In the drafting and revision of the stories, the writer explored her life experiences, dreams and various identity options. Through performing, reflecting and re-visioning, she actively worked out who she was, is and wants to become, thus revealing a complex and dynamic individual. These phases of becoming, as mediated through her (investment in) autobiographical writing, highlight the importance of creating an alternate space for multilingual writers to cross borders in literacy education.

The study, as a whole, challenges the poststructuralists' overemphasis on learner identity as constantly shifting (see Price, 1996, for a critique). As the analysis above has shown, Beth seemed to have used autobiographical writing to engage in her ongoing identity project, which, despite its diverse manifestations, converges on a theme of tension between safety and adventure. Additionally, Beth's imagined identity as a writer has persisted both through the time before and after she joined the writing group, and across both Chinese and English. Therefore, holistic understandings of learners' identity work call for researchers to reconsider identity as a dialogical notion, which entails both change and continuity (Menard-Warwick, 2005). From this perspective, text becomes a site where identity work occurs. Even if the final product is only written in English, effective pedagogical practices should consider creating an alternate space to encourage border crossing between languages, varieties of the same language and different modes of representation. That way, multilingual writers may construct their sense of self not solely in terms of some Standardized Written English, but also other communicative resources at their disposal (Canagarajah, 2006; Lam, 2000). Teaching and researching literacy are not neutral activities either. By the ways we teach literacy or do research on literacy, we shape the ways multilingual writers continue or change their identities by influencing the ways they relate to their own backgrounds and the world. Therefore, as literacy professionals, we should be mindful and reflective of the ways we "co-author" (White, 2007) our multilingual writers' identity options.

Beth's study is limited in it being a single case, and in its lack of detailed information about her language activities in Bai, her first language. Nonetheless, through autobiographical writing in the group, Beth explored both known and new territories of her life, discovered and shared an emerging sense of herself as a confident and hopeful writer. In the alternate space afforded by autobiographical writing, Beth was developing a complicated and still evolving view of her multiple identities. This view of self did not focus on what she was lacking. Instead, it was informed by her diverse experiences, imaginations and expertise, as nurtured by her multiple languages and cultures. A translingual subject, who could write "A Wonderful Book" to share with her audience about herself, thus came into being. As she claimed confidently in her unfinished draft, "If you read my book, you can saw a girl who have both rose dream and . . ." (Week-18 Writing).

## Notes

1. An earlier form of this article was published in *Autobiographical Writing and Identity in EFL Education* (Yang, 2013), revised for the current publication with the publisher's written permission. The research was sponsored by Endeavour Asia Award, Endeavour International Postgraduate Research Scholarship from the Australian government and David Myers Scholarship from La Trobe University.
2. The Bai language used to have a script modelled after Chinese characters. A new script based on Latin Alphabets was invented in recent years. However, neither script is in wide use. None of the students in the writing group knew how to write in Bai.
3. The numeral indicates sequence whereas the abbreviations indicate the data type, e.g., I 1 referring to the First Interview, and Week-1 Writing standing for the First Week's Writing Sample. Italicized texts in quotes are my translation from Chinese.

## References

Belcher, D. D., & Braine, G. (Eds.). (1995). *Academic writing in a second language: Essays on research and pedagogy*. Norwood, NJ: Ablex.

Block, D. (2002). Destabilized identities and cosmopolitanism across language and cultural borders: Two case studies. *Hong Kong Journal of Applied Linguistics, 7*(2), 1–19.

Brisk, M. E. (1998). *The transforming power of critical autobiographies*. Paper presented at the 32nd Annual Meeting of the Teachers of English to Speakers of Other Languages, Seattle, WA, March 17–21.

Bruner, J. (1986). *Actual minds, possible worlds*. Cambridge, MA: Harvard University Press.

Canagarajah, A. S. (2006). The place of world Englishes in composition: Pluralization continued. *College Composition and Communication, 57*(4), 586–619.

Casanave, C. P. (2002). *Writing games: Multicultural case studies of academic literacy practices in higher education*. Mahwah, NJ: Lawrence Erlbaum Associates.

Coffman, D. M. (2003). *A Peking University coursebook on English exposition writing*. Beijing: Peking University Press.

CCCC Statement on Second Language Writing and Writers. (2009). Retrieved from www.ncte.org/cccc/resources/positions/secondlangwriting.

Cook, V. (1999). Going beyond the native speaker in language teaching. *TESOL Quarterly, 33*(2), 185–209.

Cox, M., Jordan, J., Ortmeier-Hooper, C., & Schwartz, G. G. (Eds.). (2010). *Reinventing identities in second language writing.* Urbana: NCTE Press.

Cummins, J., Bismilla, V., Chow, P., Cohen, S., Giampapa, F., Leoni, L., . . . Sastri, P. (2005). *ELL students speak for themselves: Identity texts and literacy engagement in multilingual classrooms.* Retrieved from www.curriculum.org/secretariat/files/ELLidentity-Texts.pdf

Edelsky, C. (2003). Theory, politics, hopes, and action. *The Quarterly, 25*(3), 10–19. Retrieved from www.nwp.org/cs/public/print/resource/867.

Freiberg, S., & You, X. (2012). A multilingual and multimodal framework for studying L2 writing. *EFL Writing Teaching and Research, 1*(1), 22–33.

Haneda, M. (2005). Investing in foreign-language writing: A study of two multicultural learners. *Journal of Language, Identity, and Education, 4*(4), 269–290.

Hartley, J., & Qu, W. (Eds.). (2015). *Re-orientation: Trans-cultural, trans-lingual and trans-media studies in narrative, language, identity and knowledge.* Shanghai: Fudan University Press.

Heath, S. B., Street, B. V., & Mills, M. (2008). *On ethnography: Approaches to language and literacy research.* New York: Teachers College Press.

Holquist, M. (2002). *Dialogism: Bakhtin and his world* (2nd ed.). London: Routledge.

Hungerford-Kresser, H. (2010). Navigating early college: Literacy experiences and identity negotiations of Latina/o students. *Journal of College Literacy & Learning, 36,* 3–13.

Ivanič, R. (1998). *Writing and identity: The discoursal construction of identity in academic writing.* Amsterdam: John Benjamins.

Krāmsch, C., & Lam, W. S. E. (1999). Textual identities: The importance of being nonnative. In G. Braine (Ed.), *Educators in English language teaching* (pp. 56–72). Mahwah, NJ: Lawrence Erlbaum Associates.

Lam, W. S. E. (2000). L2 literacy and the design of the self: A case study of a teenager writing on the internet. *TESOL Quarterly, 34*(3), 457–482.

Li, X. (2007). Souls in exile: Identities of bilingual writers. *Journal of Language, Identity & Education, 6*(4), 259–275.

Liu, Y. C. (2008). Taiwanese students' negotiations with academic writing: Becoming "playwrights and film directors." *Journal of Second Language Writing, 17*(2), 86–101.

McAdams, D. P. (1995). *The life story interviews.* Retrieved from www.sesp.northwestern.edu/docs/Interviewrevised95.pdf.

McKay, S. L., & Wong, S. C. (1996). Multiple discourses, multiple identities: Investment and agency in second language learning among Chinese adolescent immigrant students. *Harvard Educational Review, 3,* 577–608.

Maguire, M. H., & Graves, B. (2001). Speaking personalities in primary school children's L2 writing. *TESOL Quarterly, 35*(4), 561–593.

Menard-Warwick, J. (2005). Both a fiction and an existential fact: Theorizing identity in second language acquisition and literacy studies. *Linguistics and Education, 16,* 253–274.

Morris, P. (1994). *The Bakhtin reader: Selected writings of Bakhtin, Medvedev, Voloshinov.* London: Arnold.

Norton, B. (2000). *Identity and language learning: Gender, ethnicity and educational change.* Edinburgh Gate: Pearson Education Limited.

Norton, B. (2001). Non-participation, imagined communities and the language classroom. In M. Breen (Ed.), *Learner contributions to language learning: New directions in research* (pp. 159–171). London: Longman/Pearson Education.

Norton, B. (2006). Identity: Second language. In K. Brown (Ed.), *Encyclopedia of language & linguistics* (Vol. 5, pp. 502–508). Oxford: Elsevier.

Norton, B., & Williams, C.-J. (2012). Digital identities, student investments and e-Granary as a placed resource. *Language and Education, 26*(4), 315–329.

Park, G. (2013). "Writing *is* a way of knowing": Writing and identity. *ELT Journal, 67*(3), 336–345.

Pavlenko, A. (2004). "The making of an American": Negotiation of identities at the turn of the twentieth century. In A. Pavlenko, & A. Blackledge (Eds.), *Negotiation of identities in multilingual contexts* (pp. 34–67). Clevedon: Multilingual Matters.

Peirce, B. N. (1995). Social identity, investment, and language learning. *TESOL Quarterly, 29*(1), 9–31.

Pennycook, A. D. (2012). *Language and mobility: Unexpected places.* Bristol, UK: Multilingual Matters.

Price, S. (1996). Comments on Bonny Norton Peirce's "Social Identity, Investment, and Language Learning": A reader reacts. *TESOL Quarterly, 30*(2), 331–337.

Shen, F. (1989). The classroom and the wider culture: Identity as a key to learning English composition. *College Composition and Communication, 40*(4), 459–466.

Snow, D. A., & Anderson, L. (1987). Identity work among the homeless: The verbal construction and avowal of personal identities. *The American Journal of Sociology, 92*(6), 1336–1371.

Starfield, S. (2002). "I'm a second-language English speaker": Negotiating writer identity and authority in sociology one. *Journal of Language, Identity & Education, 1*(2), 121–140.

Steinman, L. (2005). Writing life 1 in language 2. *McGill Journal of Education, 40*(1), 65–79.

Strauss, A., & Corbin, J. (1990). Grounded theory research: Procedures, canons, and evaluative criteria. *Qualitative Sociology, 13*(1), 3–21.

White, M. (2005). *Workshop notes. 1–25.* Retrieved from www.dulwichcentre.com.au.

White, M. (2007). *Maps of narrative practice* (1st ed.). New York: W. W. Norton.

Wu, R. (1994). *ESL students writing autobiographies: Are there any connections?* Paper presented at the Annual Meeting of the Rhetoric Society of America, Louisville, KY, May 19–22.

Yang, S. (2013). *Autobiographical writing and identity in EFL education.* New York: Routledge.

Yi, Y. (2013). Adolescent multilingual writer's negotiation of multiple identities and access to academic writing: A case study of a Jogi Yuhak student in a US high school. *The Canadian Modern Language Review, 69*(2), 207–231.

You, X. (2011). Chinese white-collar workers and multilingual creativity in the diaspora. *World Englishes, 30*(3), 409–427.

You, X. (2016). *Cosmopolitan English and transliteracy.* Carbondale, IL: Southern Illinois University Press.

# 8

# EFFECTS OF STUDY-ABROAD EXPERIENCES ON L2 WRITING

## Insights From Published Research

*Miyuki Sasaki*

### Introduction

Few studies have investigated the effects of study-abroad (SA) experiences on second language (L2) writing abilities compared to the number of studies that have investigated other forms of L2 knowledge and skills. This is regrettable because writing skills in an L2, especially in English as a Lingua Franca, is now indispensable in a highly IT-intensive world, and SA is one of the means through which L2 literacy can be acquired in a manner that is most appropriately "socio-literate" (Ferris & Hedgcock, 2014, p. 114). In response, this study critically reviews under-investigated SA literature dealing with L2 writing abilities for the purpose of exploring possible future research directions for that sub-field. Organizationally, the study first defines the two central terms "study-abroad" and "language ability." I chose to focus on linguistic aspects of SA effects because they have been most extensively studied since Carroll's (1967) seminal study reporting impacts of SA on university students' L2 proficiency. Although I am aware that there are other non-linguistic effects of SA, including changes in belief and value systems (e.g., Fraiberg, Wang, & You, 2017), these go beyond the space allowed for this chapter. After defining these two terms, this chapter first presents an overall summary of studies that have investigated effects of SA on L2 proficiency other than L2 writing abilities. The chapter then proceeds to the main part, a synthesis of past studies related to impacts of SA on L2 writing abilities. These studies are examined in greater details than studies of other L2 abilities especially in terms of their epistemological orientations and methods employed. Based on this synthesis, the chapter concludes with a discussion of how effects of SA on L2 writing abilities may be better studied in the future in terms of research targets, methods, and theoretical orientations.

This study adopts a revised version of Kinginger's (2009) definition of the term "study-abroad," namely "a temporary sojourn of pre-defined duration, undertaken for educational purposes" (p. 11). On the basis of this definition, I open this chapter with the case of the first five Japanese women who studied abroad at the end of the 19th century. Although their cases are rather unusual, they exemplify (then) rare cases of recorded SA experiences. Since "claims about 'learning' (or development, progress, improvement, change, gains, and so on) can be most meaningfully interpreted only within a full longitudinal perspective" (Ortega & Iberri-Shea, 2005, p. 26), these women's life-long stories show how their SA experiences impacted their life.

## The First Five Japanese Women Who Studied Abroad

In 1871, the fourth year of the Meiji period, five young Japanese women headed to the United States, intending to spend the following ten years learning English and American culture. They were the first Japanese women to study abroad (Terasawa, 2009). Before the Meiji period, the Tokugawa Shogunate feudal samurai warriors had ruled the country for about 260 years since 1600, when its founder, Ieyasu Tokugawa, achieved full political centralization. During the long Tokugawa period, the government allowed very limited access to foreign cultures and people, afraid of an invasion by Christianity, which was believed to be harmful to the feudal system. In 1868, the Shogunate collapsed as a result of internal nationalism, requiring it to return power to the emperor as well as repeated foreign threats (Walker, 2015). Knowing that their predecessor's fall was caused by a lack of modern knowledge and technology, the new Meiji government hastily pursued the country's modernization by inviting foreign experts and sending its own people abroad. Among these were the above-mentioned five young women.

All five were chosen from among samurai warrior families, and their mission was to westernize Japanese women upon completion of their term of study in the US. They were Shige Nagai (10 years old), Ume Tsuda (6), Sutematsu Yamakawa (11), Tei Ueda (16), and Ryo Yoshida (14). These young women fit the definition of "study-abroad" adopted in this study because the length of their stay in the US was pre-determined and they were expected to return to Japan upon completion. The Japanese government paid for all their expenses, including tuition. The five young women stayed together until Tei and Ryo had to return home after only eleven months due to illness. Up to that point, the young women's English ability did not improve much, even though they lived with an American governess for the first five months. From that point on, the remaining three young women lived with different American families in different places and remained in the US for nine to ten years, when they graduated with strong academic records from prestigious high school or colleges.

When the three young women returned to Japan at the conclusion of their terms, they had lost most of their functional Japanese. In addition, Japanese women's low social status greatly disappointed them. In response, they sought ways to contribute to their country as they felt heavily indebted to the Japanese government for their long stay overseas (Terasawa, 2009). Each one later became a major figure of their time, though in quite different ways. Shige married a Japanese navy officer with whom she had fallen in love while in the US, and taught music, her major at Vassar College, in public schools. Sutematsu married Mr. Ohyama, a high-ranking official who later became a general in the Imperial Army, and contributed to the setting up of a school for daughters of the aristocracy (*kazoku jogakkou*) and helped Ume found her own private school. Although Ume felt that "an unmarried woman can truly do very little" (cited in Furuki et al., 1991, p. 33) at the time in Japan, she remained single throughout her life, believing that it was her duty to devote herself to raising the low status of Japanese women. Having decided to found an institution of higher learning that would be open to all Japanese women, she returned to the US to receive a higher education. After studying biology and education at Bryn Mawr College from 1889 to 1892, she returned to Japan, where in 1900 she founded the Women's Institute for English Studies, which was re-established as Tsuda College after her death in 1948. It is currently one of the most prestigious women's institutes of higher learning in Japan.

Some of the key characteristics of effects of SA experiences we can glean from these women's stories are as follows:

1. The effects of SA can last a lifetime (even though Tei and Ryo stayed in the US only eleven months, their lives after returning home continued relating to English in some way);
2. The effects of SA-related L2 ability serve learners in the form of actual language use, allowing them to achieve specific goals ranging from getting their meaning across to obtaining an academic degree;
3. How the effects of SA shape learners' L2 development can differ even under similar circumstances and is influenced by various factors, including affective or cognitive and sociocultural factors.

Based on these observations, I selected two important bases on which to build this chapter: (1) the definition of the construct of "language ability," one of the most important targets of SA-related studies (Kinginger, 2009); and (2) a basic stance for interpreting the results of SA-related studies.

## *Language Ability*

As mentioned above, abilities related to the language(s) spoken by those who live in destination communities have been a major target of SA-related research. Given that learners in SA contexts need to survive in these communities, the language ability addressed by SA research should be comprehensive, covering all elements involved in language used functionally in such situations. In response, I adopt Bachman and Palmer's (2010) definition of "language ability," that is, "a capacity that enables language users to create and interpret discourse" (p. 33). This capacity consists of both "language knowledge" and "strategic competence," an executive processing function bridging language knowledge and language use. This covers all types of knowledge regarding how language is organized (grammatical knowledge) and how the language user's goals can best be achieved using the sociocultural conventions in force in the given context (pragmatic knowledge). Furthermore, language users make use of this knowledge in language use while bringing multiple attributes into the mix, including their L1, age, and gender, in addition to knowledge about the topic in question, affective characteristics such as motivation, anxiety, and other emotional states, and cognitive tactics in order to complete the given task. Bachman and Palmer's model is one of very few that assume that the ability to use language is dynamic and interactive with the environment and that it is continuously influenced by multiple factors residing both inside and outside the language user (e.g., Roever, 2011).

### Key Assumption

While defining the target construct to be investigated is necessary, it is not sufficient for conducting a thorough evaluation of past studies. Rather, the reviewer must choose a stance from which to review these studies. In this review, I choose Ortega's (2011) "non-deficit" (p. 141) view of L2 learning, which treats L2 learners not as having failed to reach native-speaker (NS) competence but as users of various types of knowledge and skills (including both their L1 and L2) in order to function as legitimate communicators in each situation. For example, although some aspects of the English of the three young women who remained in the US for ten to eleven years (e.g., pronunciation) may not have been perfectly native-like even at the end of their stay, all three earned degrees in secondary or tertiary institutions, rare accomplishments indeed even for American women at the time. Given my assumption that "L2 users are not deficient users" (Ortega, 2011, p. 171), I regard these three young women's SA experiences in the US as successful from the point of view of L2 development. This view of L2 ability as communicative functionality concurs with Bachman and Palmer's (2010) view of language ability. Consequently, I only review studies that examined the development of language use in the participants, not studies of the development of elements of knowledge (e.g., production of native-like sounds) that are not directly related to such use.

## SA Studies That Examined Aspects of Language Ability Other Than Writing Abilities

Most SA-related studies have focused on limited aspects of what Bachman and Palmer (2010) call the L2 "language ability." Even though the claim is valid in

**142** Miyuki Sasaki

the sense that language use involves multiple components of language ability that continuously adapt to ever-changing environments, it is difficult to capture changes in learners' L2 ability in a comprehensive manner. However, more recent studies have started to focus on processing aspects of L2 ability (i.e., how learners implement their knowledge and skills) while also investigating how language development interacts with other affective and external forces.

As explained earlier, I briefly summarize exemplary studies of aspects of language ability not directly related to L2 writing before I proceed to SA studies that deal with L2 writers. Findings unrelated to L2 writing skills are expected not only to reveal a broad picture of SA-related studies but also to suggest what remains to be studied about L2 writers in SA contexts. With this in mind, all these studies are presented along with information on the participants' L1 and L2, sample size(s), and SA sites. Due to space limitations, I examine only studies published from 1995, when Freed's landmark edited volume entitled *Second Language Acquisition in a Study Abroad Context* appeared, to the present. Their findings share the following three characteristics (Churchill & Dufon, 2006), which I will not repeat in the following sections unless necessary:

1. There were often significant individual differences that could not be dismissed as "outlier" cases;
2. Studies often found mixed results, which may have been caused by differences in external factors such as learning contexts, amount and quality of contact time with the target language, or the learners' personal attributes such as initial L2 proficiency, motivation, or identity. In general, highly motivated students with longer previous L2-related experiences and who had more contact with the L2 (especially outside the classroom) in SA contexts tended to do better than those who did not show these characteristics;
3. The focus and methodological orientation of these studies reflected the major trends in SLA research of their time, changing from purely product-oriented reductionist approaches to more post-positivistic approaches that emphasized individualistic and sociocultural aspects of SA contexts.

### *Listening*

Very few studies have investigated the effects of SA experiences on students' listening ability. Instead, they mostly assessed the participants' performance measured through some form of standardized testing (e.g., Brecht, Davidson, & Ginsberg, 1995, with 658 Americans learning Russian in a four-month program) or the researchers' own test (e.g., Allen & Herron, 2003, with 25 Americans learning French in a 40-day program). Many of these studies reported at least partial but significant improvements. For example, Cubillos, Chieffo, and Fan (2008) compared 48 Americans learning Spanish in a five-week SA program with 92 At-Home (AH) counterparts and found the SA program effective in improving the advanced students' listening ability.

## Reading

As with listening ability, very few studies have examined the effects of SA experiences on learners' L2 reading abilities. However, those that have examined such effects tend to report significant improvements in reading ability on at least some of the quantifiable measures, including self-assessment, as in Dewey (2004), who investigated 15 American learners of Japanese in an eleven-week SA program compared with 15 counterparts in a nine-week AH immersion program. Alternatively, they report improvements in reading in terms of student perceptions (e.g., Kaplan, 1989, with 39 Americans learning French in a six-week program). In terms of processing, as with listening, Dewey reported that the SA students came to monitor their understanding while reading more frequently than their domestic immersion counterparts, suggesting again that the SA students may have developed this strategic competence through their SA experiences.

## Speaking

Among the various language skills, speaking has been targeted most frequently in SA-related studies, along with pragmatic knowledge and processing (see below). First, the learners' speaking proficiency has often been measured through performance-based instruments such as the Oral Proficiency Interview (OPI), and SA experiences have often been found to have significantly positive effects on the participants' overall speaking proficiency (e.g., Segalowitz & Freed, 2004, with 22 Americans learning Spanish in a semester-long SA program compared with 18 AH counterparts). Meanwhile, fluency has been measured through various criteria such as total words used, words per minute, and absence of speech repetition, fillers, or L1 insertions) (e.g., Freed, Segalowitz, & Dewey, 2004, with eight Americans learning French in a twelve-week SA program, compared with eight AH counterparts who received regular formal instruction and twelve AH counterparts who received intensive immersion). Many studies have reported that SA students significantly improved their speaking fluency. More recently, several studies have examined the effects of SA on the relationship between the process and outcome of the development of speaking ability in learners. However, the results of these studies are mixed. For example, Segalowitz and Freed (2004) found that the two processing indices of "speed" and "efficiency" (how fast and accurately speakers can connect words and their meaning) showed a significantly positive relationship with fluency gains by both SA and AH students, even though there was no difference between these two groups both before and after the students' SA experiences. The only difference between the two groups

**144** Miyuki Sasaki

was the fact that the SA group showed a stronger tendency to start speaking more slowly as their attention control became more efficient than that of the AH group.

## Pragmatic Knowledge and Processing

In Bachman and Palmer's (2010) model, pragmatic knowledge is defined as the knowledge that "enables us to create or interpret discourse by relating utterances or sentences and texts to their meanings, to the intentions of language users, and to relevant characteristics of the language use setting" (p. 46). SA-related studies dealing with such knowledge are greater in number than other SA-related studies, probably because SA contexts usually have obvious advantages, compared to AH contexts, in providing students with opportunities to consider the most appropriate language to be used in a greater variety of contexts. Subsequently, many studies dealing with the development of pragmatic competence in SA students reported positive effects of SA experiences, as well as significantly greater effects relative to their AH counterparts in studies where the two were compared.

Although Bachman and Palmer further divide "pragmatic knowledge" into "functional knowledge" (related to word- and sentence-level expression and interpretation) and "sociolinguistic knowledge" (related to discourse-level expression and interpretation), in this review, I classify studies according to whether they deal with more specific or more general aspects of language use, as this type of division better reflects the types of studies conducted in this area. First, at the more specific level, after a certain duration of SA experiences, students learned to use more appropriate and varied communication devices, including address forms (e.g., measured by questionnaires and role plays in Kinginger, 2008) and opening signals, fillers, and connectors (e.g., examined through OPI speech data in Lafford, 1995, with 28 Americans learning Spanish in a semester-long program compared with 13 AH counterparts). At the more general level of pragmatic proficiency, a majority of studies targeted students' development in performing appropriate speech acts. In these studies, students' performance (in either comprehension or production or both) was usually measured through written questionnaires or spoken role plays, though other instruments such as diary entries were also used (e.g., Hassall, 2006, investigating one Australian student learning leave-taking in Indonesian). As in the case of studies focusing on more specific aspects of pragmatic abilities, SA experiences usually brought significant improvements in the participants' use of the targeted speech acts.

One issue related to these SA-related studies of pragmatic competence is the fact that many of them evaluate the students' performance with native-speaker use as the norm, which is in conflict of the non-deficit view of L2 learning adopted in the present study. Interestingly, this was not as apparent in the studies of other skills reviewed above. Lastly, although an examination of processes of speech act formation by learners would throw light on these questions, very few studies to date have investigated such processes (for one exception, see Siegal, 1996).

## Effects of SA Experiences on L2 Writing

A review of SA-related literature shows that L2 writing and L2 literacy are the least investigated. This is partly due to the strong and long-lasting influence of ACTFL's (American Council on the Teaching of Foreign Language) OPI, which since 1986 has been the most popular measure in SA-related literature (Kinginger, 2009), and partly to the fact that oral (but not literate) proficiency is commonly expected to improve through experiences such as SA (Churchill & Dufon, 2006). In this section, I chose studies that investigated the effects of SA experiences on learners' language ability as defined by Bachman and Palmer (2010), which is directly related to their L2 writing activities. Among the studies published between 2009 and the present, I identified eight representative studies according to which aspect of language use each one focused upon. Unlike the studies of other L2 abilities summarized above, these studies are explained in more detail, including their epistemological orientation and methodology, which resulted in their categorization into three groups. This categorization reveals that these SA studies of L2 writing reflect the trends found in the SLA research of their time.

### Studies That Compared Changes in Speaking and Writing Abilities Over a Relatively Shorter Period

Three studies were part of larger studies comparing the "products" (e.g., recorded role plays and compositions) of SA and AH students' language use in speaking and writing. First, Freed, So, and Lazar (2003) compared four AH American university students with four SA counterparts who spent one semester in France. Six "non-teacher NS judges" (p. 6) assessed the fluency of both groups' OPI speech subjectively (i.e., without being provided with any evaluation criteria) and concluded that the SA students were more fluent than the AH students after the former group's stay abroad. In a similar manner, "five non-teacher NS judges" (p. 7) subjectively evaluated the fluency of the same four AH and four SA students' compositions. However, unlike their speech, the AH group's compositions were judged to be more fluent at both the pre- and post-SA stages. Moreover, the SA group made no significant improvements in terms of fluency.

In contrast with Freed et al. (2003), Pérez-Vidal and Juan-Garau (2011) compared the results of two consecutive but different contexts (six-month formal English L2 instruction vs. subsequent three-month SA experiences in Britain) in terms of oral and written production in a set of 35 Catalan-Spanish bilingual university students. The results of these two contexts were compared through seven-minute role plays and 30-minute argumentative compositions. In addition, the researchers used questionnaire data to capture the participants' individual profiles, including their language use, attitude toward the L2, beliefs about L2 learning, motivation to study the L2, and experiences during their overseas stay. While all 35 participants wrote compositions, 20 of them role played at three points in time: before and after formal instruction (T1 and T2), and after the SA program (T3). The participants' speech and compositions were rated in terms of fluency (words per clause and words per minute), accuracy (ratio of grammatical, lexical, and pragmatic errors per word), and complexity (number of dependent clauses per clause, clauses per T-unit, and number of coordinate clauses divided by combined clauses, as well as lexical complexity measured by types divided by tokens and ratios of formulaic expressions per word or clause).

The results show that the participants did not significantly improve in these aspects of speaking during the formal instruction period but that they significantly improved in terms of fluency, complexity, and use of formulaic expressions during the SA period. In contrast, while the participants' writing fluency and lexical complexity decreased significantly during formal instruction, these two variables significantly improved during their SA period. However, the number of areas showing improvement during the SA period was smaller in the participants' writing than in their speaking. In terms of experiences during the SA period, those who improved the most in writing tended to engage in "extra-curricular academic activities" (p. 179) and showed evidence of "being eager to learn and being emotionally aware" (p. 181), which was not characteristic of those who achieved strong improvement in speaking during the SA period.

Llanes, Tragant, and Serrano's (2012) findings are similar to Pérez-Vidal and Juan-Garau's (2011) in that the authors compared the effects of one-semester-long SA experiences in Britain on Spanish-speaking participants in terms of fluency, complexity, and accuracy in both speaking (narratives) and writing (15-minute descriptive essays). However, Llanes et al. did not compare the effects of SA with those of formal instruction. Instead, they included a greater number of individual differences such as attitude to the L2, orientation toward learning the L2, degree pursued, registration in English classes, degree of L2 interaction, and the participants' perceptions of linguistic progress in the L2. Unlike the above studies, inclusion of the participants' own perceptions is a noteworthy addition because insider (emic) perspectives have not usually been considered in addition to traditional outsider (etic) observations and analyses by the researchers. In terms of findings, the effects of the participants' SA experiences on their linguistic performance were similar to those in the Pérez-Vidal and Juan-Garau study in that the participants' writing significantly improved only in the area of fluency, whereas their speaking improved in more aspects of fluency as well as in lexical complexity. As for relationships between the participants' linguistic improvement and their individual characteristics and perceptions, in the interest of space, I only focus here on significant results related to improvements in the participants' writing.

The findings show that humanities majors who were studying English as an elective improved in written fluency and syntactic complexity more than those who majored in translation or science. In terms of SA environments, those who lived with a family improved in written accuracy more than those who lived in an apartment or a student dorm. Those who had less contact with L1 speakers at home improved in fluency, and those who had more contact with L2 speakers improved in accuracy. In terms of the participants' perceptions, those who felt that their reading improved during the SA period also felt that syntactic complexity in their writing improved, while those who felt that their writing improved also reported that their fluency and syntactic complexity improved, and their perceptions of improvement in their accent was related to their greater perceived written fluency.

In sum, all three studies reported that speaking improved more overall as well as in a greater number of aspects than did writing, even though students tended to improve in writing fluency in all three studies. Furthermore, the two most recent studies, which examined the participants' individual characteristics and perceptions, revealed that unlike improvements in speaking, improvements in writing seem to require extra effort, including stronger intrinsic motivation, and that merely spending some time in a target language country does not suffice.

## Studies That Explored Changes in Writing Abilities, Strategies, and Motivation Over a Longer Period

The next series of studies compared Japanese university students of English who spent some time abroad with students who did not over a relatively long observation period. The three studies (Sasaki, 2004, 2007, 2011) were unique in that: (1) they observed changes in both product-oriented aspects (e.g., composition scores) and process-oriented aspects (e.g., writing strategies) of L2 writing ability; (2) they observed the participants over a relatively long period after their SA experience ended; and (3) they used both etic and emic data to explain changes over time.

Sasaki (2004) was not originally intended to investigate the effects of SA experiences but rather the L2 writing behaviors of eleven Japanese students over three and a half years, between their first and fourth year in university. When the study started in 1998, they were all 18-year-olds majoring in British and American Studies. Because six of the eleven students spent two to eight months in English-speaking countries, mainly during their third year in university, the study could also compare these six with the five who did not. All were similar in terms of L2 proficiency, L2 writing ability, and strategy use in their first year. The results reveal that the SA and AH groups developed in similar manners in terms of L2 proficiency (measured as the sum of listening and reading test scores) and L2 composition quality and fluency. In addition, both groups learned overall global planning of the content to be written. The

**148** Miyuki Sasaki

only conspicuous difference between the two groups was that 67% of the SA students became more motivated to write better in the L2 and started to use L2 writing strategies they had learned, such as overall planning, in order to enrich the content of their compositions, whereas none of the AH students mentioned motivation or strategy use.

A follow-up to Sasaki (2004), Sasaki (2007) examined more immediate effects of SA experiences on students' L2 proficiency, L2 writing ability, and strategy use by shortening the observation period to one year so that the SA group's experiences abroad took place within that one year. The SA group consisted of seven students who spent four to nine months in English-speaking countries, and an AH group consisting of six students. The participants came from a population equivalent to that used in Sasaki (2004), and the data were collected between 2001 and 2002. The results revealed that: (1) both the SA and AH groups significantly improved in overall L2 proficiency (measured as the sum of listening and grammar test scores); (2) unlike in Sasaki (2004), only the SA group significantly improved in L2 composition scores and writing fluency; and (3) as in Sasaki (2004), only the SA group became more motivated to write better in the L2, which was reflected in changes in their use of L2 writing strategies.

Following the two studies discussed above (Sasaki, 2004, 2007), I realized the importance of examining the relationship between students' L2 writing development and their motivation. Furthermore, while I collected data for these two studies (2002 to 2008), SA had become increasingly popular in Japan (Ministry of Education, Culture, Sports, Science, and Technology, Japan, 2012), which made the value of shorter stays abroad less special to students. These changes motivated me to conduct a further study (Sasaki, 2011), in which I examined the effects of lengths of SA experiences on L2 writing ability and motivation to write in the L2. I divided the 37 participants into four groups according to the lengths of their overseas stay during the three-and-a-half-year observation period: an AH group ($n = 9$), which spent no time abroad; an SA-1.5-2 group ($n = 9$), which spent one and a half to two months abroad; an SA-4 group ($n = 7$), which spent four months abroad; and an SA-8-to-11 group ($n = 12$), which spent eight to eleven months abroad. Here too, the students' major was British and American studies. Once a year during the three-and-a-half-year observation period, all participants wrote argumentative compositions and provided interview data about their L2 learning and motivation to study L2 writing. At the end of their fourth year in university, they were again interviewed about what they thought had led to changes in their L2 writing and motivation to write in the L2 over the observation period. The results revealed that: (1) as in Sasaki (2004), those who spent some time abroad saw their L2 writing ability improve over the three and a half years, while the AH students did not; (2) although the SA students were generally more motivated to study L2 writing even before their overseas stays, their motivation became stronger after coming home, and this motivational improvement seemed to be related to their formation of "L2-related imagined communities" (p. 81), where they could imagine themselves writing in the L2 for communicative purposes (see also relevant findings in You, 2016); and (3) those who spent more than four months abroad significantly improved their L2 writing ability, compared to those who spent only one and a half to two months abroad.

All three studies agree that SA had positive effects on L2 writing ability development in terms of both product and processing. However, the differences in the findings of Sasaki (2004) and those of Sasaki (2011) also suggest that by the time data collection was conducted for Sasaki (2011), or ten years later than for Sasaki (2004), the effects of shorter stays (e.g., one and a half to two months) may have become weaker because such stays had become common and therefore less special. These differences suggest that time can be a significant mediating variable in investigations of SA effects (recall how special it was when the six Japanese women studied abroad in the 1800s). Finally, the two longitudinal studies (2004 and 2011) revealed that the effects of SA experiences could last as long as one to two years after the students' SA stay was over, even though these effects were subsequently influenced by other sociocultural factors such as being busy job-hunting (Sasaki, 2011).

## Studies That Explored Changes in L2 Text Organization and Cohesion and Growth as Multi-Competent Writers

The last group of studies were spin-offs of a series of studies conducted by Kobayashi and Rinnert, who originally explored possible explanatory factors for particular rhetorical patterns emerging from texts written in Japanese participants' L1, L2, and L3 (for a summary, see Kobayashi & Rinnert, 2009). During their investigation, Kobayashi and Rinnert accidentally found that SA experiences constituted one of the factors influencing these patterns. Among their studies, I particularly focus on Kobayashi and Rinnert (2007) and (2012), which discussed the effects of the writers' past experiences and agency as they affect the writers' choices from their "repertoire of writing knowledge" (2012, p. 105). These studies are unique in that their results reveal not only the one-way influence of SA instruction on the participants' L2 writing but also interactions between L1, L2, and possibly L3 knowledge about writing.

First, Kobayashi and Rinnert (2007) compared three groups: Group 1 ($n = 10$), consisting of university students who received only L1 writing instruction mainly in high school; Group 2 ($n = 10$), consisting of university students who received L1 writing instruction mainly in high school and L2 instruction during their two-semester-long stay in L2-speaking countries; and Group 3 ($n = 5$), consisting of graduate students and teachers who spent three and a half to 14 years in English-speaking countries. All participants wrote compositions in both their L1 and L2 on one of two topics. They were also interviewed for two to three hours "about the construction of the texts and decisions made during the writing process as well as the writers' perceptions of L1 and L2 writing and possible background influences" (p. 95). The results related to effects of SA on L2 writing included the following: (1) Groups 2 and 3, which had overseas experiences, used "counterargument with refutation" (p. 96) twice as often in the L1 as in the L2 (60% in the L1 and 33% in the L2), whereas Group 1 used this strategy with the same frequency (30%) in the L1 as in the L2; (2) Groups 2 and 3's more frequent use of counterargument was transferred from the L2 writing instruction they had previously received inside and outside Japan because they knew its value, even if some of them were not confident about using it in the L2; and (3) Group 3 used specific contextualization (e.g., defining terms) in the introduction to both the L1 and L2 compositions much more frequently than did Groups 1 and 2, a finding that can be attributed to Group 3's extensive L2 writing training in their academic fields they received overseas. These findings show that the students did not simply apply the knowledge and skills they had acquired overseas to the given tasks. Rather, their final choice of the most appropriate rhetorical patterns was the result of complex decision-making processes based on their evaluation of the situation.

Turning to the second study, Kobayashi and Rinnert (2012), I focus on its second half because the first overlapped with Kobayashi and Rinnert (2007). This was a case study of Natsu, one of the Group 2 participants in Kobayashi and Rinnert (2007), which followed her development as a multilingual writer for the subsequent two and a half years after they collected her data as a Group 2 member. The authors used the first half of Kobayashi and Rinnert (2012) "to determine where Natsu stood in terms of linguistic development and text construction" (p. 11). Natsu spent three years in Australia as a high school student before entering a university in Japan, where she majored in Chinese. Kobayashi and Rinnert collected Natsu's Japanese L1 and English L2 argumentative compositions in her third year in university (Time 1), and her L1, L2, and Chinese L3 argumentative compositions two and a half years later (Time 2) after Natsu spent one year in China as a Chinese major. Kobayashi and Rinnert also interviewed Natsu for a total of 80 hours and corresponded with her by email during the two-and-a-half-year observation period. Kobayashi and Rinnert's findings related to Natsu's overseas experiences are as follows: (1) the structure of Natsu's L2 composition at Time 1 was based not only on the knowledge she had acquired in Australia but also on her knowledge of L1 writing; (2) her Time 2 essays in the L1, L2, and L3 shared a common structure of "justification" (i.e., presenting a position and supporting it with clear reasons and evidence; p. 114) because by this time, she had come to believe that this type of argumentative construction was effective across languages; however, (3) she also added some "language-specific text features . . . in order to appeal to the prospective audience" (p. 122), a strategy she had learned through formal instruction and self-training for the L2 and during her stay in China for the L3. For example, she ended her Time 2 Chinese compositions with a four-word idiom because she believed that it was a common and effective way to end a Chinese composition. These findings suggest that the effects of SA experiences become incorporated over time into learners' multi-competent linguistic "repertoire" (p. 101) and are then utilized in their evaluation of the given contexts (see You, 2016 for similar findings).

## Suggestions for Future Studies

I conclude this chapter by suggesting directions for SA-related studies of L2 writing. I agree with Cumming (2011) that L2 writing research should aim "to improve educational policies and instructional practices" (p. 223). However, suggestions for improving these practices should be tailored to each situation and time. These goals guide my suggestions. First, as regards L2 writing ability, studies should examine multiple aspects of language ability and processing, especially how these aspects interact with each other, as well as with other cognitive and environmental factors, as L2 learners develop as writers. With Llanes, Tragant, and Serrano (2012) as a rare model for such work, studies should target various aspects such as fluency, complexity, and accuracy as well as their interactions with other SA-related internal and external factors such as motivation and L2 contact hours. Inclusion of writing processes such as writing strategy use, as in Sasaki (2007), is also desirable. Furthermore, given today's rapid globalization, writing on the internet (e.g., Twitter or Facebook posts) may be another candidate as a research target. Related to this issue, SA contexts should be varied and not be confined to those already investigated (e.g., the US for Japanese learners) so as to permit more multicultural perspectives.

As regards the non-deficit view of L2 learning, I recommend that studies follow learners' development as effective L2 writers rather than as would-be native-like writers. If participants' final achievement is to be assessed against specific norms, these norms should be those of L2 users who have reached the goals the participants are currently aiming at. For example, Sasaki (2004) compared SA students with L2 writing experts who participated in Sasaki (2002), not as native speakers of that language but as L2 users regularly writing academic papers in the L2 for professional purposes. Such professional L2 use may be appropriate for the purpose of gauging the effects of SA experiences if the ultimate goal of the L2 instruction is to develop high-level academic writing abilities in non-L2 dominant contexts (e.g., academic English writing classes in Japanese universities). On the other hand, if the contexts and students are multilingual (e.g., Spanish or Basque as an L1 and English as an L2, as reported by Cenoz & Gorter, 2011), and the students' aim is to write effective messages for an online social network (e.g., part of the data used in Cenoz & Gorter), the gauge needed to assess SA impacts on the students' multilingual repertoire may be completely different (e.g., how best they can use their multilingual repertoire as resources to accomplish the given goal). However, studies of learners' L2 writing development in such multilingual contexts are few, and the topic remains to be investigated in future studies (see also Jarvis, 2013).

## 152 Miyuki Sasaki

Third, in a context where the number of quantitative or mixed-methods studies, as exemplified by Llanes et al. (2012), is increasing (e.g., Muñoz & Llanes, 2014), synthetic studies such as meta-analyses of SA-related studies of L2 writing ability would inform us regarding the general and overall effects of SA experiences on L2 writers' development. Although meta-analyses based on various types of L2 abilities, including those introduced in the present chapter, have started to appear (e.g., Yang, 2016), they need refinements, including surveying a more exhaustive number of studies (Cooper, 2017). Alternatively, as suggested above, replicating previously conducted studies can also be meaningful with time as the intervening variable. Investigation of which types of abilities and skills did (or did not) improve between the two different periods when the studies were conducted would suggest what should be prioritized when we plan effective SA programs.

Lastly, I would like to see more longitudinal SA-related case studies of L2 writers. Among the L2 writing studies reviewed in the previous section, Kobayashi and Rinnert's (2012) study of Natsu is exemplary in that it followed how a learner's knowledge of writing led her over time to become multi-competent, and how her repertoire of writing knowledge was strategically applied to writing in the L1, L2, and L3 across different contexts. In particular, this study achieves high ecological validity by using both the participant's writing in these three languages (etic data) and her accounts of how and why she wrote in them as she did (emic data). Given this ecologically sound methodology, even longer observation periods may be needed once the participants return home, as we saw in Sasaki (2011), which observed the participants for as long as two and a half years after they came home, or ideally even longer, involving learners similar to the first five Japanese women whom I introduced at the beginning of this chapter. By combining such detailed, long-term case studies with the results of large-scale meta analyses and replication studies, we may be able to see patterns shared by groups coexisting with unique cases such as Natsu, especially over longer periods of time. Recall that Tei and Ryo's discontinuation of their studies was unique and unexpected. However, the fact that none of the five improved in their English ability because they all lived together with only one English-speaking governess concurs with the findings of many SA studies (e.g., Taguchi, 2008), which emphasize the importance of contact time with the target language.

## Acknowledgments

I would like to thank Paul Bruthiaux and Hiroe Kobayashi for their valuable comments and suggestions. The preparation of this paper was aided by the 2016-2018 Abe Fellowship granted by the Social Science Research Council and the Japan Foundation Center for Global Partnership as well as Research Grant No. 20520533 for the 2012–2016 academic years from the Japan Society for the Promotion of Science.

# References

Allen, H. W., & Herron, C. (2003). A mixed-methodology investigation of the linguistic and affective outcomes of summer study abroad. *Foreign Language Annals, 36*, 370–385.

Bachman, L., & Palmer, A. (2010). *Language assessment in practice*. Oxford: Oxford University Press.

Brecht, R. D., Davidson, D. E., & Ginsberg, R. B. (1995). Predictors of foreign language gain during study abroad. In B. F. Freed (Ed.), *Second language acquisition in a study abroad context* (pp. 37–66). Amsterdam: John Benjamins.

Carroll, J. B. (1967). Foreign language proficiency levels attained by language majors near graduation from college. *Foreign Language Annals, 1*, 131–151.

Cenoz, J., & Gorter, D. (2011). Focus on multilingualism: A study of trilingual writing. *Modern Language Journal, 95*, 356–369.

Churchill, E., & Dufon, M. A. (2006). Evolving threads in study abroad research. In M. A. Dufon, & E. Churchill (Eds.), *Language learners in study abroad contexts* (pp. 1–27). Clevedon: Multilingual Matters.

Cooper, H. (2017). *Research synthesis and meta-analysis* (5th ed.). Los Angeles, CA: SAGE.

Cubillos, J. H., Chieffo, L., & Fan, C. (2008). The impact of short-term study abroad programs on L2 listening comprehension skills. *Foreign Language Annals, 41*, 157–185.

Cumming, A. (2011). The contribution of studies of foreign language writing to research, theories, and policies. In R. M. Manchón (Ed.), *Writing in foreign language contexts: Learning, teaching, and research* (pp. 209–231). Bristol: Multilingual Matters.

Dewey, D. P. (2004). A comparison of reading development by learners of Japanese in intensive domestic immersion and study abroad contexts. *Studies in Second Language Acquisition, 26*, 303–327.

Ferris, D. R., & Hedgcock, J. S. (2014). *Teaching L2 composition*. New York: Routledge.

Fraiberg, S., Wang, X., & You, X. (2017). *Inventing the world grant university: Chinese international students' mobilities, literacies, and identities*. Logan, UT: Utah State University Press.

Freed, F. B. (Ed.). (1995). *Second language acquisition in a study abroad context*. New York: John Benjamins.

Freed, F. B., Segalowitz, N., & Dewey, D. P. (2004). Context of learning and second language fluency in French. *Studies in Second Language Acquisition, 26*, 275–301.

Freed, B., So, S., & Lazar, N. A. (2003). Language learning abroad: How do gains in written fluency compare with gains in oral fluency in French as a second language? *ADFL Bulletin, 34*(3), 34–40.

Furuki, Y., Althaus, M., Hirata, Y., Ichimata, T., Iino, M., Iwahara, A., & Ueda, A. (Eds.). (1991). *The attic letters: Ume Tsuda's correspondence to her American mother*. New York: Weatherhill.

Hassall, T. (2006). Leaning to take leave in social conversations: A diary study. In M. A. Dufon, & E. Churchill (Eds.), *Language learners in study abroad contexts* (pp. 31–46). Clevedon: Multilingual Matters.

Jarvis, S. (2013). Crosslinguistic influence and multilingualism. In C. Chapelle (Ed.), *The encyclopedia of applied linguistics*. Malden, MA: Blackwell.

Kaplan, M. A. (1989). French in the community: A survey of language use abroad. *French Review, 63*(2), 290–301.

Kinginger, C. (2008). Language learning in study abroad: Case studies of Americans in France. *Modern Language Journal, 92*(s1), Monograph Issue, 1–124.

Kinginger, C. (2009). *Language learning and study abroad: A critical reading of research*. New York: Palgrave Macmillan.

Kobayashi, H., & Rinnert, C. (2007). Transferability of argumentative writing competence from L2 to L2: Effects of overseas experience. In M. Conrick, & M. Howard (Eds.), *From applied linguistics to linguistics applied: Issues, practices, trends* (pp. 91–110). London: British Association of Applied Linguistics.

Kobayashi, H., & Rinnert, C. (2009). Situated writing practices in foreign language settings: The role of previous experience and instruction. In R. M. Manchón (Ed.), *Writing in foreign language contexts: Learning, teaching, and research* (pp. 23–48). Bristol: Multilingual Matters.

Kobayashi, H., & Rinnert, C. (2012). Understanding L2 writing development from a multicompetence perspective: Dynamic repertoires of knowledge and text construction. In R. M. Manchón (Ed.), *L2 writing development: Multiple perspectives* (pp. 101–134). Boston, MA: De Gruyter Mouton.

Lafford, B. A. (1995). Getting into, through, and out of a survival situation: A comparison of communicative strategies used by students studying Spanish abroad and at home. In B. F. Freed (Ed.), *Second language acquisition in a study abroad context* (pp. 97–121). Amsterdam: John Benjamins.

Llanes, A., Tragant, E., & Serrano, R. (2012). The role of individual differences in a study abroad experience: The case of Erasmus students. *International Journal of Multilingualism, 9*(3), 318–342.

Ministry of Education, Culture, Sports, Science, and Technology, Japan. (2012, January). *Nihonjin no kaigai ryuugaku koukyou* [*Trends among Japanese studying abroad*]. Tokyo.

Muñoz, C., & Llanes, A. (2014). Study abroad and changes in degree of foreign accent in children and adults. *Modern Language Journal, 98*, 432–449.

Ortega, L. (2011). SLA after the social turn: Where cognitivism and its alternatives stand. In D. Atkinson (Ed.), *Alternative approaches to second language acquisition* (pp. 167–180). London: Routledge.

Ortega, L., & Iberri-Shea, G. (2005). Longitudinal research in second language acquisition: Recent trends and future directions. *Annual Review of Applied Linguistics, 25*, 26–45.

Pérez-Vidal, C., & Juan-Garau, M. (2011). The effect of context and input conditions on oral and written development: A study abroad perspective. *International Review of Applied Linguistics, 49*, 157–185.

Roever, C (2011). Testing of second language pragmatics: Past and future. *Language Testing, 28*(4), 463–481.

Sasaki, M. (2002). Building an empirically-based model of EFL learners' writing processes. In S. Ransdell & M-L. Barbier (Ed.). *New directions for research in L2 writing* (pp. 49–80). Amsterdam: Kluwer Academic.

Sasaki, M. (2004). A multiple-data analysis of the 3.5-year development of EFL student writers. *Language Learning, 54*(3), 525–582.

Sasaki, M. (2007). Effects of study-abroad experiences on EFL writers: A multiple-data analysis. *Modern Language Journal, 91*, 602–620.

Sasaki, M. (2011). Effects of varying lengths of study-abroad experiences on Japanese EFL students' L2 writing ability and motivation: A longitudinal study. *TESOL Quarterly, 45*, 81–105.

Segalowitz, N., & Freed, B. F. (2004). Learning Spanish in at home and study abroad contexts. *Studies in Second Language Acquisition, 26*, 173–199.

Siegal, M. (1996). The role of learner subjectivity in second language sociolinguistic competence: Western women learning Japanese. *Applied Linguistics, 17*, 356–382.

Taguchi, N. (2008). Cognition, language contact, and the development of pragmatic comprehension in a study-abroad context. *Language Learning, 58*(1), 33–71.

Terasawa, R. (2009). *Meiji no joshi ryuugakusei* [*Women who studied abroad during the Meiji period*]. Tokyo: Heibonsha.

Walker, B. L. (2015). *A concise history of Japan*. Cambridge: Cambridge University Press.

Yang, J. (2016). The effectiveness of study-abroad on second language learning: A meta-analysis. *Canadian Modern Language Review, 72,* 66–94.

You, X. (2016). *Cosmopolitan English and transliteracy*. Carbondale, IL: Southern Illinois University Press.

# 9

# FROM ACTIVITY TO MOBILITY SYSTEMS

## Tracing Multilingual Literacies on the Move

*Steven Fraiberg*

## Introduction

A wide range of scholarship in academic literacies has examined how actors develop disciplinary identities and practices as part of a process of enculturation (Bartholomae, 1986; Casanave, 2002; Haas, 1994; Ivanič, 1998; Lillis, 2003; Prior, 1998; Russell & Yañez, 2003; Spack, 1997; Zamel & Spack, 2004). In relation to teaching and learning, this approach has largely conceptualized learning as a process in which students are socialized into ways of reading, writing, researching, and being in the world. More particularly, in relation to transnational and multilingual language learners, a number of studies have traced students' literate and academic trajectories as they move in and across genres, classrooms, and disciplines. While much of this work has been critical in developing richer insight into how students learn to navigate the university as actors accumulate knowledge and literate practices in their disciplines, the academic literature as a whole has largely focused on how students move in and across *official* institutional spaces: classrooms, writing centers, student-teacher conferences, textbooks, and journals. Alternatively, less attention has been devoted to the ways that an array of other "unofficial" spaces, technologies, languages, and literacies brokers or sponsors shaping students' language and literacies. This broader unit of analysis is particularly important as part of a more holistic approach and developing a richer understanding of ways that students' out of classroom literacies mediate students' literate lives in school settings. Theoretically and methodologically, this analytic shift is furthermore critical in a challenge to structuralist and container models perpetuating static, autonomous, and fixed notions of literacy, space, and culture. Predominantly grounded in the theoretical constructs of discourse communities (Hymes, 1974) and communities of practice (CoP) (Wenger, 1998), much of the academic literacies scholarship linked to these concepts, as Prior (1998) argues, are only a partial break from this bounded approach (see also Roozen & Erickson, 2017, for a similar critique). The following case study is aimed at upending such models to better understand not only ways that students learn to "invent" the university, but also how the university itself is being reinvented. This is part of a dynamic process shaping and shaped in everyday moments of practice. In this fashion, the following case links local literacy practices to wider sociomaterial contexts.

To accomplish these aims, I align the analysis with a growing body of work in composition identified as translingualism (Canagarajah, 2013; Horner, Lu, Royster, & Trimbur, 2011). The prefix *trans-* was adopted to better articulate the dynamic, contested, and transformative nature of language practices. This approach is characterized by a theoretical shift away from monolingual ideologies and towards less discrete and bounded conceptions of language. Moreover, undergirding these moves is a shift away from deficit models toward a conception of language differences and diversity as a resource. Yet despite a broad-based focus on these analytic issues, translingual methods have yet to be fully theorized or articulated. To better conceptualize the dynamic and fluid nature of translingual activity, I draw on and extend a "mobile literacies" (Lorimer Leonard, 2013; Nordquist, 2017) approach. This frame attends to actors "on the move" as they shape and are shaped by everyday literacy practices and activities. Central to this approach is attention to the complex coordination of activity and the ways that this process affords and constrains social and geographic trajectories. This analytic lens is grounded in questions linked to the politics of mobility: who moves, when they move, how they move, and to what effect. To more closely glimpse the effects, I turn to a telling case of a first-year Chinese international student with attention to the deeply distributed, mediated, dynamic, and material nature of her literacy processes and practices. Scholars have recently argued for the need to shift from a focus on linguistic repertoires to spatial ones (Canagarajah, 2017; Pennycook & Otsuji, 2014). The case study highlights both the need for this approach and strategies attending more fully to this process.

## Mobility Systems

This analysis is taken from a long-term study focused on global shifts in higher education and the rapid increase of the Chinese international student population at Michigan State University (MSU). Founded as a land grant college under the Morrill Act in 1862, MSU's mission has been traditionally to serve the state and the local community by making education accessible to the underprivileged and working class. Linked to a sluggish Michigan economy along with disinvestment in higher education, however, the university has been forced to make up for shortages in funding by turning to out-of-state and international students who pay three times the in-state tuition. As a result, the Chinese international student population rapidly increased from 2% of the student body in 2007 to approximately 10% in 2014 (MSU Office of the Registrar). Across campus and in classrooms these large-scale shifts have disrupted traditional curricular structures, classroom practices, and pedagogies. As a result, there has been an increasing need to better understand how these students (1) think about and "do" literacy and (2) ways this process mediates the development of their academic (and non-academic) literacies and identities as they learn to navigate the university. Closely attending to these issues, a focus on the lived literacy practices of the Chinese international student community further provides broader theoretical and methodological insight into the relational, material, and spatialized nature of this process.

To map out how students' mobile practices are bound up in the construction of students' literate lives, I draw on and extend Cultural-Historical Activity Theory (CHAT) (Engeström, 1987; Prior & Shipka, 2003; Prior, 2004; Bazerman & Russell, 2003; Spinuzzi, 2008; Wertsch, 1991). Central to this framework is the notion that individual identities cannot be understood apart from tools-in-use (Wertsch, 1991). Tools are sedimented with ideologies that orient and get oriented by the actors in moments of everyday practice. This process mediates "trajectories of participation" (Dreier, 1999) across scenes of literacy as literate identities stabilize and thicken over time. To study this process in the context of increasingly transnational flows of actors across a global eduscapes (Luke, 2006), I shift from CHAT's traditionally bounded focus on an activity system (Engeström, 1987) towards a mobility system (Fraiberg, Wang, & You, 2017; Nordquist, 2017; Urry, 2003). This concept is imagined as an assemblage of texts, tools, tropes, and ideologies complexly distributed across space and time. This system in-the-making mediates actors' movements in and across social and geographic spaces as part of a complex struggle. Useful for understanding this fluid interplay is "knotworking" (Prior & Shipka, 2003), or the complex orchestration of activity involving the tying and untying of actors and objects dispersed across near and far-flung spaces. This process shapes the alignments of the participants, the coordination of activity, and the fluid networks forming the pathways through which signs, symbols, and actors circulate. Taking up this frame, space itself is imagined as a knotwork or complex entanglement of densely knotted streams of activity, analogous to Bakhtin's (1981) chronotope. Consequently, mapping literate identities necessitates the tracing of trajectories of participation across scenes of writing, or "laminated chronotopes" (Prior & Shipka, 2003), as literate actors mobilize complex webs of resources.

## Mobile Methods

Applying this perspective to international student mobility uncovers how various material resources afford and constrain student movements in and across global eduscapes. To look more specifically at how this framework serves as a lens for studying transnational actors' complex literate trajectories, I draw on and extend a longitudinal study of a Chinese international student (Fraiberg et al., 2017) who first arrived at the university in 2013. Core to the story is the ways this participant, Yisi, mobilizes a complex web of human and non-human actors (Latour, 1999) that shapes her literate pathway. To more systematically map out this process, I identify key literacy sponsors or brokers mediating her literate trajectory. Deborah Brandt (2001) defines a sponsor as "agents local or distant, concrete or abstract, who enable, support, teach, model, as well as recruit, regulate, suppress, or withhold literacy—and gain advantage of it in some way" (p. 167). Further extending the concept while situating it within the new materialism, Jon Wargo and Peter De Costa (2017) take up the term "literacy sponsorscape." The term is intended to account for the globally distributed nature of literacy sponsorship, as well as how an array of humans and non-humans broker literacy and learning. Taking up this concept as an analytic frame, I attend to key actors (people, institutions, technologies, languages, tropes) that mediated Yisi's academic pathways. More particularly, I attend to three analytically separate but intertwined moves (Latour, 2005).

First, I localized the global. This move is grounded in the notion of keeping an analysis "flat" or rhizomatic to make visible extended chains of actors without jumping, breaking, or tearing. Keeping this principle in mind, I charted transnational flows of people, imaginaries, and things as they were recontextualized or "translated" across space and time (i.e., across people, genres, language, modes, and spaces). For instance, in the writing of a student paper, one might trace how a conversation with an instructor in class (in English) is recontextualized into written notes (in a mixture of Chinese and English) and then into a conversation on a social media account (in Chinese) and then into a draft of a paper (in English and Chinese). Tracing these moments of "translation" (recontextualization) offers insight into the ways that everyday objects (e.g., student papers) and practices are stabilized over time. These are moments of struggle or friction as objects, meanings, and actors shaped and are shaped by material and social structures.

Second, I redistributed the local. This process attends to the jointly mediated nature of activity and ways it is deeply distributed across space and time. For instance, again in looking at the composing of a student paper, one might attend to how a student located in front of a laptop in coffee shop writes a question by email to a teacher, sends a text to a friend (by mobile phone), searches for the meaning of a key term or concept in an online dictionary (by laptop), and highlights in yellow marker a core point in a reading on the coffee table. In this manner, I attended to the ways a complex assemblage (or web) of actors, texts, tools, and objects is distributed across near- and distant-spaced, mediated moments of everyday practice. This was an uneven struggle as actors wove and were woven into complex sociotechnical systems (through a process of knotworking).

Third, I connected sites. In making this final move, I looked for the links, relations, and connections in the complex assemblages or networks (or knotworks) of activity.

**160** Steven Fraiberg

## One Student's Networking and Knotworking

To more specifically trace how Yisi's networks, or knotworks, of activity mediated her movement across the higher educational landscape, I turn to three key scenes shaping her literate trajectory. Illustrating the complexity of her rich network of literacy sponsors, the first was the period immediately before her departure to MSU. From the western province of Xinjiang, Yisi quickly began to mobilize a range of resources as she sought to establish a network of social connections upon learning that she was accepted to the university. Characteristic of many in her incoming class, she joined an online forum, QQ, created by a veteran student for the incoming class, as she quickly began to form a web of relationships. This included locating roommates, partners to travel together with on the plane and bus from the Detroit airport to the East Lansing campus, and others who could assist her with a range of questions and needs, covering everything from purchasing a cell phone plan to registering for classes. This process continued during her first weeks on campus and was recorded and shared on her WeChat microblog, which served to document as well as help build her growing network of connections. The following entry points to the complexity of her rich network of resources, in which she thanks eleven different people on a day in which everything seemed to go wrong. The entry serves to foreground her rapidly expanding social circle and ways it served as a distributed network, or knotwork, of actors and resources mediating her movement across the university.

> ### September 3, 2013
>
> 今天实在太糟糕了，各种巧合不好的事情。谢谢帮我指导电脑和打印的翼飞同学，帮我弄好 mail 的神烦同学，拔刀相助的kk还有铁老板，还有鼓励我的歌姐姐糖糖，自己忙数学还帮我的师傅，不认识的不收我钱的出租车司机，还有教我读阿拉伯语的很厉害的那个同学，还有kk的小伙伴，还有陪着我的毛线，还有越洋安慰的学长，真的很好。
>
> (Today was so bad, all bad things happened together. Thank Yifei who helped me with the computer and printing, thank Shenfan who helped me with email, thank kk and Tie Laoban who were willing to help me, thank Ge Sister and Tangtang who encouraged me, thank *shifu* [teacher] who helped me even when he was busy with math himself, thank the stranger cab driver who didn't charge me, thank the person who taught me to pronounce Arabic, thank kk's friend, and thank Maoxian who was with me, thank study brother who comforted me overseas. Really nice.)

Uncovered in this entry are Yisi's multilayered relational networks. This included friends, friends of friends, and even the local cab driver whom she thanked for not charging her. These varied actors also offered multiple forms of support. This included technical assistance with her computer, email, and printing. The web of support further included moral encouragement from both friends situated locally as well as her old deskmate still residing in China. Finally, she received assistance with her academic studies from two key friends who served as her "teachers." The first was someone whom she referred to as "*shifu*" (teacher). This person had helped her even when he was busy with his math homework. The second person, whose name she had not learned, would later become a central figure in her social and professional trajectory who "taught" her correct pronunciation for her Arabic course. Together this complex and dynamic web or assemblage formed part of a literacy sponsorscape. In this fashion, Yisi's networking, or knotworking, mediated the ways that she moved in and across the university.

One key cultural term or trope within Chinese society shaping (and shaped by) this process is referred to as "*guanxi.*" Broadly, the term refers to a complex system of exchanges through which one leverages a relationship with the purpose of gaining a personal advantage (Lu, 2000): e.g., finding a job, acceptance to a school, preferential treatment, and so forth. A *guanxi* relationship can involve, for instance, a friend, friend of a friend, former classmate, current associate, and so on. More broadly, *guanxi wang* (a network of connections) is embedded in the structure of society and serves as a type of "currency" (Shef as cited in Lu, 2000, p. 15). Within literacy studies the term has been most notably used by Hawisher and Selfe (2006), who link the term to Bourdieu's (1977) notions of social capital and *habitus*, as a framework for tracing two Chinese transnational students' literate trajectories and acquisition of English. In a similar fashion, this wider cultural trope served as an actant bound up in Yisi's network or knotwork. Critically, the concept *guanxi* itself is further not imagined as static, but as dynamic, contested, and continually being reconfigured in moments of everyday practice.

To more closely look at how this process influenced the development of her academic and disciplinary writing, I turn to the second scene that revolves around a first-year women's literature course Yisi took as part of her major. The course specifically focused on Western feminist literature, and for her first paper Yisi was writing an analysis of Kate Chopin's *Awakening.* Yisi had performed poorly on the assignment, and her instructor had requested a meeting in her office while encouraging her to drop the course. Unnerved and concerned that her plans to pursue a degree in creative writing were already in jeopardy, she enlisted me for assistance.

To more closely examine the activity and material nature of Yisi's literacy practices, I draw on video clips and transcripts of our interactions. Notable is my own participation as an actor who was being enlisted into her relationship web. This interaction was part of a complex exchange. Just as Yisi was leveraging my expertise and position within the university for assistance with her paper, so too was I leveraging her as a participant in the study who could offer data. In this fashion, our positions indexed broader social roles, structures, and orders of discourse. Structuring the ways we ordered our activity was my request to see a copy of her paper. However, quickly realizing that she did not have it with her, she attempted to have a friend send her a copy from another computer. As she had not yet purchased a copy of a word processing program, she had borrowed her roommate's computer where the paper still resided. The fact serves as evidence of a complex sociotechnical network, or sponsorscape, mediating her literacy practices. The fine-grained look at the following scene is grounded in the notion that contradictions and breakdowns can serve to uncover routinized processes and practices that normally remain invisible and difficult to study because they are "so fast, fluent, dense and condensed" (Prior, 2008, p. 3). The interaction is taken from a meeting on September 27, 2013, at a conference room table where we set our computers, notepads, cell phones, and other materials. As will be discussed, these texts, tools, and objects formed part of a complex sociotechnical network, or knotwork, mediating our alignments and interactions. I have specifically identified four key moments during the meeting that foreground ways Yisi drew on widely distributed networks or knotworks.

## Moment 1

Meeting about her assignment as well as a range of other issues, the first key moment begins as she realizes that her paper is on her roommate's computer. As a result, she uses her iPhone to call her roommate (Figure 9.1) only to discover that she is tied up at the social security office receiving a social security number. Her roommate's own visit to a government office points to complex ways that the students negotiated wider bureaucratic and regulatory regimes that structured their mobilities. More broadly, the everyday, mundane, and routine practice of calling

**FIGURE 9.1** Using iPhone to Contact Friend at Social Security Office

From Activity to Mobility Systems    163

**FIGURE 9.2**  Using WeChat Voice to Contact Other Roommates

her roommate by iPhone points to the ways that digital and cultural assemblages (i.e., *guanxi* networks) were complexly knotted.

## Moment 2

Continuing to trace her sociotechnical web of activity, the next key moment unfolded a few minutes later. Yisi had decided to try her other two roommates, only this time trying to contact them using WeChat voice (Figure 9.2). WeChat is a popular social media application in China that allows participants to chat (using text or video) and to leave voice messages; she left two messages in quick succession. Continuing to problem solve, she simultaneously remembered that she printed out the paper on another friend's computer, where the file also resided. Attempting to contact him from her laptop using the social media application, QQ, she rapidly typed a message using the chat feature. In this fashion, we can further glimpse part of a complex media ecology (iPhone, WeChat voice, QQ) that jointly coordinated a deeply distributed network, or knotwork, forming part of her wider literacy sponsorscape.

## Moment 3

As we engaged in other activities, our conversation was soon interrupted by a response from her friend with the printer, who explained he was at lunch, but would soon return to his room to email the essay. Once again using the QQ chat feature (Figure 9.3) to communicate, she continued to leverage various media, as part of a process through which her networks, or knotworks, were continually under construction.

**FIGURE 9.3** Use of QQ Chat

## Moment 4

Approximately an hour into our meeting, she finally received the essay, only to encounter a problem downloading the file. This caused her to troubleshoot the issue with her friend in an exchange on QQ (chat) that then shifted to WeChat (voice) (Figure 9.4). At this juncture, she explained to me her preference for WeChat since it was more portable on her iPhone, with people generally more readily available. In this manner, she voiced a media ideology recognizing the affordances and constraints of different forms of media as she mobilized them in orchestrating her relationship web. In this fashion, an assemblage of technologies and actors formed part of a complex mobility system or sponsorscape, as she strategically drew on a range of resources that helped her traverse the higher educational landscape.

Revising the paper over a period of days, Yisi further continued to draw on a rich range of resources, including meetings with me, email conversations with her former American teacher Mark who had returned to Chicago, and exchanges with her IELTS (International English Language Testing System) teacher Tina, who was still residing in China and now working at a bank. Indebted to Tina for her help, Yisi noted that her former tutor really was not obligated to assist, since her parents maintained no interpersonal connections. The sentiment indexes a wider set of obligations and cultural roles and expectations that mediated her practices and movement across the university. Yisi also continued to consult with a friend by WeChat and email, through which she received detailed responses to her paper using the Microsoft comments feature. This friend, James (whose English name was a reference to the basketball player LeBron James), who had been her deskmate in school, was a person who might be helpful for assisting with grammar. Seeking the assistance of various connections, she specifically

**FIGURE 9.4** Using QQ and WeChat Voice

assessed the talents of each as she strategically selected them according to her shifting sets of needs. In this manner, she continued to network, or knotwork, as she traversed global eduscapes.

## Networks, or Knotworks, in the Making

The following semester her in-class and out-of-class social networks became increasingly entangled, as Yisi enlisted a new actor into her relationship web. In this fashion, her social networks continued to serve as a mobility system under construction, mediating how she traversed the university. This third scene begins with a high school friend who was attending Purdue University. Through this friend, Yisi had become acquainted with an online magazine about Chinese international students living abroad, for which she began to write. Becoming friends with the magazine President, who she referred to as She Zhang (leader), she learned that he had minored in Old English literature. Recognizing him as a resource, Yisi had begun to seek his help with her academic English. For instance, Yisi was involved in an undergraduate research project with the need to create a poster presentation for an end-of-the-year conference. As it was the first time that she had engaged in such an activity and she was anxious about using her English in a professional context, she consulted with She Zhang for feedback. They developed a list of questions and rehearsed over the phone. In this fashion, she continued to extend her relationship webs as they became densely knotted into her in-class activity.

She furthermore turned to him for assistance with an end-of-the-year presentation for a composition course with the theme "women in America." Working on a draft of the presentation, she first set out to create video subtitles for her English-speaking audience with the assistance of her roommate's boyfriend, who as computer science major could provide technical support. Once the translations

**166** Steven Fraiberg

were complete, she worked throughout the night on drafting a script that she sent to She Zhang for review. Reading the draft, the "leader" did not want to simply make corrections, because he thought the next time she might run into a similar situation without having learned. Consequently, he suggested they review the script together on Google Docs, in order to work and edit the text simultaneously, as they carefully went through the structure, language, and other details into the early morning hours. With the online activity serving as an educational space, Yisi noted the process "took a long time because he tried to be the *teacher* [emphasis added]." In this fashion, the actors in her social network, or knotwork, continued to broker her learning and academic trajectory. Moving on to the revision of a paper based on the presentation, the pair again engaged in an extended feedback session. Recorded with a screen capture program, the following transcript documents the conversation unfolding in real-time (April 28, 2014).

*She Zhang:*  这句话可以改的更书面一些～
(This sentence could be changed into more formal language)

*Yisi:*  怎么改［她删除了，然后改成］我想想哦
(How to revise? [she deletes what she typed] Let me think about this.)

*She Zhang:*  还是说这是演讲稿
(Or is it a speech?)

*Yisi:*  不是，作文啦
(No, it is an essay.)

*She Zhang:*  那totally需要书面一些
(Then, it totally needs to be more formal.)

*Yisi:*  好的!
(Ok!)

*She Zhang:*  来看看这两句的区别
(Come and see the differences between these two sentences.)

*Yisi:*  好
(Ok.)

*Yisi:*  感觉更加工整了。社长你好厉害。要是有一个英语能和你一样强，我睡觉都能乐醒。
(I think the new one is neater. She Zhang, you are awesome. If one day my English could be as good as yours, I will be smiling in my sleep.)

*She Zhang:*  嘻嘻学拉丁文吧～～～
(Haha you should learn Latin.)

*Yisi:*  句子更简洁了[她删除了，然后改成] 这句好像。。。越改。。。越奇怪了
(It is simpler and clearer [she deletes what she typed]. This sentence seems like, the more I revise, the weirder it becomes.)

*She Zhang:*  因为和上面木有衔接。突然冒出来 selective display. 一开始总起，广告日益重要，广告影响三观，然后突然到了 selective display.

(Because it is not connected to the sentence above. The expression "selective display" comes from nowhere. The essay starts by making a statement that advertisements are increasingly important because they can affect people's values. Then it suddenly starts to talk about "selective display.")

*Yisi:* 所以要加阐述么。对,可以这么说。

(So I need to explain here? Yes, this is right.)

*She Zhang:* 亲爱的加点东西吧

(Dear you should add something here.)

*Yisi:* 广告影响着人们的选择,人们的价值观,但是广告为了售卖商品,在大部分情况下,选择了选择性的展示。

(Advertisements can affect people's choice, people's value, but their purpose is to sell products. So in most cases advertisements choose to display things selectively.)

*Yisi:* 广告并不是完全诚实的。选择性展示的广告对美国女性产生巨大的影响,其中包括很多负面影响。

(Advertisements are not entirely honest. Selective display also has great influence on American females, including a lot of negative influence.)

*Yisi:* [修改了文中的一句话]这样呢

(How about this?)

Working together on the revision, the exchange covered a range of issues, including organization, genre, tone, and word choice. For example, focusing broadly on the genre and mode, She Zhang clarified differences between creating a presentation and a paper, arguing that the latter was more "formal." In order to illustrate the differences, he subsequently composed a sentence so that Yisi could compare to the original. In response, Yisi lavishly praised his abilities, saying that she could only dream of one day aspiring to his level of English. However, in the background Yisi joked with her roommate: "every time when She Zhang made a revision to my essay I was trying my best to say nice things about him. I was like 'She Zhang you're so awesome.' 'She Zhang I didn't realize that a sentence could be written like this.'" While genuinely appreciative of She Zhang's help, Yisi also engaged face work and impression management as she strategically positioned herself in her complex relationship web. It is more broadly through such moves that she developed her mobile academic and literate practices.

## Conclusion

In sum, this case illustrates the need to attend to the jointly and complexly mediated activities as actors continually weave and are woven into wider social systems. As Yisi's practices illustrate, her continual networking, or knotworking, was part of a mobility system in the making. This system included an array of actors, objects, and media. It is the continual orchestration of these webs of activity that mediated how she navigated, and, in Bartholomae's (1986) terms, was learning to invent the university. As such, the study points to the need to situate writing and disciplinary enculturation in broader contexts that conceptualize them as a dynamic, embodied, and deeply distributed. Challenging national and classroom container models, Yisi's case points to how the manner in which she ordered her literacy practices was complexly linked to a wider re-ordering within a globalizing educational landscape. It is to these processes that we must turn as higher education is increasingly entangled in global contexts.

## References

Bakhtin, M. M. (1981). *The dialogic imagination: Four essays by M.M. Bakhtin* (Ed. M. E. Holquist, Trans., C. Emerson and M. Holquist). Austin: University of Texas Press.

Bartholomae, D. (1986). Inventing the university. *Journal of Basic Writing, 5*(1), 4–23.

Bazerman, C., & Russell, D. (Eds.). (2003). *Writing selves/writing societies: Research from activity perspectives*. Perspectives on Writing. Fort Collins, CO: The WAC Clearinghouse and Mind, Culture, and Activity.

Bourdieu, P. (1977). *Outline of a theory of practice*. Cambridge, UK: Cambridge University Press.

Brandt, D. (2001). *Literacy in American lives*. Cambridge, MA: Cambridge University Press.

Canagarajah, S. (2013). *Translingual practice: Global Englishes and cosmopolitan relations*. New York, NY: Routledge.

Canagarajah, S. (2017). Translingual practice as spatial repertoires: Expanding the paradigm beyond structuralist orientations. *Applied Linguistics, 39*, 1–25.

Casanave, C. P. (2002). *Writing games: Multicultural case studies of academic literacy practices in higher education*. Mahwah, NJ: Lawrence Erlbaum.

Dreier, O. (1999). Personal trajectories of participation across contexts of social practice. *Outlines: Critical Practice Studies, 1*(1), 5–32.

Engeström, Y. (1987). *Learning by expanding: An activity theoretical approach to developmental research*. Helsinki, Finland: Orienta-Konsultit.

Fraiberg, S., Wang, X, & You, X. (2017). *Inventing the world grant university. Chinese international students' mobilities, literacies, and identities*. Logan, UT: Utah State University Press.

Haas, C. (1994). Learning to read biology: One students' rhetorical development in college. *Written Communication, 11*(1), 43–84.

Hawisher, G. E., & Selfe, C. L. (2006). Globalization and agency: Designing and redesigning the literacies of cyberspace. *College English, 68*(6), 619–636.

Horner, B., Lu, M.-Z., Royster, J. J., & Trimbur, J. (2011). Language difference in writing: Toward a translingual approach. *College English, 73*(3), 303–321.

Hymes, D. (1974). *Foundations of sociolinguistics: An ethnographic approach*. Philadelphia, PA: University of Pennsylvania Press.

Ivanič, R. (1998). *Writing and identity: The discoursal construction of identity in academic writing*. Philadelphia, PA: John Benjamins.

Latour, B. (1999). *Pandora's hope: Essays on the reality of science studies*. Cambridge, MA: Harvard University Press.

Latour, B. (2005). *Reassembling the social: An introduction to actor-network theory*. Oxford, UK: Oxford University Press.

Lillis, T. (2003). Student writing as "academic literacies": Drawing on Bakhtin to move from critique to design. *Language and Education, 17*(3), 192–207.

Lorimer Leonard, R. (2013). Traveling literacies: Multilingual writing on the move. *Research in the Teaching of English, 48*(1), 13–39.

Lu, X. (2000). The influence of classical Chinese rhetoric on contemporary Chinese political communication and social relations. In D. R. Heisey (Ed.), *Chinese perspectives in rhetoric and communication* (pp. 3–24). Stamford, CT: Ablex.

Luke, C. (2006). Eduscapes: Knowledge capital and cultures. *Studies in Language and Capitalism, 1*(1), 97–120.

Michigan State University Office of the Registrar. (2014). *Geographical sources of students: Other countries.* Retrieved on December 18, 2015 from https://reports.esp.msu.edu/ReportServer /Pages/ReportViewer.aspx?%2fROReports2005%2fUE-GEOForeignand term_seq _id=1126.

Nordquist, B. (2017). *Literacy and mobility: Complexity, uncertainty and agency at the nexus of high school and college.* New York, NY: Routledge.

Pennycook, A., & Otsuji, E. (2014). Metrolingual multitasking and spatial repertoires: "Pizza mo two minutes coming." *Journal of Sociolinguistics, 18*(2), 161–184.

Prior, P. (1998). *Writing/disciplinarity: A sociohistoric account of literate activity in the academy.* New York, NY: Taylor Francis/LEA.

Prior, P. (2004). Tracing process: How texts come into being. In C. Bazerman & P. Prior (Eds.), *What writing does and how it does it: An introduction to analysis of texts and textual practices* (pp. 167–200). Mahwah, NJ: Lawrence Erlbaum.

Prior, P. (2008). *Flat chat? Reassembling literate activity.* Paper presented at Writing Research Across Borders, Santa Barbara, CA, February 22–24.

Prior, P., & Shipka, J. (2003). Chronotopic lamination: Tracing the contours of literate activity. In C. Bazerman, & D. R. Russell (Eds.), *Writing selves/writing society: Research from activity perspectives* (pp. 180–238). Fort Collins, CO: The WAC Clearinghouse and Mind, Culture, and Activity.

Roozen, K., & Erickson, J. (2017). *Expanding literate landscapes: Persons, practices, and sociohistoric perspectives of disciplinary development.* Logan: Computers and Composition Digital Press/Utah State University Press.

Russell, D., & Yañez, A. (2003). Big picture people rarely become historians: Genre systems and the contradictions of general education. In C. Bazerman, & D. R. Russell (Eds.), *Writing selves/writing society: Research from activity perspectives* (pp. 331–362). Fort Collins, CO: The WAC Clearinghouse and Mind, Culture, and Activity.

Spack, R. (1997). The acquisition of academic literacy in a second language: A longitudinal case study. *Written Communication, 14*(1), 3–62.

Spinuzzi, C. (2008). *Network.* Cambridge, MA: MIT Press.

Urry, J. (2003). *Global complexity.* Cambridge: Polity Press.

Wargo, J. M., & de Costa, P. I. (2017). Tracing academic literacies across contemporary literacy sponsorscapes: Mobilities, ideologies, identities, and technologies. *London Review of Education, 15*(1), 101–114.

Wenger, E. (1998). *Communities of practice: Learning, meaning, and identity.* New York, NY: Cambridge University Press.

Wertsch, J. V. (1991). Voices of the mind: A sociocultural approach to mediated action. Cambridge, MA: Harvard University Press.

Zamel, V., & Spack, R. (Eds.). (2004). *Crossing the curriculum: Multilingual learners in college classrooms.* Mahwah, NJ: Routledge.

# 10

# TECHNOLOGY-MEDIATED TRANSNATIONAL WRITING EDUCATION

## An Overview of Research and Practice

*Zhiwei Wu*

### Introduction

At the turn of the millennium, given the existing technical affordances and enhanced connectivity, educators have been increasingly called upon to develop learners' skills to cross geographical, linguistic, and cultural boundaries. As early as 1996, the American Council on the Teaching of Foreign Language (ACTFL) proposed a five-C model, urging foreign language educators to develop learners' skills in communication, culture, connection, contrast, and communities (ACTFL, 1996). A decade later, the call was reiterated by the Modern Language Association (MLA) Ad Hoc Committee on Foreign Languages, which highlighted the goal of foreign language education to develop learners' "translingual and transcultural competence" (MLA, 2007, p. 237). This exigency is also shared in the wider educational communities. It has been advocated that education in the age of globalization must cultivate "global citizenship" (UNESCO, 2014) and pursue internationalization of curricula and learning outcomes (De Wit, 2016).

In parallel with these calls, the definitions and views of literacy have been expanded to reflect the diverse communicative practices in different (combinations of) modalities. Notably, in 1996, the New London Group proposed the concept of "multiliteracies" to replace the monolithic understanding of literacy as the ability of reading and writing written texts. Multiliteracies underscore "the multiplicity of communications channels and media, and the increasing saliency of cultural and linguistic diversity" (1996, p. 63). Thus, literacy pedagogy in the new millennium must be repurposed and revamped to develop learners' abilities to cross linguistic and other representational boundaries.

It is in the context of rapid technological advances that two pedagogical approaches emerge to develop learners' multiliteracies or translingual and

Technology-Mediated Transnational Education **171**

transcultural competence. The first approach is conventionally referred to as "tele-collaboration" (Warschauer, 1996) or "online intercultural exchange" (O'Dowd, 2007; Thorne, 2010). This approach engages geographically distributed learners in virtual interaction and learning activities "for the purpose of foreign language learning and intercultural competence" (Belz, 2003, p. 2). The second approach is the global partnership programs launched in professional writing courses, to train future business practitioners to communicate effectively and efficiently in varying cultural and local contexts (Connor, Davis, De Rycker, Phillips, & Verckens, 1997; Herrington, 2010; Tesdell, 2013). These two approaches differ in their pedagogical goals and priorities. For instance, online intercultural exchange is primarily geared towards learning foreign languages and cultures, while global partnership programs focus more on preparing students for professional writing in industries that are highly globalized. Despite this, the two approaches share more commonalities than differences. First, both take advantage of technology-enabled learning opportunities to transcend various borders for learners, who are unwilling or unable to go abroad but still want to experience intercultural encounters, thereby contributing to the internationalization of curricula (De Wit, 2016). Second, the two approaches value, advocate, and forge transnational partnership, which supports the co-construction of knowledge and skills among participants. Third, they contribute to a larger education agenda in the New Literacies Movement (Jenkins, 2006), foregrounding the role of digital literacy in meaning making, communication, and negotiation and the participatory nature of literacy practices in glocal communities.

This chapter situates and reviews technology-mediated transnational writing education (TTWE) in the context of the New Literacies Movement. Although reviews of online intercultural exchange have been conducted (Guth & Helm, 2010; Helm, 2015; Lewis & O'Dowd, 2016; O'Dowd, 2013), these reviews tend to be West-centric, under-representing the research and practice that has happened or is happening in non-Western locales. To present an inclusive picture of TTWE, this chapter reports and examines research and practice across the globe. It is important to note that TTWE activities are inherently international, cross-national, and transnational. They are international because participants typically come from different countries. They are cross-national because participants transcend national borders and inhabit a third space. They are transnational because when participants are engaged in virtual communication, their identities projected, relations forged, and languages practiced all emerge from the context, defying any static or discrete nation-based grouping. Therefore, it is fair to say that TTWE is a rich site for participants to develop their cosmopolitan disposition and communicative repertoire in and across various discourse communities (You, 2016).

This chapter first reviews TTWE research and practice published over the last two decades, followed by a discussion of three prevalent issues that impede the enactment of TTWE projects as an integrated component in writing education.

Finally, this chapter argues for three perspectival changes, which hopefully would inform and guide future research and practice in TTWE.

## Review Procedure

To identify TTWE research and practice, three databases were consulted: Linguistics and Language Behavior Abstracts, Education Resources Information Center, and Google Scholar. The key words "online intercultural collaboration," "telecollaboration," "technical writing," "writing across cultures/borders," "virtual exchange," "e-tandem," "technical writing," and "writing across curriculum" were used to locate journal articles and chapters in edited volumes published between 1996 and 2016.[1] Initially, 227 entries were found in the three databases. After eliminating duplicates and non-empirical studies, 75 entries were retained for detailed analysis. The review process was based on an iterative reading of the 75 articles and chapters.[2] In the first reading, the studies were coded based on the metadata, such as language(s) used, countries involved, research questions, research methods, and research findings. In the second reading, research questions of each study were carefully examined and thematically analyzed. In the third reading, studies of the similar themes were grouped, and research findings were compared and coded. In the fourth reading, to check intra-coder reliability, one-third of the entries (i.e., 25 entries) were randomly chosen from the pool and re-coded again in terms of research themes and research findings. 100% agreement was found in the coded research themes and 96% agreement in the coded research findings. Inconsistencies were due to overlapping research findings in the same studies. After research outcomes were analyzed, TTWE practices reported in the 75 entries were grouped according to languages, institutions, and interactional models.

## Themes in TTWE Research

Three overarching themes are identified in TTWE research: interaction outcomes, interaction process, and power and identities. These research themes correspond to three general questions in transnational writing research: a) What are the learning outcomes? b) In the process of transnational writing, how do participants interact with each other? c) How does transnational writing reveal and shape learners' power differentials and/or identities?

### *Interaction Outcomes*

TTWE has been recognized as a powerful activity to develop participants' linguistic proficiency, intercultural competence, and digital literacies (Angelova & Zhao, 2016; Guth & Helm, 2012). In particular, TTWE enables learners to engage in authentic communication and target language immersion

(Fedderholdt, 2001; Pasfield-Neofitou, 2011), through which learners acquire lexical, syntactic (Edasawa & Kabata, 2007), pragmatic (Belz & Vyatkina, 2005), and generic knowledge (Connor et al., 1997). In addition, TTWE is able to enhance the understanding of home culture and target culture (Liaw, 2006), sensitize leaners to cultural differences (Belz & Kinginger, 2003; Jin & Erben, 2007), and develop learners' intercultural competence (Schenker, 2012; Stickler & Emke, 2011). Finally, TTWE exposes learners to an array of digital tools and engages them in multimodal practices (Hauck, 2010), thereby developing their digital literacies (MacKinnon, 2016).

## Interaction Process

Research on the process of TTWE has concentrated on peer review and negotiation of meaning. Studies on peer review have found that first-language (L1) speakers and second-language (L2) speakers differ in the quantity and quality of feedback (Ware & O'Dowd, 2008). In particular, L2 speakers provide less feedback than L1 speakers, and focus more on grammar than on content (Anderson, Bergman, Bradley, Gustafsson, & Matzke, 2010; Kramsch, 2006). In addition, L2 speakers tend to provide direct and explicit feedback, while L1 speakers provide indirect and implicit feedback (Sotillo, 2005). Finer-grained comparison further shows that L2 speakers provide more affective feedback and adopt reformation strategies in their comments, while L1 speakers focus on vocabulary and syntax and adopt metalinguistic strategies (Lee, 2011). Finally, it is important to note that the medium of communication impacts the quantity and quality of comments. For example, in synchronous communications, the percentage of corrective feedback is much lower than in asynchronous communications (Bower & Kawaguchi, 2011). Compared with wiki collaboration, online forums are more likely to evoke affective feedback (Díez-Bedmar & Pérez-Paredes, 2012).

TTWE is a fruitful site for negotiation of meaning. When peers share their opinions in the writing process, they usually negotiate content, vocabulary, and grammar (Blake, 2000; O'Rourke, 2005; Tudini, 2003). It is found that content negotiation is the most frequent, followed by vocabulary negotiation and grammar negotiation (Bradley, 2014; Edasawa & Kabata, 2007; Lee, 2006). When participants are not specifically required to make corrective feedback, they tend not to negotiate linguistic forms (Edasawa & Kabata, 2007; Ware & O'Dowd, 2008). In terms of negotiation strategies, peers adopt suggestion and evaluation strategies more often than correction or clarification strategies (Bradley, 2014).

## Power and Identities

When participants communicate online, they are not sheltered in a neutral space, but rather a space vested in power differentials. Liu (2011) brought to light the power differentials perceived by Taiwanese students when they were engaged in an intercultural email writing activity. Three discursive strategies were uncovered to "negotiate power differentials in three types of interactions—balance, endurance, and resistance" (p. 257). When Taiwanese students interacted with their American peers in the "balance" style, they presented the identities of friends or classmates by using "friendly," "informal," and "conversational" discourses. In the "endurance" style, they constructed the identities of tourist guides or cultural ambassadors by enacting "formal," "polite," "academic," and "fact-oriented" discourses. In the "resistance" style, they created the identities of cultural fighters by shifting "from open-minded and personal language to more opinionated language" (p. 267).

Despite the dissonance featured in Liu's (2011) research, studies (Prieto-Arranz, Juan-Garau, & Jacob, 2013) also point out that student writers are able to co-construct collective identities by implementing three discursive strategies: a) maintaining an informal language style in the interaction; b) resorting to orthographic pictures or emoticons; and c) sharing common interests and concerns in youth subculture.

## A Survey of TTWE Practices

This section features the practices of TTWE in Europe, Asia, Australia, and North America.[3] To balance representation, two cases are selected from each continent. TTWE typically involves institutions in multiple locations and/or continents. In the following subsections, cases are grouped based on the location where the technological platforms are housed. For example, if a transnational writing activity is a collaboration between an American and a Chinese university, and the communication platform is hosted on a Chinese server, this practice is reported under the Asia subsection. If writing activities are carried out via emails, the case is grouped based on the affiliation of the (first) author who reports the project.

### Europe

The LITERALIA project (Learning In Tandem to Encourage Reciprocal Autonomous Learning In Adults) was initiated to connect learners from Britain, Italy, Germany, and Poland (Stickler & Emke, 2011). As the name suggests, the project was implemented in a tandem model—learners from different countries pair up and spend an equal amount of time communicating in the respective target languages. Learners mainly communicate via emails, but they could also participate in synchronous chatroom discussion and collaborate on wiki entries (Stickler, 2008). Between 2006 and 2008, the LITERALIA project was able to connect over 180 learning partners across the four countries, enabling autonomous learning and enhancing their language proficiency and intercultural maturity.

Another sizable project, The Clavier Network, was initiated in 2011 between the University of Warwick in Britain and the Université Blaise Pascal Clermont Ferrand in France (MacKinnon, 2016). Students from the two institutes review their transnational peers' profiles and then pair up at their own choice. After one semester's communication on various media platforms (e.g., Twitter, Google Documents, Facebook, and the project portal platform), they were required to produce a "language learning history" in the target language with the assistance of a new telecollaborative partner. Alternatively, in another task (chain stories), students worked together to co-create stories in English and in French. So far, this project has involved 900 participants and the learning outcomes have been promising: students' engagement is prolonged and their "transversal skills such as digital literacies" are promoted (MacKinnon, 2016, p. 239).

## *Asia*

Ever since 2009, Guangdong University of Foreign Studies (GDUFS, China) and The Pennsylvania State University (PSU, United States) have been committed to a transnational activity, dubbed "Cross-Pacific Exchange in English Writing." In the early stages of the project, students uploaded their written texts (narrative, expository, or argumentative) to a self-built discussion forum and traded comments on each other's texts. In 2011, the writing task was redesigned to establish a common ground for discussion. Now, students from these two universities watch a Chinese and an American movie dealing with a similar social issue. They post their movie reviews on the discussion forum and exchange comments. They discuss linguistic, rhetorical, and socio-cultural topics from an intercultural perspective. Based on peer feedback, they revise their texts and reflect upon their telecollaborative learning. Thus far, the discussion forum has hosted 30 rounds of transnational writing activities between three Chinese universities, two American universities, and one New Zealand university, involving about 900 learners and generating a two-million-word corpus of online posts. Research based on this project has shown that TTWE is beneficial to developing learners' multilinguistic sensitivity, intercultural communication skills (Zheng, Du, & Wu, 2013), generic knowledge, and cosmopolitan disposition (You, 2016). When pre-service or in-service teachers are involved, the transnational space also serves as a useful site to link the conceptual and experiential knowledge for writing teacher development (You, 2016) and shapes teacher identities (Zhang, this volume).

Based on a long tradition of transnational email exchanges in Japan (Fedderholdt, 2001; Gray & Stockwell, 1998; Johnson & Brine, 2000), a revamped pen-pal project between Doshisha Women's College (Japan) and the University of Alberta (Canada) has been conducted since 2001 (Edasawa & Kabata, 2007). The project is implemented in a tandem model, requiring students to answer their partners' questions in their native language and ask questions in the target language. In the first stage, Japanese students form small groups and decide on a research topic of interest. In the second stage, Canadian students divide themselves into small groups and match the Japanese groups. In the interaction stage, students exchange messages on a discussion board, specifically addressing the research topics they have chosen. In the final stage, students give a presentation to their transnational partners and submit a research essay for course fulfillment. In addition to the uptake of vocabulary and syntactic structures during the interaction, the researchers identify an interesting translingual practice: the majority of participants "used both languages by adding translations to the entire message or just parts of it" (Edasawa & Kabata, 2007, p. 199), despite the task instruction requiring students to use one language in posting questions and another in answers.

## *Australia*

As an extracurricular practice, Italian-learning students from the University of South Australia were asked to interact with Italian students in chatrooms on their own time. There was no specific topic or requirement prescribed for the text chat (Tudini, 2003). The interactions lasted one year. The naturally occurring data demonstrated that this non-institutionalized, transnational written communication resulted in language development, evidenced by the modified output and negotiation of meaning in lexis and morphosyntax. However, the Australian students were also found to be inactive in seeking assistance or feedback from the Italian students. Thus, in the following round of interaction, students were specifically encouraged to solicit Italian speakers' feedback. In addition, "ability to make use of native speaker's knowledge by improving language during chat" was stipulated in the assessment criteria (Tudini, 2007, p. 601). Overall, chatrooms proved to be a valid form of virtual and social immersion to develop students' intercultural communicative competence through negotiation.

Unlike the previous case, an institutionalized project was launched in 1998–1999 at the University of Melbourne. The PrOCALL (Project-Oriented Computer-Assisted Language Learning) project transformed language classes by incorporating multimedia tools and transnational collaboration into project-based learning tasks (Debski, 2000). In particular, students were divided into small groups and each group picked a topic. Then they gathered information on this topic by consulting (online) materials and exchanging information with their intercultural peers via emails or bulletin board messages. After that, they created multimodal web pages in the target language and received comments and suggestions from their classmates and teachers. After they revised the web pages, they published them on the globally accessible project platform (Toyoda, 2001). Arguably, this project had the widest coverage in languages; it covered English, Chinese, German, Indonesian, Japanese, and Russian.

## North America

Probably the earliest pedagogical model for TTWE, the Cultura project was designed by the Massachusetts Institute of Technology (MIT) in 1996. The project was launched in 1997 between MIT (US) and Institut National des Télécommunications (France) to develop foreign language learners' linguistic and intercultural communication skills (Furstenberg, Levet, English, & Maillet, 2001). The transnational interaction is sequenced in three stages. First, American and French students answer a word association questionnaire, a sentence completion questionnaire, and a situation response questionnaire in their native languages (for details see Furstenberg et al., 2001). Second, American and French students' survey responses are juxtaposed to reveal linguistic and cultural differences, which are discussed and explained among the peers in asynchronous online forums. Third, students are given new materials (polls, books, films, advertisements, etc.) and tasked with further exploring the differences. After two decades of development, recent Cultura projects take on new forms: a) students are required to write an essay in the target language to synthesize and expound on the survey responses; b) students set up regular Skype sessions in both the native and target languages for communication, discussion, and presentation (Furstenberg, 2016). Ongoing for two decades, the Cultura project is truly "exceptional" (Levy, 2007, p. 119), considering its meticulous task design, diverse materials, and long-standing commitment.

With a view toward "developing composition classrooms that rely on computer-mediated communication to reify the writing process" (Herrington, 2010, p. 520), the Global Classroom Project was created at the Georgia Institute of Technology to connect with universities in Russia. This project is "international, experiential, and cross-disciplinary" (p. 521), with participants collaborating on projects via an array of web-based tools (see Herrington & Tretyakov, 2005 for details). For instance, students were asked to create a memorial to the victims of the Indian Ocean tsunami disaster, to compare Russian and American cartoons, and to compare the differences of news reporting of the same event. The project also involves research assignments. Students choose their research focus on a given topic and draft annotated bibliographies in their native languages. They then exchange the bibliographies and form groups based on the research focus. They collaborate on research proposals, analytical reports, oral progress presentations, and final presentations. Herrington (2010) noted that the Global Classroom Project enabled students to learn by experience and develop their synthetic thinking abilities.

## Limitations in TTWE Research and Practice

In the introduction, I argue that TTWE is inherently and simultaneously international, cross-national, and transnational. Based on the review, we are able to see that the recurring research themes and the existing interaction models largely

**178** Zhiwei Wu

focus on the international and cross-national aspects of TTWE: engaging participants from different locations in a technology-enabled space. The international/cross-national fixation is predicated on nation-based categories and leaves the transnational potential of TTWE unexplored. This section discusses three limitations caused by the international/cross-national fixation.

The first limitation comes from the (un)witting endorsement of Standard English as the preferred, privileged, and prioritized language for communication. When the languages used in TTWE activities are tallied, English takes up the lion's share (61 out of the 75 reviewed studies); German is a distant second (17 out of 75); and Spanish is the third most frequent choice (13), followed by Japanese (11) and French (seven). The bottom five languages are Chinese (three), Italian (two), Portuguese (one), Polish (one), and Indonesian (one). Given its lingua franca status, while it is understandable to adopt English as a common language for transnational interaction, Standard English is usually reified as the only acceptable variety and the ultimate goal of language learning. This monolingual ideology is evidenced in the studies focusing on how non-native speakers improve their linguistic accuracy (Belz, 2003; Sauro, 2009) through interaction with native English speakers. Non-English participants are almost always labeled as "non-native speakers" and "language learners," and their writings are considered undesirable or defective. This ethnocentric mindset is so prevalent that even participants identify themselves as "foreign" or "non-native" (Pasfield-Neofitou, 2011, p. 105) in the transnational writing process to avoid losing face because of incompetent use of language. Interestingly, in Pasfield-Neofitou's (2011) case, it was the Australian students who foregrounded their identity as foreigners in the Japanese social networking sites, a gesture to make them "more attractive to Japanese members who were actively looking for a foreign or English-speaking contact" (p. 105). Emphasizing (or flaunting) foreign status in a non-English transnational writing site carries the currency of the order, purity, and normality of English (Blommaert, Leppänen, Pahta, & Räisänen, 2012) and reinforces the English monolingual ideology.

The second limitation is the insufficient understanding of relations between different literacy practices in TTWE. Thanks to technological affordances, geographically distant learners are connected in the World Wide Web and communications are enabled on various online platforms. Despite this, learners' digital literacies in transnational writing education are under-researched (Lewis & O'Dowd, 2016) and the relationship between digital literacies and "mere literacy" (Cope & Kalantzis, 2000, p. 5)[4] is not sufficiently explored. Although researchers have claimed that TTWE is beneficial to the development of digital literacies (Guth & Helm, 2012), the evidence is largely anecdotal. In practice, recent TTWE projects usually involve a multitude of networking tools. Many teachers and students have been forced to assemble an *ad hoc* combination of technological tools, juggling and struggling between asynchronous communication applications (emails, discussion forums, blogging, Twitter, Facebook, wikis) and synchronous ones (Skype, instant messaging, Adobe Connect Pro, VoiceThread). The culmination of the projects is usually an essay, a written text product, fashioned and refined based on the multimedia-enabled intercultural communication. Thus far, it is rare to allow multimodal products (for instance, a video clip or a poster with images and texts) for project assessment (for exceptions see Toyoda, 2001 and Dooly, 2016). Although transnational writing is inherently a multiliterate practice (You, 2016), the legitimacy of submitting multimodal products for assessment is not recognized in many classroom projects, perpetuating the dominance of "mere literacy" over multiliteracies.

The third limitation is the institutional confinement of transnational writing education. Although involving international participants, some projects are conducted on course management platforms (e.g., ANGEL, Blackboard), and require sanctioned institutional access for collaborative learning, thereby creating a bounded community. This runs counter to the distributed and participatory nature of new literacies (Jenkins, 2006), and unwittingly confines learners to a predefined and prescribed readership, handpicked and prepared by teachers. Arguably, the single most important goal of TTWE is to expand learners' "communicative repertoire" (Hall, Cheng, & Carlson, 2006, p. 232). If participants are limited to a dialogue with a static and monolithic readership, it would be difficult to sensitize them to a wide range of literacy practices, contributed and distributed by global citizens. As a matter of fact, non-institutional establishments prove to be rich in opportunities for participants to experience, engage, and immerse in various literacy practices. Benson's (2015) examination of comments posted under translingual YouTube videos shows evidence of language and intercultural learning. You's (2011) ethnographic observation of a white-collar online forum in China reveals that Chinese English writers perform their linguistic creativity by coining novel English screen names, appropriating local and trans-local discourses, and mixing a variety of semiotic resources. If teachers integrate these affordances "in the wild" (Thorne, 2010, p. 144) into classroom instruction, transnational writing education will truly reflect the collaborative, distributed, and participatory nature of new literacies.

## Prospects for TTWE Research and Practice

To address the issues of Standard English bias, unexamined relation between mere literacy and multiliteracies, and institutional confinement of participants, this section argues for three perspectival changes for future research and practice in TTWE.

First, the conformist approach must be paradigmatically shifted to the cosmopolitan approach. Based on the review findings and limitation analysis, I note that there are two approaches in TTWE, the conformist approach and the cosmopolitan approach (see Table 10.1). The conformist approach valorizes and canonizes Standard English as the normative literacy practice, which L2 participants (imagined as language learners) are expected to conform to. Conversely,

180 Zhiwei Wu

**TABLE 10.1** Differences Between the Conformist Approach and the Cosmopolitan Approach

| Dimensions | Conformist | Cosmopolitan |
| --- | --- | --- |
| Attitude towards Standard English | The English style | One English style |
| Ethical implication | Ethnocentrism | Relativism |
| Understanding of literacy practice | Canonized and valorized | Dynamic and fluid |
| Characterization of L2 participants | Language learners | Language users |

the cosmopolitan approach decentralizes Standard English and highlights the dynamic and fluid nature of literacy practices, grounded in the communicative context co-determined by language users. From an ideological perspective, the conformist approach perpetuates ethnocentrism, while the cosmopolitan approach celebrates relativism. Therefore, I argue that when future transnational writing projects are pursued, it is important to design activities to develop a cosmopolitan disposition among participants. For instance, to avoid "native-speaker prejudice" (Ruecker, 2011, p. 402), learners should be advised not to uncritically accept their peers' comments simply because of the "native speaker" status. When research is conducted, the focus can shift from how learners acquire certain linguistic forms to how "native speakers" adapt their writing in response to the English styles distributed by language users from another "languaculture" (Agar, 1995). To illustrate, it has been found that native speakers are not immune from or indifferent to the language styles emerging in transnational writing interaction. They would question the legitimacy of "Standard English" in certain contexts and update their linguistic repertoire by accepting local usages of certain expressions, though deviant from the linguistic norm in their home languaculture (Zheng et al., 2013). A shift from the conformist approach to the cosmopolitan approach will enable us to understand the irreducible dynamics in transnational writing education (see Table 10.1).

Second, multilingual, multimodal, and multicultural resources must be fully incorporated into technology-mediated writing projects. Although the name "transnational writing" deceptively suggests that this is a mono-modal (i.e., text-based) endeavor, it is actually a multiliterate pursuit when linguistic, geographical, cultural, and modal boundaries are strategically crossed and transcended (You, 2016). Thus far, there have been few projects to draw upon participants' multilingual, multimodal, and multicultural resources in their interaction, thereby constraining their multiliterate development. If their multiliterate practices are enabled and encouraged in the transnational environment, or "contact zone" (Pratt, 1991), educators and researchers will be able to gauge how effectively participants employ contextual, personal, social, and textual strategies (Canagarajah, 2011) and negotiate multiple resources to achieve rhetorical effects in the transnational interaction. In addition, as discussed in the previous section, the assessment of TTWE projects could do well to allow multimodal products to complement, if not replace, the written essays. This renewed practice will invigorate learners' multiliterate practices and urge them to explore the rhetorical possibilities of different representational systems, complicated by the othering perspectives (Palfreyman, 2005) offered by intercultural partners. For instance, students' identities can be tapped as resources in the composing and interaction process. The assignment of "identity text" enables students to express, project, and re-create identities "in the creation of these texts—which can be written, spoken, signed, visual, musical, dramatic, or combinations in multimodal form" (Cummins & Early, 2011, p. 3). When intercultural participants collaborate and reflect on identity texts, they are sensitized to cross-modal and cross-cultural rhetorical and ethical implications, becoming multiliterate rhetors in glocal communities.

Third, layered institutional control must be lifted to invite participatory engagement. Many TTWE projects are operated under the model of "handshake partnership" (Rainey, 2004 quoted in Sapp, 2004, p. 271), a collaboration kicked off by individual faculty members and subsequently leading to cooperation between two institutions. Without doubt, this is an efficient model to set up and scale up TTWE projects, as coverage is progressively expanded from students who are enrolled in individual faculty members' courses to course-wide and/or program-wide student populations. Nonetheless, to ensure that writing education is transnational, we must go beyond the institutional boundary. We must not confine our interaction to a particular cohort of students in a particular participating institution. Studies have uncovered that in institutional settings multilingual students intentionally suppress their multilingualism and multiliteracies to conform to the Standard English practice, but they "consciously, knowledgeably, and creatively" enact their multilingual and multiliterate resources on social networking sites (Marshall, Hayashi, & Yeung, 2012, p. 50). It is debatable, and worth finding out, whether the bounded community created in institutionally sanctioned TTWE projects is tantamount to the high-stakes institutional setting reported in Marshall et al.'s (2012) study. Still, it would be ideal for institutions to open the community to anyone, and connect the transnational writing project to participants' daily literacy practices on social networking sites, thereby blurring the boundary between the academic and the private. In this regard, transnational writing education will expose participants to the true dynamics of participatory literacies and create a sense of in-betweenness, whereby they are constantly prompted to negotiate their meaning-making strategies, representational systems, and evolving identities. These skills and qualities fall squarely into the communicative repertoire championed by translingual literacy (Canagarajah, 2013), and yet are rarely foregrounded in existing transnational writing projects.

## Conclusion

We are living in a remarkably different world from that of 1996, when ACTFL advocated the five-C goals in foreign language education, and when the

US-France transnational project Cultura was initiated at MIT. The world is more connected, interdependent, and interactive. As Kramsch (2014) aptly pointed out, for foreign language learners in an era of globalization, "developing their own voice increasingly means developing an ear for the voices of others" (p. 309). Technology-mediated transnational writing projects, in their multifarious forms, have been able to engage intercultural participants in dialogues, to afford them the otherwise unavailable opportunities to listen to voices from the other side of the world, and to foster their abilities to express, interpret, and negotiate meanings among heterogeneous and diasporic members of discourse communities. Two decades ago, it was indeed a pioneering endeavor for a transnational writing project to wield technological tools to cross geographical, linguistic, and cultural borders. Now, for a technology-mediated project to truly benefit students in their multiliteracies development, we must additionally and simultaneously transcend ethnic, institutional, and modal borders to equip them with a cosmopolitan disposition and a globalizing communicative repertoire. Admittedly, this is no easy task, as it requires concerted efforts from individuals, institutions, and teaching and scholarly communities to recognize the necessity of crossing multiple borders in writing education. Hopefully, this chapter has provided some ideas to gear up in our journey of transnational writing education.

## Acknowledgment

This paper was supported by the research project "Transnational Collaboration and its Impact on Students' Multiliteracies," funded by the Guangdong Provincial Education Department.

## Notes

1. I decided to set the time frame from 1996 to 2016, because 1996 witnessed the launch of ACTFL's five-C model and the US-France Cultura project, representing the seminal commencement of research and practice in TTWE.
2. For the reason of space, I do not include these articles and book chapters in the reference list. Interested readers can contact me for the list.
3. Initially, I intended to select two practices from each continent, but I was unable to locate studies reporting practices in Africa and Antarctica. In addition, I was only able to locate one practice case in South America: "Teletandem Brazil: Foreign languages for all" (Telles & Vassallo, 2006). This project, however, involves primarily visual and oral interaction among intercultural learners. Therefore, it is not included in this review.
4. Mere literacy is defined by Cope and Kalantzis (2000, p. 5) as literacy that focuses on language alone, and usually predicates on a singular national form of language.

## References

Agar, M. (1995). *Language shock: Understanding the culture of conversation*. New York: William Morrow.

American Council on the Teaching of Foreign Language (ACTFL). (1996). *Standards for foreign language learning: Preparing for the 21st century*. Yonkers, NY: American Council on the Teaching of Foreign Languages, Inc.

Anderson, P., Bergman, B., Bradley, L., Gustafsson, M., & Matzke, A. (2010). Peer reviewing across the Atlantic: Patterns and trends in L1 and L2 comments made in an asynchronous online collaborative learning exchange between technical communication students in Sweden and in the United States. *Journal of Business and Technical Communication*, *24*(3), 296–322.

Angelova, M., & Zhao, Y. (2016). Using an online collaborative project between American and Chinese students to develop ESL teaching skills, cross-cultural awareness and language skills. *Computer Assisted Language Learning*, *29*(1), 167–185.

Belz, J. A. (2003). Linguistic perspectives on the development of intercultural competence in telecollaboration. *Language Learning & Technology*, *7*(2), 68–117.

Belz, J. A., & Kinginger, C. (2003). Discourse options and the development of pragmatic competence by classroom learners of German: The case of address forms. *Language Learning*, *53*(4), 591–647.

Belz, J. A., & Vyatkina, N. (2005). Learner corpus analysis and the development of L2 pragmatic competence in networked inter-cultural language study: The case of German modal particles. *Canadian Modern Language Review*, *62*(1), 17–48.

Benson, P. (2015). Commenting to learn, evidence of language and intercultural learning in comments on YouTube videos. *Language Learning & Technology*, *19*(3), 88–105.

Blake, R. (2000). Computer mediated communication, A window on L2 Spanish interlanguage. *Language Learning & Technology*, *4*(1), 120–136.

Blommaert, J., Leppänen, S., Pahta, P., & Räisänen, T. (Eds.). (2012). *Dangerous multilingualism: Northern perspectives on order, purity and normality*. London: Palgrave Macmillan.

Bower, J., & Kawaguchi, S. (2011). Negotiation of meaning and corrective feedback in Japanese/English eTandem. *Language Learning & Technology*, *15*(1), 41–71.

Bradley, L. (2014). Peer-reviewing in an intercultural wiki environment-student interaction and reflections. *Computers and Composition*, *34*, 80–95.

Canagarajah, S. (2011). Codemeshing in academic writing: Identifying teachable strategies of translanguaging. *The Modern Language Journal*, *95*(3), 401–417.

Canagarajah, S. (2013). Negotiating translingual literacy. *Research in the Teaching of English*, *48*, 140–167.

Connor, U. M., Davis, K. W., De Rycker, T., Phillips, E. M., & Verckens, J. P. (1997). An international course in international business writing, Belgium, Finland, the United States. *Business Communication Quarterly*, *60*(4), 63–74.

Cope, B., & Kalantzis, M. (2000). Multiliteracies, The beginnings of an idea. In B. Cope, & M. Kalantzis (Eds.), *Multiliteracies, literacy learning and the design of social futures* (pp. 3–8). New York, Routledge.

Cummins, J., & Early, M. (Eds.). (2011). *Identity texts: The collaborative creation of power in multilingual schools*. Stoke-on-Trent, UK: Trentham Books.

Debski, R. (2000). Exploring the re-creation of a CALL innovation. *Computer Assisted Language Learning*, *13*(4–5), 307–332.

De Wit, H. (2016). Internationalization and the role of online intercultural exchange. In R. O'Dowd, & T. Lewis (Eds.), *Online intercultural exchange: Policy, pedagogy, practice* (pp. 69–82). New York: Routledge.

Díez-Bedmar, M. B., & Pérez-Paredes, P. (2012). The types and effects of peer native speakers' feedback on CMC. *Language Learning & Technology*, *16*(1), 62–90.

Dooly, M. (2016). "Please remove your avatar from my personal space": Competences of the tellecollaboratively efficient person. In R. O'Dowd, & T. Lewis (Eds.), *Online intercultural exchange: Policy, pedagogy, practice* (pp. 192–208). New York, Routledge.

Edasawa, Y., & Kabata, K. (2007). An ethnographic study of a key-pal project: Learning a foreign language through bilingual communication. *Computer Assisted Language Learning, 20*(3), 189–207.

Fedderholdt, K. (2001). An email exchange project between non-native speakers of English. *ELT Journal, 55*(3), 273–280.

Furstenberg, G. (2016). The Cultura exchange programme. In R. O'Dowd, & T. Lewis (Eds.), *Online intercultural exchange: Policy, pedagogy, practice* (pp. 248–255). New York, Routledge.

Furstenberg, G., Levet, S., English, K., & Maillet, K. (2001). Giving a virtual voice to the silent culture of language, The Cultura project. *Language Learning & Technology, 5*(1), 55–102.

Gray, R., & Stockwell, G. (1998). Using computer mediated communication for language and culture acquisition. *On-Call, 12*(3), 2–9.;

Guth, S., & Helm, F. (2010). *Telecollaboration 2.0: Language, literacies and intercultural learning in the 21st century.* Bern, Switzerland: Peter Lang.

Guth, S., & Helm, F. (2012). Developing multiliteracies in ELT through telecollaboration. *ELT Journal, 66*(1), 42–51.

Hall, J. K., Cheng, A., & Carlson, M. T. (2006). Reconceptualizing multicompetence as a theory of language knowledge. *Applied Linguistics, 27*(2), 220–240.

Hauck, M. (2010). Telecollaboration: At the interface between multimodal and intercultural communicative. In S. Guth, & F. Helm (Eds.), *Telecollaboration 2.0, language, literacies and intercultural learning in the 21st century* (pp. 219–248). Bern, Switzerland: Peter Lang.

Helm, F. (2015). The practices and challenges of telecollaboration in higher education in Europe. *Language Learning & Technology, 19*(2), 197–217.

Herrington, T. K. (2010). Crossing global boundaries: Beyond intercultural communication. *Journal of Business and Technical Communication, 24*(4), 516–539.

Herrington, T. K., & Tretyakov, Y. P. (2005). The Global Classroom Project, troublemaking and trouble-shooting. In K. Cargille Cook, & K. Grant-Davie (Eds.), *Online education: Global questions, local answers* (pp. 267–283). Amityville, NY, Baywood.

Jenkins, H. (2006). *Fans, bloggers, and gamers: Exploring participatory culture.* New York and London: New York University Press.

Jin, L., & Erben, T. (2007). Intercultural learning via instant messenger interaction. *Calico Journal, 24*(2), 291–311.

Johnson, E. M., & Brine, J. W. (2000). Design and development of CALL courses in Japan. *CALICO Journal, 17*(2), 251–268.

Kramsch, C. (2006). From communicative competence to symbolic competence. *The Modern Language Journal, 90*(2), 249–252.

Kramsch, C. (2014). Teaching foreign languages in an era of globalization, Introduction. *The Modern Language Journal, 98*(1), 296–311.

Lee, L. (2006). A study of native and non-native speakers' feedback and responses in Spanish-American networked collaborative interaction. In J. Belz, & S. Thorne (Eds.), *Internet-mediated intercultural foreign language education* (pp. 147–176). Boston, MA: Thomson Heinle.

Lee, L. (2011). Focus on form through peer feedback in a Spanish-English telecollaborative exchange. *Language Awareness, 20*(4), 343–357.

Levy, M. (2007). Culture, culture learning and new technologies, towards a pedagogical framework. *Language Learning and Technology, 11*(2), 104–127.

Lewis, T., & O'Dowd, R. (2016). Online intercultural exchange and foreign language learning: A systematic review. In R. O'Dowd, & T. Lewis (Eds.), *Online intercultural exchange: Policy, pedagogy, practice* (pp. 21–66). New York: Routledge.

Liaw, M.-L. (2006). E-learning and the development of intercultural competence. *Language Learning & Technology, 10*(3), 49–64.

Liu, Y. (2011). Power perceptions and negotiations in a cross-national email writing activity. *Journal of Second Language Writing, 20*(4), 257–270.

MacKinnon, T. (2016). The Clavier network. In R. O'Dowd, & T. Lewis (Eds.), *Online intercultural exchange: Policy, pedagogy, practice* (pp. 235–240). New York: Routledge.

Marshall, S., Hayashi, H., & Yeung, P. (2012). Negotiating the multi in multilingualism and multiliteracies, undergraduate students in Vancouver, Canada. *Canadian Modern Language Review, 68*(1), 28–53.

MLA Ad Hoc Committee on Foreign Languages. (2007). Foreign languages and higher education, new structures for a changed world. *Profession 2007*, 234–245.

The New London Group. (1996). A pedagogy of multiliteracies: Designing social futures. *Harvard Educational Review, 66*(1), 60–93.

O'Dowd, R. (Ed.). (2007). *Online intercultural exchange: An introduction for foreign language teachers.* Clevedon: Multilingual Matters.

O'Dowd, R. (2013). Telecollaborative networks in university higher education, overcoming barriers to integration. The internet and higher education, *18*, 47–53.

O'Rourke, B. (2005). Form-focused interaction in online tandem learning. *CALICO Journal, 22*(3), 433–466.

Palfreyman, D. (2005). Othering in an English language program. *TESOL Quarterly, 39*(2), 211–233.

Pasfield-Neofitou, S. (2011). Online domains of language use: Second language learners' experiences of virtual community and foreignness. *Language Learning & Technology, 15*(2), 92–108.

Pratt, M. L. (1991). Arts of the contact zone. *Profession*, 33–40.

Prieto-Arranz, J. I., Juan-Garau, M., & Jacob, K. L. (2013). Re-imagining cultural identity, Transcultural and translingual communication in virtual third-space environments. *Language, Culture and Curriculum, 26*(1), 19–35.

Rainey, K. T. (2004). Issues in articulation agreements with international universities for a technical communication degree. Paper presented at the meeting of the Association of Teachers of Technical Writing, San Antonio, TX.

Ruecker, T. (2011). The potential of dual-language cross-cultural peer review. *ELT Journal, 65*(4), 398–407.

Sapp, D. A. (2004). Global partnerships in business communication: An institutional collaboration between the United States and Cuba. *Business Communication Quarterly, 67*(3), 267–280.

Sauro, S. (2009). Computer-mediated corrective feedback and the development of L2 grammar. *Language Learning & Technology, 13*(1), 96–120.

Schenker, T. (2012). Intercultural competence and cultural learning through telecollaboration. *CALICO Journal, 29*(3), 449–470.

Sotillo, S. (2005). Corrective feedback via instant messenger learning activities in NS-NNS and NNS-NNS Dyads. *CALICO Journal, 22*(3), 467–496.

Stickler, U. (2008). Chatting, chatten or chattare: Using a multilingual workspace for language and culture learning. *ijET (International Journal of Emerging Technologies in Learning)*, *3*(8), 69–76.

Stickler, U., & Emke, M. (2011). LITERALIA: Towards developing intercultural maturity online. *Language Learning & Technology*, *15*(1), 147–168.

Tesdell, L. S. (2013). Innovation in the distributed technical communication classroom. In K. C. Cook, & K. Grant-Davie (Eds.), *Online education 2.0, evolving, adapting, and reinventing online technical communication* (pp. 257–270). Amityville: Baywood.

Telles, J. A., & Vassallo, M. L. (2006). Foreign language learning in-tandem: Teletandem as an alternative proposal in CALL. *The ESPecialist*, *27*(2), 189–212.

Thorne, S. L. (2010). The "intercultural turn" and language leaning in the crucible of new media. In S. Guth, & F. Helm (Eds.), *Telecollaboration 2.0: Languages, literacies and intercultural learning in the 21st century* (pp. 139–164). Bern, Switzerland: Peter Lang.

Toyoda, E. (2001). Exercise of learner autonomy in project-oriented CALL. *Call-Ej Online*, *2*(2), 1–11.

Tudini, V. (2003). Using native speakers in chat. *Language Learning & Technology*, *7*(3), 141–159.

Tudini, V. (2007). Negotiation and intercultural learning in Italian native speaker chat rooms. *The Modern Language Journal*, *91*(4), 577–601.

UNCESO. (2014). *Global citizenship education: Preparing learners for the challenges of the twenty-first century*. United Nations Educational, Scientific, Education Sector. Paris: UNESCO.

Ware, P. D., & O'Dowd, R. (2008). Peer feedback on language form in telecollaboration. *Language Learning & Technology*, *12*(1), 43–63.

Warschauer, M. (1996). *Telecollaboration in foreign language learning*. Honolulu: Second Language Teaching and Curriculum Center.

You, X. (2011). Chinese white-collar workers and multilingual creativity in the diaspora. *World Englishes*, *30*(3), 409–427.

You, X. (2016). *Cosmopolitan English and transliteracy*. Carbondale, IL: Southern Illinois University Press.

Zheng, C., Du, Y., & Wu, Z. (2013). *Chinese and American student cross-Pacific interactions in English: Action research and data analysis*. Beijing: Science Press.

# 11

# ENGLISH TEACHER IDENTITY DEVELOPMENT THROUGH A CROSS-BORDER WRITING ACTIVITY

*Yufeng Zhang*

## Introduction

Teacher identity has received increasing attention in foreign language teaching in recent years. With language education theories shifting from the traditional cognitivist Second Language Acquisition (SLA) framework to sociocultural perspectives, teacher identity has become the focus of foreign language education research (Miller, 2009; Varghese, Morgan, Johnston, & Johnson, 2005). Our understanding of this concept is no longer limited to the psychological processes, but has extended to the social processes: Identity construction is more and more viewed as an ongoing process "constructed and reconstructed in interaction with others" in social contexts (Burns & Bell, 2011, p. 958). Along with the internationalization of language education and the global spread of the English language, the process of teacher identity construction has been further complicated. While effective communication in a globalized world calls for multilingual and multicultural perspectives in language teaching, current practices in this profession are still influenced and confined by traditional linguistic and cultural boundaries. Despite the rich communicative repertoire language learners bring to the classrooms, for instance, language teachers still feel the urge to teach students to conform to the norms of the target language. In the context of globalization, however, it is essential for teachers to help students develop strategies to negotiate between linguistic and between cultural codes (You, 2016a), and thus foster a translingual orientation to communication (Canagarajah, 2013). To better understand the evolution of teacher identity amidst the tensions of language teaching in a transnational frame, the present study explores American pre-service ESL teachers' identity construction through an online cross-border activity.

**188**  Yufeng Zhang

Teacher identity is a becoming process throughout teachers' professional career, but for pre-service teachers, teacher education is a critical time period in their identity development (Xie & Xiong, 2014). As pre-service ESL teachers lack real-life language teaching experience, studies about them have mainly focused on the impact and effectiveness of teacher education curriculum and activities. These studies have emphasized the significance of understanding the "other" culture (Smolcic, 2011) and enhancing intercultural competence (Byram, 2000) in teachers' identity construction. Because of the globalization of English education and the potential cultural and language differences between teachers and students, first-hand interactions have become an effective means to promote mutual understanding between language teachers and students across national and cultural borders (You, 2016a). This type of interaction can help teachers adopt a multilingual and multicultural orientation in their pedagogical practice, and thus elicit transnational teacher identity development (You, 2016b). In addition, researchers have urged teacher educators to provide more opportunities for pre-service teachers to narrow the gap between teacher education and real-life teaching (Flores, 2001; Singh & Richards, 2006). Therefore, this study explores the identity construction of pre-service American English teachers through an online cross-border activity that aims to improve ESL writing and enhance understanding between language teachers and students. Different from the traditional "direct experience" through student teaching (Guo & Wang, 2009; Xu, 2013; Li, 2015) or overseas immersion programs (Lee, 2009; Willard-Holt, 2001; Yang, 2011), the pre-service ESL teachers and students in this study interacted online.

## Identity Construction

Identity, as an ongoing process in practice, is manifold, dynamic, fluid, and shifting. Because of the numerous social and cultural roles each language teacher plays, teacher identity is also a site of competition and struggle (Peirce, 1995; Duff & Uchida, 1997). In addition, identity is relational, "constructed and altered by how I see others and how they see me" in interactions (Johnson, 2003, p. 788). Simply put, identity is constructed in discourse, practice, and activity (Miller, 2009; Lee, 2013). Lee (2013) further defines teacher identity as teachers' discussion of themselves (their knowledge, attitudes, beliefs and pedagogies), their roles, and their practical activities as teachers (identity-in-discourse and identity-in-practice), as well as their positioning of themselves in relation to the sociocultural, political, and historical environment (identity-in-activity). For ESL teachers who teach English in increasingly globalized or transnational contexts, their identity construction is also influenced by the spread of English as a global language, the internationalization of education, and the worldwide mobility and interconnectedness of people, all of which add a global facet to this process (Pennington, 2014).

English Teacher Identity Development **189**

Identity, which is inseparable from discourse, is developed through discourse in people's interactions. To gain the identity they desire, people have to learn the behaviors and written language associated with it (Gee, 2001, p. 526). Hall, Johnson, Juzwik, Wortham, and Mosley (2010) also suggest that "as people learn the characteristics associated with the identities available to them, they can adopt the language and speech patterns connected to them in order to position themselves as a certain type of person" (p. 235). In other words, discourse is a medium through which people manifest and perform their positions, attributions, and identities. In language teacher education, as teachers grow and mature, they acquire new discourse modes, or new professional discourse (Richards, 2010); when they employ them to discuss their knowledge and teaching, they establish new identities. This is identity-in-discourse.

Identity is enacted in practice. As Gee (1996) states, "It's not just what you say or even how you say it; it's who you are and what you are doing while you say it" (p. viii). Therefore, identities are constructed in people's performance and practice. As Lave & Wenger (1991) point out, identity is not brought in practice as a finished product, nor is it achieved incidentally as a result of acquisition of certain skills or knowledge; it is the primary subject throughout the process of people's practice. Identity-in-discourse also indicates the "mutually constitutive relationship between identity and discourse" (Kanno & Stuart, 2011, p. 240): identity can only be developed through participating in community activities and acquiring relevant behavior patterns in real contexts. At the same time, the evolution and transformation of people's identities influence their practice methods and knowledge system. For language teachers, their personal and professional identities may turn into pedagogical performance, and thus become part of language teaching and learning (Morgan, 2002; Varghese et al., 2005). Broadly speaking, identity-in-discourse is part of identity-in-practice, because discursively constructed identities are "verbal expressions of the ongoing mutual relationship between the self and the practice of a teacher" (Kanno & Stuart, 2011, p. 240); therefore, identities-in-practice can be further divided into narrated identities (based on teachers' self-reports) and enacted identities (based on teachers' practice).

In its constant forming process, teacher identity is not an isolated individual activity; instead, it is a mediated social activity shaped by social, cultural, and historical factors (Cross & Gearon, 2007; Lee, 2013), including constraints from specific settings such as work conditions, curriculum goals, language policies, cultural differences, and student demographic structure. Identity construction is self-development in shared cultural experiences and social activities (Cross & Gearon, 2007, p. 54). This is identity-in-activity.

Based on Lee's definition of identity (2013), this study investigates the construction of pre-service teachers' identity-in-discourse, identity-in-practice, and identity-in-activity in a transnational context through a cross-border activity between American and Chinese college students.

## Research Method

### *Background*

In spring 2016, 14 college students from Guangdong University of Foreign Studies (GUFS) in China corresponded online with 14 students from Millersville University (MU) in the United States in a cross-border activity. GUFS students were first-year English majors, while MU students were pre-service ESL teachers in my TESOL seminar. 12 out of 14 MU participants were undergraduate juniors and seniors, and two were Master's students; none of them had worked with ESL students, although two had taught American students previously. MU has the lowest percentage of international students among the 14 Pennsylvania state system universities: 1.2% ("Millersville University Admissions," 2017). Due to a predominantly monolingual learning environment, these pre-service teachers' knowledge of English learners was limited to textbook discussions; therefore, one of the purposes of this cross-border activity is to promote these teachers' multilingual and multicultural awareness through first-hand interaction.

As part of the course requirement, the pre-service ESL teachers (referred to as "MU teachers" below) read and critiqued English essays written by GUFS students, which were narratives with a surprise ending or based on personal experience. Then they discussed their reflections on this activity in class and shared their teaching philosophy with GUFS students by the end of the semester. All interactions between the two parties took place online primarily through a website; some participants also communicated with each other via email and Skype. Having taken one or two writing classes previously (as required by the MU curriculum), all pre-service teachers were familiar with the peer review method in teaching writing. In this activity, each teacher read and commented on at least one English essay, using guidelines provided by me focusing on aspects such as unity, development, organization, and language (see Appendix I).

### *Data Collection and Analysis*

The data for the present study came from the following three sources: first, MU teachers' written materials, including their feedback on GUFS students' essays, their reflections on this activity, and their teaching philosophy; second, the teachers' class discussion; and third, online posts and the correspondence between the students and MU teachers.

For the purpose of the study, which is to explore teacher identity construction from the aspects of discourse, practice, and activity through this cross-border activity, I read and analyzed the data closely, selected and categorized MU teachers' written materials and student posts from both universities (the first and third data source), and transcribed and categorized relevant class discussions (the second data source). MU teachers' identity-in-discourse (how they discussed themselves and their teaching, such as their perceptions, attitudes, and teaching philosophy, as presented through discourse) can be manifested through the following categories: (1) their perceptions of Chinese students' needs; (2) their perceptions of themselves as native English-speaking teachers; (3) their perceptions of teaching ESL; (4) their perceptions of Chinese students' English writing; (5) their perceptions of the varieties of English as a global language; and (6) their relevant teaching philosophy formed through this activity. MU teachers' identity-in-practice (how they performed their teaching responsibilities in practice) can be manifested through their feedback on GUFS students' essays, including treatments of English variations. Also investigated in this study are social factors that impacted MU teachers' identity construction (identity-in-activity). Due to overlaps between identity-in-discourse and identity-in-practice, some categories are applicable to both; for instance, MU teachers' teaching philosophy formed through this activity can be categorized as both identity-in-discourse and identity-in-practice. To avoid repetition, such data were discussed only in one kind of identity construction in the study.

## Results

### Pre-Service Teachers' Identity-in-Discourse

Through their reflections, teaching philosophy, class discussions, and interactions with GUFS students, the teachers constructed their identity-in-discourse by discussing their perceptions of ESL students, ESL writing, and the teacher's role in language education.

First, the teachers transformed their perceptions of ESL students. Prior to this cross-border activity, MU teachers' understanding of language students, which mainly came from their own foreign language learning experience, was limited and abstract. With little to no first-hand interactions with ESL students previously, many MU teachers were initially concerned about GUFS students' English proficiency and communication skills. In many American public schools, foreign language study is not included in the school curriculum until high school; without a rich multilingual environment, many students are poorly motivated, and after four years of high-school study their foreign language proficiency is still limited. However, after interacting with GUFS students, 13 (93%) MU teachers expressed their amazement at the students' high English proficiency and motivation. For instance, Sidney noted in his reflection that these English learners' writing was "incredible"; Jenn also changed her notion of ESL students after this activity:

> My preconceived notion of ESL learners was that they almost wouldn't be literate. I thought it would be very disconnected speech and very simple sentences. I did not realize that learners that legitimately wanted to know

a language would be so advanced so early in their language learning experience, since I was nowhere near their fluency levels during my second semester of Spanish at Millersville.

*(Reflection)*

Jenn believed that the students' English proficiency showed they genuinely wanted to learn the language. Concurring with this viewpoint, Laura added that the status of English as a global language had increased these English learners' motivation. During the cross-border activity, GUFS students positively responded to the pre-service teachers' feedback on their writing, and further inquired about the latter's comments they were uncertain of. Their level of enthusiasm for learning English deeply impressed the teachers.

MU teachers also reflected on foreign language education, inspired by their new perceptions of ESL students' English proficiency and language learning motivation. First, they realized that their assumptions about language learners are mostly unreliable and inaccurate; instead, they have to rely on scientific need analysis to evaluate students' language skills, needs, and goals. Two teachers clearly expressed this understanding in their teaching philosophy: "At the start of each class cycle, I think it is important to perform a diagnostic test so that I am aware of my students' proficiency levels and problem areas and know what to focus on during the course" (Laura); "I want to critically conduct need analyses, so that I am able to know what students value, and what accommodations they need to effectively learn" (Ariel).

Second, new perceptions of Chinese English learners also caused two MU teachers (who had taught mainstream American students) to reflect upon current ESL curricula in the United States. For instance, Andrew came to realize that the current ESL curriculum in some school districts did not meet the needs of ESL students. Andrew was an English teacher in a public elementary school, which comprised a small number of ESL students. His school district did not offer systematic ESL courses, and in his mind, ESL students were low-achieving, low-motivation learners. However, the interactions with GUFS students helped him realize that ESL students could be highly motivated and high-achieving learners who would require a more rigorous ESL program to guide them; unfortunately, his school district was unable to provide this kind of program. Through this activity, he came to recognize the necessity of "quality L2 instruction domestically" and the significance of "strong ESL programs in public schools" (Reflection). Andrew's reflection also demonstrated the impact of historical and environmental factors on language teachers' identity construction (see further in the section "Pre-Service Teachers' Identity-in-Activity").

Third, through this cross-border activity, 10 (71%) MU teachers developed a deeper understanding of the differences between two familiar concepts, ESL and EFL, and their impact on language study. In China, where English is not a dominant language, appropriate and accurate word choice and language style proved

English Teacher Identity Development **193**

to be a major challenge for Chinese ESL students, despite their positive attitudes and hard work. They could have learned numerous language rules, but the lack of context for practice was a gap hard to bridge. As Chantelle noted,

> When I first began this class, I did not see the real applicable difference between EFL and ESL. Doing this exercise made me realize that English in China is really a foreign language. The fact that students there are learning both British and American side by side also drives this [concept of] EFL home.
>
> *(Reflection)*

Inspired by this perception, 11 (79%) MU teachers emphasized in their teaching philosophy the significant role of context in vocabulary and grammar teaching; in order to help students use English appropriately in both formal and informal settings, teachers should also minimize students' reliance on bilingual dictionaries and literal translation.

Therefore, MU teachers' new perceptions of students' learning environment and needs were manifested in their language teaching philosophy and pedagogy. This demonstrates their construction of both identity-in-discourse and identity-in-practice; at the same time, it shows teacher's dialogic response to students (Hallman, 2015), or the relational nature of teacher identity.

Fourth, during this activity, MU teachers (10, 71%), deeply impressed by GUFS students' active pursuit of "authentic English," became more aware of their identity as native English-speaking teachers. Among them, seven teachers recognized their advantage in the target language, for instance, their sense of language appropriateness based on intuition. On the other hand, three teachers realized that native speakers cannot explain *what* the problem is and *how* to fix it simply based on intuition (Class Discussion). Although native English is no longer the only language model in a world that recognizes different varieties of English, undeniably, the "native speaker" identity is part of pre-service teachers' resources (Miller, 2009; Morgan, 2004), making them language authorities in the eyes of students. In the meantime, MU teachers recognized the necessity of professional knowledge and training to the construction of professional identity.

In short, through this cross-border activity, MU teachers developed new perceptions of Chinese ESL students, their own identity as language teachers, and English teaching. These new perceptions shaped their own language teaching philosophy and pedagogy, enabling them to construct their identities-in-discourse.

## *Pre-Service Teachers' Identity-in-Practice*

MU teachers also gained a deeper understanding of Chinese students' writing through this activity. They recognized the strengths of their writing and provided constructive suggestions to address their needs. Doing so, they enhanced their own professional knowledge both theoretically and practically, built up their professional confidence, and constructed their identity-in-practice.

First, almost all MU teachers (13, 93%) considered the GUFS students' English writing exceptional and exceeding their expectations. In both their feedback and class discussions, they commented on unity, creativity, descriptive language, fresh imagery, sophisticated vocabulary, and clear plot structure in the student writings. For instance, Danielle stated that the metaphors created by the students were original and poetic, although they were not idiomatic in terms of American English. She found certain expressions refreshing, such as "as if someone pumped an extra hundred liters air in [the classroom]" (to highlight the heavy atmosphere in the classroom) and "as if we had a glue to stop time from rolling us forward" (to emphasize the slowdown of time), as she wrote in her feedback: "You have beautiful poetry in your writing! It is easy for native speakers of English to resort to cliché phrases; your fresh imagery makes your writing invigorating." Some teachers also commended the writers' ability to connect with readers: "The author used various techniques such as imagery, providing personal details and creating an emotional response from the reader in order to create empathy" (Marie, Feedback). In addition, they were impressed by the structure and transition of the student writings: "It has a clear plot structure including exposition, rising action, climax, falling action and resolution, and it flows smoothly with necessary transitions" (Ariel, Feedback).

On the other hand, the teachers discussed the recurring issues (or features) in the student writings, made an effort to locate the causes of the issues, and made suggestions to improve the papers. They found that some of the problems in the Chinese student writing were similar to those found among American students, such as grammar errors and insufficient development of ideas, but due to cultural and linguistic differences, some ESL issues, such as word choice, sentence structure, and register, seemed unique to ESL students.

Despite their amazement at the students' large vocabulary and advanced word choice, nine teachers (64%) pointed out that some words were used inappropriately or inaccurately. In their online interaction with the students, the teachers learned that the vocabulary issues mainly came from students' over-reliance on bilingual dictionaries and their neglect of context and word connotations: One Chinese word may correspond to several English words in Chinese-English dictionaries, which usually do not provide sample sentences or further explanations on usage. Accordingly, the teachers recommended that ESL students rely less on literal translation; instead, they should seek opportunities to learn how words are used in real life. ESL students can overcome this vocabulary issue with more language exposure and practice.

Seeing grammar errors as an inseparable part of language learning, MU teachers did not correct each error in their feedback; instead, they paid more attention to the patterns, causes, and treatment of students' grammar errors throughout the cross-border activity. In their communication with students, the teachers also acquired first-hand information about ESL students' misconceptions of sentence structures and word choice and the impact of L1 on L2 study.

MU teachers also pointed out recurring errors in GUFS students' writing, such as shifts in tense and run-on sentences, and asked students to revise their writing based on the intended meaning and goals. For instance, they advised students to double check the time of events when conjugating verbs; they also recommended using short sentences to create suspense and build up to the surprise ending in the students' stories. The teachers further rectified ESL writers' misconceptions about long sentences, telling them that longer sentences are not always more sophisticated, and thus do not always mean better grades; instead of length, students should pay more attention to the purpose of writing and sentence structures. These in-depth interactions allowed these teachers to pin-point students' needs more accurately and thus to provide feedback more effectively. As a teacher commented, "I understood why the errors were made, so I was able to better explain to the writer why in the English language it was not correct" (Yaliza, Reflection).

Eight (57%) MU teachers noted inappropriate use of register in the students' writing. For instance, when creating dialogs to develop plot in their stories, many GUFS writers failed to adjust the style and formality according to the setting and interlocutor. For instance, to the dialog below between a mother and daughter: "'You are my only treasure. You mean everything to me. Please keep clear-minded and don't repeat my mistake,' Luna exhorted Lily. 'I won't let you down, mama. You have my word,' Lily assured Luna," Haley responded: "You may try to use less formal language when having Luna and Lily talking. Some of the words you used wouldn't traditionally be used in this setting" (Feedback). In a class discussion, pre-service teachers associated this issue with students' English proficiency, foreign language context, and lack of practice. To resolve this issue, they believed that teachers should expose students to contextualized, instead of isolated, language.

In this cross-border activity, MU teachers also gained first-hand experience with the varieties of English in a global context, an experience that made them reflect upon the treatment of language variations in students' writing. Should expressions with "accents" (or those that "sound a little off") be treated the same way as "errors"? What is the difference between the two? 11 (79%) teachers shared their thoughts on these questions in their Reflection and Class Discussion; among them, eight (73%) indicated that the key difference between "accents" and "errors" is that the former does not interfere with the intended meaning and comprehension, but the latter may prevent readers from perceiving the focus of the writing. For instance, "Our friendship didn't fade out as the sun rose" and "You really brought me surprise" (instead of You surprised me) may impact the flow of the essays but not the intended meaning, so they are examples of "accents." On the other hand, "was" in "Can we turn on the air-conditioner? I was [am] roasting!" belongs to the category of "errors," because the incorrect verb conjugation makes the meaning confusing. Due to the differences between the two, most teachers agreed that it is not necessary to fix the accents; instead of simply telling students the "correct" answer, teachers may take the opportunity to discuss with students the diversity of language and culture. Moreover, the teachers believed that the English writers' original, non-cliché imagery adds to the flavor of their writing, and therefore should be encouraged. However, common errors such as verb conjugation should be pointed out and corrected, not only because of their interference with writers' purposes but also the un-negligible social implications resulting from the errors. At the same time, some teachers pointed out that although accents are "not incorrect," they are not "conventional" or "typical" (Kyra, Reflection). When discussing how to address students' needs, three teachers mentioned the importance of native English exposure; for instance, "I would try to facilitate substantial interaction with native English speakers . . . and expose [students] to a lot of native English movies and even books" (Danielle, Reflection).

As discussed above, this activity has motivated MU teachers to deliberate over the English variations in ESL writing. They did not assume the role of grammar police, or simply "correct" GUFS students' language "errors," nor did they preconceive the deficiency of the students' writing (You, 2012). As readers, they tried to respect the writers' purposes and intended meaning. Border-crossing activities should not be limited to one party fixing language issues for the other party, but should focus on the purpose of communications (see Wu's chapter in this volume). Therefore, this eye-opening experience allowed the teachers to see the diversity and creativity of English as a global language; their focus on meaning rather than form and their treatment of learners' languages as resources manifested their translingual awareness and practice (Canagarajah, 2013). On the other hand, some teachers' resorting to native English to address students' accents showed their deeply ingrained monolingual mindset shaped by their previous learning experience.

Through analyzing GUFS students' essays and interacting with the writers, MU teachers developed a deeper understanding of ESL writing, teacher feedback, and teachers' roles as mediators of learning. They identified ESL writers' strengths and recognized their innovative language use; at the same time, they diagnosed writers' issues, located the causes and patterns of these issues, and provided constructive feedback to resolve them. This means the teachers' feedback met the criteria of mediated learning interaction: intentionality (which is to help ESL writers improve their writing), reciprocity (which is the active online interactions between teachers and students), and meaning (which refers to the significance of the interactions: the identification of strengths and weaknesses in students' writing, and strategies to improve the weaknesses) (Feuerstein, Rand, & Rynders, 1988), making these teachers effective mediators of learning. In this activity, pre-service teachers also realized the importance of language learners' active participation in the feedback activity system (Lee, 2014), and thus fostered a deeper understanding of the roles teachers and learners play in language learning.

In short, MU pre-service teachers advanced their perceptions of ESL writing, teacher/learner roles, and the different varieties of English through this cross-border activity. The enhancement of their professional knowledge further promoted their professional confidence: more than half of the teachers (57%) indicated that this activity elevated their interest and confidence in teaching ESL; they also wished to gain more opportunities to learn other aspects of ESL learning, such as listening and speaking. Therefore, this activity helped the teachers position themselves professionally in practice, foster their "relational self" in negotiations with peers and students (Liu, 2015), and eventually construct their identity-in-practice.

## Pre-Service Teachers' Identity-in-Activity

Although most MU teachers did not have much real-life teaching experience, this cross-border activity shaped their identity construction from social, cultural, and historical perspectives. First, before participating in this activity, the teachers' notions (or preconceptions) of language learners mainly originated from their own foreign language learning experience; their previous monolingual, monocultural learning environment and mindset also contributed to their misconception of ESL students (see section "Pre-Service Teachers' Identity-in-Discourse"). They benefited substantially from the online interactions with GUFS students, enhancing perceptions of themselves, their students, and their future careers. Second, for the few MU teachers who had taught American students before, this activity made them realize the limitations of their current ESL programs and the necessity of high-quality ESL programs in the public school system (see section "Pre-Service Teachers' Identity-in-Discourse"). This reflection demonstrates the restrictions of school environment on teacher identities. As a result, sociocultural factors such as the teachers' personal experience (foreign language learning experience), educational environment (monolingual student body), educational system (foreign language policies), and work environment played a role in their identity construction.

Furthermore, in this transnational activity, MU teachers also gained a firsthand understanding of the different rhetorical conventions in English and Chinese writing, and therefore saw the close connection between language and culture. For instance, eight (57%) teachers found a unique feature in GUFS students' writing: expressing emotion with an analogy to nature, which is a significant rhetorical strategy in traditional Chinese essay writing (Li, 1996) but rarely used in academic writing in English. Some teachers expressed puzzlement at this strategy; for instance, Marie mentioned several times in her feedback that she was not sure how the scenery descriptions fit into the writer's story. In contrast, others, such as Kyra, regarded it a beautiful way to express feelings. Either way, these pre-service teachers all recognized the presence of culture, hence students' cultural identity, in ESL writing: "I definitely saw cultural leakage into writing" (Marie, Reflection); "The biggest thing I learned was about their culture and how present it was in their writing" (Jenn, Reflection). This inspiration also helped them realize the inseparability of language, culture, and identity, the complicated nature of English education, and the transnational nature of English writing instruction.

Through this cross-border activity, MU teachers adjusted their preconceptions of ESL students and ESL writing that resulted from influences such as their history, culture, conventions, and educational environment and system. By enriching and complicating their perceptions, pre-service teachers took initial steps in crossing national, linguistic, and cultural borders in language education, and constructed their identity-in-activity.

## Discussion and Conclusion

To sum up, this cross-border activity is a "fresh" and "authentic" (Sidney; Yaliza) experience for MU teachers that facilitated their ESL teacher identity construction through discourse, practice, and activity. It also demonstrated the intertwined relationship between teachers' perception, knowledge, pedagogy, and identity (Miller, 2009): By reading GUFS students' essays and interacting with the writers, MU teachers updated their perceptions of ESL students' attitudes, needs, and language environment. These new perceptions allowed them to further understand teacher/student roles in language education and inspired them to develop their own ESL teaching philosophy. They constructed their professional identities in discourse and practice, which is a process impacted by social, cultural, and historical factors. In addition, the teachers interacted with GUFS students in various roles, which showed the shifting and fluid nature of identity: The teachers were peers as well as teachers; they were American readers that respected writers' purposes as well as effective mediators of learning; they were native English speakers with certain language authority, but not grammar police that simply caught and corrected errors. The teachers also exhibited multiple teacher identities (Racelis & Matsuda, 2014) in this activity: language teacher, writing teacher, and L2 writing teachers.

In his book *Language Teacher Education for a Global Society*, Kumaravadivelu (2011) urges teacher educators to "create the conditions necessary for teachers to know, to analyze, to recognize, to do, and to see what constitutes learning, teaching, and teacher development" (p. 122). This border-crossing activity provided such an opportunity for pre-service ESL teachers to better *know* varieties of English and rhetorical strategies across cultures, *analyze* students' needs and attitudes, *recognize* their own strengths and weaknesses as teachers, *do* the right kind of teaching, and *see* language education from different perspectives. This activity helped pre-service teachers move away from a monolingual and monocultural ideology to a global orientation to English teacher identity (You, 2016a,

2016b). However, despite their recognition of different varieties of English and their awareness of student needs, the solutions some teachers proposed to address student needs revealed the superiority of native English over other varieties and a monolingual mindset deep down. The global facet of transnational identity construction requires not only an awareness of worldwide trends of language and people (their diversity and mobility), but also incorporation of the trends into instruction (Pennington, 2014); from this perspective, the teachers have not achieved a truly translingual or transnational approach to language teaching.

Moreover, in this era of globalization, foreign language education calls for multi-channel, multi-mode methods of foreign language study (Zheng, Du, & Wu, 2013, p. 2). This applies not only to ESL students, but also to foreign language teachers (You, 2016a). Unlike traditional overseas immersion programs, Chinese students and American pre-service teachers in this study interacted with each other and gained first-hand experience online, without traveling abroad. Open, accessible, and convenient, this mode allows more teachers and students to see beyond the limitations of their physical environment, to challenge their own preconceptions of the cultural other, to improve their intercultural competence, and to thus evolve their identities in a transnational context. To truly benefit from these new channels and modes for border-crossing, however, both teachers and students should be wary of the power differentials between speakers of different varieties of English and learn to respect and "appreciate each other's accented English" (Liu, 2011, p. 268).

Admittedly, due to pre-service ESL teachers' limited teaching activities, this research mainly relied on their narrations and reflections (narrated identity) when studying teacher identity construction. In addition to analyzing pre-service teachers' feedback on the student essays and their correspondence with the student writers, if observations of their teaching performance were available, this study could better investigate the consistency between teachers' narrated identity and enacted identity (Kanno & Stuart, 2011). Furthermore, a semester-long course project would be useful for understanding the teacher identity construction, as the teacher-student interactions in this activity were only short-term. Since identity construction is a long-term activity, teacher identities will evolve over time with influence from school, colleagues, and parents in day-to-day interactions. If conditions allow, a longitudinal follow-up study could further enlighten us on the sociocultural impact on teacher identity construction.

## References

Burns, E., & Bell, S. (2011). Narrative construction of professional teacher identity of teachers with dyslexia. *Teaching and Teacher Education, 27*, 952–960.

Byram, M. (2000). Assessing intercultural competence in language teaching. *Sprogforum, 18*, 8–13.

Canagarajah, S. (2013). *Translingual practice: Global Englishes and cosmopolitan relations.* New York, NY: Routledge.

Cross, R., & Gearon, M. (2007). The confluence of doing, thinking, and knowing. In A. B. Clemans, & A. Kostogriz (Eds.), *Dimensions of professional learning* (pp. 53–67). Dordrecht: Sense Publishers.

Duff, P., & Uchida, Y. (1997). The negotiation of teachers' sociocultural identities and practices in postsecondary EFL classrooms. *TESOL Quarterly, 31*(3), 451–461.

Feuerstein, R., Rand, Y., & Rynders, J. (1988). *Don't accept me as I am.* New York, NY: Plenum.

Flores, M. (2001). Person and context in becoming a new teacher. *Journal of Education for Teaching, 27*(2), 135–148.

Gee, J. P. (1996). *Social linguistics and literacies: Ideology in discourses* (2nd ed.). London: Taylor & Francis.

Gee, J. P. (2001). Literacy, discourse, and linguistics: Introduction. In E. Cushman, M. Rose, B. Kroll, & E. R. Kintgen (Eds.), *Literacy: A critical sourcebook* (pp. 525–544). Boston, MA: Bedford/St. Martins.

Guo, X., & Wang, Q. (2009). Jiaoyu shixi yu zhiqian yingyujiaoshi zhuanye fazhan guanxi tanjiu 教育实习与职前英语教师专业发展关系探究 [A study on the relationship between internships and preservice teachers' professional development]. Waiyu yu waiyu jiaoxue 外语与外语教学 [*Foreign Languages and Foreign Language Education*], *3*, 28–33.

Hall, L. A., Johnson, A. S., Juzwik, M. M., Wortham, S. E. F., & Mosley, M. (2010). Teacher identity in the context of literacy teaching: Three explorations of classroom positioning and interaction in secondary schools. *Teaching and Teacher Education, 26*(1), 234–243.

Hallman, H. (2015). Teacher identity as a dialogic response: A Bakhtinian perspective. In Y. L. Cheung, S. B. Said, & K. Park (Eds.), *Advances and current trends in language teacher identity research* (pp. 3–15). New York: Routledge.

Johnson, K. (2003). "Every experience is a moving force": Identity and growth through mentoring. *Teaching and Teacher Education, 19*, 787–800.

Kanno, Y., & Stuart, C. (2011). Learning to become a second language teacher: Identities-in-practice. *The Modern Language Journal, 95*(ii), 236–252.

Kumaravadivelu, B. (2011). *Language teacher education for a global society.* New York, NY: Routledge.

Lave, J., & Wenger, E. (1991). *Situated learning: Legitimate peripheral participation.* Cambridge: Cambridge University Press.

Lee, I. (2013). Becoming a writing teacher: Using "identity" as an analytic lens to understand EFL writing teachers' development. *Journal of Second Language Writing, 22*, 330–345.

Lee, I. (2014). Revisiting teacher feedback in EFL writing from sociocultural perspectives. *TESOL Quarterly, 48*(1), 201–213.

Lee, J. F. K. (2009). ESL student teachers' perceptions of a short-term overseas immersion programme. *Teaching and Teacher Education, 25*, 1095–1104.

Li, J. (2015). *Xiaoxue yingyu shixi jiaoshi zhuanye shenfen renzhi yanjiu* 小学英语实习 教师专业身份认知研究 [*A study on the perceptions of elementary school student teachers' professional identity*]. Master's Thesis, Ningbo University.

Li, X. (1996). *"Good writing" in cross-cultural contexts.* Albany: State University of New York Press.

Liu, Y. (2011). Power perceptions and negotiations in a cross-national mail writing activity. *Journal of Second Language Writing, 20*, 257–270.

Liu, Y. (2015). Jiaoshi shenfen rentong jiangou wenti xintan 教师身份认同建构问题新 探 [Issues in teacher identity construction]. Jiaoyu lilun yu shijian 教育理论与实践 [*Educational Theories and Practice*], *33*, 42–44.

Miller, J. (2009). Teacher identity. In A. Burns, & J. C. Richards (Eds.), *The Cambridge guide to language teacher education* (pp. 172–181). Cambridge: Cambridge University Press.

Millersville University Fast Facts. (2017). Retrieved June 9, 2017, from www.millersville.edu/admissions/undergrad/basics/index.php

Morgan, B. (2002). Critical practice in community-based ESL programs: A Canadian perspective. *Journal of Language, Identity, and Education, 1*, 141–162.

Morgan, B. (2004). Teacher identity as pedagogy: Towards a field-internal conceptualization in bilingual and second language education. In J. Brutt-Griffler & M. Varghese (Eds.), *Re-writing bilingualism and the bilingual educator's knowledge base* (pp. 80–96). Clevedon, England: Multilingual Matters. Peirce, B. (1995). Social identity, investment and language learning. *TESOL Quarterly, 29*(1), 9–31.

Pennington, M. C. (2014). Teacher identity in TESOL: A frames perspective. In Y. L. Cheung, S. B. Said, & K. Park (Eds.), *Advances and current trends in language teacher identity research* (pp. 16–30). London: Routledge.

Racelis, J. V., & Matsuda, P. K. (2014). Exploring the multiple identities of L2 writing teachers. In Y. L. Cheung, S. B. Said, & K. Park (Eds.), *Advances and current trends in language teacher identity research* (pp. 203–216). London: Routledge.

Richards, J. C. (2010). Competence and performance in language teaching. *RELC Journal, 41*(2), 101–122.

Singh, G., & Richards, J. (2006). Teaching and learning in the language teacher education course room. *RELC, 37*(2), 149–175.

Smolcic, E. (2011). Becoming a culturally responsive teacher. In K. Johnson, & P. Golombek (Eds.), *Research on second language teacher education: A sociocultural perspective on professional development* (pp. 15–30). New York: Routledge.

Varghese, M., Morgan, B., Johnston, B., & Johnson, K. (2005). Theorizing language teacher identity: Three perspectives and beyond. *Journal of Language, Identity and Education, 4*, 21–44.

Willard-Holt, C. (2001). The impact of a short-term international experience for pre-service teachers. *Teaching and Teacher Education, 17*(4), 505–517.

Xie, S., & Xiong, M. (2014). Zhiqian jiaoshi zhuanye shenfen rentong de lilun fazhan yu yanjiu zhanwang 职前教师专业身份认同的理论发展与研究展望 [Theoretical developments and research perspective in professional identification of the preservice teachers]. Jiaoshi jiaoyu xuebao 教师教育学报 [*Journal of Teacher Education*], *6*, 10–17.

Xu, Q. (2013). *Huayu shijiao xia gaozhong zhiqian yingyu jiaoshi shenfen rentong de pipanxing renzhongzhi yanjiu* 话语视角下高中职前英语教师身份认同的批判性人种志研究 [*A critical ethnographic study on high school preservice teachers' identification from the discourse perspective*]. Master's Thesis, Zhejiang Normal University.

Yang, C. C. (2011). Pre-service English teachers' perceptions of an overseas field experience programme. *Australian Journal of Teacher Education, 36*, 92–104.

You, X. (2012). Towards English writing research with Chinese characteristics. *Chinese Journal of Applied Linguistics, 35*, 263–270.

You, X. (2016a). *Cosmopolitan English and transliteracy*. Carbondale, IL: Southern Illinois University Press.

You, X. (2016b). Historical knowledge and reinventing English writing teacher identity in Asia. *Writing & Pedagogy, 83*, 409–431.

Zheng, C., Du, Y., & Wu, Z. (2013). *Zhongmei xuesheng yingyu kuayang hudong: Xingdong yanjiu yu yuliao fenxi* 中美学生英语"跨洋互动": 行动研究与语料分析 [*Cross-Pacific exchange: Action research and data analysis*]. Beijing: Kexue chubanshe 北京: 科学出版社 [Beijing: Science Press].

## Appendix: Reader Response Guide

**Overall Response** (State your general reaction to the text; your main observation; strength of the essay)

**Focus** (State what you think the focus/thesis statement is; indicate whether all sections of the text fit the focus)

**Development for Readers** (Discuss whether the text supplies enough, too much, or too little detail for the focus/thesis)

**Organization and Coherence** (State what organization you see; identify what parts fit and what parts don't; comment on coherence—how helpful or not helpful the transitions are between sections)

**Design** (Comment on the overall visual effectiveness of the text; indicate whether the layout of the page is consistent with the audience, genre, and purpose of the text)

**Language, Grammar, Conventions** (Point out significant or repeated errors in these categories)

**Main Emphasis for Revision** (State the most important thing to change for the next version)

# 12

# THE AFFORDANCES OF FACEBOOK FOR TEACHING ESL WRITING

*June Yichun Liu*

## Introduction

With the rapid development of information technology and the growing demands of digital natives, social media has been increasingly viewed by educators as indispensable for teaching and learning. Web 2.0 technology allows users to interact and collaborate with each other in social media dialogues where they create user-generated content. One of the compelling benefits of Web 2.0 technology for second language (L2) learning is that it offers students a platform for interacting with diverse users of the target language, giving them exposure to target contexts and resources. Studies suggest that Web 2.0 technology has the potential to motivate students (Blattner & Fiori, 2009; Shih, 2011), enhance collaborative learning (Maloney, 2007), promote critical thinking (Bugeja, 2006), and develop a sense of learning community and socio-pragmatic competence (Blattner & Fiori, 2009). Specific to the teaching of L2 writing, studies suggest that Web 2.0 technology, such as weblogs, Wiki, and Facebook, supports cross-cultural communication (Blattner & Fiori, 2009; Wang, 2012), improves EFL learners' writing skills (Shih, 2011, 2013), advances informal learning (Madge, Meek, Wellens, & Hooley, 2009; Selwyn, 2009), and promotes learners' agency and identity (Pasfield-Neofitou, 2011).

Among the various social media, Facebook has enjoyed wide use in teaching L2 writing. Influenced by cognitively oriented Second Language Acquisition (SLA) scholarship, classroom studies tend to focus on testing the effectiveness of Facebook groups for improving student writing; writing is often assessed as a product based on monolingual assumptions. In contrast, influenced by New Literacy Studies, researchers of students' extracurricular Facebook use tend to adopt a multilingual perspective, focusing on their deployment of multilingual and multimodal resources for responding to rhetorical situations and for performing social functions (Depew, 2011; DePew & Miller-Cochran, 2010; Schreiber, 2015; Lee, 2011). As Facebook use is both a cognitive and social activity, I argue that scholars and teachers of L2 writing should also take a New Literacy Studies approach to explore the pedagogical affordances of Facebook.

In this chapter, I adopt a New Literacy Studies approach to explore the affordances of Facebook for academic literacy development. This approach emphasizes that reading and writing are not just cognitive but also social activities, situated in specific social contexts and shaped by sociopolitical and material forces (Street, 2003). In a first-year English course at a Taiwanese university, I created a Facebook group where fifty students shared drafts of their academic writing as well as their life experiences. The writing strategies used by students on Facebook show their awareness of genre and register; they consciously moved across genre or register boundaries for creativity and identity work. Such language practice demonstrates translingual subject positions among some students. After sorting students' Facebook posts into academic and non-academic writing categories, I found that these two types of Facebook discourse shaped students' academic writing in distinct ways.

## Facebook and L2 Writing

Published studies on Facebook and L2 writing can be roughly divided into classroom and out-of-school-based research. In most of the classroom studies, Facebook has been used as a technological tool for discussing and practicing writing, and writing has been understood as a product. Influenced by cognitively oriented SLA scholarship, these studies tend to adopt experimental designs, using pre-tests and post-tests to assess the effectiveness of the technological intervention (Shih, 2011, 2013; Shukor & Noordin, 2014; Suthiwartnarueput & Wasanasomsithi, 2012). Implicitly embracing monolingual assumptions, the researchers focus on the formal features of the student texts and evaluate them based on native speaker norms. For instance, Suthiwartnarueput and Wasanasomsithi (2012) examined the use of Facebook among eighty-three first-year Thai college students. They created a Facebook page where students could discuss English grammar and writing with the teacher and their peers. On Facebook, students left messages, posted their writings, or chatted about the problems they had encountered with grammar and writing. Most discussions dealt with issues of sentence structure, word meaning, parts of speech, and relative clauses. Based on the students' posts, scores from a pre-test and a post-test, and student interviews, the study found that Facebook discussions were helpful to the students' learning of grammar and to their writing competence. Similarly, Shih (2013) studied the effects of Facebook in a Business English course in a Taiwanese university. As part of the course, participants (111 students) completed four writing tasks on Facebook; they also provided feedback on each other's writings posted

Facebook for Teaching ESL Writing **205**

on Facebook, focusing on tense, spelling, and structure. Comparing students' pre-test and post-test scores, Shih found that the participants made significant progress on their writing. This result was confirmed in a survey questionnaire and interviews, showing that Facebook was effective in enabling the participants' English learning.

Classroom studies also examined writing from a process perspective, focusing on students' writing strategies and challenges (Barrot, 2016; Razak, Saeed, & Ahmad, 2013; Razak & Saeed, 2014). These studies took a socio-cognitive perspective to writing. For instance, in Razak and Saeed's (2014) study, they examined the strategies the students used in collaborative revision activities. They collected the original writing tasks, revised paragraphs, online feedback, and student responses to the post-revision. They identified three common types of errors, i.e., language (form and meaning), unity, and content. The strategies students adopted in correcting errors include addition, substitution, deletion, permutation, consolidation, distribution, negotiation, and scaffolding. These findings show that Facebook was helpful in the learners' revision process. It encouraged peripheral learners' (i.e., new members of the group) participation in the revision activities by creating social ties, a supportive learning environment, and a sense of autonomy among its members.

In contrast, studies of L2 students' use of Facebook and other social media programs in extracurricular contexts tend to view writing as a socially-constructed meaning making process, involving multi-literate practice and identity construction. Scholars tend to take a multilingual, transnational perspective rather than a monolingual perspective in studying language use (DePew, 2011; DePew & Miller-Cochran, 2010; Lee, 2011; Schreiber, 2015; You, 2008, 2011). For instance, You (2008, 2011) examined the rhetorical strategies used by Chinese youths when they exchanged messages on an English-based bulletin board in China. He found that the youths used different languages (English and Chinese), dialects (Mandarin and regional Chinese dialects), and images in their online communication. Further, they were able to respond to different rhetorical situations by selecting different discursive patterns for meaning making and for identity construction. Focusing on identity construction as well, Schreiber (2015) examined Aleksandar's, a Serbian college student, literacy practice on Facebook. She found that as a hip-hop fan, this student constructed a fluid transnational identity by capitalizing on the affordances of multimodality. He used Serbian or English and posted images and links to video clips to mark his local and global membership. Studies of L2 students' extracurricular use of social media demonstrate that they are capable of using multilingual and multimodal resources in social-networking in ways that deviate from the bounded, monolingual assumptions of language and nation.

The studies reviewed above have examined L2 students' Facebook use in school and extracurricular contexts. When Facebook is used in school, teachers and researchers tend to treat it as a neutral tool for improving student's school/

academic writing. They tend to focus on its benefits as measured by the extent to which features of student texts match native-speaker norms. When Facebook use is studied outside of school, scholars have focused on students' multilingual and multimodal literacy practice. They tend to highlight and celebrate students' agency in using multi-literate resources in constructing fluid identities. It is important to note that studies on Facebook and L2 writing seem to assume that school and extracurricular settings constitute two distinct sociocultural spaces which demand different uses of Facebook. While Facebook could be used as a technological tool for improving formal features of student writing, it could also serve diverse social functions inside and outside school. However, there are few classroom studies that have actively collapsed the boundaries of these two sociocultural spaces by tapping into both Facebook's impact on formal features of student texts and its social functions in school.

Therefore, in the present study, like some of the previous studies, Facebook was integrated into a traditional ESL writing class. Adopting a New Literacy Studies approach, two questions were raised for the present study. First, what are the features of the texts produced by students on Facebook? Second, what do these texts mean for the students' identities and academic socialization? To understand students' L2 use on Facebook and to find out whether their informal learning in social media has an impact on their academic writing, I conducted teacher research, which will be reported below.

## Community of Practice and a Biosocial Perspective to Writing

Aligned with New Literacy Studies, the present study adopts "community of practice" and a biosocial perspective to writing as the key constructs for examining the affordances of Facebook for teaching L2 writing. Observing how novices gain legitimate peripheral participation, Wenger (1998) defines learning as "a social participation" (p. 4). Learning takes place when a group of people in a shared domain of interest are engaged in meaningful social interaction or participating in collaborative activities. Through negotiation with the community discourse and community values, learners could be enabled to acquire the domain knowledge and be empowered to construct their identity. An L2 writing class can be viewed as a community of practice; sharing the same purpose of acquiring writing conventions and improving one's writing ability, students collaborate online or in-person on reading and writing activities.

Learning in online communities takes place through written language, often informal or non-standard. Challenging the conventional Anglo-American speech community that sets Standard English as the norms, Canagarajah (2007) proposes a biosocial paradigm of the communicative practice of multilinguals. Due to globalization, multilingual communities have been emerging and developing. This new context features "transnational affiliations, diaspora communities, digital communication, fluid social boundaries, and the blurring of time-space distinctions" (p. 924). Thus, in a multilingual community, the dichotomies of language constructs need to be reexamined, such as grammar and pragmatics, determinism and agency, individual and community, purity and hybridity, fix and fluidity, cognition and context, and monolingual and multilingual acquisition (p. 923–924). Linguistic variations used by multilinguals may be unintelligible to some but may make perfect sense to others. Although variants may be linguistically inappropriate to the norms and have little normative consistency, they emerge through social interaction and through pragmatic negotiation for effective communication. Therefore, Canagarajah argues that these variants, which are indeterminate, open, and fluid, should not be regarded as secondary to the traditional norms. Effective communication is the responsibility of all interlocutors. Therefore, a seemingly failed communication could be viewed as the communicators' strategies that go awry rather than as one's language deficit.

## Methodology

### Participants and Context

The study was conducted at a national university in Taiwan, involving fifty first-year students. They took a two-semester course called "College English" with me. Their English proficiency fell within the range of intermediate B1 level according to the Common European Framework of Reference (CEFR) bands of EF Standard English Test. I created a Facebook group for the course in the first semester to provide a virtual platform for students to use English for everyday communication and for discussing academic writing. To give students time to become acquainted with each other, data collection started in the second semester. This online community was semi-public: a user's profile was only visible to his or her Facebook friends. Students could create a new account or use their existing ones to participate in this community. Although it was designed by the teacher-researcher, the community very much operated bottom-up because it was developed and shaped by the students' discourse, experiences, and problem solving strategies. Students' Facebook participation counted for 5% of the total grade in the second semester, enough to serve as an incentive but without creating high-stakes pressure for students. To create a friendly English environment, I regularly posted course-related materials, such as articles, links to films, music, and pictures, as well as non-course-related materials, such as jokes and humorous cartoons. Additionally, my teaching assistants and I frequently posted questions related to classroom writing instruction. We also provided comments and suggestions on students' writing exercises posted on Facebook. Students were encouraged to share their essay drafts, diaries, course reflections, comments, pictures, and anything else that they were willing to share. Other than the requirement that students should use English, they were free to interact in whatever way made them comfortable.

In the second semester, the students were required to write one argumentative essay. In the classroom, I lectured on writing conventions and strategies, including thesis statement, topic sentence, organization, authorial position, supporting evidence, argument and counter-argument, coherence, and logic. The students were expected to stake their positions based on supporting evidence, to organize their ideas by following the writing convention and logical reasoning, and to make arguments by analyzing both the pros and cons. On Facebook, students were encouraged to brainstorm with their peers to generate ideas, share drafts, invite peer comments, and offer comments to each other. My teaching assistants and I interacted with students by providing feedback on Facebook as well. At the end of the semester, the students turned in the final draft of their argumentative essay.

## Data Collection

Data came from multiple sources, including perceptual data (one reflection journal, one survey, and one interview) and performance data (drafts of student writings and Facebook messages). In the middle of the second semester, the students were first asked to turn in a reflection paper, designed to elicit their perceptions and reflections on Facebook use. After the midterm exam, a survey was conducted among the students about the effects of Facebook on their English writing, motivation, and attitude. Moreover, a semi-structured interview was conducted after students had submitted their writing projects to assess what they had learned and how they had learned it. Given that the students might be sensitive to cues related to Facebook but insensitive to their acquisition of writing knowledge, I avoided asking questions about Facebook. To solicit the students' responses but avoid misleading them, I adopted Eraut's (2004) suggestion by asking indirect questions about their attitudes towards and habits of learning. For example, I asked students to describe their habits and attitudes, and then their evolution throughout the school year. Students were also asked what types of knowledge, skills, or competence they used to complete their writing tasks, how they prepared for their writing project, solved their writing problems, came up with their writing strategies, and what and how they would like to change about their writing strategies.

## Data Analysis

To answer the two research questions, I took four major steps in my analysis of the data. First, I divided the texts the students produced into three kinds: (1) the academic writing drafts (AWD) and student comments posted on Facebook; (2) non-academic writing (NAW) posts on Facebook related to chatting, diary, status updates, sharing (articles, pictures, and videos), and so on; (3) the final draft of the argumentative essay.

Second, I studied the features of language use on Facebook, language used in both the drafts of the argumentative essay and the non-academic posts on Facebook. I compared the two types of texts to identify their distinct features.

Third, I examined the three types of texts to identify the affordances of Facebook for the students' academic English writing. I compared the students' first and last drafts of the argumentative essay. The changes made in the final draft were taken as the revisions generated partly due to peer interaction on Facebook.

Finally, to answer the research questions, students' performance data (i.e., the texts they produced) was triangulated with their perceptual data in order to understand the writers' rhetorical choices and identity work. To enhance the reliability in data analysis, two trained research assistants examined the perceptual data using an open-coding method. They first scrutinized the data and marked each meaningful chunk with summary words. Exhaustive data analysis was used for categorization, grouping similar comments. If the existing category did not fit the data, a new category was created. After sorting out the categories, the two assistants compared and discussed inconsistencies with me to reach consensus.

## Results

### *Features of Students' Language Use on Facebook*

The students reshaped the native speaker norms through their socio-pragmatic negotiations. This Facebook community was little monitored, thus it was less judgmental and less form-constrained than a traditional writing class. The naturally emerging discourse, a mix of Chinese structure with English and other language codes, though sometimes lacking linguistic consistency, was well intelligible to the participants. The community of practice allowed the participants to test their "peculiar" discourse or develop their personal styles.

The discourse of AWD on Facebook sometimes featured an informal style and a distinct personal voice. Transitioning from early drafts of the argumentative essay posted on Facebook to the final draft, some students showed awareness of register. The following example of Zen's AWD on Facebook shows her distinct voice and style.

> News has become a tool of placement marketing. **It's most unforgiveable** that government **officals** are joining this business. **I'm really disapprove** of the government's breaking the independence of news.

The expressions "It's most unforgiveable that . . ." and "I'm really disapprove of . . ." show her strong and disfavored position. However, the misspelled word "officals," the contractions (e.g., "It's" and "I'm"), and grammar errors (e.g. "I'm really disapprove of") also reveal her informal style and suggest a careless or undisciplined writer identity. Although no one provided detailed feedback on her draft on Facebook other than making encouraging comments with three "Likes," the language style in Zen's final draft was changed. It became more formal and more balanced in opinion:

> Most people believe that news is produced independently and honestly. As a result, I disagree that government broke the independence of news to promote policies through news placement marketing.

Zen used "most" to qualify the referent "people." She also inserted a transition phrase, "as a result," to bridge the first and the second idea. Furthermore, she used "disagree" to replace "I'm really disapprove of . . ." to show her firm, formal, and grammatically appropriate voice.

Facebook served as a contact zone where Zen shuttled between Chinglish and Standard English, between a relaxed and a disciplined writer. The informal Facebook context allowed Zen to enjoy the agency and ownership of her English variation rather than satisfying the native-speaker norms. Writing informally did not impede her from transitioning to formal writing in her final draft. Her ability to shift from informal to formal discourse demonstrates her awareness of register and identity, as well as a translingual writing competence.

The NAW on Facebook also featured an informal style with clear traces of colloquialism. Comparing AWD and NAW, some informal characteristics of NAW were identified. For example, the length of each paragraph in the NAW texts was shorter than that in the AWD. The flow of NAW usually was less coherent than that of AWD. The discourse of NAW showed fewer transitional devices, such as "on the contrary," "as a result," or "additionally," but NAW contained more colloquial forms, such as using the first person pronoun to make statements (e.g., "I miss my dog"), incomplete sentences (e.g., "tired, but happy today"), spontaneous response (e.g., "oh, yes, cutting off the extras words are necessary"), and oral language markers (e.g., "ha ha," "ya," "so cool").

The NAW also featured translanguaging; Chinese English was frequently incorporated in the NAW texts. Some students used the particle "lar," "bar," and "der" at the end of an English sentence; for example, "your sharing is so cool lar." "lar" (啦 [la]), "bar" (吧 [ba]), and "der" (的 [de]) are common ending interjections in Mandarin. Code mixing of Mandarin into English sentences, which has become popular among young people in Taiwan, creates a sense of humor and colloquialism facilitating the formation of group membership. Some common Chinglish is generated from literal translation of Mandarin. For example, "cheer up" or "come on, go!" is "add oil" in Chinglish; "turning on TV/light" is "opening TV/light." "Let me think" sometimes is intentionally written as "let me think-think" because in Mandarin, "think-think" (想想) is an idiomatic expression. Some English phrases were displaced by homophonic Mandarin (including its acronyms), Taiwanese, or numbers; for example, "bye-bye" is often replaced by "88 [ba ba]" or "881 [ba ba yi]." Mandarin "wo-ai-li" ("I love you") shares the homophony of "520 [wu.er.ling];" "thank you" is homophonic to "3Q [san.kʰju];" "TMD" refers to Mandarin swear words [ta.ma.de]; "BJ4" is the acronym close to the Mandarin pronunciation of "不解釋 [bu.jie.shi]" ("no explanation"). Some expressions came from computer games, for example "GG" ("good game") refers to "game over" or "you are toast" (完蛋了). Some unique characteristics of NAW texts also include acronyms or abbreviations (e.g., "thx," "LOL," "OMG," "GF"), emoticons (e.g., :D, ;(, :P, XD, QQ, TT), and code borrowings from other languages, such as Kuso (糞, くそ), a Japanese expression referring to ridiculous parodies on the Internet.

In addition to crossing language and dialectal boundaries, the students' translanguaging practice also took place across genre and modal boundaries. In their posts, they often inserted hyperlinks, images, and video clips into the body of their texts, making their texts multimodal. Ding, an education major, often shared his life experiences on Facebook because, as he explained in an interview, his Facebook friends were his real-life friends. He found that, in response to his friends' messages, "translat[ing] what I want to say into English" was "interesting." He had enjoyed Japanese manga, comics, and video games since high school. Several times, he appropriated manga strips creatively to express his feelings and his identity. Take the following post as an example.

> It is so hard to express my feelings these day. So I try to modify some picture in manga to show my mood. I know it should be translated to English, but I don't have that skill to finish it. So I hope more people can see it. I believe I am not lonely.
> I have to sleep now. I will get busy and busy.

In this post, Ding inserted two manga panels into his status update to represent his feelings at the end of the semester (see Figure 12.1, 12.2). In these two panels, he replaced the original dialogue with his own, using Chinese instead of Japanese. The dialogues on the two panels tried to capture the conversations he had or he imagined he had with his classmates. They talked about how much effort they had devoted to preparing for the final exams, and how relieved and excited they were as the semester wound down. Crossing language and genre boundaries, Ding not only shared his feelings with his friends, but more importantly asserted his identity within the Japanese manga world. Doing so, like Aleksandar in Schreiber's (2015) study, Ding came to establish both a local and a global membership. Facebook enabled Ding to find his place in the new place (the university), a step critical for his academic socialization in the long run. The importance of Facebook in his initiation into the university was confirmed a few years later. After his undergraduate studies, Ding went to Japan to pursue his Master's

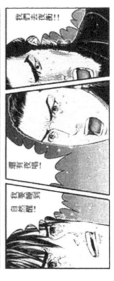

FIGURE 12.1 Ding's Japanese Manga Remix 1

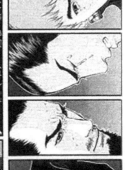

FIGURE 12.2  Ding's Japanese Manga Remix 2

degree in teaching Chinese as a foreign language. In retrospect, he agreed that the Facebook community enabled him to fit in his undergraduate studies.

## The Affordances of Facebook for Students' Learning of Academic Writing

The affordances of Facebook for students' learning of academic writing can be divided into the affordance of AWD and the affordance of NAW. Analysis of the data suggests that the practice of AWD on Facebook contributed to the participants' improvement in academic discourse, informal learning, autonomous learning, and identity reconstruction. However, the affordances of the NAW on Facebook for academic writing were minimal.

The practices of AWD on Facebook seemed to have improved students' academic writing. 87% of the students chose to post their argumentative essay drafts on Facebook to receive feedback from their peers, the teaching assistants, and myself. The comments on Facebook, especially those from the teaching assistants or the teacher-researcher, were effective for students' revisions. The survey results show that 85% of the participants considered the Facebook community beneficial to their writing assignment. Apart from local errors dealing with spelling and grammar, the peer feedback also focused on genre conventions including thesis statement, topic sentence, supporting evidence, and transition. For example, when Zen posted her first draft on Facebook, I suggested to her that her essay lacked topic sentences and transitions. In her final draft, both issues were fixed. Global issues (e.g., organization) and conceptual issues (e.g., rhetorical style and logical fallacy) were rarely raised in the feedback.

The practices of AWD seemed to have enhanced students' informal and self-learning due to the public nature of Facebook posts. According to the survey, 85% of the students agreed that the Facebook community facilitated self-learning. The survey also showed significant results on self-evaluation through Facebook-ing; 83% (mean = 3.85) of the participants agreed or strongly agreed that reading others' posts and discussions encouraged them to evaluate their own English use by comparing it with that of their peers. In their reflections, for instance, Yen and Kei explained how Facebook motivated them in English learning: "When reading some good works, some people really shocked me by their level of English. That motivated me to study hard to catch up" (Yen). "I can see others' writings and compare them with mine. By this way, I can know my learning situation. Even though I didn't post my writings on FB (I was too lazy to type), I could know where should be noticed from teacher's comments on others' writings. Then, I will check if there is the same mistake in my writings" (Kei).

The peer comments exchanged on Facebook, as well as the student essay drafts, served as important academic writing resources for the students. They especially benefited those who were shy about asking questions in class but Facebook savvy. For example, Hui was quiet in class and only lurked on Facebook. Before reading his reflections and interviewing him, I had viewed him as a passive learner. However, in the interview, he explained how Facebook helped him learn about English writing: "Facebook helped me solve writing problems though I never posted any question. I visited Facebook almost every day. Reading my classmates' posts and the teacher's comments helped me solve my own problems." His reflections were consistent with his comment in the interview: "If I encountered any writing-related questions, I would first surf the FB to find solutions. Unlike others, I think I'm less creative. Thus, I sometimes can't come up with the content to write my own article. At this moment, I would go to Facebook to watch how other people comment on the same topic, and then figure out my own opinion." I checked his essay drafts and noted a few instances that corroborate his reflective report. Hui borrowed a few ideas and expressions from Facebook discussions, which enhanced his writing quality to a certain extent. The Facebook community enabled him to gain legitimate "peripheral participation" (Lave & Wenger, 1991). Yu also reported that she gained knowledge about writing by reading the Facebook posts traded between students, and between students and the teacher. In an interview, Yu revealed that she had acquired knowledge about topic sentence and thesis statement by mining the resources shared by the Facebook community: "I didn't really understand what a topic sentence was when the teacher taught us in class, but I got the idea through reading the writing samples and discussions posted by the other students."

Through community of practice, the students not only acquired the language forms and writing conventions others shared, but also tested what they had learned through interacting with other students online. That is, Facebook allowed situated learning for legitimate peripheral participation, as illustrated by the following case. Lai, a law major, claimed that he was a "passive lurker." Based on his Facebook data, he had interacted with his classmates and me several times. One of his most engaged interactions took place with a discussion on media freedom and privacy. He posted his opinion at the very bottom of a series of messages posted by his classmates. He took a strong position on privacy, and explained why the practice of freedom of speech should not violate privacy:

TW's Constitution No.22 involves privacy protection:

www.judicial.gov.tw/constitutionalcourt/p03_01.asp?expno=603

Yah, I kind of agree people discussed here that media have the "fourth estate," but the "Fourth Estate", so-called mass media's freedom of speech, does not exist. The word "Estate" means social classes: noble, clergy and civilian. Where is the "Fourth Right"? It's just a power that does not really exist, not being protected. Even the western countries don't have a concrete Constitution or law to protect this "Fourth rihgt". The only thing being protected is the freedom of speech. But as the freedom of speech and Privacy are both "Rights" in the Constitution class, these two rights' use should be confined by each other.

*(Lai)*

First, it seemed that Lai had been following the discussion for a while. Second, through reading posts by other participants, he learned related information. Being motivated, he researched this issue and then argued for his position. As a law major, he demonstrated his professional knowledge with an authorial voice. Finally, in his final draft, he incorporated other students' opinions as counterarguments to his own, and he borrowed information from others' posts which he considered professional or academically appropriate. Likewise, others in their writing projects incorporated the information and opinions Lai had shared. The Facebook discussion motivated Lai to do research, to consider opposing views, to read, analyze, and synthesize information, to share and comment, and to take a position. During this invention process, Lai was engaged and transformed from a lurker into a peripheral participant. With his legal knowledge and authorial voice, his informed opinion earned him a community membership. Moreover, Lai's participation and the collective knowledge benefited not only himself, but also all the participants and silent viewers. To sum up, the writing resources, collective feedbacks, and stimuli for self-evaluation promoted informal and autonomous learning.

The practice of AWD encouraged some participants to construct specific identities. The participants came from different disciplines. Not knowing each other well at first, they became better acquainted in the second semester. Since they were required to use English in the Facebook community and to show their real names, this made their English proficiency discernible and some felt face-threatened. Based on the survey, over half of the students (56%, mean=2.7) considered their English not good enough to comment on others' posts, while the others were not comfortable with offering comments in English (18%), or felt it was time consuming to reply in English (17%). In other words, most students seemed hesitant with their English. This hesitation, coupled with their lack of writing knowledge, in turn, molded them into the identity of "learners," which made most of the participants quiet and passive on Facebook in the first half of the semester. The following student comments show how such a mindset helped to construct a learner identity.

> Though I don't dare to post anything, I go to Facebook about once a week. The main purpose is to see others' writings, especially Lee's. His posts really deserve to be read and learned by us.
>
> *(Reflection, Chen)*

> I never provide comments on other's writings because I think I don't have the ability, and I'm afraid of leaving something wrong and absurd.
>
> *(Survey)*

> Some classmates' posts were written excellently. My English is not as good as them, so I usually feel pressure to reply in English.
>
> *(Survey)*

> Though I like to read the others' posts, I am afraid of making comments because I think I am not qualified to do so. I am not an expert, and I don't want to provide wrong opinions that would mislead my friends, and it is embarrassing.
>
> *(Reflection, Cheng)*

> My English is not good so usually it takes me a lot of time to write responses in English. Since not so many people log in the College English FB, my response may not be seen and replied. So, why bother to write and post it?
>
> *(Reflection, Ping)*

Most participants preferred reading the posts quietly. Their lurking and sparing voice revealed their anxiety and unease. They were unable to see their "sharing written opinions" in other identities such as a friend, a writer, a brother/sister, or an expert.

This learner identity evolved over time, however. In the second half of the semester, as students' familiarity with the Facebook community and its discourse improved, they constructed diverse identity roles. Take the abovementioned case of Lai as an example. He had stayed reticent for quite a while before participating in the heated debate about speech freedom and privacy. The debate motivated him to conduct research, to read and analyze information, to consider counter-arguments, to generate critical insights, to make judgement, and to take a position. Lai was empowered by the Facebook community, which encouraged him to voice his thoughts without much concern about formal writing conventions and rules. This experience transformed his identity from a passive learner to a critical writer and reader, from a lurker to an active community member.

In contrast, the practice of NAW on Facebook hardly transferred to students' academic writings. The shared discursive strategies of NAW in the Facebook community, used in status updates, casual chats, or diaries, did not seem to benefit students' academic writing directly. For example, Ding was an active Facebook participant, who held all his conversations in English. He posted twenty-two diary entries on his Facebook timeline within eighteen weeks, including the one with Japanese manga strips. According to his reflection, he spent "loooots of the time" on diary writing, and he considered that keeping a diary in English "really helps to practice writing skill most." Unfortunately, he failed to present an effective thesis statement and did not maintain coherence or proper organization in the final draft of his argumentative essay. He even plagiarized in his paper. Ding regretted in his interview that he copied some sentences from the Internet because he was unable to express himself well. Ding's case suggested that the communicative competence embodied in diary-writing and chatting was hardly transferred to an academic register.

However, Ding's plagiarism might, to a certain extent, be associated with his developing translingual writing competence. Ding received the most messages/

comments and "Likes" from other participants. He frequently updated his status, left messages to others, shared part of his life in diary entries, and generously gave others' posts a thumbs-up. His participation and interaction on Facebook revealed that he had a keen sense of the readers' concern, and he seemed to enjoy his identity as a friend or a writer when sharing his diary and responses. He was the most productive writer on Facebook, yet he decided to plagiarize when working on the final draft of his essay. His plagiarism suggested the following possibilities: He did research and read some topic-related materials. He might have suffered much anxiety, as suggested in his manga post, and was greatly concerned about academic genre and discourse, which he was unfamiliar with and which the Facebook activity did not necessarily support. He might have struggled with writing in an academic identity and voice. Unfortunately, he was unable to transfer his sense of readership, autonomous learning, genre concern, and identity construction to an academic register.

## Discussion and Conclusion

The present study has tried to tap the affordances of Facebook for teaching L2 writing. Previous classroom studies tended to adopt a monolingual perspective and used social media as an intervention for enhancing students' L2 writing. The present study has adopted "community of practice" and a biosocial perspective as theoretical constructs when incorporating Facebook into the writing class. The study viewed students as members of a community of practice, who learn about writing conventions and rules through collaborative activities. Students mobilized their multiliterate resources to construct local and global identity roles on Facebook, a "transliteracy" (You, 2016) practice crucial for novice writers probing in the academic world. Taking community of practice and a biosocial perspective to writing as constructs reveals not only how students acquire writing conventions and formal linguistic features critical for academic writing, but also the multiple identities that they would need to construct in this particular stage of their life. Guided by these constructs, the writing class metamorphosed into a nurturing social space for students' individual development.

The study reveals that the students were keenly aware of register in their language use on Facebook. When they posted the first drafts of their argumentative essay online, their style tended to be informal and opinionated. When they communicated with each other on matters unrelated to the essay assignment, their translingual practice was in a full array—mixing languages, blending dialects, and crossing genre and modal boundaries. These ways of translanguaging practice make perfect sense to the young digital natives. As Canagarajah (2011) suggested, translanguaging has become a natural and inevitable activity for multilingual students nowadays. The students' language use suggests that Facebook has provided a space where norms can be socially redefined and users' linguistic repertoire is at their full disposal (DePew, 2011; Lee, 2011; Schreiber, 2015).

Further, as the case of Ding shows, such translingual practice contributed to the students' identity roles in the first year of college.

Echoing previous studies (DePew, 2011; Razak & Saeed, 2014; Schreiber, 2015; Shih, 2013; Suthiwartnaruepu & Wasanasomsithi, 2012), the present study confirms that Facebook can benefit students' academic writing competence. In the present study, Facebook encouraged informal and autonomous learning about academic writing due to its public nature. The essay drafts posted on Facebook and feedback provided by the community members became important resources for some students. Exploring these resources, they came to understand the expectations of the writing assignment, gained ideas for developing their own topics, and deepened their understanding of writing-related topics initially introduced in the classroom. However, as Ding's case also reveals, the communicative competence embodied in updates, diary-writing, and chatting could hardly transfer to the academic writing assignment for some students. This finding is consistent with the findings from previous studies (Anderson, Reder, & Simon, 1996; Wilson, 1993) that language knowledge acquired situationally can only be transferred to similar situations.

The transfer of translingual writing competence to support academic writing requires a writing teacher's explicit scaffolding. Ding's case suggests that transfer does not take place automatically; there is a minimum threshold in academic writing competence. A teacher can provide instruction in paraphrasing and summary writing to scaffold novice writers like Ding for borrowing others' ideas. Direct and explicit exercise on revising colloquial expressions into academically appropriate ones can be helpful for novice writers too. For example, a sentence like "I **got** the information from internet" can become more formal if "got" is replaced by "obtained." The teacher can also provide writing exercises, such as narrative essay or descriptive essay assignments, that may enable students to shuttle between registers more easily. These pluriliteracy or transliteracy exercises can gradually remove the stigma imposed on non-standard English writing by orthodox teachers, encourage multilingual writers to shuttle between languages, genres, modes, and registers, and enable students to positively view non-standard English writing as a legitimate means of meaning making rather than a linguistic deficit.

## References

Anderson, J. R., Reder, L. M., & Simon, H. A. (1996). Situated learning and education. *Educational Researcher, 25*(4), 5–11.

Barrot, J. S. (2016). Using Facebook-based e-portfolio in ESL writing classrooms: Impact and challenges. *Language, Culture and Curriculum, 29*(3), 286–301.

Blattner, G., & Fiori, M. (2009). Facebook in the language classroom: Promises and possibilities. *Instructional Technology and Distance Learning, 6*(1), 17–28.

Bugeja, M. (2006). Facing the Facebook. *Chronicle of Higher Education, 52*(21), C1–C4.

Canagarajah, S. (2007). Lingua Franca English, multilingual communities, and language acquisition. *Modern Language Journal, 91*, 293–939.

Canagarajah, S. (2011). Codemeshing in academic writing: Identifying teachable strategies of translanguaging. *Modern Language Journal*, *95*(3), 401–417.

DePew, K. E. (2011). Social media at academia's periphery: Studying multilingual developmental writers' Facebook composing strategies. *The Reading Matrix*, *11*(1), 54–75.

DePew, K. E., & Miller-Cochran, S. K. (2010). Social networking in a second language: Engaging multiple literate practices through identity composition. In M. Cox, J. Jordan, C. Ortmeier-Hooper, & G. Shwartz (Eds.), *Reinventing identities in second language writing* (pp. 273–295). Urbana, IL: National Council of Teachers of English.

Eraut, M. (2004). Informal learning in the workplace. *Studies in Continuing Education*, *26*(2), 247–273.

Lave, J., & Wenger, E. (1991). *Situated learning: Legitimate peripheral participation*. New York: Cambridge University Press.

Lee, C. K. M. (2011). Micro-blogging and status updates on Facebook: Texts and practices. In C. Thurlow, & K. Mroczek (Eds.), *Digital discourse: Language in the new media* (pp. 110–130). New York: Oxford University Press.

Madge, C., Meek, J., Wellens, J., & Hooley, T. (2009). Facebook, social integration and informal learning at university: "It is more for socializing and talking to friends about work than for actually done work." *Learning, Media and Technology*, *34*(2), 141–155.

Maloney, E. (2007). What Web 2.0 can teach us about learning. *Chronicle of Higher Education*, *53*(18), B26.

Pasfield-Neofitou, S. (2011). Online domains of language use: Second language learners' experiences of virtual community and foreignness. *Language Learning & Technology*, *15*(2), 92–108.

Razak, N. A., & Saeed, M. A. (2014). Collaborative writing revision process among learners of English as a foreign language in an online community of practice. *Australasian Journal of Educational Technology*, *30*(5), 580–599.

Razak, N. A., Saeed, M. A., & Ahmad, Z. (2013). Adopting social networking sites (SNSs) as interactive communities among English Foreign Language (EFL) learners in writing: Opportunities and challenges. *English Language Teaching*, *6*(11), 187–198.

Schreiber, B. R. (2015). "I am what I am": Multilingual identity and digital translanguaging. *Language Learning and Technology*, *19*(3), 69–87.

Selwyn, N. (2009). Faceworking: Exploring students' education-related use of Facebook. *Learning, Media and Technology*, *34*(2), 157–174.

Shih, R. C. (2011). Can Web 2.0 technology assist college students in learning English writing? Integrating Facebook and peer assessment with blended learning. *Australasian Journal of Educational Technology*, *27*(5), 829–845.

Shih, R. C. (2013). Effect of using Facebook to assist English for business communication course instruction. *The Turkish Online Journal of Educational Technology*, *12*(1), 52–59.

Shukor, S. S. B., & Noordin, N. (2014). Effects of Facebook collaborative writing groups on ESL undergraduates' writing performance. *International Journal of English Language Education*, *2*(2), 89–99.

Street, B. (2003). What's "new" in New Literacy Studies? Critical approaches to literacy in theory and practice. *Current Issues in Comparative Education*, *5*(2), 77–91.

Suthiwartnarueput, T., & Wasanasomsithi, P. (2012). Effects of using Facebook as a medium for discussions of English grammar and writing of low-intermediate EFL students. *Electronic Journal of Foreign Language Teaching*, *9*(2), 194–214.

Wang, C. M. (2012). Using Facebook for cross-cultural collaboration: The experience of students from Taiwan. *Educational Media International*, *29*(1), 63–76.

Wenger, E. (1998). *Communities of practice: Learning, meaning, and identity.* Cambridge: Cambridge University Press.

Wilson, A. (1993). The promise of situated cognition. *New Directions for Adult and Continuing Education, 57,* 71–79.

You, X. (2008). Rhetorical strategies, electronic media, and China English. *World Englishes, 27*(2), 233–249.

You, X. (2011). Chinese white-collar workers and multilingual creativity in the diaspora. *World Englishes, 30*(3), 409–427.

You, X. (2016). *Cosmopolitan English and transliteracy.* Carbondale, IL: Southern Illinois University Press.

# 13

## TEACHING ENGLISH ACADEMIC WRITING TO NON-ENGLISH MAJOR GRADUATE STUDENTS IN CHINESE UNIVERSITIES

### A Review and a Transnational Vision

*Yongyan Li, Xiaohao Ma*

### Introduction

This chapter aims to present an overview of a body of Chinese-medium literature on the teaching of English academic writing (EAW) to non-English major graduate students in mainland Chinese universities. The growing volume of publications by English language professionals in both Anglo-American and more regional English-medium journals is opening a window on local practices of English education to the outside world. However, it would be fair to say that the general academic work published in languages other than English, such as the publications reporting English-writing-related teaching practices at the tertiary level in China, is hidden to the English world to a large extent. This is a situation that needs to be redressed in order to bring about a more balanced perspective on how writing is framed and taught in contexts other than Anglophone countries (Donahue, 2009). This literature includes the research and discussions surrounding the teaching of EAW to non-English major graduate students, a pedagogical concern which has arisen in Chinese universities in the past decade with the growing demands for these students to write for publication in English.

As dictated by the Chinese literature that we were able to put together through a systematic search, the kind of EAW under question in this chapter is discipline-based academic writing, specifically concerning EFL novices learning the genre of the English research article. Our topic thus falls within the field of English for Academic Purposes (EAP). In the definition of Hyland and Hamp-Lyons (2002), EAP "refers to language research and instruction that focuses on the specific communicative needs and practices of particular groups in academic contexts" (p. 2). More specifically, it can be said that the kind of EAW instruction featured in our target literature addresses the growing field of English for

Research Publication Purposes (Cargill & Burgess, 2008), an area of scholarship in the broader sphere of EAP.

In the following, we will first sketch a backdrop for the germination of the body of Chinese literature that we aimed to review in our study, and characterize a line of previous overviews of the Chinese scene of English writing instruction that our study followed. We will then present our findings from analyzing a body of Chinese literature on the teaching of EAW to non-English major graduate students. In discussing our findings, we will incorporate an ecological perspective that emphasizes the impact of local influences on educational initiatives (e.g., Van Lier, 2004), and then contemplate how the vision of transnational writing education could inform English for Research Publication Purposes pedagogy. We will conclude the chapter by speculating on the future of EAP teaching and research in China, emphasizing the importance of professional development for Chinese EAP practitioners.

## Context

In mainland China, publishing in English-medium journals included in the Science Citation Index (SCI) by Thomson-Reuters is an expectation with important ramifications for graduate students at universities. Doctoral students in science and engineering disciplines, for example, usually need to publish a number of papers before they can graduate with a PhD degree. Since the normative duration of doctoral candidature is three years, the requirement is found to be onerous and frequently leads to extension of candidature (Li, 2016). While Master's students (with the same length of candidature) in these disciplines do not necessarily have such a graduation requirement, they are encouraged to aim for SCI publication and are expected to achieve such a target if they go on to pursue doctoral studies. In humanities and social sciences disciplines, although there is generally no English publication requirement, the situation varies somewhat across disciplines. For instance, students in schools of business may participate in English writing and publishing with their supervisors who have an overseas education background. Against this backdrop, EAW has become a concern of high importance in the tertiary education sector in China, and yet at the same time, it is recognized that the students are not prepared to meet the challenge by traditional English language teaching, which is characterized by a focus on consolidating basic English knowledge and skills and helping students to pass standardized English tests (Cai, 2012; Cargill, O'Connor, & Li, 2012; Li, 2016).

Amidst a sense of urgency perceivable amongst students, supervisors, and English teachers, a trend of transforming the traditional English curricula to a new design aimed at addressing students' needs for using English for academic purposes has been initiated at Chinese universities, at both undergraduate and graduate levels. This endeavor is captured in the academic literature published in

## Previous Literature

Our chapter extends the scholarship of some existing overviews addressing the teaching of English writing in mainland China. Such overviews have often been conducted by overseas Chinese researchers (e.g., Cheng, 2016; Ding, 2010; Fu & Matoush, 2012; Hu, 2005; You, 2010). With his long-standing commitment to researching English composition in China, You (e.g., 2008, 2010, 2012) garnered extensive historical evidence to illustrate how sociocultural and historical factors have always been implicated in the teaching and practice of English writing in China. Hu (2005) investigated the impact of the sociocultural milieu on English pedagogical practices in different parts of the country, pointing out that China's EFL writing instruction has been dominated by an analytic and linguistically controlled approach characterized by language exercises. Fu and Matoush (2012) echoed Hu's observations, drawing upon their findings derived from a question-naire survey aimed to understand the nature of English writing instruction at the primary and secondary levels in China. Ding (2010), examining technical communication practices in the Chinese contexts, likewise emphasized that "one has to pay close attention to the impacts of local cultural, educational, political, and economic contexts" on such practices (p. 300). Gao, Liao, and Li (2014) sur-veyed English language education articles published in leading Chinese journals between 2008 and 2011 to provide a close-up analysis of 60 articles, pointing to both the growing methodological diversity as reflected in the literature and room for improvement. Cheng (2016), in a recent overview of "EAP at the ter-tiary level in China," addressed the burgeoning field of EAP instruction, includ-ing EAP writing instruction, at both the undergraduate and graduate levels in Chinese universities. Yet Cheng's review apparently gave much more weight to EAP at the undergraduate level than that at the graduate level. In discussing EAP writing instruction for Chinese graduate students, Cheng cited just one study, namely, Huang's (2012) report (which was published in English) on teaching engineering Master's students (at Chongqing University) to write journal articles by adopting a genre-based approach (Swales & Feak, 2012).

Two reports of the writing research presented at two ELT conferences in China are also worth mentioning. From attending the 4th International Confer-ence on ELT in China (May 2004, Beijing), You (2004) characterized 49 pre-sentations that focused on English writing instruction concerning English and non-English majors at the undergraduate level (about one-tenth of the total pre-sentations at the conference). From attending the 7th International Conference on ELT in China 10 years later (October 2014, Nanjing), Zhang, Yan, and Liu (2015) (the first two authors being graduate students studying in the U.S.) gave an updated report on the development of EFL writing instruction and research in

China. In neither of the reports, however, did we find mention of EAW instruction at the graduate level in Chinese universities.

## Method

Our literature research was guided by this question: How is English academic writing (EAW) taught to non-English major graduate students at the tertiary level in China? We conducted the search for the relevant literature in the China Academic Journals Full-text Database (CJFD), limiting our search to the papers published in CSSCI journals.[1] Specifically, we first searched for 英语写作 (*yingyu xiezuo*, English writing), 学术英语写作 (*xueshu yingyu xiezuo*, academic English writing), 英语论文写作 (*yingyu lunwen xiezuo*, English paper writing), and 论文写作 (*lunwen xiezuo,* paper writing) respectively, in conjunction with 教学 (*jiaoxue*, teaching). We then combined 非英语专业 (*feiyingyu zhuanye*, non-English majors), 研究生 (*yanjiusheng*, graduate students), 硕士 (*shuoshi*, Master's students), 博士 (*boshi*, doctoral students) in turn with 写作 (*xiezuo*, writing), 英语写作 (*yingyu xiezuo*, English writing), and 写作课 (*xiezuo ke*, writing course). Finally, we searched on other terms such as 体裁分析 (*ticai fenxi*, genre analysis) and 科技英语 (*keji yingyu*, English for science and technology). This wide-net searching returned around 1,700 titles (with redundancies included), which were thoroughly gone through to look for papers relevant to our focus of interest.

In our rounds of filtering, we looked for those papers that described pedagogical practices concerning the teaching of EAW either as a separate course or a component of a broader academic English course targeting non-English major graduate students. Discussion papers that only made proposals were excluded. As a result, a total of 26 papers (with an average length of three and a half pages), published over the span of a decade, i.e., 2005–2016, were selected (see Appendix for a complete list of these 26 papers). These papers can be characterized along a continuum from focusing on suggestions and only giving an overview of the teaching practices involved, through reporting pedagogical strategies with some details (e.g., showcase of teaching material, or report of student evaluation or improvement in student writing), to reporting pedagogical strategies with details of the procedure and/or being presented as classroom-based empirical research. The right end of the continuum, i.e., papers reporting pedagogical strategies with details of the procedure and/or being presented as classroom-based empirical research, was a clear minority in our collection. Seven out of the 26 papers were published between 2005 and 2010, while all the rest came out during 2012–2016, indicating that teaching EAW to graduate students is a rising trend at Chinese universities. On the other hand, noticeably, only five of the 26 papers were published in the so-called *hexin qikan* (key journals).[2] This presumably implies a relatively peripheral status of this modest body of literature. Without exception, it can be seen that the authors themselves were the teacher practitioners directly involved in the EAW instruction reported.

These papers report practices from 23 universities and two institutes. Nevertheless, we should emphasize that this sample of featured institutions are likely to only account for a small proportion of a wider range of Chinese universities/institutes where EAW has become part of the English curriculum for graduate students. Neither is there guarantee of "representativeness" of the practices reported in these papers, although what is found in these papers does provide a valuable entry point for us to begin to understand EAW instructional practices targeted at graduate students across disciplines at Chinese universities.

Treating the collection of 26 papers as our "core" documentary "data," we scrutinized them repeatedly, combining a grounded, inductive approach with a literature-informed deductive approach. Naturally, we were above all interested in teasing out some basic facts concerning the EAW instruction portrayed in these papers: namely, target students and the curriculum location, and timing and duration. Taking hints from discussions in the literature (e.g., Casanave, 2003; Dudley-Evans, 2001; Cargill & O'Connor, 2013), we also aimed to find out how Chinese teachers might deal with mixed-discipline classes and collaborate with content specialist teachers. At the same time, as we pored through the collected papers, we easily noticed the frequent references to the notion of "genre," with "genre pedagogy" often applied to teaching abstract writing; we therefore tried to understand the relevant teaching practices.

In the following section, which reports our findings, we will focus on the five dimensions highlighted above which constituted the focus of our literature analysis: namely, target students and the curriculum location, timing and duration, dealing with the challenge of multidisciplinary classes, collaboration with content specialist teachers, and implementing genre pedagogy in teaching abstract writing. In addition to the 26 "core" papers, we also looked into other relevant papers which came up in the process of our literature search, so as to enrich our background knowledge and draw upon information to confirm, modify, or extend our understandings derived from the 26 texts. This additional pool of literature consists of discussion papers that reflected upon the current problematic situation and made proposals of pedagogical strategies to cultivate graduate students' EAW or EAP abilities. Thus, while centering on the 26 core papers, where appropriate, we will cite these other papers as instances in "the wider literature" in the following section on findings.

## Findings

### *Target Students and the Curriculum Location*

Seven of our 26 core papers addressed EAW teaching targeted at doctoral students; ten papers focused on that for Master's students; the rest of the papers did not specify either, but referred to *yanjiusheng* (graduate students) in general.[3] In most cases, the course including a component of, or devoted to, the teaching of EAW seems compulsory for the target students, although sometimes it is an elective course (Gu, Shi, & Gao, 2008; Liu, 2013; Zhang, 2010). The average target students also have equal opportunities to access such instruction. Li (2005), however, reported that an academic English course which included a writing component at Renmin University was only open to those doctoral students with stronger English proficiency. Gu et al. (2008) suggested that setting an entry level as practiced at Li's (2005) university could be useful, given that 50% of their participants at Nanjing Agricultural University, after attending an elective course for doctoral students, Academic Paper Writing in English, reported that their understanding of how to write a paper had developed, but still had major difficulty in expressing themselves in English.

EAW is often installed as a separate course at the universities featured in our collection of 26 core papers. However, sometimes it may be part of a broader course, or is one of several related modules. At South East University, English Academic Writing and English Academic Communications were the two components of Academic English, a one-semester compulsory course for Master's students (Zhang, 2013). At North East University, Academic Paper Writing was one of the three writing modules (together with General Writing and Practical Writing) taught in 18 weeks to Master's students (Wang, 2014). At Beijing University of Technology, English Academic Paper Writing and Publication Workshops, together with Academic English Literature Reading and Evaluation, and Academic Communication at International Conferences, constituted the three modules of an academic English curriculum (Shao, 2015). Whether EAW is a separate course or a course component, it has tended to be developed at the individual universities as part of a new English curriculum for graduate students, introduced by stages from the early 2000s or a little later to replace a traditional curriculum which focused on the training of basic English knowledge and skills (Gu et al., 2008; Huang, 2010; Sun & Chen, 2009; Sun, Wang, & Yin, 2015; Wu, 2015; Yang, 2012; Zeng, Su, & Ren, 2014; Zhang, 2013).

## Timing and Duration

EAW instruction is typically provided to graduate students across disciplines in one semester in the first year of their study program (the normative duration of which is three years at both Master's and doctoral levels, as noted earlier) (Fan, 2016; Feng, 2014; Huang, 2010; Liu, 2013; Lu, 2016a, 2016b; Zeng et al., 2014; Zhang, 2013). At Chongqing University, for example, English Academic Writing and Communication was taught as an 18-week course for Master's students across disciplines (Huang, 2010).

At several universities, students were prepared for the challenge of academic writing by stages. At Chongqing Jiao Tong University, Master's students learned about English academic writing through reading in Semester 1, before opting for an elective course English Academic Writing in Semester 2 (Zhang, 2010). Similarly, at National University of Defense Technology, English Science Paper Writing was offered in Semester 2 after newly enrolled graduate students have taken English Academic Paper Reading in Semester 1 (Zeng et al., 2014); and at Academy of Military Equipment (Beijing), where continuity of training from Master's to doctoral study was emphasized, training focuses moved from literature reading, through writing the English abstract of a degree thesis, to practicing writing sections of a research article (Wang & Hou, 2013).

Two universities practiced a systematic scheme of differentiated levels. At China Science & Technology University, English S&T Paper Writing was started as a compulsory course for Master's and doctoral students in 2006 (Sun & Chen, 2009); then, from September 2010, it spread into Levels I, II, and III, respectively, to target students who had not yet decided their topic, those who were in the process of conducting research, and those who had finished research and were ready to write (Sun, Chen, & Xing, 2012). At Beijing Forestry University, EAW was taught in the context of four levels of English classes (A being the highest level and D the lowest) for Master's students, who were moved up or down the levels depending on their performance; the scheme aimed to extend the English support to cover the students' entire candidature (Wu, 2015). These two universities' level schemes addressed a problem in the traditional timing of English courses for graduate students (hence of EAW instruction, when this started to replace traditional courses). That is, the period of time when these students attend English classes (i.e., in Year 1) mismatches the time when they have conducted research and need to write, later in their candidature, and thus presumably would need English support most. Other papers in our core collection (Huang, 2010; Qian, 2011; Sun & Chen, 2009) as well as the wider literature (Lu & Wang, 2015; Zhang & Li, 2015; Zhou, 2011) have likewise observed on this misalignment in timing, emphasizing that it is important for students to continue to receive English training when they start to focus on research, and suggesting that EAW support can be most effectively provided when students have had some research experience, possibly with research data which they can write about.

## Dealing With the Challenge of Teaching Multidisciplinary Classes

The EAW teachers in our core collection of papers generally had to deal with large graduate student populations. For example, Wu (2015) mentioned an intake of about 720 Master's non-English major students in September 2013 at Beijing Forestry University, and Zhan, Liao and Chen (2010) referred to an enrollment of 109 new doctoral students in 2009 at the Third Military Medical University. Reported class sizes ranged from around 25 (Gu et al., 2008; Lu, 2016a) to around 40 (Huang, 2010; Zhang, 2013; Wu, 2015). Understandably, mixed-discipline classes seemed to be the norm, although there were efforts of dividing classes by broad disciplinary areas. Li (2005) noted that at Renmin University, students were divided into classes by disciplinary groups: economics and management, law, and other arts disciplines; Zhang (2013) likewise reported that at South East University, students were divided into classes by related disciplines as far as possible.

Collaborative, task-based, and autonomous learning was emphasized (e.g., Wang, 2014; Zhang, 2013). In mixed-discipline classes, students were commonly expected to work in discipline-based study groups, to collaboratively finish tasks, to give presentations on the journal articles they read, or to select a topic to jointly finish a paper to present at the end of the semester, simulating the format of an international conference (Huang, 2010; Shi & Cui, 2015; Wang, 2014; Zhang, 2013). For example, at Nanjing University of Agriculture, a "collaborative task completion" approach was implemented in EAW teaching to doctoral students, whereby a class of 25 students, together with the English teacher, played the role of the co-authors of a manuscript draft composed by a student, by collaboratively reviewing, revising, and editing the manuscript according to a target journal's requirements for submissions (Gu et al., 2008).

QQ, a highly popular social media website in China (www.QQ.com), was sometimes used to facilitate communication in a class, within groups, and between students and teachers, to enable sharing of resources, and to submit and share work (Huang, 2010; Liu, 2013; Shi & Cui, 2015). Web-based platforms were set up for similar purposes and for enhancing autonomous learning. China Science & Technology University constructed an "autonomous exploratory learning system" for graduate students; a web-based self-access courseware was developed to include self-study materials, annotated articles from different disciplines, discipline-based corpora of journal articles which students could search with a corpus tool, and a demo version of a small corpus for demonstrating how to search a corpus (Sun & Chen, 2009; Sun, Chen, & Xing, 2012). Likewise, at Ningbo University, a web-based platform was designed to expand students' learning space where students could view case histories of paper writing and submission, and search both the English- and Chinese-medium corpora of journal articles built for them, as well as a range of free online corpora provided by some universities in other parts of the world (Huang & Yang, 2010).

## Collaboration With Content Specialist Teachers

The challenge for English teachers who lack content knowledge to teach EAW to students across disciplines was recognized (Qian, 2011; Sun et al., 2015). Not surprisingly, collaboration with content specialist teachers or students' supervisors seems a potentially important issue for Chinese authors. Yet more proposals than actual reports of such collaboration can be found.

Of the 26 core papers in our collection, six papers mentioned involvement of content teachers. In four of the scenarios, content teachers did not directly participate in class teaching, but were involved in other ways: firstly, content teachers contributing to the design of "problems" in a Problem-Based Learning (PBL) EAW course for doctoral students at Fujian Medical University (Feng, 2014); secondly, supervisors making comments on students' selection of (discipline-based) research topics in the EAW class at National University of Defense Technology (Zeng et al., 2014); thirdly, both English and specialist teachers giving feedback on students' journal paper drafts, focusing on language and content respectively, at Chongqing Jiao Tong University (Zhang, 2010); and finally, English teachers and content teachers jointly providing hands-on support to student writers through writing and publication workshops at Beijing University of Technology (Shao, 2015). Just two cases of a specialist teacher contributing through class teaching were found: independently teaching EAW classes (Yang, 2012), or co-teaching with an English teacher (Wu, 2015). Specifically, Yang (2012) reported that at Guangzhou University of Traditional Chinese Medicine, a specialist teacher took charge of teaching two classes of doctoral students, while a third class was taught by an English teacher with a background in medical English. Based on student evaluation, Yang (2012) commented: "the specialist teacher was familiar with the SCI paper publication process and with the medical terminologies, but the analysis of the rhetorical structure of the papers and the teaching of writing strategies was a weak point" (p. 93). Wu (2015) described a differentiation mode of teaching at Beijing Forestry University, whereby Master's students went into four levels of classes (from A to D) according to their academic performance and English ability, as mentioned earlier in the present chapter. Level A classes were taught by an equal number of English and content teachers, focusing on academic English and academic publication; Level B classes had more English teachers than content teachers, with the proportion of academic English growing over time; Level C classes had more content teachers than English teachers, and moved from basic to higher-level academic English; and finally, an equal number of English and content teachers were allocated to Level D classes, and the grasp of basic English knowledge was set as the initial target, and academic English was introduced gradually (Wu, 2015, p. 44).

Beyond our collection of core papers, we also tended to find proposals for English and content teachers' collaboration and emphasis on its importance (Han & Wang, 2010; Jiang, 2012), rather than actual reports of how such collaboration plays out in a particular institutional setting. In addition, it is worth noting that we also found two papers authored by content specialists. Liu (2010), a specialist professor at Henan Polytechnic University, described how his School of Material Sciences cultivated graduate students' ability in using English through a systematic content-based training plan, adopting English textbooks and journal articles as the teaching materials and assigning content teachers with overseas study or work experience to take up the instruction. There was no mention of collaboration with English teachers. Likewise, Zhang and Li's (2015) paper, ostensibly co-authored by an English teacher and a professor of engineering thermophysics (as seen from their affiliations), did not emphasize such collaboration, but suggested that graduate students' supervisors should shoulder the main responsibility in training students' EAW ability.

## Implementing Genre Pedagogy in Teaching Abstract Writing

In terms of the pedagogical theories, our core collection of papers often mentioned task-driven learning (Gu et al., 2008; Qian, 2011; and Shi & Cui, 2015), reflecting an interest in task/project-driven learning in the wider literature (e.g., Zhou, 2011); three papers adopted the notion of Content-Based Instruction (CBI) (Gu et al., 2008; Shao, 2015; Wu, 2015); one paper reported using a Problem-Based Learning (PBL) approach (Feng, 2014); and another paper reported adopting an "Analysis, Awareness, Acquisition, and Achievement" cyclic model proposed by Swales and Feak (2012, p. ix) in teaching abstract writing (Lu, 2016b). Many more papers (14 in total), however, declared reliance on the notions of genre and genre pedagogy, particularly as conceptualized in the ESP tradition (e.g., Bhatia, 1993; Swales, 1990) and the Australian tradition (e.g., Feez, 1998), two of the three main areas of genre scholarship widely acknowledged in the literature (Hyon, 1996), with the third being New Rhetoric studies (e.g., Freedman & Medway, 1994). While genre pedagogy in the ESP tradition is characteristically based on move analysis and analysis of lexico-grammatical features, the Australian approach emphasizes scaffolded instruction, fulfilled through a Teaching Learning Cycle aiming to move learners from supported learning to more independent processing and production of texts.

Somewhat surprisingly, where some details about the actual teaching process were available, the focus was almost always on the teaching of abstract writing (Han & Hou, 2012; Hu & Ma, 2012; Huang, 2010; Lu, 2016a; Shi & Cui, 2015; Sun & Chen, 2009). Papers that described an EAW course in more general terms also alluded to the teaching of abstract writing (Jia & Jia, 2013; Liu, 2013; Wang, 2014; Wang & Hou, 2013; Zhang, 2013). It can be seen that the featured instructions on abstract writing commonly adopted the practices of genre pedagogy in the ESP tradition (e.g., Hu & Ma, 2012; Huang, 2010; Sun & Chen, 2009). A few papers, however, reported an integration of the ESP approach and the Australian approach. Han and Hou (2012) built on Feez's (1998) five-stage Teaching Learning Cycle (building the context, modeling and deconstructing the text, joint construction of the text, independent construction of the text, and linking related texts), but argued that it is necessary to add a stage of "comparative analysis" (e.g., analysis of abstracts from different journals and different disciplines) after the first two stages, to enhance students' analysis and holistic understanding of the target genre. They dropped Feez's last stage, thus still having a five-stage model. In an action research project on teaching abstract writing, Lu (2016a) adopted Han and Hou's (2012) five-stage model and likewise integrated it with genre analysis in the first round of her action; the integration continued in her second round of action, but she found it necessary to increase the amount of input for students and giving them more support, by modeling and deconstructing more abstract texts with the students and jointly writing an abstract for a paper with the students. Shi and Cui (2015) referred to both Hyon's (1996)[4] and Feez's (1998) models of genre pedagogy, and worked out a set of stages to meet their students' needs. These include building the context, modeling, task design and completion (joint analysis, independent analysis and peer feedback in groups, and independent construction and peer feedback in groups), teacher feedback, and language focus (student presentation and teacher summary).

Other than an apparent interest in teaching abstract writing, we can only find general remarks on the structures and linguistic features (e.g., the use of tenses and voices) of other sections of a research article being analyzed in EAW teaching (e.g., Shao, 2015; Sun et al., 2015), and broad-strokes mention of students being required to write and compare their writing with published texts (e.g., Gu et al., 2008; Wang & Hou, 2013; Wang, 2014).

## Discussion

Our review of Chinese literature in the previous section, based on a collection of 26 core papers with reference to the broader literature, seems to indicate that EAW has increasingly become a pivotal component in the English curriculum for non-English major graduate students at Chinese universities. Previous discussions addressing ELT, or more specifically, English writing research and pedagogy in EFL contexts, have emphasized an ecological perspective (Van Lier, 2004) to fully take into account the impacts of local, contextual factors on teaching practices (Casanave, 2009; Hu, 2005; You, 2008). In trying to interpret the findings reported in the previous section, we likewise found it necessary to assume such a stance. In what follows, we will first discuss several issues implicated in the current developments of EAW instruction to non-English majors at the graduate level at Chinese universities, in light of local conditions; we will then consider how a vision of transnational writing education might inform EAW instruction in the context of English for Research Publication Purposes.

### EAW Instruction to Non-English Majors at the Graduate Level at Chinese Universities

Firstly, EAW instruction in China echoes EAW pedagogical support reported in other contexts in the literature, and at the same time manifests some Chinese characteristics. In terms of the nature of the institutions involved, our core collection of 26 papers mostly features universities/institutes that specialize in science, engineering, agriculture, or medicine. This is understandable, given that these disciplines are characterized by high levels of Englishization in written scientific communication at the global level. Reform of the traditional English curriculum at these universities seems to have been particularly urgent for the Chinese practitioners. The kinds of EAW support described in this chapter were typically scheduled in the early stage of the students' candidature in a graduate program. This resembles the general practice found in universities in other parts of the world, such as North America (e.g., Cheng, 2006), Australia (e.g., Cargill, Cadman, & McGowan, 2001), and Hong Kong (e.g., L. Flowerdew, 2016). However, the effort at a couple of Chinese universities to provide writing support to students throughout their entire candidature is both innovative and laudable, and potentially provides a useful curriculum model for reference by other Chinese universities. The need to support graduate students in their communication development throughout their candidature has likewise been recognized and responded to accordingly at some North American universities (Feak, 2016). There is thus a space for experience-sharing between Chinese practitioners and their overseas counterparts. It can also be seen that Chinese teachers commonly teach multidisciplinary classes, a challenge long documented in the literature (e.g., Casanave, 2003; Leki & Carson, 1997). Although a common recommendation is to teach classes of students who share a broad disciplinary area so as to practice the principle of specificity in EAP pedagogy (Cargill et al., 2001; Hyland, 2002), this can be difficult to implement at Chinese universities where the student population is large and there is a shortage of instructors. The Chinese papers we reviewed do not usually seem to directly acknowledge the challenge posed for English teachers, but they report a range of instructional strategies that tackle the challenge, including fostering collaborative, task-based, and autonomous learning, using disciplinary texts as teaching materials, and involving content specialist teachers in providing EAW support or instruction. Apart from being recommended practices in ESP/EAP pedagogy, these strategies also serve to overcome, to some extent at least, potential local constraints in resources and staffing.

Secondly, collaborating with content specialist teachers, as a crucial feature of EAP pedagogy in general (Dudley-Evans, 2001) and EAW instruction in particular (Cargill & O'Connor, 2013), seems a salient issue for discussion amongst Chinese practitioners. In the papers we reviewed, the involvement of content specialists ranged from playing a more marginal to a more hands-on role, reflecting different kinds of collaborative relationships between language specialists and content specialists as conceptualized in the literature (e.g., Dudley-Evans, 2001). On the whole, however, more proposals for such collaboration than reports of practice exist. From our perspective, such collaboration can be deterred by a number of factors at a Chinese university: the traditional compartmentalization between disciplines that has discouraged communication and collaboration between English teachers and content teachers (Cargill et al., 2012), lack of proficiency in English on the part of the content teachers (Ding, 2010), and sizable student populations that potentially create large multidisciplinary classes as a common reality and in turn could make collaborative teaching "infeasible" (Qian, 2011, p. 57). Yet the very existence of the cases of collaboration, and even of the instances of papers authored by specialist professors (in the wider literature we explored) which introduced local methods of training graduate students' EAW ability, demonstrate the possibility of overcoming the traditional separation between language and content teachers. Initiatives at the level of individual teachers, as well as of institutions, in the form of encouraging interdisciplinary collaboration and deploying resources, can help to break down silos in institutional contexts (Cargill et al., 2012).

Thirdly, our literature research revealed a strong interest among Chinese practitioners in genre pedagogy, characterized as "the most popular approach to teaching EAP to graduate students" by Cheng (2016, p. 104). It can be seen that since its introduction into China, genre pedagogy has engaged the interest of many English teachers at Chinese universities. The teachers were keen to apply the insights from the relevant applied linguistics research to their teaching, in particular those concerning move analysis and analysis of lexico-grammatical features in the ESP tradition, while the Teaching Learning Cycle in the Australian genre approach (Feez, 1998) was found by Chinese practitioners to provide a stage-model compatible with the needs of the Chinese students. The literature we reviewed tended to give similar reiterations about genre and genre analysis across papers, citing a similar range of references. This seems to indicate that the early introductory papers on genre pedagogy in the Chinese literature (Fang, 1998; Han & Qin, 2000; Qin, 2000; Wang, 1998), which detailed the conceptualizations of genre in different traditions of genre theory (citing, among others, Bhatia, 1993; Martin, 1992; and Swales, 1990) and gave examples of pedagogical applications (citing, for instance, Feez, 1998; J. Flowerdew, 1993; and Hyon, 1996), probably served as a primary source of reference for subsequent authors' engagement with the notion of genre. At the same time, efforts of modifying existing stage models of the Teaching Learning Cycle to better cater to the needs of Chinese students, as seen in a few papers (Han & Hou, 2012; Lu, 2016a; Shi & Cui, 2015), signal attempts at localizing Western pedagogical ideas in the Chinese context (Gao et al., 2014).

Finally, we believe that while demonstrating great promise of future development in EAW pedagogy at Chinese universities, the body of literature we reviewed in this chapter suggests that EAP pedagogy training, as well as EAP-related research methodology training, are urgently needed for the average Chinese teachers entrusted to undertake EAW instruction targeted at students across disciplines. As noted earlier, in our literature research we found abstract writing consistently being used to demonstrate genre pedagogy in Chinese classrooms. The emphasis upon abstract writing is understandable, given its potential importance across disciplines (even the students in the humanities and social sciences, for whom there may not be an English publication requirement, should learn how to write an abstract in English: an English abstract is required in degree theses/dissertations written in Chinese and in many Chinese journals). Yet the general absence of the specifics of teaching the genre of research article in its complete form (or sections other than abstracts) may indicate a gap in the relevant genre knowledge and training on the teachers' part, which may have stopped them from implementing genre pedagogy more systematically. English teachers at Chinese universities commonly hold degrees in English linguistics or applied linguistics (in the tradition of second language acquisition) or English literature (Ding, 2010; Li, 2016). Contemporary genre theories, EAP classroom pedagogy, and related research methodology have yet to become a common feature of the current applied linguistics degree programs that train English teachers for Chinese universities. In addition, from the perspective of research, as far as we could see, only a small number of the 26 papers were presented as classroom-based empirical research, while a majority were characterized by a combination of description of practice (varying in the level of detail) and discussion/recommendation, rather than featuring a clear research design. This seems to echo Gao et al.'s (2014) observation that most articles on ELT published in leading Chinese journals are not empirical, despite a rising number of empirical papers. While we do not wish to repudiate the value of non-empirical literature in representing different voices of discussion in academia, we would suggest that the dominance of such papers in a particular domain of education (teaching EAW to graduate students at Chinese universities, in this case) points to an academic sphere that needs be developed. We believe a difference can be made through the practitioners receiving systematic training, on the fronts of both classroom practice and empirical research. In essence, this is about the professional development of EAP practitioners. At a time when international literature on this very topic is surprisingly sparse (Ding & Campion, 2016), Chinese experience can make valuable contributions to the discussion and practice surrounding this important issue.

## *EAW Instruction and Transnational Writing Education*

Our chapter highlights local practices of graduate-level pedagogy and speaks to the growing field of English for Research Publication Purposes (Cargill & Burgess, 2008). The landscape we sketched in this chapter is therefore distinguished from the setting of an undergraduate general-purpose EAP summer course that Xiaoye You taught in Shanghai, which "was designed as an equivalent of first-year writing offered in American universities" (You, 2016, p. 144). You (2016, Chapter 6) illustrated how an EAP teacher in that context may take a "transliteracy perspective" and "do two key things in class": to "intervene in students' writing processes by directing their attention to resources, audiences, and consequences across languages" (p. 143) and to "encourage students to engage discourses across languages both in and outside their majors" (p. 144). Such transliteracy/translingual pedagogical strategies suggested by You were not found in the collection of Chinese papers we reviewed. This is perhaps not surprising, given the traditional compartmentalization between disciplines at Chinese universities and the typical training background of English teachers, as noted earlier. Yet developing a commitment to transnational writing education, as envisioned by You (2016, and his introductory chapter in this book), will probably have important implications for the development of EAW, or English for Research Publication Purposes, pedagogy more generally at Chinese universities.

Margaret Cargill, an Australian English for Research Publication Purposes specialist who has been travelling to China since 2001 to deliver publication skills workshops and short courses to scientists (Cargill et al., 2012), and who meanwhile has worked tirelessly to promote take-ups of her work by local English teachers, emphasized that Chinese colleagues can contribute in ways that she has not been able to achieve.[5] For instance, she observed on the tendency among early-candidature students to show greater interest in improving listening comprehension and practicing speaking by attending the class of a native English speaker like her, than in acquiring the content that she tried to get across about how to write an English paper successfully; she also noted that, in the stage of helping a student to revise a draft, a Chinese colleague may potentially be able to better understand why the writing of a novice has appeared in the way it has. Cargill's comments suggest that teachers can capitalize on their own and/or their students' multilingual status in identifying students' difficulties and resources, and steering students' attention to developing discipline-specific meaning making competencies (see, e.g., Xu, Huang & You, 2016; You & You, 2013). More broadly, in the context of envisioning a future of transnational writing education in the context of English for Research Publication Purposes-oriented EAW pedagogy, Cargill's comments also point to the value of collaboration between local teachers and international colleagues in creating new spaces of learning for students, as has been powerfully illustrated by such collaboration in the context of teaching writing to undergraduate English majors in China (Zheng, Du, & Wu, 2013). In the emerging enterprise of discipline-oriented EAW instruction in China, there are signs that such cross-cultural exchange and collaboration between local and overseas EAP/English for Research Publication Purposes practitioners is growing (e.g., through overseas EAP/English for Research Publication Purposes specialists becoming advisors or visiting professors at universities, or giving keynote speeches at the international conferences held in China). Chinese teachers' local knowledge and bilingual advantage, coupled with international colleagues' potentially greater familiarity with the target English genres and discourse practices, are likely to bring maximum benefit to the novices seeking successful international publication.

At the institutional level, other than installing initiatives to encourage interdisciplinary collaboration, as we suggested earlier, policy makers, by creating international exchange programs and study-abroad opportunities (see Sasaki's chapter in this book), can work to promote graduate students' engagement in transnational academic literacy practices as well as enhance their awareness of intercultural rhetoric (Connor, 2011), experience that will help to cultivate in them cosmopolitan and translingual perspectives in meaning making in diverse academic and professional contexts. In short, a new vision of transnational writing education on the part of policy makers and teachers would prepare local students well as they embark on a career path that is necessarily transnational, by fostering "critical academic communication that can provide a strategic edge" to them, as Suresh Canagarajah has consistently argued (2014, p. 101; see also his chapter in this book).

## Conclusion

In this chapter we conducted a survey of the emerging EAW instructional practices targeted at graduate students at Chinese universities, drawing upon a body of recent literature published in Chinese journals. It is important to bear in mind that this body of literature only reported what was happening in particular classrooms at some universities at certain points in time, roughly within the span of a decade or so between the mid-2000s and mid-2010s. We also do not know how sustainable the reported efforts have been at the individual institutions. To chart out a broader, state-of-the-art picture with in-depth understandings, case studies of EAW instruction at particular settings and large-scale surveys should be conducted. Obtaining insights into the current practices, with our literature review presented here constituting only a preliminary step, will crucially inform endeavors of educational reform and policy-making, as well as future research.

Although the existing literature featuring the emerging EAW instructional practices at Chinese universities seems to have a peripheral status by appearing mostly in non-"key" journals, a growth in both the number of the papers along the line and their status in China's ELT publishing world in the coming years can be anticipated. For one thing, this emerging field seems to be gaining ground in terms of resource support. A majority of the papers we surveyed in preparing this chapter acknowledged a funding source for the work reported—ranging from the national to the university-level grants, which may indicate growing awareness at administrative and institutional levels for the strategic importance of investing in curriculum construction dedicated to graduate-level EAW support.

Within the professional community of the ELT practitioners in China, some concerted efforts are also helping to make EAW, or EAP more broadly, a promising field of practice and research in China. Such initiatives include the inauguration of the international academic conferences such as "ESP in Asia" (annual since 2009) and the annual conferences of the China EAP Association (CEAPA) (since 2015), and the launching of the journal of *China ESP Research* in 2010. Particularly worth mentioning is the leadership of CEAPA, based at Fudan University in Shanghai and led by Jigang Cai, a champion of the EAP movement in China in the past decade (e.g., Cai, 2012). As we write the present chapter,

## 238 Yongyan Li, Xiaohao Ma

training in both EAP pedagogies and research methodologies in the form of professional development seminars and workshops is unfolding under the sponsorship of CEAPA, with the participation of Chinese scholars based outside of mainland China in collaboration with mainland colleagues. Propelled by the great enthusiasm of the ELT practitioners at Chinese universities, these many endeavors will be shaping the direction that EAW instruction and research at the tertiary level in China will take in the years to come. In the long run, EAP education on Chinese soil will contribute to the dynamic and diversified enterprise of transnational writing education envisioned in this book.

## Notes

1. CJFD is part of the knowledge network system of CNKI (China National Knowledge Infrastructure) (www.cnki.net/), a mega cross-disciplinary database of Chinese academic literature. CNKI is typically accessible through Chinese university libraries and it is also accessible through the library of our university in Hong Kong. CSSCI (Chinese Social Sciences Citation Index) is a database of academic journals in humanities and social sciences that meet a high standard of quantity and quality of citations.
2. "Key journals" here refer to the most authoritative journals in the field of foreign language studies and education in China, all of which are included in CSSCI. At the time of our writing, there were altogether 15 such key journals.
3. From our experience, when the term *yanjiusheng* (graduate students, or literally, research students), is used on its own in the Chinese literature, instead of *shuoshi yanjiusheng* (Master's students) or *boshi yanjiusheng* (doctoral students), it often primarily refers to the former, although it may also imply a combination of both types of graduate students.
4. A multi-stage model adopted by Hyon (1996) in genre-based pedagogy for teaching reading comprehension was described by Han and Qin (2000) and Qin (2000) in their papers, which were among the earliest papers that introduced genre pedagogy into China.
5. The first author of this chapter conducted a series of interviews with Margaret Cargill, when the latter was teaching a 32-hour course on "Writing a Life-Science Research Article for International Submission" to a class of graduate students at the School of Life Sciences and Technologies at Shanghai Jiao Tong University, China, in the summer of 2016 (see Li, 2017).

## References

Bhatia, V. K. (1993). *Analysing genre: Language use in professional settings.* London: Longman.

Cai, J. (2012). *Zhongguo daxue yingyu jiaoxue: Lu zai hefang [A way out for EFL at tertiary level education in mainland China].* Shanghai: Shanghai Jiao Tong University Press.

Canagarajah, S. (2014). EAP in Asia: Challenges and possibilities. In I. Liyanage, & T. Walker (Eds.), *English for Academic Purposes (EAP) in Asia: Negotiating appropriate practices in a global context* (pp. 93–102). Rotterdam, Boston, and Taipei: Sense publishers.

Cargill, M., & Burgess, S. (2008). Introduction to the special issue: English for Research Publication Purposes. *Journal of English for Academic Purposes, 7,* 75–76.

Cargill, M., Cadman, K., & McGowan, U. (2001). Postgraduate writing: Using intersecting genres in a collaborative content-based program. In I. Leki (Ed.), *Case studies in*

*TESOL: Academic writing programs* (pp. 85–96). Alexandria, VA: Teaching English to Speakers of Other Languages (TESOL).

Cargill, M., & O'Connor, P. (2013). *Writing scientific research articles: Strategy and steps* (2nd ed.). Oxford: Wiley-Blackwell.

Cargill, M., O'Connor, P., & Li, Y. (2012). Educating Chinese scientists to write for international journals: Addressing the divide between science and technology education and English language teaching. *English for Specific Purposes, 31*(1), 60–69.

Casanave, C. P. (2003). Multiple uses of applied linguistics literature in a multidisciplinary graduate EAP class. *ELT Journal, 57*(1), 43–50.

Casanave, C. P. (2009). Training for writing or training for reality? Challenges facing EFL writing teachers and students in language teacher education programs. In R. M. Manchón (Ed.), *Writing in foreign language contexts: Learning, teaching, and research* (pp. 256–277). Bristol: Multilingual Matters.

Cheng, A. (2006). Understanding learners and learning in ESP genre-based writing instruction. *English for Specific Purposes, 25*(1), 76–89.

Cheng, A. (2016). EAP at the tertiary level in China: Challenges and possibilities. In K. Hyland, & P. Shaw (Eds.), *The Routledge handbook of English for academic purposes* (pp. 97–108). London and New York: Routledge.

Connor, U. (2011). *Intercultural rhetoric in the writing classroom.* Ann Arbor: University of Michigan Press.

Ding, A., & Campion, G. (2016). EAP teacher development. In K. Hyland, & P. Shaw (Eds.), *The Routledge handbook of English for academic purposes* (pp. 547–559). London and New York: Routledge.

Ding, H. (2010). Technical communication instruction in China: Localized programs and alternative models. *Technical Communication Quarterly, 19*(3), 300–317.

Donahue, C. (2009). "Internationalization" and composition studies: Reorienting the discourse. *College Composition and Communication, 61*(2), 212–243.

Dudley-Evans, T. (2001). Team-teaching in EAP: Changes and adaptations in the Birmingham approach. In J. Flowerdew, & M. Peacock (Eds.), *Research perspectives on English for academic purposes* (pp. 225–238). Cambridge, UK: Cambridge University Press.

Fang, Y. (1998). Qiantan yulei [On genres]. *Wai Guo Yu [Journal of Foreign Languages], 1,* 18–23.

Feak, C. B. (2016). EAP support for post-graduate students. In K. Hyland, & P. Shaw (Eds.), *The Routledge handbook of English for academic purposes* (pp. 489–501). London and New York: Routledge.

Feez, S. (1998). *Text-based syllabus design.* Sydney, NSW: National Centre for English Language Teaching and Research, Macquarie University.

Flowerdew, J. (1993). An educational, or process, approach to the teaching of professional genres. *ELT Journal, 47*(4), 305–316.

Flowerdew, L. (2016). A genre-inspired and lexico-grammatical approach for helping postgraduate students craft research grant proposals. *English for Specific Purposes, 42,* 1–12.

Freedman, A., & Medway, P. (Eds.). (1994). *Genre and the new rhetoric.* Bristol: Taylor and Francis.

Fu, D., & Matoush, M. (2012). Teacher's perceptions of English language writing instruction in China. In C. Bazerman, C. Dean, J. Early, K. Lunsford, S. Null, P. Rogers, & A. Stansell (Eds.), *International advances in writing research: Cultures, places, measures* (pp. 23–39). Fort Collins, CO: The WAC Clearinghouse.

Gao, X., Liao, Y., & Li, Y.-X. (2014). Empirical studies on foreign language learning and teaching in China (2008–2011): A review of selected research. *Language Teaching*, *47*(1), 56–79.

Han, J., & Qin, X. (2000). Ticai fenxi yu ticai jiaoxue fa [Genre analysis and genre pedagogy]. *Wai Yu Jie* [*Foreign Language World*], *1*, 11–18.

Han, S., & Wang, J. (2010). Dui feiyingyu zhuanye yanjiusheng xueshu yingyu xiezuo jiaoxue de duoyuan sikao [Some thoughts on teaching English academic writing to non-English major graduate students]. *Xuewei Yu Yanjiusheng Jiaoyu* [*Academic Degrees and Graduate Education*], *8*, 45–49.

Hu, G. (2005). Contextual influences on instructional practices: A Chinese case for an ecological approach to ELT. *TESOL Quarterly*, *39*, 635–660.

Huang, P. (2012). A genre-based approach to teaching Chinese engineering graduates writing research articles. *Asian ESP Journal*, *8*(4), 30–62.

Hyland, K. (2002). Specificity revisited: How far should we go now? *English for Specific Purposes*, *21*, 385–395.

Hyland, K., & Hamp-Lyons, L. (2002). EAP: Issues and directions. *Journal of English for Academic Purposes*, *1*, 1–12.

Hyon, S. (1996). Genre in three traditions: Implications for ESL. *TESOL Quarterly*, *30*, 693–722.

Jiang, Y. (2012). Yanjiusheng zhongyingwen xueshu lunwen xiezuo kecheng de goujian [Constructing a course of Chinese and English academic paper writing for postgraduates]. *Xueshu Tansuo* [*Academic Exploration*], *10*, 186–188.

Leki, I., & Carson, J. (1997). Completely different worlds: EAP and the writing experiences of ESL students in university courses. *TESOL Quarterly*, *31*, 39–69.

Li, Y. (2016). "Publish SCI papers or no degree": Practices of Chinese doctoral supervisors in response to the publication pressure on science students. *Asia Pacific Journal of Education*, *36*(4), 545–558.

Li, Y. (2017). *Teaching Chinese graduate students of science to write for publication: An interview with Margaret Cargill*. Retrieved from www.ceapa.cn/d.asp?id=261

Liu, Q. (2010). Xue yong jiehe, xue yi zhiyong—tan shuoshi yanjiusheng yingyu yingyong nengli de peiyang [Integrating learning with using, and learning to use—on developing Master's students' performance in using English]. *Jixu Jiaoyu Yanjiu* [*Continuing Education Research*], *6*, 69–70.

Lu, Y., & Wang, X. (2015). Tigao yixue yanjiusheng yingwen keji lunwen xiezuo nengli de jiaoxue fangfa tansuo [Exploring a pedagogy for improving medical graduate students' performance in writing scientific papers in English]. *Nanjing Yike Daxue Xuebao* [*Acta Universitatis Medicinalis Nanjing: Social Sciences*], *4*, 324–326.

Martin, J. R. (1992). *English text: System and structure*. Amsterdam: John Benjamins.

Qin, X. (2000). Ticai Jiaoxuefa shuping [A review of genre-based pedagogy]. *Waiyu Jiaoxue Yu Yanjiu* [*Foreign Language Teaching and Research*], *32*(1), 42–46.

Swales, J. M. (1990). *Genre analysis: English in academic and research settings*. Cambridge: Cambridge University Press.

Swales, J. M., & Feak, C. B. (2012). *Academic writing for graduate students: Essential tasks and skills* (3rd ed.). Ann Arbor, MI: University of Michigan Press.

Van Lier, L. (2004). *The ecology and semiotics of language learning: A sociocultural perspective*. Dordrecht: Kluwer Academic.

Wang, S. (1998). Cong *genre* chufa jinxing yuedu jiaoxue—jieshao meiguo mixiegen daxue Sunny Hyon de shiyan [Genre-based approach to teaching reading: An introduction of Sunny Hyon's experiment at University of Michigan]. *Wai Yu Jie* [*Foreign Language World*], *4*, 54–55.

Xu, M., Huang, C., & You, X. (2016). Reasoning patterns of undergraduate theses in translation studies: An intercultural rhetoric study. *English for Specific Purposes, 41,* 68–81.

You, X. (2004). New directions in EFL writing: A report from China. *Journal of Second Language Writing, 13,* 253–256.

You, X. (2008). Goujian yige shengtaixing de EFL xiezuo lilun—cong zhongguo yingyu xiezuo jiaoxueshi tanqi [Constructing an ecological theory of EFL writing: From the historical perspective of English writing instruction in China]. In L. Wang, & Z. Zhang (Eds.), *EFL writing research: Chinese perspectives and practice* (pp. 26-32). Beijing: Foreign Language Teaching and Research Press.

You, X. (2010). *Writing in the devil's tongue: A history of English composition in China.* Carbondale, IL: Southern Illinois University Press.

You, X. (2012). Towards English writing research with Chinese characteristics. *Chinese Journal of Applied Linguistics, 35,* 263–270.

You, X. (2016). *Cosmopolitan English and transliteracy.* Carbondale, IL: Southern Illinois University Press.

You, X., & You, X. (2013). American content teachers' literacy brokerage in multilingual university classrooms. *Journal of Second Language Writing, 22,* 260–276.

Zhang, C., Yan, X., & Liu, X. (2015). The development of EFL writing instruction and research in China: An update from the International Conference on English Language Teaching. *Journal of Second Language Writing, 30,* 14–18.

Zhang, L., & Li, Y.-R. (2015). Fei yingyu zhuanye yanjiusheng keji lunwen yingyu xiezuo nengli peiyang moshi yanjiu [The training mode research on the scientific English writing ability for non-English major graduate students]. *Gaodeng Jianzhu Jiaoyu* [*Journal of Architectural Education in Institutions of Higher Learning*], *2,* 97–100.

Zheng, C., Du, Y., & Wu, Z. (2013). Zhongmei xuesheng yingyu "kuayang hudong" xingdong yanjiu yu yuliao fenxi [*Cross-Pacific exchange: Action research and data analysis*]. Beijing: Science Press.

Zhou, M. (2011). Lun xiangmu qudong xia yanjiusheng yingyu lunwen xiezuo nengli de peiyang [Project-driven approach to developing English academic writing performance among graduate students]. *Xuewei Yu Yanjiusheng Jiaoyu* [*Academic Degrees and Graduate Education*], *3,* 41–46.

# Appendix: The 26 Papers in Our "Core" Collection

Fan, Y. (2016). Ticai jiaoxue fa zai nongye keji yingyu xueshu lunwen xiezuo zhong de yingyong [Application of genre-based teaching approaches in academic writing of agricultural science and technology English]. *Jilin Nongye Keji Xueyuan Xuebao* [*Journal of Jilin Agricultural Science and Technology University*], *25*(1), 88–91.

Feng, X. (2014). PBL zai feiyingyu zhuanye boshisheng xueshu yingyu xiezuo nengli fazhan zhong de xiaoyong [The application of PBL for developing non-English major doctoral students' English academic writing performance]. *Kaifeng Jiaoyu Xueyuan Xuebao* [*Journal of Kaifeng Institute of Education*], *34*(6), 136–138.

Gu, F., Shi, G., & Gao, S. (2008). Boshi yanjiusheng xueshu yingyu xiezuo jiaoxue "hezuo wancheng renwu fa" de lilun yu shijian [Theory and practice of teaching English academic writing to doctoral students: A collaborative task completion approach]. *Zhongguo Nongye Jiaoyu* [*China Agricultural Education*], *2,* 41–43.

Han, P., & Hou, L. (2012). Cong ticai fenxi jiaodu tansuo yanjiusheng xueshu yingyu xiezuo nengli peiyang [A genre analysis approach to developing graduate students' facility in English academic writing]. *Wai Yu Jie* [*Foreign Language World*], *6,* 74–80.

Hu, Y., & Ma, M. (2012). Yupian ticai jiegou fenxi zai yanjiusheng xueshu yingyu xiezuo jiaoxue zhong de yingyong [The use of genre analysis in teaching English academic writing to graduate students]. *Zhongguo Chengren Jiaoyu* [*China Adult Education*], *10*, 124–126.

Huang, D., & Yang, W. (2010). Jiyu huodong lilun de xueshu yingyu xiezuo litihua kecheng de jiaoxue moshi [On the teaching mode of cubic course of academic English writing on the basis of activity theory]. *Anhui Gongye Daxue Xuebao: Shehui Kexue Ban* [*Journal of Anhui University of Technology: Social Sciences*], *27*(5), 67–69.

Huang, P. (2010). Yanjiusheng xueshu yingyu jiaoliu jineng de peiyang [On developing the communicative competence in academic English among graduate students]. *Xuewei Yu Yanjiusheng Jiaoyu* [*Academic Degrees and Graduate Education*], *8*, 55–59.

Jia, X., & Jia, Y. (2013). Jiyu guocheng ticai jiaoxuefa de junxiao xueshu yingyu xiezuo yanjiu [Teaching English academic writing to students in military universities: A genre-process approach]. *Xiaoshuo Pinglun* [*Novel Reviews*], *S2*, 348–351.

Li, G. (2005). Feiyingyu zhuanye boshisheng xueshu yingyu de shizheng jiaoxue [An empirical study of teaching English academic writing to non-English major doctoral students]. *Zhongguo Daxue Jiaoxue* [*University Teaching in China*], *4*, 47–49.

Liu, L. (2013). Jiyu ticaifa he wangluo de yanjiusheng xueshu yingyu xiezuo jiaoxue [Web-and-genre-based English academic writing course for graduate students]. *Anhui Gongye Daxue Xuebao: Shehui Kexue Ban* [*Journal of Anhui University of Technology: Social Sciences*], *30*(6), 88–91.

Lu, L. (2016a). ESP lilun shijiao xia nongye xueshu yingyu xiezuo kecheng shezhi ji jiaoxue moshi tanxi [On the design and implementation of an academic writing course for students of agriculture from the ESP perspective]. *Hebei Nongye Daxue Xuebao: Nonglin Jiaoyu Ban* [*Journal of Agricultural University of Hebei: Agriculture & Forestry Education*], *18*(2), 93–96.

Lu, L. (2016b). Yanjiusheng xueshu yingyu xiezuo jiaoxue xingdong yanjiu—yi nongye keji lunwen zhaiyao ticai fenxi jiaoxue weili [An action research study on teaching English academic writing to graduate students: Writing abstracts in agricultural disciplines based on genre analysis]. *Gaodeng Nongye Jiaoyu* [*Higher Agricultural Education*], *2*(2), 99–104.

Qian, Y. (2011). Feiyingyu zhuanye duoxueke daban boshisheng yingyu lunwen xiezuo jiaoxue moshi chutan [Exploring a teaching mode of research writing courses for non-English major doctoral students in a multidisciplinary class]. *Tianjin Waiguoyu Daxue Xuebao* [*Journal of Tianjin Foreign Studies University*], *18*(5), 56–60.

Shao, H. (2015). Jiyu CBI lilun de feiyingyu zhuanye yanjiusheng xueshu yingyu jiaoxue tanjiu—yi Beijing Gongye Daxue de yanjiusheng yingyu jiaoxue gaige weili [An innovative CBI-based approach to teaching English academic writing to non-English major graduate students—The case of Bejing University of Technology]. *Dongjiang Xuekan* [*Dongjiang Journal*], *32*(3), 101–104.

Shi, J., & Cui, X. (2015). Jiyu ticai fenxi de renwuxing yanjiusheng xueshu xiezuo ketang goujian [Task-oriented academic writing class construction for non-English major graduate students based on genre analysis]. *Haiwai Yingyu* [*Overseas English*], *24*, 257–259.

Sun, J., Wang, Y., & Yin, Y. (2015). Yanjiusheng xueshu yingyu xiezuo jiaoxue yu hudong moshi tansuo [Exploring the teaching and interactional mode of English academic writing for graduate students]. *Jiaoyu Jiaoxue Luntan* [*Education and Teaching Forum*], *42*, 109–110.

Sun, L., & Chen, J. (2009). Yanjiusheng yingyu keji lunwen xiezuo tanjiushi xuexi tixi de sikao yu goujian [Reflections on and construction of exploratory self-access learning system for graduate students' English academic writing]. *Zhongguo Waiyu* [*Foreign Languages in China*], *6*(4), 66–71.

Sun, L., Chen, J., & Xing, H. (2012). Yanjiusheng yingyu keji lunwen xiezuo nengli peiyang de tansuo yu shijian [An exploration and practice of developing graduate students' performance in writing research papers in English]. *Xuewei Yu Yanjiusheng Jiaoyu* [*Academic Degrees and Graduate Education*], 7, 23–26.

Wang, J., & Hou, L. (2013). Yanjiusheng xiezuo kecheng shezhi yu jiaoxue yanjiu [Design and implementation of a writing course for graduate students]. *Kaoshi Zhoukan* [*Weekly Journal of Testing*], *72*, 55–56.

Wang, Y. (2014). Jiyu xuqiu fenxi de yanjiusheng xueshu yingyu xiezuo jiaoxue moshi [A teaching mode of English academic writing for graduate students based on needs analysis]. *Shenyang Shifan Daxue Xuebao: Shehui Kexue Ban* [*Journal of Shenyang Normal University: Social Science Edition*], *38*(1), 127–129.

Wu, T. (2015). Nonglin yuanxiao feiyingyu zhuanye shuoshi yanjiusheng xueshu yingyu xiezuo jiaoxue de youhua—yi Beijing Linye Daxue wei li [Improving English academic writing instructions for non-English majors in agricultural and forestry universities: Bejing Forestry University in focus]. *Zhongguo Linye Jiaoyu* [*Forestry Education in China*], *33*(1), 42–44.

Yang, Z. (2012). SCI lunwen xiezuo yu zhongyiyao yanjiusheng yixue yingyu xiezuo kecheng jianshe tanxi [SCI paper writing and curriculum construction in medical English writing for graduate students of Chinese medicine]. *Zhongguo Gaodeng Yixue Jiaoyu* [*China Higher Medical Education*], 7, 92–94.

Zeng, X., Su, J., & Ren, F. (2014). Yanjiusheng yingyu xueshu lunwen "yuedu xiezuo chenshu" yitihua jiaoxue moshi [A pedagogy of 'reading, writing, and presenting' research papers in academic English for graduate students]. *Yuwen Xuekan: Waiyu Jiaoyu Yu Jiaoxue* [*Journal of Language and Literature: Foreign Language Teaching and Learning*], *2*, 83–85.

Zhan, X., Liao, R., & Chen, M. (2010). Yixue boshisheng yingwen SCI lunwen xiezuo kecheng de kaishe [Teaching SCI paper writing to doctoral students of medicine]. *Yixue Jiaoyu Tansuo* [*Research in Medical Education*], *9*, 1183–1185.

Zhang, P. (2013). Xiaozu xiezuo xiangmu qudong renwu fenjie—shuoshi yanjiusheng xueshu yingyu jiaoliu nengli peiyang de jiaogai shijian [Group work, project-driven, and task-based: A pedagogical initiative to develop Master's students' communicative competence in academic English]. *Xuewei Yu Yanjiusheng Jiaoyu* [*Academic Degrees and Graduate Education*], 7, 33–37.

Zhang, Z. (2010). Yanjiusheng yingyu xueshu lunwen xiezuo jineng peiyang moshi tansuo [Cultivating graduate students' ability in writing English academic papers]. *Haiwai Yingyu* [*Overseas English*], *11*, 15–16.

# 14

## EPILOGUE

### A Perspective on Transnational Writing Education From a New York City Subway Train

*Brooke Ricker Schreiber*

In the fall of 2016, I began teaching as an assistant professor at Baruch College, part of the City University of New York (CUNY). I found myself living in a part of southern Brooklyn known as Gravesend, which is an eclectic mix: a traditionally Italian neighborhood recently shaped by waves of immigration from East Asia and the former Soviet republics. This deep hybridity is evidenced by the food landscape, in which Georgian and Azerbaijani restaurants stand beside Chinese grocery stores, coffee shops with names like "Café La Notte" echo with Russian dialects, and cars still line up every weekend outside a legendary pizzeria where a "Sicilian half tray" and homemade spumoni are on the menu. After five years living in a tiny, almost exclusively white town in rural Pennsylvania, I had landed in the heart of urban superdiversity (Vertovec, 2007; Blommaert, 2010), and its accompanying range of linguistic repertoires and varieties of English.

Perhaps nowhere is this superdiversity more evident than on my subway commute. Traveling the hour from south Brooklyn to midtown Manhattan, the train collects my neighbors, speaking Chinese, Italian, and various Slavic languages, then Orthodox Jews speaking Hebrew, Black teenagers on their way to school, laughing and joking in AAVE, and mothers corralling their children with Spanish commands. Day by day, ride by ride, crammed into one of the D train's orange plastic seats, I have read drafts of the chapters of this edited collection with these intermingled languages and dialects in my ears (some days more dramatically than others, such as the day that two Italian grandmothers sat down next to and across from me and proceeded to argue across my laptop, gesturing emphatically). This experience has struck me as fundamentally transnational and translingual. Surrounded by people communicating in multiple and hybrid forms all around me, I am literally crossing borders—ethnic, socioeconomic, and geographic—simply by moving through the urban space.

Yet as new as this has all been for me, my own crossings are minimal compared to the ones I ask my students to do. My second language writing courses are populated by international and immigrant students, many of whom have undergraduate degrees in their home countries and are transporting their literacy practices into a new context. Even in "mainstream" courses, my students are constantly crossing linguistic and cultural borders, as more than 40% of Baruch students report that English is not their first language (CUNY, 2012). In an upper division class I taught in the spring of 2017, students' primary languages included Chinese, Spanish, Russian, Arabic, Gujarati, Burmese, Serbo-Croatian, Tagalog, and Haitian Creole, as well as AAVE and Brooklynese. In addition, Baruch students, like those across CUNY, are highly likely to be working-class and to be the first in their families to attend college (Leonhardt, 2016). Thus, within the classroom, especially the writing classroom, we are asking students to cross class borders as well: to imagine themselves into a community of academics by taking on a persona of individual authority, a process which demands emotional labor from students (Iten, 2016) and critical reflection on class-based positioning from teachers (Lindquist, 2004). In environments like this, the myth of linguistic homogeneity (Matsuda, 2006)—or indeed of any homogeneity—absolutely implodes, and even mundane class discussions become acts of linguistic and cultural negotiation. For me, these experiences have demonstrated the necessity of a writing pedagogy that goes beyond ESL, one which grapples directly with students' lived experiences in and between cultures and languages and works to break down simplistic definitions of nationality and identity: a transnational pedagogy, drawing on and extending principles of translingualism.

The goal of this edited collection is to ask how we as teachers can best facilitate our students' crossing of multiple, overlapping boundaries within and beyond the classroom, and how we ourselves will need to shift in our ideologies and practices. In this concluding chapter, I will outline the specific insights I see in this collection which can support these processes. In particular, I aim to mine the knowledge generated by these scholars for concrete pedagogical suggestions: specific ways of engaging students in the work of negotiating language standards, reflecting on their own experiences, and working for institutional change.

## Moving Past Standard English

The translingual writing approach has been critiqued within the field of second language writing for being overly idealistic: that is, for emphasizing a "happy hybridity" and valuation of language difference that does not attend to students' desires (and expectations) to acquire Standard English in their writing classes. Certainly, even in contexts of visible superdiversity like New York City, where the environment both in and out of the classroom is deeply translingual, monolingual frames hold tremendous power, shaping standardized testing and other gatekeeping practices, as well as the beliefs of many students and teachers.

Particularly in educational settings, it is still assumed that we communicate with a homogenous community, "sharing a national language and a national culture" (You, this volume, p. 3). Thus, when we teach writing in English, we may create for our students an imagined Anglo-American audience which has specific rhetorical expectations; while this simplifies pedagogy, it also supports standard language ideology and the need to write (exclusively) in standard English. The goal of transnational writing pedagogy is not to hold back "the codes of power" from students who need or want them (Delpit, 1995; Young, 2004), but rather to interrogate the nature and origins of those codes. As this collection demonstrates, we need to break down for ourselves and for our students the myth of the monolingual audience—to recognize, deconstruct, and transcend monolingual assumptions and to view language standards as always negotiated, rather than fixed. We can best help students to do so through two paths: investigation of external language standards and reflection on their own language experiences.

Key to counteracting standard language ideologies, Donahue notes in her chapter, is to focus on the inherent instability of any one form of English. In particular, we must ourselves consider, and offer our students the opportunity to consider, how languages both are and are not "real": language boundaries, like national boundaries, both exist and do not exist, as they are socially constructed and constantly redefined. For Donahue, this process begins with research which captures changing linguistic norms beyond the walls of the institutions, as with research on English as a Lingua Franca (ELF), and more importantly which clarifies empirically "the difference between new linguistic norms in everyday practice, across multiple contexts, and the . . . expectations in particular high-stakes settings" like academia. Donahue suggests that we might share research on linguistic change with our students, "generating insights with them about the implications" (p. 34).

Surma's critique of the Grammarly program and its monolingual, neoliberal framing is an excellent example of such research. Surma's chapter demonstrates that Grammarly is not only often inaccurate, but also reinforces the idea that correct grammar is simply a matter of mechanical conformity, rather than a rhetorical act—that the value of writing can be "quantitatively measured," and that grammatical accuracy "can be calculated in an essentially instrumental fashion" (p. 69). Students might be invited to respond to the use of such programs, to "talk back" to the feedback they receive and consider how such programs position them. Similarly, students might be invited to compare grammar handbooks from different eras and reflect on how language standards have shifted; they might write about their own experiences with grammar correction, especially moments where authorities have presented conflicting rules.

In my own teaching context, students are often aiming towards careers in business, and associate success in the business world with the acquisition of prestige forms of Standard English. In my classes, I have asked students to read and respond to research on both ELF norms and on business people's reactions to accented writing (Wolfe et al., 2016), comparing their own life experiences to the conclusions of these scholars, as a way of articulating and confronting their beliefs about the linguistic expectations of the business world.

## Investigating Students' Language Experiences

For many students, transnational border crossings can promote cosmopolitan dispositions, including a desire to write in "genres, grammars, and voices that go beyond territorialized and autonomous languages" (Canagarajah, this volume, p. 43). Yet the monolingual ideologies students internalize from schooling and general life experiences compete with these ambitions and structure their goals in the writing class. To encourage and facilitate students' existing aspirations towards cosmopolitanism, we need to provide students spaces to articulate and grapple with this tension.

One such space is in autobiographical writing. Both Canagarajah's and Yang's chapters demonstrate that autobiographical writing offers a place for students to struggle productively with multiple identities. Outside of class and away from a strict focus on grammar correction, autobiographical writing gave Yang's participant Beth an opportunity for expanded personal agency and deeper investment in writing. In Yang's study, this opportunity hinged on the expanded audience for students' writing (including peers as well as a researcher), providing content-driven feedback, and the freedom to code-mix. Ultimately, "looking back, as afforded by autobiographical writing, may provide opportunities for multilingual writers to reconnect with their multilingual resources," and to overcome deficit positioning (p. 133).

Finally, teachers should set aside their assumptions about students' experiences with and relationships to languages. As You shows us in his introduction (and Wu furthers in his chapter), individual students' language knowledge and use may not reflect the "officially sanctioned codes" (p. 3) of the monolingual nation state. It's important for teachers to understand that just as languages and language communities are not homogenous, so students' emotional and ideological experiences of languages are not identical. As Canagarajah's chapter demonstrates, students may find writing in their second language to be a liberating experience, one which permits the development of new identities. As teachers, therefore, we should work actively to "inquire into the policies, pedagogies, and ideologies accompanying the languages used in order to interpret their identity and expressive implications" for our students as individuals (Canagarajah) (p. 49). These investigations can be incorporated into class assignments: teachers might start with simple written or oral surveys, and move on to autobiographical reflections and class investigations of minority languages in the local context.

## Create Opportunities for Sustained Interactions With Linguistic/Cultural Others

One crucial element in developing cosmopolitan attitudes is direct and extended contact with linguistic others, particularly speakers of other languages and dialects (i.e., You, 2016). This direct experience can, of course, occur through physical transnational movement, as with study abroad. Sasaki's chapter reminds us that study abroad experiences, even brief ones, support the development of sensitivity to the expectations of diverse audiences and the ability to shuttle between and negotiate with rhetorical conventions. Yet for many students this may simply not be feasible. Sustained contact, as multiple chapters demonstrate, can be effectively created through digital communication. Teachers can support sustained cross-cultural interactions without physical transnational movement through what Wu (this volume) calls technology-mediated transnational writing education (TTWE).

To be fully effective, TTWE activities must be specifically designed to develop a cosmopolitan disposition, positioning the participants as language users rather than learners, and to deconstruct the valorization of Standard English. Wu therefore recommends that TTWE activities should have several features: first, an explicit non-deficit linguistic stance, so that, for example, feedback from "native speakers" is not accepted uncritically. Second, TTWE activities should have an openness towards multimodality and multilinguality in writing, including code-mixing and use of video and image. Third, where possible, teachers should move beyond digital platforms such as course management systems which are supported but also bounded by institutions. Students in institutional settings are not only more likely to "intentionally suppress their multilingualism and multiliteracies to conform to the Standard English practice" (p. 181), but these platforms limit access to only specific classes, rather than creating opportunities to communicate with (and develop rhetorical awareness of) broader audiences.

This kind of transnational interaction is especially important for monolinguals and pre-service teachers (You, 2016), especially those who are not able to have direct experience. In Zhang's border-crossing activity, pre-service ESL teachers were able to recognize and reevaluate their limited perceptions of EFL learners grounded in monolingual ideology, realizing that their "assumptions about language learners are mostly unreliable and inaccurate" and questioning native-speaker privilege (p. 192).

Perhaps most importantly, in being exposed to varieties of English, these pre-service teachers began to think more deeply and critically about classifying language variation versus language error, while developing respect and appreciation for translingual creativity. The border-crossing activity helped the pre-service teachers realize that "it is not necessary to fix the accents" and motivated them to open up dialogue about language diversity (p. 196). The key to this benefit was structuring the interaction so that pre-service teachers focused on communicative purpose, which meant

Epilogue **249**

that they were able to adopt a teacher identity beyond that of "grammar police" and to have concrete, contextualized debates about error versus written accent.

Surma's work also reminds us that as teachers, the writing we do ourselves and the writing we ask our students to do has ethical implications. To push back against neoliberal conceptions of the self as a singular, a-cultural individual, competing with everyone, we can promote with students a feminist "ethics of care," considering how the writing done in the classroom privileges some discourses above others and hides ethical connections between the self and the world. One such project might involve asking students to tell stories of those in their linguistic communities that might otherwise go unheard. Writing projects based on conducting interviews in students' other languages can be designed to elicit life narratives from elders or expose social issues in the community, which can then be published in a wider forum (see, for example, Alvarez, 2017; Marko, 2012; You, 2016). This is one way in which transnational writing classes can, as Donahue suggests, "call out students' vast knowledge, to invite re-use" of their linguistic and writing abilities" (p. 36).

## Use Scholarship to Promote Egalitarian Educational Practices at a Policy Level

Where possible, teachers can couple individual transnational pedagogical activities such as those outlined above with efforts to work against monolingual institutional cultures at a policy level. Certainly, these chapters demonstrate that even within an institution steeped in monolingual ideologies, an individual teacher can have an impact: Yang's project, conducted outside of class with a group of ethnic minority students, worked counter to the "persistent disvalu[ation]" of their culture on campus, supporting students' efforts to assert their ethnic identities through translingual writing. At an individual level, Sharma suggests, teachers can adopt innovative pedagogies which not only "make translanguaging a natural process of teaching and learning" (p. 88), but may include the use of social media, teaching world languages, and promoting "citizen journalism" in the writing class—which, when focused on community issues, could tie in Surma's "ethics of care." And at an institutional level, he suggests, teachers may open up dialogue through organizing workshops and conferences, and drawing on "social science research about the benefits of multilingualism and translanguaging" to make arguments at a policy level for educational practices such as bilingual testing and providing teacher training which "bring[s] translanguaging out of hiding and away from shame" (p. 89). Likewise, Wu's chapter suggests that while transnational collaborations can most effectively start with a "handshake" partnership between individual teachers, teachers should then look to "scale up" their projects to expand the numbers of students able to participate, which requires work at the program level.

As teachers, we need to carefully consider what boundaries our own institutional practices (for example, writing class placement) place on students, knowing how deeply such labels impact students' identities (Ortmeier-Hooper, 2008). Arnold's study of students' extracurricular published writing in Arabic at the turn of the century finds that when given a public forum for their writing, multilingual students eagerly engage in "a constant and oftentimes productive negotiation of educational, linguistic, and cultural borders," borders that are "often reinforced or constructed by us" (p. 108). Similarly, Yang notes that students' identities are formed in relationship "be it broad conceptions such as languages and cultures, or others' words", including institutional labels for multilingual writers" (p. 119). On an individual level, teachers may offer alternatives to the ESL label (multilingual, English-dominant), and ask students to identify for themselves their first and dominant languages. At the institutional level, this suggests a need for guided self-placement into writing classes, allowing students to exercise agency in course selection by providing resources for accurate information about the content and expectations of writing classes (Saenkhum, 2016).

## Cross Borders Between Fields

The implementation of a transnational approach to writing instruction demands the crossing not only of linguistic and cultural borders, but as with translingual scholarship, the crossing of disciplinary borders. Thus, I would like to add to this collection a consideration of one more border to be crossed: that between basic writing and L2 writing scholarship. These two disciplines have long been separate, as each has worked to professionalize and codify a body of knowledge (e.g., Silva & Leki, 2004). Yet the two disciplines serve students populations that, where they do not directly overlap, have profound similarities. As Canagarajah points out, multilingual students' creativity can be motivated by the "tensions and alienations" they experience writing in academic English—emotions certainly amplified for L2 writers, but not unknown to those often placed into basic writing courses who come from backgrounds of literacy and epistemology vastly different from those assumed as the norm in academia (Iten, 2016). Likewise, both multilingual writers and basic writers can be deeply harmed by neoliberal beliefs which, Surma notes, place responsibility for self-improvement solely on the individual and thereby disguise "the structural inequalities that continue to distinguish so-called successful from unsuccessful students as they go through their school education" (p. 63). Transnational writing, then, with its goals of creating cosmopolitan citizens, can benefit from considering how writers confront and cross class borders, and what skills are required to do so—as in Fraiberg, Wang, and You (2017), where Chinese students grapple with class identity within a transnational writing course.

A practical activity which elegantly fulfills the pedagogical goals outlined in this book comes from a recent issue of the *Journal of Basic Writing*. In "Noticing the Way: Translingual Possibility and Basic Writers," Sarah Stanley (2013) describes a "sentence workshop," in which students select sentences to write on the board for the whole class to comment on, opening up a dialogue about the writer's choices and options. Her first workshop is unsuccessful—Stanley jumps in to read *through* the student's error and provide implicit, rather than explicit, feedback. In response, the student edits without actually clarifying the meaning of the sentence. Stanley goes on to conclude that, despite backlash against SLA-informed theories of error often associated with English-only policies, students cannot negotiate linguistic forms without explicit noticing: "given that conscious access to neither systematic English rules nor rhetorical traditions and cross-cultural understanding is equitable in our classrooms, we need to reorient ourselves and our students towards noticing and talking about error as enabling further possibilities for basic writers" (p. 43).

For me, this is precisely the sort of work which this volume calls on us as teachers to take up. This activity fulfills Donahue's call in this volume for pedagogy that supports "students' values, including their possible interest in linguistic and rhetorical flexibility" (p. 35). Students in Stanley's class are neither forced to conform to monolingual expectations, nor forced to ignore them, but are ultimately given the space and the support to explore language as it is for them at the moment. Arnold suggests that we might ask of ourselves how our writing tasks "encourage students to both acknowledge and negotiate linguistic, institutional, and cultural boundaries" (p. 108). I would argue that translingual writing tasks can simultaneously scaffold acquisition of Standard English and the development of the creativity and aptitude to transgress language norms. And this is what students need to be successful in a deeply transnational world, as this volume makes clear: not only the straightforward mastery of prestige forms of English, but rather both the skill and the confidence to deploy their linguistic resources to maximum effect and to relate to others with compassion and tolerance. This is what transnational writing seeks to promote.

## References

Alvarez, S. (2017). *Community literacies en confianza: Learning from bilingual after-school programs.* Urbana, IL: NCTE.

Blommaert, J. (2010). *The sociolinguistics of globalization.* Cambridge: Cambridge University Press.

CUNY Office of Institutional Research and Assessment. (2012). *A profile of undergraduates at CUNY senior and community colleges: Fall 2012.* Retrieved from http://cuny. edu/about/administration/offices/ira/ir/databook/current/student/ug_student_pro file_f12.pdf

Delpit, L. (1995). *Other people's children: Cultural conflict in the classroom.* New York: The Press.

Fraiberg, S., Wang, X., & You, X. (2017). *Inventing the world grant university: Chinese international students' mobilities, literacies, and identities.* Logan, UT: Utah State University Press.

Iten, M. (2016). *Argument and social class: Differences before the curriculum*. Presentation at the International Writing Across the Curriculum Conference, Ann Arbor, MI.

Leonhardt, D. (2016, January 18). America's great working-class colleges. *New York Times*. Retrieved from www.nytimes.com/2017/01/18/opinion/sunday/americas-great-working-class-colleges.html?_r=0

Lindquist, J. (2004). Class affects, classroom affectations: Working through the paradoxes of strategic empathy. *College English, 67*(2), 187–209.

Marko, T. (2012). *Proyecto Boston Medellín as pedagogscape*. Retrieved from http://mobility17.com/wp-content/uploads/2013/09/MarkoPBMasPedagogscape.pdf.

Matsuda, P. K. (2006). The myth of linguistic homogeneity in US college composition. *College English, 68*(6), 637–651.

Ortmeier-Hooper, C. (2008). English may be my second language, but I'm not "ESL." *College Composition and Communication*, 389–419.

Saenkhum, T. (2016). *Decisions, agency, and advising: Key issues in the placement of multilingual writers into first-year composition courses*. Logan, UT: Utah State University Press.

Silva, T., & Leki, I. (2004). Family matters: The influence of applied linguistics and composition studies on second language writing studies: Past, present, and future. *The Modern Language Journal, 88*(1), 1–13.

Stanley, S. (2013). Noticing the way: Translingual possibility and basic writers. *Journal of Basic Writing, 32*(1), 37–61.

Vertovec, S. (2007). Super-diversity and its implications. *Ethnic and Racial Studies, 30*(6), 1024–1054.

Wolfe, J, Shanmugaraj, N, & Sipe, J. (2016). Grammatical versus pragmatic error: Employer perceptions of nonnative and native English speakers. *Business and Professional Communication Quarterly, 79*(4), pp. 397–415.

You, X. (2016). *Cosmopolitan English and transliteracy*. Carbondale, IL: Southern Illinois University Press.

Young, V. A. (2004). Your average nigga. *College Composition and Communication, 55*(4), 693–715.

# ABOUT THE EDITOR

**Xiaoye You** is Professor of English and Asian studies at The Pennsylvania State University, USA, and Yunshan Chair Professor at Guangdong University of Foreign Studies, China. His first monograph, *Writing in the Devil's Tongue: A History of English Composition in China*, won the 2011 Conference on College Composition and Communication (CCCC) Outstanding Book Award. His recent book, *Cosmopolitan English and Transliteracy*, arguing for ethical use of English in everyday life and for cultivating global citizens in English literacy education, received the 2018 CCCC Research Impact Award.

# ABOUT THE CONTRIBUTORS

**Lisa R. Arnold** is Assistant Professor of English and Director of First-Year Writing at North Dakota State University.

**Suresh Canagarajah** is Edwin Erle Sparks Professor of Applied Linguistics, English, and Asian Studies at Penn State University.

**Christiane Donahue** is Associate Professor of Linguistics and Director of the Dartmouth Institute for Writing and Rhetoric, and a member of the research group Théodile-CIREL at l'Université de Lille.

**Steven Fraiberg** is Assistant Professor of Writing, Rhetoric, and American Culture at Michigan State University.

**Yongyan Li** is Associate Professor of English Language Education at the University of Hong Kong.

**June Yichun Liu** is Associate Professor of English at National Chenchi University, Taiwan.

**Xiaohao Ma** is a PhD student in applied linguistics at the University of Hong Kong.

**Miyuki Sasaki** is Professor of Applied Linguistics at Nagoya City University, Japan.

## About the Contributors   255

**Brooke Ricker Schreiber** is Assistant Professor of English at Baruch College, City University of New York.

**Shyam Sharma** is Assistant Professor of Writing and Rhetoric at Stony Brook University, State University of New York.

**Anne Surma** is Associate Professor in the School of Arts at Murdoch University, in Western Australia.

**Zhiwei Wu** is Associate Professor of English at Guangdong University of Foreign Studies, China.

**Shizhou Yang** is Associate Professor and Chair of the English Department at Yunnan Minzu University, China.

**Xiaoye You** is Professor of English and Asian Studies at Pennsylvania State University, USA, and Yunshan Chair Professor at Guangdong University of Foreign Studies, China.

**Yufeng Zhang** is Associate Professor of English at Millersville University of Pennsylvania.

# INDEX

Abasi, A. R. 9
academic literacy xii, xiii, 31, 116–117, 156–158, 204, 222
Arabic 8, 96–99, 106–110, 160–161
argumentation 101–102, 121, 150, 208–209, 216–218
Arnold, L. xii, 8, 97, 250, 251
assessment: formative 86; in neoliberal times 61, 65, 70–71; in technology-mediated transnational writing education 176, 179–180; in writing research 151, 203–204, 208
autobiographic writing: in the classroom xi, 45, 52–58, 117, 247; its impact on writer identity xii, 57, 129–132

Bachman, L. 141, 144, 145
Bakhtin, M. M. 30, 43, 158
Blackledge, A. 25, 30
Britain 7, 25, 79, 145–146, 174–175

Canagarajah, S. xi, 5, 11–12, 27, 34–35, 41, 88, 115, 206, 207, 218, 237, 247, 250
Cargill, M. 236, 238
Cheng, A. 224
China: ELT conferences in xv–xvi, 224; English writing instruction in 224; ethnic university in 120; graduate education in 223; in student literacy narrative 53–56; in student social network 163–164; transnational writing education in 3–7
Chinese English 179, 209–214

citizenship 6, 63, 170
Colombia 10
Common European Frame of Reference 22, 36, 207
communicative repertoire: conceptualization of 5, 41–44, 52, 82; mobilized in composing process 3, 34, 53, 57–59, 132–133, 151–152, 179–182
community of practice 156, 206, 215, 218
Connor, U. 9, 11
container model xii, 156, 168
contrastive rhetoric 4, 9, 23, 32–33
Cook, V. 27, 33
cosmopolitan disposition: cultivated through writing education 171, 180, 247–248; manifest in student writing 41, 43, 52, 56–57
cosmopolitan English 11, 29
cosmopolitanism xi, 5–7, 11, 29–30; see also critical cosmopolitanism
Creese, A. 25, 30
critical cosmopolitanism: its challenge to instrumental approach to writing 68–73; definition 65; disposition 66; its orientation to writing 65–68
cross-border activity: benefits for teacher education 198; description of 190; power differentials in 199
Curry, M. J. 22, 34

data analysis: in study of affordances of Facebook for academic writing 208–209; in study of student identity

work 122; in study of teacher identity 190–191
Davies, A. 79–80, 81
diaspora 6, 42, 55, 87, 117
Donahue, C. x, xii, 13, 22, 246, 249, 251

English academic writing in China: of Chinese characteristics 232–235; collaborating with content specialists 229–230, 233; genre pedagogy 231–232, 234; students and curricula 226–227; teacher training 234; teaching abstract writing 231–232; teaching multidisciplinary classes 228–229; timing and duration 227–228
English as a Foreign Language 4, 192–193, 224, 232, 248
English for Academic Purposes 222–224, 233–238
English-only instruction 80, 84, 86, 90, 251
ethics: discussed in student writing 104–106; in multilingual education 84–85; in teaching writing in globalization 2, 6–7, 29, 48–49; in writing in neoliberal times 61, 65–73
ethnicity 1, 42, 52, 81, 120–121, 249
Europe 1, 22, 27, 62, 87, 174–175
extracurricular writing 98–100, 120, 146, 165, 203, 205–206

Facebook: its affordances for academic writing xiii, 175, 214–218; in the classroom 203–204, 207; and features of student language 209–214; and L2 writing 204–206; and neoliberalism 65
feedback: in shaping identity work 53, 130; in teacher training 190–193, 194–197; in technology-mediated writing instruction 173, 175–176, 204–205, 214–215; in writing outside classroom 101–102, 165–166
Fraiberg, S. xii, 22, 34, 250
Fu, D. 224

Garcia, O. 37, 82
genre pedagogy xii, 32, 58, 224–226, 231–232, 234
global citizen x, 2, 11, 170, 179
globalization: and critical cosmopolitanism 66; and language policy 170; and reconceptualization of language and writing 21, 25, 29, 182, 206; and teacher identity 187–188; and transnational writing education xi, 5–7, 10–11

global partnership program 10, 171
graduate students 222
grammar: and Facebook 193–194, 204; in student writing 103, 122–123; and technology 62, 69–70; in technology-mediated transnational writing projects 173
Grammarly 65, 69, 74, 246

Hamp-Lyons, L. 222
Hawisher, G. E. 161
heteroglossia xi, 30
historical inquiry xi–xii, 3, 7–9, 83–86, 95–96
history: Arabic student publications at Syrian Protestant College 97–106; English literacy education in Nepal 83–86; Japanese women in study abroad 139–140; transnational writing education 7–8
Horner, B. 22, 33, 35
hybridity 28, 34, 45–46, 244–245
Hyland, K. 222

identity construction: in academic writing 216–217; a dynamic model 116, 134; implications for pedagogy 134–135; process 124–129; in teacher education 187–192; in transnational social field 41, 44–48, 58–59
immigrants 3–5, 7–8, 116–117, 245
intercultural rhetoric 9, 11–12, 23, 237
international students 4, 8, 34, 52, 157, 165
interview 85, 121–122, 124, 129, 131, 148–150, 204–205, 208, 211, 215, 238
Introna, L. D. 68–70, 73, 74
investment: financial 63; in language learning 45, 118–119, 122–123, 128, 132, 134, 147

Japan 7, 139–140, 147–152, 175–176, 178, 211
Japanese manga 211–213

Kaplan, R. 4, 9, 23
Kinginger, C. 139
knotworking 158, 167
Kobayashi, H. 149–150, 152
Kramsch, C. 25, 28, 36, 44–49, 182

language ability: affected by study abroad 141–151; definition 140–141
language ideology: monolingual 8, 43; multilingual 33; non-deficit view 141,

**258** Index

151; related to English-only instruction 79–80, 87; related to local languages 133; related to Standard English 246; transnational 48–51, 53, 56, 58–59
language policy 79–80, 82–83, 88, 90–91, 170, 236–237, 249
Lee, I. 188, 189
Leki, I. 84
lexical complexity 146
Liebman, J. 9
Lillis, T. 22, 34
literacy autobiography 48, 52–58, 132
literacy sponsors 159–161, 163
Liu, Y. xii, 13, 173–174
local languages 26, 80–83, 85, 87–88, 90; attitudes to 121, 133

Mandarin 3, 53, 56, 120–121, 210–211
Marko, T. 10, 11
meta-analysis: of reports on technology-mediated transnational writing education 172; of scholarship in teaching English academic writing to Chinese graduate students 225; of study abroad scholarship 142, 152
metrolingualism xi, 28–29
mobile methods 158–159
mobility systems: an illustration 160–167; introduction to 157–158
Molina, C. 28, 35–36
monolingualism 3–4, 50
morality 104–108
multicompetence 27, 33–36, 149
multilingualism: in classroom 245; a framework in scholarship 33; a literate art x; in Nepal 80–82, 86–88; in New York City 244; in university 120
multiliteracies 117, 170, 179, 181–182, 248
multimodality: critique of 44; in student writing 117, 129, 173, 176, 179–181, 204–206, 211

narrative theory 119–120
nationalism 1–5, 24, 29, 97, 139
native speaker 4, 43, 45, 48, 50–51, 180, 193–194, 248
neoliberalism: definition 62–63; its impact on writing and writing studies 10–11, 62, 64–66
Nepal 79
Nepali 81–83, 85–86
New Literacy Studies 171, 203–204, 206
newspaper 95, 97–101, 105–106, 110

Ortega, L. 141
Otsuji, E. 28, 33

Palmer, A. 141, 144, 145
pedagogy: examples of transnational writing education 9–11; implications drawn from Arabic student publications for 108; implications of a transnational perspective for 10, 35–37, 58–59, 245–250; nationalist 3–4; for sustaining interaction with linguistic/cultural others 248–249; teacher education 188, 190–191; for teaching English academic writing for graduate students in China 228–232, 235–236; technology-mediated transnational writing education 170–171
Pennycook, A. 28, 33
plagiarism 65, 69, 74, 218
plurilinguisme xi, 26–28
policy *see* language policy
Poststructuralism 118, 134
Prendergast, C. 87
pre-service teacher: identity development 190–198; studies on 188–189
Prior, P. 157
Professional Communication 9–10, 171

QQ 160, 163–164, 229

racism 1–2
register 194–195, 209–210, 218–219
research: future directions 11–13, 34, 151–152, 199, 234–235, 250–251; transnational values in 32
rhetoric: classical 13, 96–97; current-traditional 4; strategies 58, 68, 104, 149–150, 197–198, 205
Rinnert, C. 149–150

Sasaki, M. xii, 147–149, 151–152, 248
Schreiber, B. R. xiv, 205, 211
second language acquisition 37, 142, 187, 203, 204
second language writing 49, 245
Selfe, C. L. 161
social media 1, 65, 159, 163, 203–205, 218, 229
sociolinguistics 32, 44
Standard English xiii, 26, 178–181, 245–246, 248
Starke-Meyerring, D. 9
study abroad: definition 139; its impact on L2 learning in general 142; on L2

listening 142–143; on L2 pragmatic knowledge and processing 144–145; on L2 reading 143; on L2 speaking 143–144; on L2 writing 147–152
superdiversity 25–26, 244–245
Surma, A. xi, 7, 61
syntactic complexity 147

Taiwan 174, 204, 207, 210–211
teacher education 49, 187, 190, 198
teacher identity: in activity 197; in discourse 191–193; in practice 193–197
teacher research 207–209
technology-mediated transnational writing education: in Asia 175–176; in Australia 186; definition 171; in Europe 174–175; its interaction process 173; limitations in its practice 178–179; in North America 177; its outcomes 172–173; power and identities in 173–174; prospects 179–181
telecollaboration 171, 175
theory: critical cosmopolitan approach to writing 65–68; identity work 118–120; mobility systems 157–159; translingual subject 41–49; transnational writing education x–xi, 1–7; trans-understandings of language and writing 23–25
transfer of writing competence 217–219
translanguaging: definition 82; as everyday practice 81; in instructional practice 85; in relation to translingualism 26
translation: studies of 5; as translingual practice x, 124, 133, 159, 165, 176, 193–194, 210; in transnational scholarship 13, 85, 96, 109–110

translingual disposition xi, 44–45, 48, 51, 54, 56, 204
translingualism xi, 157; in scholarship 96, 109
translingual practice 9, 42, 44, 170
transliteracy 6, 11, 218–219, 235
transnational historiography 95–96
transnational identity 12, 199, 205, 211–213
transnationalism: definition 2, 23, 41; in graduate education 236; in scholarship 91, 205, 222, 225, 250–251; in teacher education 236
transnational social space xi, 42–44, 56
transnational writing education: definition x, 2; in the future 11–13; in the past 7–8; pedagogical suggestions 245–251; in the present 8–11; see also technology-mediated transnational writing education
Turnitin 65, 69, 74
Twitter 65, 69, 151, 175, 178

voice: in Bakhtin 30–31, 43, 119; scholarly 32; student 9, 53–54, 96, 126, 209–210, 216–217; in telecollaborative activities 182; in writing in neoliberal times 71

WeChat 160, 163–165
Wible, S. 88
World Englishes 195–196, 209–214
writing assessment see assessment
writing group xii, 120–123
writing studies x–xi, 2, 6–12, 26, 32, 64

Yang, S. xii, 3, 12, 135
You, X. x, 11, 28–30, 34, 66, 84, 85, 95, 117, 179, 205, 224, 235–236, 247